The
Lake District

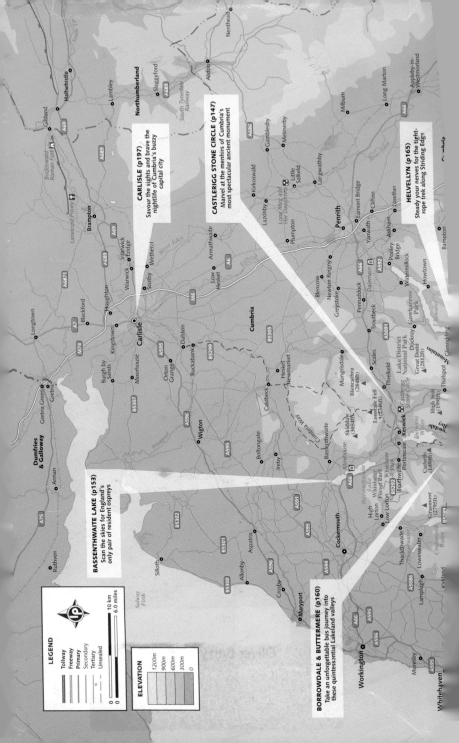

CARLISLE (p197)
Savour the sights and brave the nightlife of Cumbria's buzzy capital city

CASTLERIGG STONE CIRCLE (p147)
Marvel at the menhirs of Cumbria's most spectacular ancient monument

HELVELLYN (p165)
Steady your nerves for the tight-rope trek along Striding Edge

BASSENTHWAITE LAKE (p153)
Scan the skies for England's only pair of resident ospreys

BORROWDALE & BUTTERMERE (p160)
Take an unforgettable bus journey into these quintessential Lakeland valleys

LEGEND

Tollway
Freeway
Primary
Secondary
Tertiary
Unsealed

ELEVATION

1200m
900m
600m
300m
0

0   10 km
0   6.0 miles

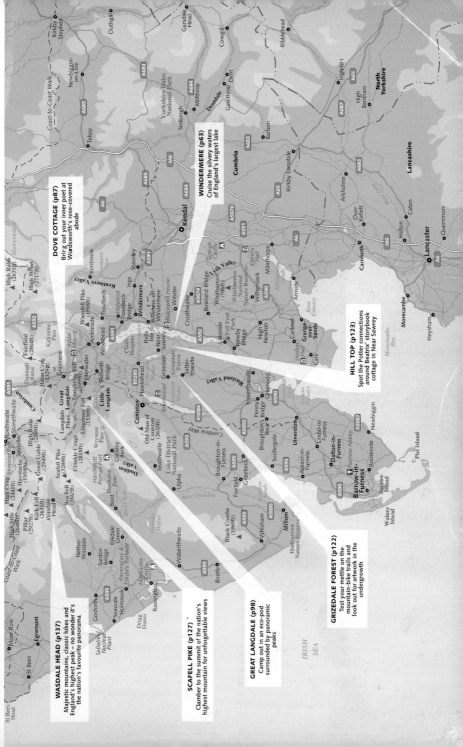

DOVE COTTAGE (p87)
Bring out your inner poet at Wordsworth's rose-covered abode

WINDERMERE (p63)
Cruise the silvery waters of England's largest lake

HILL TOP (p123)
Spot the Potter connections around Beatrix's storybook cottage in Near Sawrey

GRIZEDALE FOREST (p122)
Test your mettle on the mountain-bike trails and look out for artwork in the undergrowth

GREAT LANGDALE (p98)
Camp out in an eco-pod surrounded by panoramic peaks

SCAFELL PIKE (p127)
Clamber to the summit of the nation's highest mountain for unforgettable views

WASDALE HEAD (p137)
Majestic mountains, classic hikes and England's highest peak – no wonder it's the nation's favourite panorama

On the Road

LONDON BOROUGH OF
WANDSWORTH

9030 00000 4502 5	
Askews	23-Jul-2009
914.278 BERR	£10.99
	WWX0005145/0032

OLIVER BERRY Author

I could have chosen any number of classic fells for this picture, but I thought I'd go for one of the lesser-known ones. I'm standing on top of Sergeant Man (p92), looking north towards Easedale Tarn – you can just see the silvery flash of Windermere behind me. It's a pretty tough climb up there, but the views are out of this world.

MY LAKE DISTRICT

There's nothing quite like hiking on a clear autumn morning when there's mist in the valleys and frost on the fell-tops. I like to set out early, and I always remember to stock up on goodies to keep me going – my current tips for trail treats are Good Taste (p151) in Keswick and the Honeypot (p121) in Hawkshead. As for top walks, it's almost impossible to pick one. Skiddaw (p143), the Langdale Pikes (p86) and Helvellyn (p165) are all definitely on the list, but for me the fells around Buttermere (p163) have that extra touch of magic that keeps drawing me back.

For post-hike recuperation, a pint in a Lakeland inn is an essential ritual – the Kirkstile Inn (p157), the Old Dungeon Ghyll Hotel (p100) and the Wasdale Head Inn (p139) are all long-term favourites.

ABOUT THE AUTHOR

Oliver Berry graduated with a degree in English from University College London, and now lives and works in Cornwall as a writer and photographer. His travels for Lonely Planet have carried him from the snowy mountains of Canada to the beaches of the Cook Islands, but no matter how far he goes, he just can't seem to stay away from his home shores for long. He has covered Cumbria for several editions of Lonely Planet's bestselling guides to England and Britain, and swaps the windswept Cornish cliff tops for the equally windswept Cumbrian fells whenever time and work allow.

Skiddaw
Kirkstile Inn Keswick
Buttermere Helvellyn
Wasdale Head Inn
Old Dungeon Langdale Pikes
Ghyll Hotel Hawkshead

HIGHLIGHTS

The Lake District is where England's scenery takes an unexpected walk on the wild side. Nowhere in the nation packs such an instant panoramic punch: rivers rush, forces tumble, lakes glimmer and lonely fells glower along every horizon. But the Lake District is much more than just a sum of grandstand views. It's a historic textbook, a rural heartland, a pastoral haven, a foodie heaven, an outdoor playground and a literary landmark all rolled into one breathtakingly scenic bundle. Trek the trails, stalk the fells, cruise the lakes, sample the tucker and savour the views – inspiration is sure to follow.

Views

Mountain grandeur, coastal sweep, drystone walls and country meadows – the Lake District is famous for having some of England's best views. If you're a sucker for scenery, you won't find anywhere to top it.

① Great Langdale & the Langdale Pikes

Tramped by generations of hill walkers and Herdwicks, the valley of Great Langdale (p98) and the peaks of the Langdale Pikes (p86) have been a favourite target for peak baggers since Wainwright first put pen to paper in the 1950s.

② Derwent Water

This picturesque lake (p147) is one of the district's loveliest and was a longstanding favourite of Beatrix Potter. Seen on a crisp autumn day when the wooded islands are ablaze with colour, it's not too tough to understand why.

③ Wasdale Head

It's official: Wasdale Head (p137) is the nation's favourite view. England's loftiest summits loom along the skyline, and if the weather takes a turn for the worse, there's no better place to snuggle down than the historic Wasdale Head Inn (p139).

④ Borrowdale & Buttermere

The neighbouring valleys of Borrowdale and Buttermere (p160) are right up there in the scenic stakes; Alfred Wainwright loved the view from Haystacks (p163) so much he decided to stay there for keeps.

⑤ Haweswater

The lakes don't get much more remote than Haweswater (p175), which still has a frisson of wildness many of the other lakes lost long ago.

⑥ Whinlatter Forest

England's only true mountain forest (p156) is now a haven for osprey watchers and red squirrel spotters – just watch out for the mountain bikers on the woodland trails.

Literary Lakes

There's a literary landmark almost everywhere you look in the Lakes, and if you've ever pondered a Wordsworth poem or fantasised about your very own *Swallows and Amazons* adventure, you should feel right at home.

❶ Dove Cottage & Rydal Mount
William Wordsworth's first Lakeland home (p87) is a spiritual mecca for the Romantic movement, but the poet actually spent most of his life at Rydal Mount (pictured, p91).

❷ Hill Top
This fairy-tale farmhouse (p123) in tiny Near Sawrey is a must-see for any self-respecting Potterite – it's where Beatrix penned many of her most famous tales.

❸ Brantwood
Art critic, philosopher, lace enthusiast and environmental campaigner, John Ruskin is one of the most inspiring of the Lakeland characters, and his former home at Brantwood (p112) makes a fascinating introduction to his life and work.

❹ Wordsworth House
This is the place where the Romantic brand began. After years of neglect, Wordsworth's childhood home in Cockermouth (p157) has been painstakingly restored to its former glory thanks to the National Trust.

❺ Mirehouse
Wordsworth, Tennyson, Southey, Thomas Carlyle and John Constable all stayed at this country house (p153) on the shores of Bassenthwaite. Literary memorabilia abounds.

❻ St Oswald's Churchyard
Along with his beloved family, William Wordsworth is buried beneath the old yew trees of Grasmere's parish church (p89).

History

Cumbria is a haven for history lovers; hilltop forts, crumbling castles, ruined abbeys and eerie stone rings stand as reminders of the region's long and sometimes troubled past.

2

① Carlisle Castle

Carlisle's crimson fortress (p197) bears the scars of several centuries of border conflict. Clamber the battlements and cast your mind over the city's war-torn past.

② Furness Abbey

This tumbledown abbey (p187) might be a shell of its former self, but its rosy-red ruins make it one of Cumbria's most romantic spots.

③ Castlerigg Stone Circle

Wow – those ancient Britons sure knew a good location when they saw one. Avebury and Stonehenge steal the limelight, but this hilltop circle (p147) is one of the most awe-inspiring in Britain.

④ Hardknott Roman Fort

The old Roman fort of Mediobogdum (p135) once guarded the vital supply route from the coast to the forts along Hadrian's Wall.

⑤ Holker Hall

The Lake District has its share of stately homes, but none can match the pomp and ceremony of Holker Hall (p183). Keep your eyes peeled for fallow deer, longhorn cattle and salt marsh sheep around the grounds.

⑥ St Olaf's Church

Britain's teeniest house of worship (p137) occupies a fabulous spot in the Wasdale Valley; rumour has it the roof-beams were carved from a Viking longboat.

Food & Drink

Whitewashed inns and gastropubs, farmers markets and frilly teashops, organic food halls and designer delis – the Lake District is a place to feed your soul and your stomach all at once.

❶ Grasmere Gingerbread
Is it a biscuit? Or is it a cake? Who cares! It's delicious, and still baked to the very same carefully guarded recipe laid down by Sarah Nelson in the mid-19th century (p89).

❷ Cumberland Sausage
Cumbria's trademark coil-shaped banger (p45) is a staple feature on many a Lakeland menu.

❸ Food Shops & Farmers Markets
If you like your produce fresh from the farm and brimful of flavour, pick up some local goodies from one of the region's markets or delis (p45). Whether it's chutneys, cheeses, jams or gingerbreads, you're guaranteed to find something that tickles your fancy.

❹ Pubs & Inns
There's nothing quite like warming your toes in front of a flickering fire, pint of warm ale in hand, and the Lake District has some of the most atmospheric inns in England (p47).

❺ Tea & Cake
After a long day on the fells, what could be more cockle-warming than a hot mug of tea and a thick slab of crumbly homemade cake? Go on. You deserve it.

❻ Ale
Wry'Nose, Bluebird Bitter, Sneck Lifter and Chesters Strong & Ugly – the names are almost as much fun as the ales in this corner of England, and there are loads of marvellous microbreweries (p49) and atmospheric inns to seek out.

Contents

Regional Map Contents

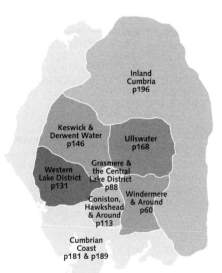

Inland Cumbria p196

Keswick & Derwent Water p146

Ullswater p168

Western Lake District p131

Grasmere & the Central Lake District p88

Coniston, Hawkshead & Around p113

Windermere & Around p60

Cumbrian Coast p181 & p189

Destination Lake District

There is a blessing in the air,
Which seems a sense of joy to yield
To the bare trees, and mountains bare,
And grass in the green field.

William Wordsworth, 1798

In terms of sheer natural splendour, nowhere in England can hold a candle to the sky-topping vistas and wide-angle views of the Lake District. For centuries, poets, painters, polymaths and perambulators alike have been tramping around the region's fells and sunlit ravines in search of inspiration and escape, and it's still the nation's favourite place to revel in the mighty majesty of the English landscape.

'No part of the country is more distinguished by its sublimity,' mused the grand old bard of the lakes, William Wordsworth, and two centuries on his words still ring true. Wordsworth, Coleridge and their Romantic contemporaries famously emigrated to the Lakes in search of their collective poetic muse in the early 19th century, and a host of other literary luminaries followed in their footsteps: John Ruskin, Harriet Martineau, Beatrix Potter, Arthur Ransome and, of course, John Cunliffe, creator of the classic children's TV series, *Postman Pat*. It's not too hard to understand what drew them all here. Every bend in the road seems to reveal a fresh panorama of astonishing views: deep valleys and plunging passes hollowed out by long-extinct glaciers, plummeting fell-sides coated with orange bracken, granite boulders and twisted trees, and misty mountain lakes illuminated by sudden shafts of sunlight breaking through the cloud. It's a place where you can almost hear the creak and grind of Mother Nature's cogs at work, where stout cob-walled cottages huddle beneath overarching crags, hardy Herdwick sheep wander the fell-tops and saw-tooth summits trace a jagged course against the horizon.

Unsurprisingly, with some of the nation's loftiest peaks clustered within its borders, the Lake District is considered by many to be the spiritual home of British hiking. Ever since the accountant-turned-author Alfred Wainwright first put pen to paper in the 1950s and began the seven-book, 14-year, 214-peak odyssey of the *Pictorial Guides to the Lakeland Fells* (still the bestselling Lakeland hiking guides almost 50 years after their initial publication), walkers of every age and ability have been flocking to the Lake District to tackle the mountains, tarns and hilltop trails for themselves.

But surprisingly few stop to consider the fact that despite its wild, windswept aspect, the Lake District is a long way from an untouched wilderness. In fact, it's one of the most intensively cropped, cultivated and managed corners of the country, shaped and moulded by generations of Cumbrian hill farmers (not to mention several million Herdwick, Swaledale and Rough Fell sheep). Hill farming has been a vital local industry here since the arrival of the Norse settlers in the 10th century, and probably long before: many of the drystone walls stretching out across the fell-sides date back to the days when doublets and hose were still considered the height of contemporary fashion.

As in many rural corners of England, however, those employed in traditional industries such as agriculture and hill farming are finding it increasingly tough to make ends meet. The fallout from the devastating outbreak of foot-and-mouth in 2001, which closed down much of Cumbria and led to the enforced slaughter of hundreds of thousands of sheep and cattle, forced

CUMBRIA FAST FACTS

Area: 2630 sq miles

Population: 498,900

Unemployment: 2.1%

Number of people employed in the tourism industry: 63,020

Number of sheep: 2.05 million

Ratio of grey to red squirrels: 66:1

Percentage of dwellings used as holiday or second homes: 15%

Number of peaks over 3000ft: 4

Estimated length of drystone walls: 9400 miles

many already struggling farmers to the wall, and raised fears not just for the survival of this age-old industry, but for the very future of the beloved Lakeland landscape. Without sheep to graze the high country, there are very real concerns that the Lake District's distinctive fells might look very different in years to come. Hill farming is more than just a local industry – it's a way of life that's stitched into the fabric of the Lake District landscape, and for many people its future survival is inextricably linked with the long-term welfare of the wider national park.

And while the formation of the national park in 1951 has undoubtedly helped protect the landscape for future generations, it hasn't been without its teething troubles. Spiralling visitor numbers and hundreds of thousands of extra boots tramping the fells have inevitably had consequences for the fragile Lakeland environment, leading to ongoing problems of litter, habitat damage and fell erosion, as well as a huge rise in road traffic, with all the attendant problems of noise, tailbacks and air pollution. And as in many other scenic pockets of the English countryside, many Lakeland villages have found themselves swamped by an ever-rising tide of holiday cottages, seasonal lets and second homes, which have helped push house prices to sky-high levels and prevented local families from taking their first tentative step onto the housing ladder.

While there are undoubtedly problems ahead, there are also plenty of positive signs for the future too. The designation of the Lake District as an Environmentally Sensitive Area (ESA) in 1993 recognised for the first time the unique importance of traditional agriculture to the local environment, and helped farmers to diversify into new areas in order to supplement their income, providing funding for the restoration of drystone walls, farm buildings and hedgerows and paying local landowners to protect sensitive areas such as marshland, moorland, lakes and riverbanks.

So in a world facing up to the stark realities of climate change, the Lake District has in many ways set the course for the rest of the nation to follow. Local businesses have been actively encouraged to take advantage of the growing green economy, and a host of environmentally friendly schemes, ranging from the car-free Cross-Lakes Shuttle to the solar-powered launches plying Coniston Water, have helped place Cumbria and the Lake District at the forefront of the search for greener and more sustainable ways of life.

Similarly, projects to protect the native red squirrel, restore heavily eroded footpaths and return areas of landscape to unmanaged wilderness (most obviously around the valley of Ennerdale) all bode well for the future. And perhaps most encouragingly of all, the return of Britain's first breeding pair of wild ospreys to Bassenthwaite Lake (p153) in 2001 is seen by many as a sign that after years of hanging in the balance, crucial Lakeland habitats are slowly starting to regain their natural status quo.

Getting Started

Covering an area of 885 sq miles and measuring just 30 miles from edge to edge, the Lake District's compact dimensions are both a boon and a curse: you're never more than a bus ride away from the next trailhead or town, but unfortunately the narrow lanes, crowded trails and sardine-can car parks can make that all-important cloudlike feeling seem frustratingly elusive on the busiest days. By timing your visit and pre-planning your trip, you'll be able to dodge the crowds and appreciate the Lakeland scenery at its best.

WHEN TO GO

There's no getting around it – overcrowding can be a serious headache in the Lake District. By far the most hectic period is from July to late August, but Bank Holiday weekends and school vacations (especially around Christmas and Easter) might also be worth avoiding: on the busiest days it can feel like half of northern England has joined you in a headlong dash to admire the Lakeland scenery. See p22 for a calendar of Lakeland events.

'Wordsworth thought the Lakeland colours were most vivid on a crisp winter's day'

Regardless of when you visit, the notoriously fickle Lakeland weather is bound to play a part in your travel plans. All those green pastures and lush dales come at a price: according to the Met Office, the Lake District is officially the wettest place in England and receives twice the national rainfall average, so you're likely to experience a dose of good old English rain at some point during your stay. But the region's topography means that the weather can vary widely – while one fell summit could be cloaked in cloud and drenched by drizzle, another nearby valley might be bathed in brilliant sunshine.

All things considered, early spring and late autumn are the most settled times to visit. Arrive in March and early April and you'll be treated to a dazzling display of fresh greenery and spring blossoms, while in late October the woodlands are a blaze of autumnal reds, oranges and ochre-browns. The post-Christmas period can be another lovely season – Wordsworth thought the Lakeland colours were at their most vivid on a crisp winter's day, and glimpsing the fell tops brushed with a fresh covering of snow is one sight you won't forget in a hurry.

COSTS & MONEY

Travelling in the Lake District certainly isn't as cheap as many other destinations, but thankfully there are options to cater for all comers, whether you're busting the budget on a full-blown luxury Lakeland experience or bunking down in a hostel or B&B. Booking ahead, dodging the peak seasons and using public transport are good ways of bringing costs down, and of course (unlike in many countries) you won't have to fork out a penny to visit the national park itself – although you might well find the costs ratchet up once you've forked out for a few days' of car-parking fees.

At the bottom end, backpackers and campers can expect to pay around £15 to £20 a night at most campsites, including two people and a car, while hostels generally charge between £12 and £18 per person for a dorm bunk and a hearty breakfast fry-up. By self-catering and using public transport, you could scrape by on £30 to £35 a day.

At the other end of the scale, romantic-weekend splurgers could find themselves shelling out a small fortune at some of the more upmarket country hotels. The cheapest rooms start at around £100 to £120 for a double, but you won't get anything special for that kind of cash; bump up to between £180 and £250 and you're entering boutique territory, while fork out £300

DON'T LEAVE HOME WITHOUT...

- Good hiking boots with plenty of tread
- A waterproof, breathable rain jacket – Gore-Tex is best
- A comfortable rucksack or day pack to carry your gear
- An up-to-date 1:25,000 map if you're doing any hiking or biking
- Binoculars, camera and a spare memory card (or spare film for traditionalists)
- Plenty of spare socks
- A healthy appetite
- A taste for warm ale
- A calm attitude to queues

---

or more and you can expect an establishment of aristocratic standing. Count on £30 to £60 a head at the top-rated restaurants, excluding wine.

The vast majority of visitors end up falling into the midrange price bracket. A double room in an average B&B (including breakfast) will set you back £50 to £80; singles are often a reduced rate on a double room (generally 75%). Splash out more than £80 and you'll buy a few luxury touches (designer decor, flat-screen TVs, gourmet breakfasts and bath goodies), while under £50 you'll be looking at dowdy decor, battered tellies and a bathroom shared with your next-door neighbour. A decent bistro meal will set you back £10 to £15 for lunch, or £15 to £25 for supper; factor in admission charges and travel costs and you'll be looking at £120 to £150 per day for a really comfortable holiday. If you're travelling as a family, renting your own cottage can be a cost-effective option – see p217 for some recommended operators.

Membership of the National Trust is a worthwhile investment, since you'll be entitled to free entry to its Lake District properties and car parks. US-based visitors belonging to the White Oak Foundation (see p221) benefit from the same privileges.

TRAVELLING RESPONSIBLY

Sustainable travel is a hot topic in the Lakes, and you'll find a strong selection of environmentally friendly initiatives, from yurt campsites to carbon-neutral B&Bs and solar-powered cruise boats. But the best thing you can do is to bite the bullet and leave the car at home. It might not be as convenient, and you'll have to juggle around your travel plans, but you'll be doing your bit to reduce the traffic problem as well as cutting down on your carbon footprint. Practically everywhere in the Lakes is accessible by bus or train, so there's really no excuse not to give it a go. Cycling is also worth considering, although the Lake District hills might spring a few nasty surprises if you don't plan your route carefully.

Food is another area where you can exercise your green pound: shopping locally at small suppliers and farmers markets puts your cash directly into the pockets of local suppliers rather than supermarket conglomerates. Many cafes, hotels and restaurants are starting to source their goods from closer to home, so keep your eyes peeled for locally sourced ingredients on menus.

If you're walking on the fells, avoid picking, breaking, snapping, trampling or sitting on anything – the landscape might look rugged, but it's a surprisingly fragile environment and needs to be looked after. Most importantly, stick to the trails and avoid walking across countryside or cutting trail corners if you can to prevent unnecessary erosion.

TRAVEL LITERATURE

For many visitors the Lake District is as much a literary landscape as a natural one, so here's a selection of books we think make good bedtime companions. We've concentrated mostly on recent titles – for classic authors, jump over to our Literary Lakes chapter on p41.

AS Byatt's *Unruly Times* is a fantastically readable account of the mutually inspiring but frequently stormy relationship between two of the great Lakeland figureheads, William Wordsworth and Samuel Taylor Coleridge.

Feet in the Clouds: a Story of Fell-Running and Obsession by Richard Askwith provides an overview of one of the most brutal (and baffling) sports, told from the firsthand perspective of an ex-London journalist. If you've ever wondered what drives apparently sane men and women to run full pelt up and down a mountainside, this is for you.

Haweswater by Sarah Hall is a fictional work set in the 1930s during the creation of the Haweswater Reservoir and the drowning of the village of Mardale. It's a finely crafted study of a farming community facing up to progress and the loss of their traditional ways of life. Highly recommended.

Dorothy Wordsworth's *Grasmere Journals* make a fascinating travel companion. Her tender descriptions paint a vivid portrait of everyday life in Grasmere at the turn of the 18th century, and it's intriguing to see how much things have (or haven't) changed over the last couple of centuries.

No visit to the Lake District would be complete without a well-thumbed copy of *Swallows and Amazons* by Arthur Ransome, not just one of the classic British children's tales, but also a kind of *roman-à-clef* to the Lakeland scenery.

Melvyn Bragg, the urbane Cumbrian-born broadcaster and presenter of the long-running *South Bank Show,* is also a prolific novelist. One of his best tales is *The Maid of Buttermere,* which centres on the celebrated beauty Mary Robinson and her encounter with the con man John Hatfield.

And finally what better companion to the Lakes could there be than the most famous fell walker of them all? *Wainwright: a Biography* by the veteran Lakeland author Hunter Davies was written with the cooperation of Alfred's beloved widow Betty, and is stuffed with anecdotes and insights about the great man. Also by the same author is the classic Lake District travelogue, *A Walk Around the Lakes,* which mixes keen observation with an obvious passion for the area.

INTERNET RESOURCES

There's loads of information on the net to help you plan your Lakeland adventure, but your first stop should be the comprehensive site **Go Lakes** (www.golakes.co.uk) run by the Cumbrian tourist authority or the more general countywide **Visit Cumbria** (www.visitcumbria.com).

Cycling Cumbria (www.cyclingcumbria.com) Excellent online resource for cyclists, with archived routes for on- and off-road biking graded according to strenuousness and difficulty.

Lake District National Park Authority (www.lake-district.gov.uk) Official website for the National Park Authority (NPA), with background on the history, ecology and geology of the national park, as well as webcams and up-to-date weather reports.

Lake District Outdoors (www.lakedistrictoutdoors.co.uk) Fancy trying a spot of canoeing or ghyll scrambling? This is the place to start.

Lake District Walks (www.lakedistrictwalks.com) Encyclopaedic reference site to Lakeland walks run by the internet's answer to Alfred Wainwright, John Dawson.

TOP PICKS

LAKE DISTRICT

CAMPSITES

Whether you're a 100% committed camper or this is your first time spent kipping under the stars, there's a campsite to suit you. Some are tap-and-toilet sites, others luxury getaways; world-class views are standard.

- **Full Circle** (p96) Yurts and wood-burning stoves in the grounds of Rydal Hall.
- **Quiet Site** (p169) Ever camped in an eco-pod? Now's your chance.
- **Syke Farm** (p163) Beautiful site in the heart of Buttermere.
- **Great Langdale** (p98) Scenery stretches in every direction.
- **Gillside Farm** (p172) Farm camping in the shadow of Helvellyn.

- **4 Winds Lakeland Tipis** (p72) Camp Sioux-style near Windermere.
- **Wasdale Head** (p138) One for wild campers.
- **Low Wray** (p80) Lake camping on the shores of Windermere.
- **Bowkerstead Farm** (p122) Simple field site on the doorstep of Grizedale Forest.
- **Fisherground Farm** (p134) Family friendly site handy for the La'al Ratty railway.

STATELY HOMES

Country estates have been an integral part of Lakeland life for centuries: lord it up in some of our favourites.

- **Holker Hall** (p183) Glorious grounds, a fantastic food hall and aristocratic architecture.
- **Muncaster Castle** (p130) The nation's most haunted castle. Nice gardens, too.
- **Brantwood** (p112) John Ruskin's country hideaway on the shores of Coniston Water.

- **Blackwell** (p71) Arts and Crafts aplenty at this 19th-century mansion.
- **Levens Hall** (p214) The most ostentatious topiary in England.

WALKS

You really haven't seen the Lake District until you've conquered a few fells, so try these bad boys out for size.

- **Scafell Pike** (p127) England's highest mountain.
- **Helvellyn** (p165) Dizzying drops made this peak Wordsworth's favourite.
- **Black Combe** (p178) Often-overlooked fell with panoramic views in all directions.

- **Skiddaw** (p143) The northern Lakes' best hike.
- **The Langdale Pikes** (p86) Peak-bagging aplenty in the Langdale Valley.

Lonely Planet (www.lonelyplanet.com) Destination guides and travel tips from our own good selves.
Mountain Weather Information Service (www.mwis.org.uk) Provides a weekly download-able forecast for all of Britain's mountain parks, including the Lake District.
Striding Edge (www.stridingedge.net) Online photo diary run by Sean McMahon, with wonderful photos of practically every fell in the Lake District seen from every conceivable angle. Fantastic, inspirational stuff.

Events Calendar

FEBRUARY

KESWICK FILM FESTIVAL mid-Feb
www.keswickfilmfestival.org
Keswick's cinematic spectacular with film premieres and directors' talks.

DALEMAIN MARMALADE FESTIVAL mid-Feb
www.marmaladefestival.com
Annual jam-makers joust: separate categories for Seville orange, chunky, citrus and organic marmalades, with special prizes for chaps, kids, soldiers and (bizarrely) clergymen.

MARCH

WORDS BY THE WATER early Mar
Annual celebration of the written word in Keswick.

DAFFODIL & SPRING FLOWER SHOW end Mar
www.ambleside-show.org.uk
Springtime flower festival in Ambleside.

MAY

ULVERSTON WALKING FESTIVAL early May
Hikers hit Ulverston for organised walks, talks and events.

ULLSWATER WALKING FESTIVAL mid-May
www.ullswater.com/walkingfestival
Organised hikes around Helvellyn, Fairfield, Gowbarrow, and Ullswater's other summits.

KESWICK JAZZ FESTIVAL mid-May
Saxophones and snare drums at Keswick's five-day jazz-fest, with top names from the Brit, European and world circuits.

KESWICK MOUNTAIN FESTIVAL mid-May
www.keswickmountainfestival.co.uk
Celebrity hikers, bikers and climbers congregate at Keswick for this four-day celebration of the great outdoors.

BRATHAY WINDERMERE MARATHON mid-May
Iron-lunged competitors cover 26.2 miles around the shores of Windermere.

FRED WHITTON CHALLENGE mid-May
www.fredwhittonchallenge.org.uk
Gruelling 112-mile slog over the Lake District's six highest passes. On a bike.

HOLKER GARDEN FESTIVAL end May
Local food, horticultural displays and blooms in the grounds of Holker Hall.

JUNE

KESWICK BEER FESTIVAL early Jun
www.keswickbeerfestival.co.uk
Can't tell your Ram Tam from your Cheeky Pheasant? Then it's time you downed some brews at Keswick's annual ale-fest.

BOOT BEER FESTIVAL early Jun
Much smaller beer festival held in Boot's three hugger-mugger inns – but at least you won't have to queue up for a pint.

ULLSWATER COUNTRY FAIR end Jun
Pedigree hunting dogs and terriers take centre stage at Ullswater's historic country fair.

JULY

AMBLESIDE RUSHBEARING 1st Sat in Jul
Rushes and wreaths are carried with pomp and ceremony around Ambleside to St Mary's Church.

CONISTON WATER FESTIVAL early Jul
www.conistonwaterfestival.co.uk
Sailing, windsurfing, stone skimming and general larking about on Coniston Water.

CUMBERLAND COUNTY SHOW mid-Jul
www.cumberlandshow.co.uk
The big 'un: Cumbrian wrestlers jostle for space with dressage displays, prize bulls and handsome Herdwicks at the county's main agricultural show.

CARLISLE FESTIVAL mid-Jul
www.carlislefestival.org.uk
Concerts and recitals come to town for this classically orientated celebration.

SCARECROW FESTIVAL mid-Jul
Scarecrows cover the streets of Langwathby, Millom, Haverigg and several other Cumbrian villages.

COCK ROCK mid-Jul
www.cockermouthrockfestival.com
Popsters and rock-chicks boogie to hot new bands at Cockermouth's provocatively titled rock festival.

AMBLESIDE SPORTS last Thu in Jul
Fell runners hit the trails, hounds sniff the scents, and wrestlers in long johns battle for supremacy at this traditional sports day.

AUGUST

LOWTHER HORSE DRIVING TRIALS & COUNTRY FAIR early Aug
www.lowther.co.uk/events/
Showjumping and carriage races are the main attractions at this popular country fair.

GRASMERE RUSHBEARING Sat nearest to 5 Aug
More rushbearing antics, this time centring on St Oswald's in Grasmere.

SHEEPDOG TRIALS mid- to end Aug
Come by! Away! Sheepdogs outwit the Swaledales and Herdwicks at competitions in Rydal, Gosforth, Threlkeld, Skelton and Patterdale.

KENDAL MINTFEST Aug Bank Holiday
www.mintfest.org
Artists, street performers and plenty of odd costumes congregate on the Auld Grey Town.

GRASMERE SPORTS & SHOW Aug Bank Holiday
www.grasmeresportsandshow.co.uk
As per Ambleside Sports but on Grasmere's green.

KESWICK AGRICULTURAL SHOW Aug Bank Holiday
Historic pastoral affair, held every year since 1860.

SEPTEMBER

HELVELLYN TRIATHLON early Sep
A mile swim across Ullswater, a 38-mile cycle over Kirkstone Pass, and a 9-mile run to the summit of Helvellyn. Yes, they probably are insane.

WESTMORLAND COUNTY SHOW 2nd Thu in Sep
www.westmorlandshow.co.uk
Westmorland puts its comeliest sheep and cattle on show near Kendal.

KENDAL TORCHLIGHT CARNIVAL mid-Sep
www.kendaltorchlightcarnival.co.uk
Kendal's answer to the Notting Hill Carnival: daft costumes, street processions and decorated floats.

BORROWDALE SHEPHERDS' MEET mid-Sep
www.borrowdaleshow.org.uk
Hounds trail, fell runners race, shepherds shear and sheepdogs strut their stuff at Rosthwaite in Borrowdale.

EGREMONT CRAB FAIR & SPORTS mid-Sep
www.egremontcrabfair.co.uk
See the world's ugliest mugs battle it out in this historic gurning competition.

ESKDALE SHOW end Sep
Farmers' show in Eskdale valley.

OCTOBER

TASTE DISTRICT early Oct
www.tastedistrict.com
Gourmet gala celebrating Cumbria's best beer brewers, chutney bottlers, sausage stuffers and bread kneaders, held at Rheged near Penrith.

NOVEMBER

KENDAL MOUNTAIN FILM FESTIVAL mid-Nov
www.mountainfilm.co.uk
The best new films and documentaries from the adrenaline-fuelled world of adventure sports.

BIGGEST LIAR IN THE WORLD mid-Nov
www.santonbridgeinn.com/liar
You little liar… Hear improbable tales of flatulent sheep and giant turnips at the Santon Bridge Inn's porky-telling contest.

CARLISLE BLUES FESTIVAL mid- to end Nov
www.carlislebluesfestival.com
Blues and rock acts hit stages around Carlisle.

ULVERSTON DICKENSIAN FESTIVAL end Nov
Meet Bob Cratchits, Ebenezer Scrooges and Oliver Twists on the streets of Ulverston in this Christmassy procession.

Itineraries
CLASSIC ROUTES

LAND OF THE LAKES
Two Weeks / Windermere to Ullswater

Kick-start the trip in historic **Windermere** (p59) with a classic cruise from the jetties at **Bowness-on-Windermere** (p62). Then it's grub galore and views aplenty at **Ambleside** (p76), before venturing into Wordsworth country at **Grasmere** (p87) and the poet's former homes at **Dove Cottage** (p87) and **Rydal Mount** (p91). Take a scenic spin around the valleys of **Great Langdale** (p98) and **Little Langdale** (p96), before heading south to picture-perfect **Hawkshead** (p118), Beatrix Potter's house at **Hill Top** (p123) and the trails of **Grizedale Forest** (p122), followed by a solar-powered cruise on **Coniston Water** (p114). Heading back west, take a detour to admire the nation's favourite view at **Wasdale Head** (p137). Then travel north to visit Wordsworth's birthplace at **Cockermouth** (p157), before cutting back inland via the gorgeous valleys of **Buttermere** (p163) and **Borrowdale** (p160) en route to **Keswick** (p145) and the tree-clad islands of **Derwent Water** (p148). Wind things up with a trip around the grand old lake of **Ullswater** (p167) and (if you're brave enough) a jaunt up **Helvellyn** (p165), England's most spectacular hike.

A whistle-stop circuit packing in the Lake District's essential sights – picturesque villages, plunging fells, snowy peaks and stately lakes (with a dose of Wordsworth and Beatrix Potter thrown in for good measure).

PAST SPLENDOURS
Two Weeks / Carlisle to Kendal

Begin your historic circuit in Cumbria's capital, **Carlisle** (p197). Get some textbook perspective at the **Tullie House Museum** (p198) before strolling the battlements of **Carlisle Castle** (p197) and visiting the city's **cathedral** (p198). Head down to **Penrith** (p204), once the centre of the Celtic kingdom of Rheged, before detouring via the aristocratic splendour of **Dalemain** (p167) en route to **Keswick** (p145), a thriving hiking hub. Don't miss an unforgettable sunset at **Castlerigg Stone Circle** (p147).

Spend a day exploring elegant **Mirehouse** (p153) and the Georgian streets of **Cockermouth** (p157) before heading along the **Cumbrian Coast** (p177) to the salty old seaport of **Whitehaven** (p189), once England's third-busiest harbour. Visit the spooktastic castle of **Muncaster** (p130) before travelling back in time aboard the **Ravenglass and Eskdale Railway** (p130), built to carry iron ore from the Eskdale mines.

Stop off at the Roman fort at **Hardknott Pass** (p135), spot ancient drystone walls around the **Langdale Valley** (p95) and spend time by idyllic **Elterwater** (p97). Juggle the charms of town and countryside around busy **Ambleside** (p76) and even-busier **Grasmere** (p87), visit the quirky yeoman's cottage of **Townend** (p75), before descending to **Windermere** and **Bowness** (p59) for a trip aboard the Lake District's oldest **cruise boats** (p62) across to **Lakeside** (p71) or the Victorian grounds of **Fell Foot Park** (p71).

Further south, stroll through the ruins of **Furness Abbey** (p187), pop into the medieval priory at **Cartmel** (p182), visit the antique-packed manor of **Holker Hall** (p183) and stroll the seafront promenade of **Grange-over-Sands** (p180) before finishing up in **Kendal** (p210), home of the county's favourite minty treat and a handy launch pad for **Sizergh Castle** (p214) and **Levens Hall** (p214).

A two-week trip back in time around some of the district's historic landmarks and market towns, taking in derelict abbeys, country houses and the county's only city: red-brick Carlisle.

TAILORED TRIPS

QUIRKY CUMBRIA

Weary of Wordsworth? Bored with Beatrix? Had it with hiking? Then try this specially tailored spin around some of Cumbria's more off-kilter attractions.

Our first curiosity stop is an underground tour into the murky depths of the **Honister Slate Mine** (p163), followed by a head-spinning clamber along the **Via Ferrata** (p163), a cliff-top system of fixed ropes and ladders modelled on those used by Italian troops during WWI. Down in the Borrowdale Valley, you can climb up to the top of the house-sized lump of rock known as the **Bowder Stone** (p160), visit the wettest place in England at **Styhead Tarn** (p162) or take to the lake in a **Viking longboat** (p160). Nearby Keswick has a wealth of weirdo sights, ranging from a geological piano and an ancient mummified cat at the **Keswick Museum** (p145) to the world's biggest pencil at the **Cumberland Pencil Museum** (p147) and a filmic fleet of cinematic cars at the **Cars of the Stars Motor Museum** (p145) – keep your peepers peeled for Mr Bean's Mini, the A-Team van and a triumvirate of original Batmobiles.

More curious filmic connections can be found out on the coast in Ulverston, where a **museum** (p185) has been established in honour of the town's most famous son, Stan Laurel. Along the coast you can see a painstaking recreation of a 1930s petrol station at Holker Hall's **Lakeland Motor Museum** (p184), or have your chi cleansed and your chakras realigned at the **Conishead Priory** (p187), home to Europe's largest Kadampa Buddhist temple. Over in Whitehaven, the weird waxworks at the **Rum Story** (p190) include a recreation of a 19th-century punch tavern and Nelson's body being pickled in rum after the Battle of Trafalgar, while budding spook hunters can indulge in their very own overnight ghost sit at nearby **Muncaster Castle** (p130), supposedly the most haunted house in England. Don't forget to stop for a spin aboard England's most elaborate train set at **Ravenglass** (p130) before paying your respects at Cumbria's tiniest **church** (p137) in Wasdale Head, boning up on the nation's nuclear industry at **Sellafield** (p192) and wandering around the replica Victorian shopfronts of the **Millom Folk Museum** (p188).

Still not weirded out yet? Then travel back to the **Wordsworth Museum** (p89) in Grasmere, where the offbeat exhibits include Thomas de Quincey's walking stick along with spooky life masks of William Wordsworth and John Keats. Alternatively the **Ruskin Museum** (p112) in Coniston houses the original tail fin and engine from Donald Campbell's doomed jet boat *Bluebird,* dredged up from the bottom of the lake after 50 years (along with Campbell's mortal remains, which are now buried in the nearby churchyard of St Andrew's). Over in Penrith you can see the Monocled Mutineer's monocle at the **Penrith Museum** (p204) and wander around one of England's strangest stone circles, **Long Meg and Her Daughters** (p206), near Little Salkeld. Round things off with a trip up to Carlisle, whose curious attractions include the city's medieval stocks at the **Guildhall Museum** (p198), a Roman cataract needle at the **Tullie House Museum** (p198) and the celebrated licking stones of **Carlisle Castle** (p197), supposedly lapped by parched prisoners during the Jacobite siege of 1745.

A GREEN ADVENTURE

There's a long tradition of environmental campaigning in the Lakes, so why not join the green crusade? Your first contribution is to ditch the car: you can catch **trains** (p227) between Kendal and Windermere and along the Cumbrian Coast, while nearly every Lakeland village has its own scenic **bus route** (p226). The **Cross-Lakes Shuttle** (p70) enables car-free travel between Coniston and Windermere, while the Coniston Water **cruise boats** (p114) run on nothing but sunshine. Or, of course, there's good old carbon-neutral **cycling** (p104), which is still one of the best ways to explore the Lakeland countryside.

For eco-friendly accommodation, you're spoilt for choice. Vegetarians should make a beeline for **Lancrigg** (p94) in Grasmere or **Yewfield** (p121) in Hawkshead, while carbon-conscious travellers can sleep easy at Grasmere's luxurious **Moss Grove Hotel · Organic** (p95), cottagey **Cote How Organic Guest House** (p81) just north of Ambleside, or the refurbished **Howe Keld** (p150) in Keswick.

Campers can kip in **yurts** (p96) near Grasmere, **tipis** (p72) near Newby Bridge, or **eco-pods** (p98) in the Langdale Valley, before stocking up on local goodies from **Lucy's Specialist Grocery** (p82) and the wonderful farm shops at **Low Sizergh Barn** (p214) and **Howbarrow Organic Farm** (p183). Or, if you prefer letting someone else do the cooking, how about the wholefood cafes of **Lakeland Pedlar** (p151), **Waterside Wholefoods** (p213), **Wilf's** (p74) or the **World Peace Cafe** (p186)? Go on – green is good.

ROMANTIC RETREATS

Whether you're a chintz lover or a boutique devotee, the Lake District is brimming with romantic boltholes tailor-made for spoiling your nearest and dearest.

First you need the perfect hideaway. Prefer things posh? Then you'll want a country house hotel – perhaps the ivy-clad **Holbeck Ghyll** (p68), the splendid sophistication of **Gilpin Lodge** (p68) or the swag-draped showiness of **Sharrow Bay** (p170). Too stuffy? Don't fret. Try the **Waterhead Hotel** (p81) for cool contemporariness, **Linthwaite House** (p68) for country pampering or the **Samling** (p68) for all-out celeb splendour. Too pricey? No probs. **Summer Hill Country House** (p116), **No 43** (p180) and the **Drunken Duck** (p121) all have lashings of style without the sky-high price tag, while the **Wasdale Head Inn** (p139) is the ideal place for that dreamy end-of-the-world feel.

Next you need the perfect table. You could dine under mill machinery at the **Glass House** (p82), among cosy clutter at the **Jumble Room** (p95), amid clean lines at **Rogan and Company** (p183) or shiny pine at **Lucy's on a Plate** (p82). Veggies should plump for the **Quince & Medlar** (p159), but for culinary fireworks there's only one choice – **L'Enclume** (p183) in Cartmel.

Last you need that all-important magic moment – and what could be more romantic than a **twilight cruise** (p148) across the island-studded lake of Derwent Water?

THE WILD SIDE

Looking to give the civilised world the slip? Top spot in the wildness stakes has to go to **Wasdale Head** (p137), whose untamed peaks have long provided a proving ground for ambitious hikers and mountain climbers. Many Lakes visitors overlook the nearby **Cumbrian Coast** (p177), but if you choose your spot it can make a wonderfully remote refuge from the hustle and bustle of the busier corners of the national park. There are rich wildlife reserves around **Hodbarrow** (p188), **St Bees** (p191) and the **Solway Coast** (p192), as well as around the dramatic vales of **Eskdale** (p133) and the **Duddon Valley** (p135), where sheep and cattle still outnumber the human inhabitants by a rather considerable margin. Meanwhile the return of ospreys to **Bassenthwaite** (p153), red squirrels to **Whinlatter** (p156) and golden eagles to **Haweswater** (p176), together with the 'rewilding' of **Ennerdale** (p139), has brought a sliver of lost wilderness back to the Lakeland landscape.

As for unruly views, you're spoilt for choice: try the windswept summits of **Black Combe** (p178), **Scafell Pike** (p127) and the **Langdale Pikes** (p86), or the high mountain passes of **Kirkstone** (p174) and **Honister** (p163). And if you fancy a night out in the wilds, you won't find anywhere better than the mountain hostels of **Black Sail** (p140), **Coppermines** (p115) and **Helvellyn** (p172), or the splendidly isolated and marvellously ivy-clad **Haweswater Hotel** (p176), built in the 1930s and still the only accommodation option in the Haweswater valley.

GOURMET GETAWAY

Passionate pubbers, organic advocates and fine-dining diehards will all find culinary Cumbria a highlight. For traditional grub and ale, the **Britannia Inn** (p97) and the **Pheasant Inn** (p155) are hard to beat, but if you prefer your pints in more contemporary surroundings, try the beautifully beamed **Yanwath Gate Inn** (p207) or the organic-orientated **George and Dragon** (p175). Meanwhile the homely **Black Bull** (p117) in Coniston and the **Bitter End** (p159) in Cockermouth have established themselves as two of northern England's top microbreweries.

As for afternoon tea, **Bryson's** (p151) in Keswick turns out the crumbliest of scones and tastiest of cakes, while the **Hazelmere Cafe** (p181) in Grange-over-Sands is the top choice if you're a sucker for bone-china teapots and frilly doilies. For a funkier spin, try **Good Taste** (p151) in Keswick, or for slate-floored cosiness make a beeline for the **Yew Tree Farm** (p117) near Coniston or the **Jumping Jenny** (p114) at Brantwood.

Not full yet? Don't worry – you've still got to pick up handmade gingerbread from **Sarah Nelson's** (p89) in Grasmere, tender venison from **Holker Hall** (p183), mintcake from **Kendal** (p213), fresh bread from **Munx** (p74) in Staveley, spicy chutneys from the **Hawkshead Relish Company** (p121) and royally approved bacon from **Woodall's of Waberthwaite** (p189), not forgetting of course the stickiest of sticky toffee puddings from the **Cartmel Village Shop** (p182).

History

Jammed along the tempestuous frontier between England and Scotland, and sandwiched between the rolling grey Irish Sea and the northern English counties, Cumbria has a long and turbulent history stretching back over seven millennia. Relics of the county's past litter the surrounding hilltops, from eerie stone circles left behind by ancient Britons to Viking crosses, ancient abbeys, stately houses and crenellated castles. Even if you're not a hardcore history enthusiast, it's fascinating to see how the past has shaped both the county's landscape and its unique character, customs and traditions.

This chapter provides an overview of Cumbria's pivotal historic periods. For a quick low-down on the key events you can consult the timeline running along the bottom of the page.

EARLY PEOPLE

Until the end of the last ice age much of what is now the Lake District was covered by a series of vast glaciers. It was only when the ice sheets finally began to melt that humans arrived on the scene in any considerable numbers. Hunter-gatherer tribes first started moving into the area around the time of the great thaw, seeking shelter in the area's caves while pursuing game – deer, mammoth, wild pigs and aurochs (a forerunner of modern-day cattle). The earliest concrete evidence of human settlement has been found around the Cumbrian coastline; small flints and mesolithic arrowheads dating from around 7000 BC have been found at various coastal locations, including Cartmel, St Bees and the Isle of Walney.

By around 5000 BC, humans were well established, clearing the dense forest that had grown up on the mountain slopes as the ice sheets retreated, and setting up simple arable farms and cattle enclosures. One of the densest Neolithic sites centred on the area around Great Langdale (p98), which served as a kind of prehistoric 'axe factory'; around 40% of Neolithic axes found in Britain were fashioned from Langdale stone, and examples have been discovered everywhere from eastern Scotland to Land's End in Cornwall.

Around this time, as in many other areas of Britain and Europe, the strange practice of henge building seems to have taken root in the Lake District. Possibly as a result of the area's importance as a quarrying centre and tool factory, the area has an unusually high number of monuments and stone circles, most notably at Castlerigg (p147), near Keswick, believed to have been erected sometime around 3500 BC (roughly around the same time as Stonehenge and Avebury in Wiltshire). The area's other well-known circles, including Long Meg (p206) near Penrith and Swinside near Broughton-

Budding genealogists can try tracing their Cumbrian ancestors through the Cumbria County Council's online archive at www .cumbria.gov.uk/archives/ familyhistory.

TIMELINE

15,000–10,000 BC	5000 BC	500 BC
Following the melting of the ice sheets, humans settle sporadically around the area of present-day Cumbria, especially along the Cumbrian Coast.	Humans establish settlements in inland Cumbria. Langdale becomes a key 'factory' site for the manufacture of stone tools and hafted axes, which are traded widely throughout the British Isles and further afield.	Celts move into Cumbria from southern areas of Britain, establish defensive hill forts and form new tribes.

in-Furness, were probably built later around 1500 BC (possibly on the foundations of earlier sites). Quite what these prehistoric builders were up to with their stone rings and upstanding menhirs is anyone's guess; some scholars have suggested they may have served as celestial clocks to mark the changing seasons, while others believe they were used as trading sites, religious centres or public monuments, with each stone perhaps commemorating a great warrior or fallen chieftain. One thing's for sure – despite popular myths, they certainly weren't built by the Druids (who only arrived on the scene with the Celts, and probably appropriated already existing circles for their own religious ceremonies).

Around 2000 BC, a new race of people arrived in Britain from central Europe. These new settlers, known as the Beaker people after their distinctive decorated pottery, introduced bronze tools, weaponry and metalworking to native Britons. Archaeological evidence has indicated that the Beakers established a network of trading links between Cumbria and Ireland, Yorkshire and the rest of mainland Britain.

But it was the arrival of the Celts, who pushed up from their established strongholds in the south around 500 BC, that brought the greatest change. The introduction of iron tools, coupled with the increasing threat of aggression from Pictish raiders from the north, and a new, more warlike tribal culture, encouraged the local people to move into protective hill forts such as the one at Carrock Fell. Over the next half-millennia, Celtic settlers developed a sophisticated society of crop cultivation, cattle farming and intertribal trading, as well as a distinct pantheon of religious beliefs, epitomised by their many sacred barrows and burial mounds. Various tribes occupied the area, including the Carvetii, who mainly occupied the Eden Valley, and the Setantii, who had their stronghold in Lancashire and southern Cumbria. Both were eventually subsumed into the more powerful Brigantes tribe, which had taken control of most of northern England by the 1st century AD. Their dominion, however, was short-lived; the all-conquering Romans set foot on British soil in AD 43, and the days of the Celts were numbered.

ROMANS RULE OK

Initially the Brigantes, under the rule of the warrior-queen Cartimandua, cooperated with the Roman invaders, providing a handy buffer between advancing Roman forces and the troublesome Picts further to the north. But all was not well in the Brigantian aristocracy; Cartimandua's own husband, Venutius, led a rebellion against his wife in AD 57 (which was summarily quashed by the queen's Roman chums).

The tempestuous couple reconciled briefly, refusing to participate in Boudicca's failed rebellion in AD 60, but Venutius led a second rebellion in AD 69, no doubt piqued by the fact that his wife had divorced him for his own armour-bearer, Vellocatus. Cartimandua took flight and Venutius

Sprinkling Tarn in Borrowdale holds the record for the wettest year ever recorded in Britain - in 1954, it received over 6528mm (around 21ft) of rainfall.

AD 43	**122**	**573**
Romans invade mainland Britain and begin to push north towards Cumbria. Petilius Cerialis commands northern armies against the Brigantes and builds first timber fort in AD 72.	Emperor Hadrian visits Britain and orders the construction of a great wall stretching across the north of England between Bowness-on-Solway and the Tyne River. The wall is mostly completed within six years.	St Kentigern (or St Mungo) undertakes the first recorded Christian mission in Cumbria, probably preaching in the village of Caldbeck and several other areas.

assumed the throne, leading to several decades of bloody warfare between the Brigantes and their Roman occupiers.

British governors, including Petilius Cerialis (the son-in-law of the Emperor Vespasian) and the gifted military tactician Agricola, waged several campaigns, dividing and weakening the northern English tribes, and controlling their territorial gains through a string of forts at Ambleside (known as Galava, p76), Hardknott (Mediobogdum, p135) and Ravenglass (Glannaventa, p130), where you can still visit the remains of a Roman bathhouse. The Romans also constructed roads to facilitate the transport of troops and supplies; one key route from Ambleside to Brougham known as 'High Street' is still used as a hiking trail, while the Hardknott–Wrynose route (p135) now forms one of the nation's most spectacular roads.

Following his visit to Britain in AD 122, and frustrated by the continuing resistance of the domestic Britons, Emperor Hadrian ordered the construction of one of the great Roman engineering projects; the Vallum Aelium, a vast wall stretching from Bowness-on-Solway in western Cumbria all the way to Wallsend on the River Tyne. Initially the western section was turf, later reinforced in stone; it's still possible to visit one of the wall's garrison forts at Birdoswald (p203). Carlisle, known to the Romans as Luguvalium, became a key administrative centre for the occupation, but within a hundred years the great Romano-British adventure lay in tatters. By AD 410 the last remaining legion had been withdrawn to protect the crumbling empire back home and Britain was left to fend for itself. The Dark Ages had begun.

RHEGED, ANGLO-SAXONS & VIKINGS

Following the fall of Rome, a series of Celtic kings reassumed control over various areas of northern England; remnants of this brief Celtic revival survive in various place names (Derwent, Blencathra), and most notably in the county's modern-day name of Cumbria (which derives from the Celts' name for themselves, *Cymry*). By the 6th century a distinct kingdom, known as Rheged, had grown up around the Eden Valley. Its earliest kings included Coel Hen (possibly the ruler commemorated in the popular British nursery rhyme 'Old King Cole') and Urien, who re-established a stronghold on the site of present-day Carlisle. But Rheged was dwarfed in size and power by the neighbouring realm of Northumbria, ruled by its own kings and warlords, and sometime around the end of the 7th century Rheged seems to have been annexed by its rival (whether peacefully or by force is not known). As a result, the native Cumbric dialect gradually gave way to Anglo-Saxon, which was increasingly gaining ground as the 'national' language.

The missionary St Cuthbert arrived in Cumbria in 685, and planted the seeds of Cumbria's slow conversion to Christianity. Many Cumbrian churches are dedicated to the saint, and it's still possible to view some of the original crosses erected by early worshippers, most notably the stunningly

Hadrian's Wall: an Historic Landscape, published by the National Trust, provides a comprehensive overview of the history of one of the greatest engineering projects ever attempted in England.

875	945	1315
The Danish Viking chief, Halfdan, razes Carlisle to the ground; it remains in ruins for the next 200 years.	King Dunmail defeated by Saxon forces under King Edmund. The county of Cumberland is mentioned for the first time in a document ceding the county to Malcolm of Scotland.	Fresh from his victory at the Battle of Bannockburn, Robert the Bruce lays siege to Carlisle Castle, but is eventually forced to withdraw when the city's commandant, Andrew de Harcla, refuses to surrender.

carved example at Bewcastle (p203). Alongside the Anglo-Saxons, Norse Vikings had also begun to settle in the area in large numbers, though they seem to have mainly concentrated on crop farming and cattle raising, rather than the indiscriminate raping and pillaging favoured by their Danish cousins. The Norse settlers left a lasting mark on the Cumbrian landscape and language; the tradition of hill farming was first begun by the Norsemen, and the area is littered with Nordic-derived place names – *force* (waterfall), *ghyll* (ravine), *beck* (stream), *thwaite* (settlement) and *fell* (mountain), to name a few. Relatively few traces of Viking settlement remain, although there are some fascinating Viking artefacts on display at Tullie House (p198) in Carlisle, and there's a wonderful Viking cross at Gosforth (p136), which blends figures from both the Bible and Nordic legend.

TROUBLED TIMES

In 945 the last traces of the original Cumbrian tribes were wiped out when the warlord Dunmail was annihilated by the Saxon king, Edmund, who granted control over Cumbria to Malcolm, heir to the Scottish throne. This unfortunate decision sowed the seeds for several centuries of ongoing conflict between the Scots and English, more often than not played out along the fractious border area between the two nations.

Following their invasion in 1066, the Normans founded a motte-and-bailey stronghold on the ruins of the Roman fortress at Carlisle in 1093, which was then rebuilt as a stone castle by Henry I in 1122. Many religious houses were also established, starting in 1127 with a grand abbey at Furness (p187), followed by priories and abbeys at Lanercost, Cartmel, Shap and Carlisle. The monks also developed many key Lakeland industries, including sheep and dairy farming, coppicing (for timber and charcoal), and the production of wool and cloth – not to mention that age-old Cumbrian staple, beer brewing. The long history of Lakeland mining can also trace its roots to around this time; Borrowdale and Keswick became key quarrying areas for slate, stone and (later) graphite, while Coniston became a centre for the mining of copper and other minerals.

Throughout the medieval period, the Scots–English frontier continued to be a source of considerable tension. Following the Scottish victory over the English at the Battle of Bannockburn in 1314, the area descended into lawlessness (earning the area its ominous nickname of the 'Debatable Lands'). Rival families known as the Border Reivers indulged in a bloodthirsty campaign of violence, looting and pillaging meted out against the unfortunate local inhabitants (inadvertently bringing the words 'bereaved' and 'blackmail' into the English language). In an effort to protect themselves against the Reivers, many manor houses were fortified against attack with stout pele towers, examples of which can be seen at Muncaster Castle (p130), Sizergh (p214) and Levens Hall (p214).

Find out whether you have Reiver relatives in *The Reivers: the Story of the Border Reivers* by Alistair Moffat, a romping historical read with plenty of family vendettas and blood-curdling raids to sink your teeth into.

1537	1745	1799
Following Henry VIII's order to dissolve the monasteries of England, Furness Abbey is forced to surrender its land and wealth to the Crown. The abbey is ransacked and dismantled and its monks are forced into retirement.	Start of the Jacobite uprisings under the Scottish pretender to the English throne, Bonnie Prince Charlie. Carlisle surrenders after six days. The Jacobite rebellion is overthrown the following year at the Battle of Culloden.	The year after the publication of *Lyrical Ballads*, Wordsworth moves into Dove Cottage, near Grasmere, with his sister Dorothy, joined later by his wife Mary, whom he marries in 1802.

A brief interlude of calm followed the coronation of James I as the first joint ruler of Scotland and England in 1603, but the region was plunged into yet more divisive conflict with the advent of the Civil War. Broadly, the neighbouring districts of Cumberland and Westmorland declared for the king, while the Scots sided with the Parliamentarians. Carlisle became the site of yet another bloodthirsty siege when the 700-strong Royalist garrison was starved into submission by the Roundhead commander General Lesley. The prospect of peace heralded by the Act of Union in 1707, which brought Scotland and England under one flag for the first time, proved to be equally short-lived; the Scottish-born pretender to the throne, Charles Edward Stuart (popularly known as Bonnie Prince Charlie), led a series of Jacobite uprisings against the rule of George II, including yet another siege at Carlisle Castle. The Jacobites, however, found little support further south, and were defeated in devastating style at the Battle of Culloden in 1746, where the English armies were commanded by the king's own son, the Duke of Cumberland.

Fletcher Christian, the rebellious leader of the mutiny on the *Bounty*, was born in Cockermouth in 1764. His brother subsequently worked at Hawkshead Grammar School and may have taught young John and William Wordsworth.

THE SPIRIT OF THE AGE

During the late 18th century the Lake District found itself at the centre of another revolution, although this time of a more peaceful kind. The ground-breaking artists and poets of the Romantic movement (p41) drew inspiration from the majestic local scenery, which offered new avenues of artistic expression in opposition to the staid, ordered values of classical aesthetics. The grand old man of the Lakeland Romantics was undoubtedly the poet William Wordsworth, born in Cockermouth in 1770. Surrounded by a loose circle of like-minded writers and artists, Wordsworth laid down the blueprint for the Romantic movement through a series of landmark poems celebrating the wonders, mysteries and spiritual consolations of the natural world.

While the Romantics were busy forging new artistic ground, for most ordinary people it was the industrial, rather than the artistic, revolution which had a more immediate effect on their daily lives. For centuries the vast majority of people had been employed in traditional local industries – mainly sheep farming, agriculture, wool and cloth making – but as England's industrial machine gathered steam in the early 19th century, the abundant natural resources of the Lakes proved an irresistible draw for a swathe of new investors and manufacturing magnates. Quarrying and mining exploded across Cumbria; farming, manufacturing and agriculture became increasingly organised and mechanised; the region's coastal ports around Workington, Maryport and Whitehaven bustled with ships bound for the far-flung corners of the British Empire; and factories and mills sprang up to feed the nation's growing need for mass-manufactured goods (one of which, a restored 'bobbin' factory, you can visit at Lakeside on Windermere, p72).

The construction of a 470m dam at the lake of Haweswater submerged the village of Mardale in the 1930s. During periods of dry weather some of the drowned buildings occasionally reappear above the surface.

Perhaps most importantly of all, Britain's rapidly expanding railway network finally pushed west into the Lakes in 1847, when a branch line

1850	**1902**	**1931**
William Wordsworth dies at home in Rydal Mount aged 80, and is buried in the church-yard of Grasmere's St Oswald's Church alongside his children Dora, Catherine and Thomas.	National Trust makes its first purchase of land in the Lake District at Brandelhow Woods on Derwent Water, laying the foundations for the future protection of the Lakeland landscape.	Youth Hostelling Association (YHA) purchases its very first hostel at Thorney How in Grasmere, the first of over 20 established in the Lake District.

connected Kendal with Windermere (despite vehement opposition from Wordsworth and many other proto-environmentalists, who feared the area's fragile natural environment would be irrevocably damaged). Other railways soon followed, including lines from Penrith to Cockermouth, Ravenglass to Eskdale and around the Cumbrian Coast, bringing with them another new phenomenon that was to have a lasting effect on the area's future: tourism.

> The Haig Colliery Mining Museum website (www.haigpit.com) outlines the history of Cumbrian coal mining and the industry's many mining accidents, such as the 1947 William Pitt disaster, which killed 104 men.

A NATIONAL PARK IS BORN

Flush with the wealth provided by Britain's growing industrial power and the opportunities their newfound prosperity afforded for enjoyment and 'self-improving' leisure, Victorian and Edwardian tourists flocked in huge numbers to admire the Lakeland scenery. Charabancs and coach trips ferried passengers around the district, stopping off at a series of established viewpoints, where visitors were encouraged to admire the landscape backwards using a mirrored device (known as a 'Claude glass', after the 17th-century French landscape painter Claude Lorrain) in order to better 'frame' the view. More energetic types set out to explore the high fells in the company of local guides, while a gaggle of adventurous gents (including Will Ritson, the proprietor of the Wasdale Head Inn, p139) tackled the more challenging cliffs and peaks, starting the long tradition of rock climbing in the Lakes.

Local towns mushroomed to cater for the booming tourist trade. Grand hotels and picturesque promenades sprang up in coastal resorts such as Grange-over-Sands and Arnside, while hitherto modest villages such as Ambleside, Bowness-on-Windermere and Keswick found themselves swamped by a rash of new guest houses and holiday villas. Lavish country mansions began to pop up all over the countryside, an ostentatious sign of the seemingly limitless wealth of Britain's industrial elite.

But not everyone was content to watch the Lakeland scenery reduced to a glorified leisure park for the nation's upper classes. A growing band of forward-thinking campaigners began to speak out against uncapped industrial expansion, calling for the protection of the area's unique natural environment. One of the most vociferous campaigners was the critic, thinker and polymath John Ruskin, whose dedication to traditional artisanship over mass-manufactured goods became a key inspiration for the Arts and Crafts movement. Ruskin's tireless championing of the value of unspoilt natural environments played a huge part in preventing the overdevelopment of the Lake District, and helped kick-start the modern environmental movement.

> Windermere and Bowness were the second areas of England to be supplied with electric street lighting. Power was initially supplied by a hydro-electric generator at Troutbeck Bridge.

The green torch was later picked up by writer Beatrix Potter, who set up home in the Lake District in the early 1900s, and used the proceeds from her bestselling books to purchase houses, farmsteads and huge tracts of land in order to protect them from development. Following her death in 1943, she bequeathed nearly all her property – some 4000 acres of land – to the National Trust, a colossal gift that helped pressure the government to secure

1951	1956	1974
The Lake District becomes one of the UK's first national parks alongside the Peak District, Snowdonia and Dartmoor. By the end of the decade a further six regions have also received national park status.	UK's first commercial nuclear power station opens at Windscale and is severely damaged by fire the following year, causing widespread environmental damage. The same year, the Queen makes her first official visit to the national park.	Cumberland, Westmorland and parts of northern Lancashire are incorporated into the newly founded county of Cumbria.

the Lake District's unique environment for future generations. Finally in 1951, after over a century of campaigning, the Lake District became one of the UK's first national parks.

RECENT HISTORY

The establishment of the national park may have ensured the protection of the landscape from overdevelopment, but in many ways it also sowed the seeds for future problems. While tourism has mushroomed within the Lake District, other corners of Cumbria have borne the brunt of industrial expansion as a result. Undoubtedly the most controversial issue since the park's foundation was the decision to site the UK's first commercial nuclear power station at Windscale on the Cumbrian Coast in 1956 (see p54) – a subject that still stirs up passionately opposing opinions among local people. Equally controversial was the decision to join the historic counties of Cumberland, Westmorland and part of northern Lancashire together into the new combined administrative region of Cumbria in 1974, which for many people was symptomatic of the high-handed approach of local authorities and their apparent unwillingness to listen to popular opinion.

Tourism has grown at an exponential rate over the last half-century. Within 20 years of the park's opening, visitor numbers and traffic had nearly doubled, and have continued to spiral upwards at a steady rate ever since. The first dedicated visitor centre was established at the former stately home of Brockhole (p61) in 1969, while the arrival of the M6 motorway in the late '60s and early '70s opened up the park to a fresh wave of new visitors from the south, not to mention a rather less welcome new phenomenon: the traffic jam. And while tourism has boomed, other traditional industries such as manufacturing, timber, agriculture and, most importantly, hill farming have endured a long, slow period of decline – a pattern that's sadly become all too familiar right across England's rural counties. Catastrophic outbreaks of mad cow disease (BSE) in the late 1990s and foot-and-mouth in 2001 were the final nail in the coffin for many Cumbrian farmers already struggling to cope with plummeting revenues, increasing competition and spiralling costs.

Park authorities and local residents have generally managed to coexist fairly peacefully, but not every initiative receives a warm welcome. One of the most contentious decisions of recent years was the imposition of speed limits on several lakes, including Coniston Water, Derwent Water and Ullswater, followed in 2005 by the new 10mph speed limit on Windermere – an edict that caused howls of protests from both lake users and local tourism bosses, who feared the potential impact on visitor numbers. Other polemic issues include the ban on hunting with hounds, which came into effect in 2005, the establishment of new reservoirs to prevent over-drainage from the main lakes, and the strategy of opening up the countryside to ramblers as part of the government's controversial Right to Roam policy.

Long before Lonely Planet there was Ward Lock's *Red Guide to the Lake District,* recently reissued. The recommendations are a bit out of date, but it certainly makes a fascinating companion to peruse on the road.

2001	2000–2005	2005
Foot-and-mouth disease devastates farms across the UK; Cumbria is one of the worst affected areas. Ospreys return to Bassenthwaite Lake.	Countryside and Rights of Way (CRoW) Act passed in 2000, opening up new areas of state and privately owned land to the general public. The act is enforced in stages before reaching completion in 2005.	Damaging storms sweep across Cumbria and the northwest. Carlisle is swamped by the worst floods in living memory and many other areas of the county are also badly affected.

Culture

REGIONAL IDENTITY

What does it mean to be Cumbrian? Well, first you have to find someone who agrees the county really exists. Historically, this corner of England was divided into three separate districts – Cumberland, Westmorland and Lancashire – each defined by its own dialects, customs and political affiliations. The decision to squish the three seperate counties into the all-encompassing region of Cumbria in 1974 predictably met with fierce opposition from many quarters. Thirty years on, you'll find many locals still doggedly sticking to the old county boundaries, while the historic names linger on in many areas, from the Cumberland banger you'll eat at the breakfast table to the copy of the *Westmorland Gazette* you'll peruse while munching your cornflakes.

As in many rural areas of England, there's a strong tradition of self-reliance and down-to-earth pragmatism in these parts, borne of centuries of eking out a living from the land. Like other counties up north, Cumbrians tend to be a tough, no-nonsense bunch – a mite gruff on the outside, perhaps, but with a razor-sharp sense of humour not too far beneath the surface. A strong sense of community spirit still endures, and the county remains fiercely proud of its customs and traditions, many of which stretch back for centuries. Agricultural fairs, village sports days and community festivals such as rushbearing (p80) remain important events in the local calendar and, with some of the nation's finest hills and stateliest lakes on their doorstep, many Cumbrians unsurprisingly share a passionate devotion to the great outdoors. Hill walking is more a way of life in these parts than a leisure activity: strike up a conversation in any local boozer and you're bound to be swapping route tips and trail tales before too long.

LIFESTYLE

Things move at their own good speed out in the Cumbrian countryside, so rather than getting hot and bothered by those inevitable tractor-induced traffic-jams, you're better off just sitting back, enjoying the scenery and going with the rural flow. But while the county's winding lanes and quiet villages naturally lend themselves to a more laid-back pace, don't expect some kind of Potteresque idyll locked in a turn-of-the-century time warp. Daily life for the average Cumbrian, as in the rest of England, revolves around a standard nine-to-five routine, often with a hefty commute thrown in at the end of the working day – a necessary evil of living in a county where well-paid work rarely goes hand in hand with a rural postcode.

The Lakeland Dialect Society (www.lakeland dialectsociety.org) is dedicated to preserving traditional Cumbrian dialect – its website includes a handy online glossary of some of the Cumbrian words still in everyday use.

CHAT LIKE A CUMBRIAN

Celtic, Norse, Anglo-Saxon and the ancient Cumbric language have contributed to a wonderful repository of local words, many of which you're bound to hear on your travels. As well as the commonly used *beck* (river), *ghyll* (ravine) and *force* (waterfall), keep your ears peeled for *la'al* (little), *lowp* (jump), *gander* (look), *yat* (gate), *cowie* (thing), *yam* (home), *lewer* (money), *blether* (gossip) and our personal favourites, *jinnyspinner* (daddy-long-legs) and *snotter-geggin* (idiot).

Cumbria even had its own system of counting, sometimes called 'sheep counting numerals' since they were once widely used by local shepherds. Although the exact words can vary, nearly all start with *yan* (one), *tyan* (two), *tethera* (three) and climb up to *dick* (10), *bumfit* (15) and *giggot* (20).

In comparison to the rest of the nation, Cumbria fares pretty well on the liveability scale: school attainment, educational provision and job satisfaction are all rated above the national average, while crime rates, unemployment and environmental pollution all fall slightly below the national mean. Fittingly for an outdoors-orientated county, the region also scores highly on the physical activity scale, with a significantly higher proportion of adults taking regular exercise than in the rest of England. Unfortunately, all this gung-ho activity is counterbalanced by some of the nation's worst figures for binge drinking and obesity, which perhaps explains why the life expectancy for Cumbrians of both sexes is significantly worse than for many other areas of England.

A whopping 48% of visitors to the Lake District cite walking as the main reason for their stay, while 5% have apparently come for the fresh air.

ECONOMY

Love it or loathe it, there's no getting around the fact that tourism plays a crucial role in the local economy. Well over 15.5 million people visit the county every year, contributing £1.2 billion to the county's coffers. Around 30% of the total workforce is employed in the tourism and service sectors, compared to about 25% in the public sector, 17% in manufacturing, 12% in banking and finance and just 1.5% in the once-important industries of fishing and agriculture, which have both suffered a long, slow decline over the last century.

Historically, coal mining, mineral extraction and quarrying were huge local employers, but there are now only a couple of working mines left; a few, such as Nenthead (p210) and Honister (p163) have reinvented themselves as tourist attractions. But heavy industry hasn't entirely disappeared from the Cumbrian economy: Barrow-in-Furness remains a major shipbuilding centre, and the nation's largest nuclear-reprocessing site can be found at Sellafield (p192) on the Cumbrian Coast.

County-specific news, interviews and cultural happenings can be found at the BBC's Cumbria pages at www.bbc .co.uk/cumbria.

Unemployment in Cumbria is marginally better than in the rest of Britain, hovering around 2.1%, but the massive boom in property prices over the last decade, exacerbated by an explosion in holiday lets and second homes, has caused major headaches for local people looking to get on the housing ladder. The median house price in 2008 was just over £164,000 – six times the average Cumbrian income of around £25,000 – making the county one of the least affordable places to live in the British Isles.

POPULATION

Officially speaking, Cumbria has fewer people per square foot than almost anywhere else in England: on average, there are just 70 people for every square kilometre of land (compared to a whopping 4671 per square kilometre in London). But the official statistics fail to take into account another sobering statistic: Cumbria's resident population is outnumbered by the annual influx of tourists by around 31 to one, so it's hardly surprising that the local populace occasionally gets a little cheesed off with the summer trippers and traffic jams. In contrast to many areas of Britain, most Cumbrians seem to prefer the peace and quiet of the countryside to the hustle and bustle of the big city – less than half of the county's population live in urban areas, compared to 80% across the rest of England.

Australians are the most frequent overseas visitors to the Lake District, followed by Americans, Germans, Canadians and Japanese.

There's been a general upward curve in the county's population over the last decade, a trend that looks set to continue over the coming years, but there's a worrying statistic underpinning these headline figures. Cumbria has one of the fastest ageing demographics of any English county, with spiralling house prices and comparatively low wages forcing many people of working age out of the county in search of higher-paid jobs. Cumbria is also one of England's least ethnically diverse counties – just 1.9% of the population is of black or ethnic-minority origin.

SPORT

Cricket

Unlike its neighbours in Yorkshire and Lancashire, Cumbria's county cricket team has never hit the heights, but cricket is still a popular local sport. For details of forthcoming fixtures, pick up a local newspaper or consult the **Cumbria Cricket Board** (www.cumbriacb.play-cricket.com) website.

Football

The county's main football team is **Carlisle United** (www.carlisleunited.co.uk), which was founded back in 1904 and plays its home fixtures at Brunton Park in Carlisle. The club has had mixed fortunes in recent years; in 2006, they were promoted from League Two as season champions, but two short seasons later lost in a tight play-off against Leeds United for promotion into the Championship, and have since been dogged by player problems and managerial upheaval. Tickets are usually available for home games and cost upwards of £20.

Lakeland Walker is a magazine devoted entirely to the special joys of getting out and about in the Lake District, with interviews, gear reviews and, of course, plenty of detailed route guides.

Fell Running

One of Cumbria's oldest sports is the gruelling pursuit of fell running, in which competitors charge up and down a set course of Lakeland peaks in the fastest possible time (hopefully without bursting a blood vessel or shattering a limb in the process). Famous races are held in Borrowdale, Ennerdale and Wasdale, while shorter 'guides' races' often feature at local sports days.

For more on this lunatic sport, visit the websites for the **Fell Runner's Association** (www.fellrunner.org.uk) and the **Bob Graham Round** (www.bobgrahamround.co.uk), and see our special boxed text on p161.

Sheepdog Trials & Hound Trailing

Come by! Away! Lie down! There are few more quintessentially Cumbrian sights than watching a farmer at work on the fell-sides, rounding up a herd of Swaledales or Herdwicks with the able assistance of an obedient sheepdog. Over the centuries Cumbrian hill farmers have refined this necessary pastime into a minor art form, with directional commands delivered from farmer to dog using a sophisticated system of calls and whistles. Sheepdog trials are a regular feature at country gatherings, and you can see sheepdogs in regular action at Cockermouth's Lakeland Sheep & Wool Centre (p159).

Trained canines also feature in the sport of hound trailing, in which dogs race across a countryside course marked in advance using a rag soaked in paraffin and aniseed. The sport probably has its roots in the training of foxhounds during the 18th century.

The Cumbrian wrestler's arsenal of moves includes the back-heel, the hank, the inside-click and the excruciating-sounding full buttock.

Cumbrian Wrestling

Many corners of England have their own forms of wrestling, but nowhere is the pastime more proudly practised than Cumbria. Dressed in their distinctive outfits of white long johns, white vests and brightly patterned trunks (designed to avoid competitors gaining an unfair advantage by grabbing loose clothing), Cumbrian wrestlers stand face to face and 'tekk hodd' by linking their arms across their opponent's back, and then attempt to trip, spin, twist or throw each other to the ground, employing a series of intricate and highly technical manoeuvres. Bouts are usually contested on a best-of-three basis, and always begin and end with a sporting handshake. You'll see Cumbrian wrestlers in action at local fairs and at the annual Grasmere Sports Day (p93).

ARTS
Architecture

Cumbria might be better known for its natural attractions, but building buffs will find plenty to pique their interest, not least the many different stones used for local building materials. Penrith and the Eden Valley are notable for their distinctive red sandstone, for example, while Ambleside and Kendal predominantly use the sombre grey stone and slate from local quarries. But even more unmissable are the county's seemingly endless drystone walls; in total, Cumbria has over 9400 miles worth, enough to stretch from the Lake District all the way to the Australian coast. As its name suggests, this traditional form of wall building uses no cement, relying instead on the integral strength of the 'cavity wall' (a tightly packed double wall topped by capstones). A well-built wall can last hundreds of years – some of the oldest examples even date back to the Middle Ages.

One of the longest-running British TV series was the sheepdog-themed *One Man and His Dog*, which ran for over 23 years between 1976 and 1999 and which still makes sporadic appearances on UK screens.

Long before the first farmers started building their drystone walls, ancient Britons had already left their own architectural mark through an astonishing string of stone circles, most notably at Castlerigg (p147) and Long Meg (p206). The Romans followed in their footsteps, constructing the old forts of Hardknott (p135) and Galava (p76), as well as the epic sweep of Hadrian's Wall, which stretches across the county's northern border near Brampton (p203).

Much later, monasteries were founded at Shap (p176) and Furness (p187), while sturdy castles and defensive towers were built to resist raids from across the Scottish border; the most obvious fortress is undoubtedly Carlisle Castle (p197), although Muncaster (p130) and Sizergh (p214) also have architectural interest. Many of these old strongholds were later expanded into stately homes for the region's feudal landowners – Dalemain (p167) boasts an astonishing mix of architectural periods, while Holker Hall (p183) is perhaps the most lavish of all the Cumbrian country houses. The landowning elite were later followed by a string of rich Victorian industrialists keen to show off their newfound wealth – Lowther Castle (p175) went for all-out splendour, while Brantwood (p112) and Blackwell House (p71) both showcased an altogether more restrained Arts and Crafts style.

Literature

For the literary low-down on the Lakes, see our special chapter on p41.

Painting

Writers and poets certainly weren't the only ones to be inspired by the Lake District landscape – generations of artists have translated the area's natural scenery onto their canvases. The first to arrive were the so-called 'Sublime' artists who, like their Romantic contemporaries, drew their inspiration from wild, unspoilt natural vistas – the bigger and moodier the better. JMW Turner and Thomas Gainsborough, and later John Constable, were among the earliest Lakeland devotees. One of Turner's most atmospheric canvases (now owned by the Tate in London) depicts a lonely vision of Buttermere Lake, overlooked by glowering clouds and the faint arc of a rainbow.

The *Westmorland Gazette* (www.thewestmorland gazette.co.uk) is one of the county's oldest newspapers, and has been reporting on local events since its foundation in 1818.

But it was the prodigiously talented polymath (and ardent Turner devotee), John Ruskin, who did more than anyone else to popularise the scenery of the Lakes. He was a passionate student of nature, and lavished countless hours on botanical studies and scenic landscapes inspired by the countryside around his house at Brantwood (p112). Another notable figure

Cumbria Life (www.cum brialife.co.uk) is a glossy bimonthly of all things Lake-related. Feature stories include everything from social history to contemporary Lakeland life, and the photography is always stunning.

is the Kendal-born artist George Romney, who became one of the most important portraitists of fashionable 19th-century society, and whose work features heavily in the collections of the Abbot Hall Art Gallery (p210) in Kendal.

Meanwhile, you can view the work of one of the best-known dynasties of Lakeland artists at the Heaton Cooper Studio (p89) in Grasmere, and no artistic tour would be complete without taking in at least a few canvases by the artist most closely associated with the flora and fauna of the Lake District – Beatrix Potter. You'll find a series of her fascinating botanical sketches at the Armitt Museum (p77), along with original watercolours at the Beatrix Potter Gallery (p119) in Hawkshead.

Literary Lakes

Few corners of England have as rich a literary tradition as the Lake District, and even if you're not a book buff it's well worth taking the time to get to grips with the area's best-known writers. The most famous literary residents of the Lakes were obviously the Lake Poets – Wordsworth, Coleridge and Southey – and the wildly popular children's writer Beatrix Potter, although for many Lake District visitors there's one other towering figure without whom the list just wouldn't be complete, the man affectionately known to generations of fell walkers as AW – Alfred Wainwright.

THE ROMANTICS

The coterie of writers who became known as the Lake Poets were part of a much wider literary, artistic and philosophical awakening that gained ground across European society during the late 18th and early 19th centuries. Until this time notions of 'natural' beauty had largely played second fiddle to the 'classical' aesthetics of architecture, sculpture and art, each of which seemed to epitomise humankind's mastery over chaos and disorder. Rugged mountain landscapes, wild forests and other untamed outdoor expanses were seen as symbolic of a world unshaped by human hands. An artist's job was to try to make sense of that world, and to lay down structure, order and harmony according to a predefined sense of classical principles.

Eminent essayist William Hazlitt penned *The Spirit of the Age* covering the great Romantic figures - Wordsworth, Coleridge, Southey - along with pioneering philosophers, scientists and social reformers of the day.

But in a post-Enlightenment world struggling to come to terms with the loss of long-held values – aristocratic monarchy, organised religion and the notion of divine order – a growing body of artists across Europe began to reappraise these notions of nature and landscape, finding awe and joy in scenes that had hitherto inspired fear and horror. This new fascination with transcendental experience, creative inspiration, the potential of the subconscious mind and, most importantly, the transformative power of the natural world, underpinned the development of Romanticism in the late 18th century.

The jagged peaks of the French Alps became the centre of this new artistic movement, but British artists increasingly looked closer to home for their own sources of inspiration, and found ideal subjects among the grand vistas and majestic fells of the Lake District. The poet Thomas Gray was the first to visit the area. He made two trips in 1767, and was followed soon after by the writer Thomas West, who penned the first official *Guide to the Lakes* in 1778, beginning the long tradition of Lake District travel which continues today.

It wasn't until 1799, however, that the Romantics gained a proper foothold in the Lakes. Following brief stints in London, Cambridge, Europe and Somerset, a 29-year-old Cumberland-born lad by the name of William Wordsworth returned to his native county in search of inspiration and escape, accompanied by his artistically minded younger sister, Dorothy. Together they set up home in a converted inn near Grasmere, previously known as the Dove and Olive Bough, which they renamed Dove Cottage (p87). Here Wordsworth was joined by his closest contemporary, the young poetic firebrand Samuel Taylor Coleridge, with whom he had published the unofficial manifesto of the Romantic movement, *Lyrical Ballads*, in 1798 (the collection was later reprinted with a new preface by Wordsworth in 1800 in order to capitalise on the booklet's impressive sales).

Frances Wilson explores the passionate, sensitive and rather strange figure of Wordsworth's beloved sister in her fascinating biography, *The Ballad of Dorothy Wordsworth*.

Over the next decade, Wordsworth and Coleridge welcomed another literary heavyweight to the Lake District, the Poet Laureate Robert Southey (who also happened to be Coleridge's brother-in-law – the two men had married

TOURING THE LITERARY LAKES

Where would the Lake District be without its literary luminaries? This wordsmith's tour begins with the grand old man of the Lakes himself, William Wordsworth. Start with a visit to his birthplace in **Cockermouth** (p157), his school in **Hawkshead** (p118) and his cosy country hideaway at **Dove Cottage** (p87), then bone up on the Romantics' backstory at the **Wordsworth Museum** (p89). Have a wander around his family home at **Rydal Mount** (p91) and the daffodils of nearby **Dora's Field** (p91) before calling on the poet's peaceful grave in **St Oswald's Churchyard** (p89). If you've got time, it's worth detouring via the little-visited **Duddon Valley** (p135), renowned as one of Wordsworth's favourite corners of the Lakes.

But even old WW can't match the global phenomenon that is Beatrix Potter. You can see some of her early botanical watercolours in **Hawkshead** (p119) and at the **Armitt Museum** (p77) in Ambleside, before braving the crowds at her former house at **Hill Top** (p123) and stopping for lunch at the nearby **Tower Bank Arms** (p124), which featured as the backdrop in *The Tale of Jemima Puddle-duck*. Confront a life-size Benjamin Bunny at the **World Of Beatrix Potter** (p61) before tucking into afternoon tea at **Yew Tree Farm** (p117), which doubled as Beatrix' farmhouse in the 2006 film *Miss Potter*.

With the big two ticked off, it's time to discover some of the Lake District's lesser-known writers. There are Arthur Ransome connections aplenty around **Coniston** (p114), **Windermere** (p63) and the **Lyth and Winster Valleys** (p73); while the philosopher, art critic and compulsive shell collector John Ruskin lived at the lakeside mansion of **Brantwood** (p112), overlooking the shores of Coniston Water. Have a *Postman Pat* up-hill, down-dale moment in **Kentmere Valley** (p74) and take time to visit **Buttermere** (p163), which provided the setting for one of Melvyn Bragg's most celebrated novels. The creation of **Haweswater** (p175) informed a lyrical novel by Sarah Waters, while the coal-pits, iron mines and fishing shacks around the briny coastal town of **Millom** (p188) provided inspiration for the much-loved Cumbrian poet Norman Nicholson.

You couldn't possibly finish your bookworm's tour without paying homage to Alfred Wainwright, whose *Pictorial Guides* are closer to works of art than dusty old walking guides. Wainwright was honorary clerk and curator at the **Kendal Museum** (p210), and you can visit a reconstruction of his office, complete with battered rucksack and pipe, but the best way to appreciate his work is (of course) out on the fells. **Helvellyn** (p165), **Scafell Pike** (p127) and **Blencathra** were three of his favourite peaks, and you can follow an MP3 walking tour of Wainwright's route to the top of **Helm Crag** (p92), but you'll feel closest to the man himself on the summit of **Haystacks** (p142), where AW's ashes were scattered following his death in 1991.

sisters Edith and Sarah Fricker in 1795 and 1800). Later they were also joined by the opium-eating essayist Thomas de Quincey, who produced a fascinating account of the period in his comprehensive (if rather catty) memoir *Recollections of the Lake Poets*, and lived in Dove Cottage after Wordsworth and family moved to a new house in Allan Bank in 1808.

Collectively, Wordsworth, Coleridge and Southey became known as the Lake Poets (a soubriquet that was often used disparagingly in contemporary reviews as a byword for the poets' provincialism and countrified concerns). Together they produced a prodigious output of poems, pamphlets and literary essays: over the course of his lifetime, it's estimated that Wordsworth alone wrote in excess of 70,000 lines of poetry, almost double the output of any other English poet.

Wordsworth's most celebrated doctrines are his notions of 'emotion recollected in tranquillity' and 'spots of time' – vivid moments of experience that continued to provide poetic inspiration throughout the writer's later life. The locations and landscapes of the Lakes feature heavily in his work; famously, he got many of his best ideas while out walking, and much preferred to compose on the hoof rather than sitting in his study (de Quincey estimated that Wordsworth walked between 175,000 and 180,000 miles during his

While in France in 1791, Wordsworth courted a young French woman, Annette Vallon. She gave birth to his first child, Caroline, in 1792, but was prevented from travelling to England due to the French Revolution.

lifetime). Wordsworth also seems to have relied heavily for inspiration on the journals kept by his sister Dorothy; her delicate and perceptive descriptions of nature, wildlife and the Lakeland countryside are a clear indication of her own poetic sensibilities, while her lifelong filial devotion to her brother has led to much biographical speculation about just how deep the relationship between the two Wordsworths went.

The best indication of Wordsworth's inextricable connection with his Cumbrian homeland is given in his epic autobiographical poem *The Prelude*, but you'll find Lakeland events and locations scattered throughout his work; he penned poems for everything from daffodils and yew trees to derelict abbeys and faithful fox terriers, and managed an entire book of sonnets on the delights of the Duddon Valley (p135). Intriguingly he even found time to pen his own *Guide to the Lakes* in 1810, but later regretted it for encouraging tourism and spoiling the peace and quiet.

Linda Lear's *Beatrix Potter: the Extraordinary Life of a Victorian Genius* is one of the best Potter biographies, tracing the author's life from her first Lakeland visit through to her years as an environmental campaigner and sheep breeder.

CHILDREN'S LITERATURE

Along with the lofty concerns of the Romantics, the Lakeland landscape has inspired several much-loved children's writers. The most famous, of course, is Beatrix Potter, who first visited the Lake District aged 16, and later swapped her gentrified Kensington lifestyle for the altogether more down-to-earth life of a Herdwick sheep breeder and hill farmer. Her charming, hand-drawn tales of mischievous bunnies and flustered puddle-ducks are brimming over with Lakeland scenery; any self-respecting fan will be able to spot countless locations from her books, especially around Hill Top and Near Sawrey.

The places which influenced Arthur Ransome, who lived in the Lake District between 1924 and 1934, are tougher to spot, but with a bit of lateral thinking you should be able to spy several locations from his quintessentially English tale of childhood adventure, *Swallows and Amazons*, around Coniston, Windermere and Derwent Water. A section of the Museum of Lakeland Life (p211) in Kendal contains a reconstruction of Ransome's writing room with his writing desk and artefacts, and you can take a tailored Swallows and Amazons tour courtesy of the Coniston Launch (p115). There's some dispute regarding the exact inspiration for Captain Flint's houseboat – some Ransome scholars maintain it was modelled on the steam yacht *Gondola* (p114), while others think it's more likely to have been a boat known as the *Esperance* (owned by the Windermere Steamboat Museum, which at the time of writing was closed for refurbishment).

Arthur Ransome based the children in *Swallows and Amazons* on the children of his close friend, Ernest Altounyan: Taqui, Susan, Mavis, Roger and Brigit.

Meanwhile the sleepy Kentmere Valley, east of Windermere, provided the model for the humpbacked hills and up-and-down valleys of John Cunliffe's classic BBC TV series, *Postman Pat*. Accompanied by his long-suffering black-and-white cat, Jess, Pat's adventures in and around the valley of Greendale have been a staple feature on British screens since the early 1980s, but the recent decision to promote him to the local sorting office in Pencaster has caused howls of protest – see our Postman Pat box on p75.

Postman Pat (www.postmanpat.com) isn't just a British phenomenon. In Israel, he's known as Dar Ha'davar, in the Faroe Islands he's called Pedda Post, and in Iran he goes by the name of Pat-e Postchi.

CONTEMPORARY WRITERS

More recent writers have continued the long literary Lakeland tradition. Perhaps the best-known local writer is the extravagantly coiffured broadcaster, academic and man of letters Melvyn Bragg, who was born in Wigton in 1939 and has set several of his novels in Cumbria, including 'The Cumbrian Trilogy' *(The Hired Man, A Place in England* and *Kingdom Come)* and the critically acclaimed *Soldier's Return*.

Another notable Cumbrian writer is Hunter Davies, who has turned his attention to everything from travel writing to biography over the years;

THE REAL SWALLOWS & AMAZONS

Figuring out which Lakeland site inspired which place in *Swallows and Amazons* isn't always easy, and the task isn't helped by the fact that Arthur Ransome tended to jumble his influences together in the final book. But here's the general consensus on what's what and where's where:

- **Wild Cat Island** and its secret harbour is mainly modelled on Peel Island on Coniston Water (p114), although Blake Holme and Ramp Holme on Windermere also seem to have added some features.
- The mountain of **Kanchenjunga** is almost certainly the Old Man of Coniston (p110).
- **Cormorant Island** is most likely to be Silver Holme Island on Windermere (p64).
- **Holly Howe Farm** is based on Bank Ground Farm in Coniston (p116).
- The **Peak of Darien** is probably the viewpoint of Friars Crag on Derwent Water (p147).
- The town of **Rio** is pretty clearly modelled on Bowness-on-Windermere (p61).

---

his funny and affectionate memoir of his journey along Hadrian's Wall, *A Walk Along the Wall*, was followed by further travel memoirs including *A Walk Around the Lakes* (detailing a trip around the Lake District) and *A Walk Along the Tracks* (exploring some of Britain's disused railways). More recently, his authorised biography of Alfred Wainwright was written with the cooperation of AW's second wife, Betty, who died in August 2008. Davies has also written biographies of the Beatles, Wordsworth and (in a ghost-written capacity) the Man Utd footballer Wayne Rooney.

Other names to investigate are the Millom-based poet Norman Nicholson, whose work echoes with the sights, sounds and speech patterns of everyday life on the Cumbrian Coast; the famous British mountaineer Chris Bonington, a long-time resident of Caldbeck; and the writer Sarah Hall, whose novel *Mardale* explored the drowning of a Cumbrian village during the creation of Haweswater reservoir.

But by far the best-known, best-loved and certainly most-read modern Cumbrian author is the inveterate fell-walker, painstaking cartographer and accountant-turned-author Alfred Wainwright, the man behind the landmark seven-volume guidebook series *The Pictorial Guides to the Lakeland Fells*. The first guide was published in 1955, and over 50 years later they've sold well over a million copies and are still the bestselling Lake District guidebooks by a long chalk, not to mention some of the most reliable.

Walking the fells with a Wainwright is a longstanding Lakeland tradition, and these days the guides have even gone digital. Check out *Wainwright: the Podcasts* for eight classic walks.

Food & Drink

If ever there was a place for travellers who think with their stomach, this is it. As in many rural corners of England, traditional Cumbrian cuisine centres on hale and hearty dishes – rich stews, gravy-heavy pies, calorific cakes – tailored for farmers, shepherds and country folk who spent large chunks of time outdoors as a matter of everyday necessity.

But there's been a minor gastronomic revolution in this corner of England over the last few years, and these days you're just as likely to find yourself sitting down to a plate of teriyaki trout as the traditional staples of Cumberland sausage and steak-and-ale pie. The Lake District has long had a reputation for top-quality produce, and the explosion of interest in locally sourced food has been a boon for Cumbrian chefs; the standard of cuisine has come on in leaps and bounds in recent years, and these days you'll find village pubs are just as capable of serving up a top-class culinary experience as any traditional fine-dining emporium. Organic produce and farm-sourced ingredients are becoming increasingly common on Lake District menus, as are lip-smacking local brews, and if you're a sucker for teatime treats you'll be spoilt for choice – Cumbria's sugary smorgasbord of buns, gingerbreads, sticky toffee puddings and home-baked cakes have provided a post-hike sugar hit for generations of Lakeland fell walkers.

For a comprehensive list of Cumbrian farmers markets, check out www .madeincumbria.co.uk.

STAPLES & SPECIALITIES
Meat

Unsurprisingly for one of the nation's farming heartlands, meat features heavily in many Cumbrian dishes, whether it's stewed, fried, broiled, grilled or wrapped up in pastry and baked in a pie. Cumbria's oldest and hardiest breed of sheep, the Herdwick, is renowned for its mutton – grazing free-range on the high fells in all weathers gives the meat a distinctive rich,

---

WHERE TO BUY THE BEST...

- Kendal mintcake – 1657 Chocolate Shop, Kendal (p213) or pretty much anywhere in Kendal
- Gingerbread – Sarah Nelson's Gingerbread Shop, Grasmere (p89)
- Sticky toffee pudding – Cartmel Village Shop (p182)
- Bread – Staff of Life, Kendal (p213) or the Village Bakery, Melmerby (p209)
- Cakes – Bryson's, Keswick (p151)
- Organic produce – Howbarrow Organic Farm, Cartmel (p183)
- Afternoon tea – Hazelmere Cafe, Grange-over-Sands (p181)
- Condiments – Hawkshead Relish Company, Hawkshead (p121)
- Bacon, meat and sausages – Higginsons, Grange-over-Sands (p181)

And for general all-round Lakeland rations, try the following lip-smacking suppliers:

- Low Sizergh Barn, near Kendal (p214)
- Holker Food Hall, near Cartmel (p183)
- The Honeypot, Hawkshead (p121)
- Lucy's Specialist Grocers, Ambleside (p82)

CUMBRIAN CONDIMENTS

Fittingly for a county chock-a-block with chops, steaks, meats and stews, Cumbria has plenty of sauces to spice up the dinner table. You'll see plenty of homemade chutneys, pickles and mustards in local delis and food shops. Two varieties to look out for are Cumberland sauce, a fruity accompaniment made with redcurrants, port and spices, served cold with meats and game; and Cumberland mustard, a spicy-sweet honey mustard. There are more adventurous varieties too – the Hawkshead Relish Company (p121) sells everything from traditional Westmorland chutney and piccalilli to gooseberry chutney, Indian pepper pickle and tomato and chilli jam.

---

gamey flavour. Herdwick lamb or 'fellbred mutton' is customarily used in the Cumbrian 'tatie hotpot' – a cockle-warming concoction of mutton, potatoes, onions and winter vegetables.

Another longstanding staple is the Cumberland sausage, stuffed with herbs and coarsely chopped pork, and sold in a long ring-shaped coil. Spicy, seasoned and meaty, it's more reminiscent of a German wurst than an English sausage; some scholarly foodies think it was developed by homesick German miners who arrived in the 16th century to work in the Lakeland mines. Like several other English delicacies, Cumberland sausage is currently lobbying for official protection by the EU, giving it the same status as a fine French wine or a gourmet Italian cheese. Unfortunately the Cumberland pig after which the sausage was named died out in the 1960s, so it's not quite as authentic a banger as it once was.

Mutton and sausages aren't the only meaty treats on offer. Cuts of locally reared beef, ham, bacon and pork are becoming increasingly championed by local chefs. Higginsons in Grange-over-Sands (p181) is one of the county's best-known butchers, while Woodall's of Waberthwaite (p189) is famous for its sausages, pies, bacon and hams, and numbers HM the Queen among its celebrity clients. Meanwhile Holker Hall, near Cartmel (p183), has carved out a culinary niche thanks to its estate-reared game (particularly venison) and salt marsh lamb, raised on the tidal grasses around the fringes of the Holker estate.

According to recent statistics, Cumbria's farms contain 2,150,591 chickens, 2,007,748 sheep, 474,472 cattle, 45,759 pigs, 6141 ducks, 1754 goats and a paltry (poultry?) 1175 geese.

Fish

The Lake District is one of the few places where you're able to tuck into Arctic char, a rare member of the salmon family. The char probably became trapped in Cumbria's lakes following the melting of the glaciers around 15,000 years ago; several lakes have evolved their own distinct species, but Windermere char is the one you're most likely to see on menus, either pied, potted or served whole.

Brown and rainbow trout are farmed by several fisheries, including Esthwaite, Bessy Beck and Hayeswater, while Morecambe Bay is famous for its cockles and shrimps (traditionally served potted in butter and best eaten on hot toast).

Cheese

Unlike its near neighbours, Lancashire and Yorkshire, Cumbria is not really known for its cheeses, but over the last few years the county has slowly been developing its cheesy credentials. Strong, mature cheddars are the mainstay; the **Lake District Cheese Company** (☎ 01697-320218; www.lakedistrictcheesecompany.co.uk) is a farmer-owned cooperative that produces three award-winning cheddars. The **Wardhall Dairy** (☎ 01697-321917; www.wardhalldairy.co.uk) near Wigton produces good blue and goat's cheeses, while **Thornby Moor Dairy** (☎ 016973-45555) at Crofton Hall near Carlisle produces nine different varieties, including ewe's, smoked and unpasteurised farmhouse cheeses. Meanwhile the Bridge End Farm Shop in Santon Bridge, near Wasdale, is the only producer of Lingmell cheese, made in small quantities from unpasteurised ewe's milk at a tiny dairy in Murt.

Puddings & Cakes

Cumbria's foremost sweet treat is Kendal mintcake, the calorific sugar bar that sustained several landmark British expeditions including Shackleton's Antarctic expedition in 1914 and Edmund Hilary and Tenzing Norgay's trek to the top of Everest in 1953. The real McCoy is a slab of hard sugar flavoured with peppermint oil, but these days you can also buy it in buttermint, rum butter and chocolate-covered versions.

Kendal mintcake was discovered by accident at Joseph Wiper's confectioners in 1869 when a pan of ingredients for making glacier mints was mistakenly left to burn on a stove.

There are some fantastic artisan bakeries dotted around the Lakes – Bryson's in Keswick (p151) and the Village Bakery in Melmerby (p209) are particularly worth seeking out. One of the county's oldest recipes is Borrowdale teabread, a sweet, fruity cake filled with sultanas, raisins and currants, while two other sweet specialities hint at the county's rum-running connections – Cumberland Rum Nicky, a latticed tart filled with butter, dates, rum, spices and sugar; and Rum Butter, a fine accompaniment to mince pies and Christmas pudding. The Toffee Shop (p207) in Penrith also produces great fudge and toffees.

Grasmere gingerbread – half crumbly biscuit, half sticky cake – was invented by the enterprising young baker Sarah Nelson in the mid-1850s and has been produced to the same top-secret recipe ever since. Admirably, Sarah Nelson's descendants have refused any temptation towards supermarket stardom, so the original store in Grasmere (p89) is still the only place in the world where you can buy authentic Grasmere gingerbread (although these days you can also buy from their online shop).

Following close behind in the indulgence stakes is Cartmel's sticky toffee pudding, a delicious blend of cane sugar, dates, eggs, cream and butter, best eaten piping hot with a good dollop of vanilla ice cream (sourced, of course, from the Windermere Ice Cream Company, which uses organic milk from the dairy herd at Low Sizergh Farm). Practically everyone has their own sticky toffee recipe, but connoisseurs wouldn't think of buying anywhere other than the Cartmel Village Shop (p182), which now produces ginger, chocolate and banana variations on the original sticky toffee theme.

DRINKS

Like much of England, Cumbria's tipple of choice is undoubtedly ale – preferably pumped warm from the barrel. The main name is Jennings, a large family-run enterprise based in Cockermouth (p158), which supplies many local pubs with beers and bitters including Cumberland Ale, Cocker Hoop and the fantastically named Sneck Lifter. Cumbria also boasts an impressive number of microbreweries – small, independent breweries (often based in local pubs), which produce their own distinctive brews – see p49 for some of our favourites.

TOP FIVE PUBS FOR SUNDAY LUNCH

- Yanwath Gate Inn, near Penrith (p207)
- Britannia Inn, Elterwater (p97)
- Punch Bowl Inn, Crosthwaite (p73)
- Pheasant Inn, Bassenthwaite Lake (p155)
- Queen's Head, Troutbeck (p76)

WHERE TO EAT & DRINK
Cafes & Teashops

Whether it's frilly teashops, greasy spoons or metropolitan coffee shops, you'll find a cafe to suit somewhere in Cumbria. Afternoon tea is an essential post-hike ritual for many walkers, so you're bound to find a convenient teashop within striking distance of nearly every trail, serving a selection of cakes, puddings, salads and sandwiches. In general, most Cumbrian teashops and cafes feel traditional – expect pine, potted flowers and even the occasional doily or two – although you'll find more contemporary establishments in most of the larger towns.

Pubs & Inns

Cumbria's pubs have been slaking the thirst of farmers, travellers and hikers alike for centuries, and you'll find endless slate-roofed inns nestled in among the fells, as well as a few flashy numbers where the ambience is almost as important as the ale. If you like nothing better than warming your feet by a crackling fire, then you're in luck – most pubs have retained at least a flavour of their pre-20th-century trappings, and hefty beams, slate floors and wood-panelling are all very much in evidence. Eating out in pubs can be a matter of pot luck – some still revolve around pre-prepared meals warmed through in a microwave, while others make a real virtue of their culinary offerings.

Restaurants

There's a restaurant to suit every taste and budget in the Lake District. The traditional fine-dining, Michelin-starred type establishments are found at the longstanding country hotels – including Sharrow Bay (p170), Gilpin Lodge (p68) and Miller Howe – but they're starchy, silver-service affairs, so not necessarily ideal if you prefer things more laid-back and informal. You'll find decent restaurants in all the major Lakeland towns, ranging from top-quality modern Brit bistros to Indian, Thai, French and Italian; expect to pay between £15 and £25 a head for a good meal including main, pudding and wine.

The nearest thing to a Cumbrian celebrity chef is Lucy Nicholson, who has built up her own miniature culinary empire in Ambleside and Windermere. Her cosy, chatty approach to cuisine is symbolic of her championing of honest unpretentious cooking and her fondness for local produce. At the opposite end of the spectrum is the gastronomic magician Simon Rogan, Cumbria's very own answer to the scientist-cum-chef Heston Blumenthal. His fabulous restaurant in Cartmel, L'Enclume (p183), is a favourite among the culinary cognoscenti and regularly graces the top food guides.

VEGETARIANS & VEGANS

While Cumbria's cuisine is predominantly meat-focused, practically every menu has at least a few alternative options for vegetarians, although the range of 'choices' is sometimes not terribly impressive – pastas, salads and cheese-based dishes are the most likely culprits, and if you're happy to eat fish there are usually a few more options. Shopping at local supermarkets, wholefood shops and delis will allow you to cater for your own tastes while still experiencing Cumbrian produce, but for a truly stellar meat-free meal, Cockermouth has one of the country's top vegetarian restaurants in the Quince & Medlar (p159), where the menu of Wensleydale gateau and Cumberland cheese and mushroom roulade is a world away from nut cutlets and lentil stews.

TOP FIVE MICROBREWERIES

Hankering after something more adventurous than the usual Budweiser or Becks? Try these marvellous Cumbrian microbreweries, all of which brew their very own trademark ales (and think up daft names to match).

▪ **Barngates Brewery** (p121) In-house brewery at the Drunken Duck Inn – try the Cracker, Tag Lag or Chester's Strong and Ugly.

▪ **Bitter End** (p159) The smallest brewery in Cumbria. Cockermouth Pride is always on tap, supplemented by seasonal ales.

▪ **Coniston Brewery** (p117) Home of the original Bluebird Bitter (now available in a pale XB variety) as well as the rich, red Old Man Ale.

▪ **Great Gable Brewing Company** (p139) Lots of choice at the Wasdale Head Inn. All the ales are named after local peaks – try pale, malty WryNose or the hoppy Great Gable.

▪ **Hawkshead Brewery** (p74) One of the original and best microbreweries, with a classic hoppy bitter, red and gold ales, and the dark, fruity Brodie's Prime.

Vegans will have a harder time – there are no vegan-specific restaurants in the county, and Cumbrian milk, cheese and dairy products feature just as heavily in many restaurant menus as locally sourced meats.

COOKING COURSES

There are lots of cooking courses on offer in Cumbria if you're looking to sharpen up your knife skills.

Cumbria on a Plate (☎ 01900-881356; www.cumbriaonaplate.co.uk) Annette Gibbons' 'Food Safaris' offer a slightly different approach to cookery courses, and include a visit to local farms and producers coupled with a slap-up feed (£120). Themed cookery demos are also available.

Food & Company (☎ 01697-478634; www.foodandcompany.co.uk; Wigton) Cookery school run by two sisters in the stately surroundings of Mirehouse on Bassenthwaite Lake. Options range from dinner party desserts to courses on Mexican, Spanish and Indian cuisine. Prices start from £35.

L'Enclume (☎ 01539-536362; www.lenclume.co.uk; Cartmel) Want to meet the magician behind the curtain? Book in for a course at Simon Rogan's stellar foodery and your dinner parties will never be the same again. The day course costs £179.

Lucy Cooks (☎ 015394-32288; www.lucycooks.co.uk; Mill Yard, Staveley) Huge range of courses run by the Lakes' culinary superstar, Lucy Nicholson. Foundation courses cover the basics, while high-fliers can graduate to baking their own bread, shucking oysters and tackling choux pastry. Day courses cost between £100 and £140 or half-day taster sessions range from £40 to £70.

Watermill (☎ 01768-881523; www.organicmill.com; Little Salkeld, Penrith) Bread baking, children's cookery and vegetarian food are all covered in the programs at this award-winning bakery. Day courses cost £55.

The Made in Cumbria website (www .madeincumbria.co.uk) lists local producers and farmers markets in the Lake District, as well as details of craftspeople, artisans and artists all over Cumbria.

Environment

Many first-time visitors struggle to come to terms with the fact that the fields, fells and dales of the Lake District are actually far from a natural environment: centuries of hill farming, land management, quarrying and agricultural cultivation have left an indelible mark on the surrounding landscape, and without them the empty fells and open valleys so beloved of generations of British hill walkers would quickly revert back to a more 'natural' habitat of scrub, heath, moor and low-level woodland.

But while agricultural practices and local industry have undoubtedly played a huge part in shaping the present-day Lake District, it's also one of the few corners of England where there's still a whiff of real wildness on the breeze. The Romantics were among the first to champion the unique qualities of the Lake District landscape and the need to preserve it from industrial overdevelopment, but the area only received formal governmental protection in 1951, when the Lake District became one of Britain's first national parks. The ever-increasing importance of issues such as global warming and environmental damage have helped refocus attention on the Lake District's delicate natural environment. Pioneering projects to clean up the area's lakes, protect native wildlife, champion environmentally friendly technologies and, perhaps most importantly, to restore areas of cultivated land to unmanaged wilderness have pushed the Lake District to the forefront of the British green movement, and spearheaded the drive for a more sustainable and eco-conscious way of life in the 20th century.

For all you ever wanted to know about Cumbria's flagship sheep, visit the Herdwick Sheep Breeders Association website at www.herdwick-sheep .com, which has background on the best breeders and lists of forthcoming shows.

THE LAND

Around four million years ago, great ice sheets and glaciers covered much of northern Europe, etching out the distinctive shapes of the Lakeland fells and U-shaped valleys such as Borrowdale and Buttermere, Langdale and Wasdale. When the ice began to retreat between 15,000 and 10,000 years ago, the area's hard, non-porous volcanic rock meant that much of the glacial meltwater became trapped at the bottom of the valleys, forming the great lakes that are now such a characteristic feature of the Lakeland landscape. While the glaciers may be gone, their effects are still plainly visible: rock piles (known as 'moraines') and incongruous lumps of stone (known as 'erratic boulders') that were carved out, carried and later dumped by the glaciers can be seen dotted all over the Lake District, while the crinkled humps (known as 'drumlins') that mark many mountain slopes were caused by rocks and boulders being dragged along the surface of the land beneath the massive weight of the glaciers.

The oldest rocks in the Lake District are the Skiddaw slates, which date back around 500 million years.

For several thousand years after the great thaw, the Lake District – like much of the rest of Britain – was covered by thick forests of oak, ash, beech and yew. Around 7000 BC to 5000 BC, Stone Age settlers began to clear the area's woodland for agriculture, and to make use of the area's rich natural resources. Trees were felled to create timber, crop fields and grazing land; stone quarries were established to provide the raw materials for building and tool manufacture; and open-cast mines were developed to extract the region's rich reserves of copper, graphite and other minerals.

The surface of Windermere has frozen solid four times in the last 150 years: in 1864, 1946 and 1963, as well as the great freeze of 1895, when the lake remained frozen for six straight weeks.

All these practices had a profound and lasting effect on the surrounding landscape, and laid the foundations for many of the traditional industries that have supported Cumbrian people for hundreds of years. Perhaps the most important of these is hill farming, which has been a staple industry in this corner of England for at least a millennium.

SAVE SQUIRREL NUTKIN!

Cumbria and the Lake District is one of the last bastions for the native red squirrel in England. The star attraction of Beatrix Potter's classic children's fable, *The Tale of Squirrel Nutkin*, this cute scarlet-coated tree-scurrier was once widespread in Britain, but had suffered a massive decline in numbers by the turn of the 20th century – down from around 2.5 million to just 140,000 today. The main threat to the reds' survival is posed by their own transatlantic cousin, the grey squirrel, which was introduced from North America in the late 19th century. The introduction had a devastating effect on the smaller, more reticent reds, who soon found themselves bullied off their traditional territories and eaten out of house and home by their Yankee relatives.

But while competition for food and habitat is a major factor in the success of the greys, they also carry a much more serious threat – the deadly 'squirrel pox' virus. Most greys have developed an inbuilt resistance over the centuries, but the introduced disease is lethal to the reds and has caused widespread devastation in many British red squirrel populations.

The vast majority of the UK's remaining red squirrels live in Scotland, with just 20,000 in England and fewer than 1000 in Cumbria. Recent programs to establish 'buffer zones' to protect key red squirrel habitats against incursion by the greys have caused considerable controversy, since the only way to effectively ensure the reds' survival is to trap and cull any greys that enter their habitat. Red populations are carefully monitored, and people are encouraged to report any sighting to the Red Squirrel Hotline on ☎ 0845 347 9375 or online at www.saveoursquirrels.org.uk.

But according to a recent scientific report, things may just be looking up for Squirrel Nutkin and his crimson chums. A survey of more than 500 red squirrel corpses recently collected in England suggested that some animals seem to be developing their own antibodies against the virus, leading to hopes of a possible vaccine or – even more promisingly – that the wild reds may be able to generate their own immunity against the disease if left to their own devices. Keep your fingers (and paws) crossed…

WILDLIFE
Plants

The Lake District is one of the most heavily forested areas in England, with the majority of the park's woodland made up of broadleaf species such as sessile oaks, along with scattered patches of beech, ash, yew, elm and hazel. Remarkably little of this, however, is classed as 'native' woodland, as early settlers had chopped down most of the trees by the time of the Roman occupation, and most of the forest you'll see today has been replanted over the last couple of centuries. The largest areas of woodland are Grizedale Forest (p122) near Hawkshead, Whinlatter Forest Park (p156) and Ennerdale Forest (p139) to the north of Wasdale. Conifers were previously the main species employed in replantation projects, but more recently there have been moves to introduce different species to support a wider variety of wildlife and to provide greater biodiversity. The moist woodlands are also an important habitat for many native mosses and lichens.

The tallest tree in Cumbria is thought to be a silver fir near Aira Force in Ullswater, which reaches a height of around 160ft.

Thanks to the area's prodigious annual rainfall, plants of every persuasion grow in abundance all across the national park. In spring and summer, the hedgerows, woodlands and meadows are thick with grasses and colourful wildflowers, including primroses, pennyworts, wood sorrel, dogwort, ox-eye daisies, bluebells and wood anemones. Butterfly orchids are one of the loveliest Lake District flowers, but you'll have to keep your eyes peeled to spot them. Some of the rarest species can be seen around the Whitbarrow Nature Reserve (p73), west of Windermere.

But the Lake District's most famous flower is unquestionably the daffodil, an unofficial symbol of the park ever since it was immortalised in Wordsworth's famous poem. You can still view the dense stands of daffodils that inspired Wordsworth along the shores of Ullswater in Gowbarrow Park

ALL HAIL THE HERDWICK

Few creatures sum up the Lake District better than that shaggy symbol of the fells, the sheep. In total there are some two million sheep in Cumbria, outnumbering the resident human population by about 50 to one. The most distinctive Cumbrian breed is the Herdwick (distinguished by its thick black fleece and chalk-white face), which is thought to have been introduced to the area by Norse settlers around the 10th century, but it's just one of several hardy breeds that you'll see grazing the fells (other strains include the Swaledale and the Rough Fell). The Herdwick is less prized for its fleece than for its hardy nature – Herdwicks are happy in practically any weather, making them ideally suited to the fickle Lakeland climate – although their rich, gamey meat is also becoming increasingly common on local menus. Perhaps the most celebrated champion of the Herdwick is Beatrix Potter, who established her own flock in the 1920s and '30s and became a passionate supporter of the breed.

Sheep grazing has been the traditional method of managing the upland fells for many centuries; every flock has its own specific 'heaf' or territory, passed down the generations from ewe to lamb. The 2001 foot-and-mouth outbreak led to the compulsory culling of around a quarter of Cumbria's Herdwicks, jeopardising not only the long-term livelihoods of many hill farmers but also the age-old heaf boundaries; those farmers who stayed on the land had to 're-heaf' their new flocks by hand.

(p170) every spring, although recently there have been fears that the native species *(Narcissus pseudonarcissus)* is under increasing threat from larger and more robust cultivars.

Chilly temperatures and strong winds ensure only the hardiest plant species survive at higher altitudes. The high fells are a haven for moorland plants such as heather, bogweed and sphagnum moss, which support populations of red deer and birds of prey, while the lower slopes are largely covered by bracken, ferns and grasses. Peat bogs are another important habitat – you can visit one of the largest at Foulshaw Moss (p74), near Witherslack, east of Windermere. Towards the Cumbrian coast, the salt marshes around Morecambe Bay are good places to see marine plants such as scurvy grass, thrift and sea lavender.

Victorian gardeners established many lavish country estates around the Lake District, introducing exotic plants from faraway climes including Nepal, Bhutan, Northern India and China. Species such as rhododendron, camellias, hydrangeas and magnolias flourished in the cool, wet valleys; see p106 for a list of the district's loveliest patches and plots.

Animals

Along with the ever-present sheep and cattle, keep your eyes peeled for another shaggy inhabitant on the hilltops, the Cumbrian fell pony. This hardy little horse generally reaches between 13 and 14 hands high, and is thought to be descended from the pack ponies introduced to Cumbria during the Roman occupation. It was later employed for activities such as ploughing, harvesting and 'snigging' (transporting felled timber), and before the advent of roads was the traditional Cumbrian form of transport.

The name for a castrated male sheep is a 'wether', while a 'hogget' refers to a sheep between the ages of weaning and shearing.

The Lake District's other furry inhabitants include badgers, foxes, rabbits and voles, as well as a sizeable population of red deer, and smaller herds of fallow and roe deer. Look out too for weasels, stoats and otters, which are slowly re-establishing themselves along the riverbanks of the national park.

The hedgerows and fields are also good places to spot moths, butterflies and dragonflies. Some of the more unusual butterfly species you might spy include the mountain ringlet, the purple hairstreak, the painted lady, the northern brown argus and the holly blue, but you'll have to be seriously lucky to spy the super-rare marsh fritillary – once common across the whole of England, but now highly endangered thanks to the drainage of natural marshland. Eagle-eyed entomologists might also be able to spot around 20 of the 24 species of British ladybird.

Common frogs, newts and toads are widespread, and the county supports two of England's largest colonies of the endangered natterjack toad at Drigg and Sandscale Haws. Glow-worms (actually a beetle, not a worm) were once also prevalent across Cumbria – Dorothy Wordsworth mentions them several times in her *Grasmere Journals* – although these days the incandescent little critters are confined to quiet limestone ridges and grassy coastal areas.

The lakes also support several rare species of fish, including the Arctic char; the schelly, a whitefish only found in Ullswater, Haweswater and Brotherswater; and the highly endangered vendace, only found in Derwent Water and Bassenthwaite Lake. More common species to be found are the rainbow and brown trout, the pike and, if you're really lucky, even wild Atlantic salmon.

BIRD LIFE

More than 200 species of bird frequent the Lake District, ranging from the diminutive wood warbler to the elegant whooper swan, which winters in considerable numbers around Elterwater (p97) and the Eden Valley (p204). The best place for bird spotting is along the coast, especially around Morecambe Bay and the Solway Coast, where you might spot pink-footed geese, scaup, wigeon, grey and golden plovers; and the well-known bird reserve at St Bees Head (p191), which supports populations of guillemots, kittiwakes, razorbills, shearwaters and even a few breeding pairs of puffins.

Further inland, the once-common kingfisher and nightjar are becoming increasingly rare, although the news is happier for many birds of prey – once persecuted by local farmers, several species are now making a comeback, including honey buzzards, hen harriers, merlins and goshawks. Even more excitingly, since 2001, Bassenthwaite Lake (p153) has been the summertime home for the only breeding pair of ospreys this side of the Scottish border, while Haweswater (p176) supports England's only resident golden eagle.

THE NATIONAL PARK

The formation of two of the great English environmental movements – the National Parks and the National Trust – can both trace their roots to the Lake District in the mid- to late 19th century. Ever the trailblazer, Wordsworth was the first to ponder the concept of a national park in his 1810 *Guide to the Lakes,* in which he famously described the Lake District as a 'sort of national property in which every man has a right and interest who has an eye to perceive and a heart to enjoy'. Inspired by the poet's passionate defence of the Lakeland landscape against unnecessary industrial expansion, the clergyman, campaigner and sonnet-writer Hardwicke Rawnsley joined forces with Octavia Hill and Robert Hunter to form the National Trust in 1895. One of their first purchases was Brandelhow Woods on Derwent Water in 1902. Rawnsley also founded one of the first green lobby groups, the Lake District Defence Society (later The Friends of the Lake District), and inspired a young Beatrix Potter, whom he met during a family holiday to Wray Castle in 1895.

Thus by the time the government finally bowed to popular pressure and formed the UK's first batch of national parks in 1951 there was already a strong tradition of environmental campaigning in the county. Predated only by the Peak District, the Lake District was (and still is) the largest national park in England, covering a total area of 885 sq miles. Unlike many other countries, Britain's national parks are protected landscapes rather than strict nature

The last wolf in England is said to have been shot near Cartmel in the 14th century. A weathervane in the shape of a wolf's head on top of Cartmel Priory (p182) commemorates the event.

The passionate local naturalist Peter Wilde runs a fascinating website detailing all his favourite Cumbrian bugs and beasties, with details of where, when and how you can see them – check it out at www.cumbria -wildlife.org.uk.

reserves. Domestic building, commercial activity, agriculture and certain heavy industries (such as timber felling and quarrying) are all theoretically allowed within the park's boundaries, but strict planning rules and environmental regulations ensure that all development is carefully managed and in keeping with the spirit and traditions of the wider national park. All of Britain's national parks are managed and administered by government funded National Park Authorities (NPAs), although intriguingly, the Lake District NPA actually owns only around 3.9% of the total land – the vast majority is in private ownership (58.8%), with the remainder taken up by the National Trust (24.8%), United Utilities (6.8%), the Forestry Commission (5.6%) and the Ministry of Defence (0.2%).

In addition to the wider national park itself, Cumbria also boasts more Sites of Special Scientific Interest (SSSIs) than any other English county, a testament to the area's rich biodiversity and varied habitats. Many smaller national and local nature reserves have been established around the county to give extra protection to specific species and habitats; the Royal Society for the Protection of Birds (RSPB) also operates five reserves at Hodbarrow, St Bees, Campfield Marsh, Haweswater and Geltsdale.

ENVIRONMENTAL ISSUES

While the new national park helped secure the future for the land within its borders, it inadvertently caused problems for the rest of the region. Rigidly enforced planning restrictions within the park pushed heavy industry outwards, leading to a concentration of large-scale industrial development around the cities of Carlisle and Barrow-in-Furness, now a major centre for shipbuilding and aeronautics.

Even more controversial was the decision to locate the world's first commercial nuclear power station at Windscale on the Cumbrian coast. Four Magnox reactors were opened at Calder Hall in 1956, but shut down just a year later in October 1957, when a major fire ripped through the reactor core and released vast quantities of radioactive particles into the air, contaminating hundreds of hectares of local farmland, and drifting all the way to the Isle of Man and Northern Ireland. Despite public concern, a second generation of reactors was built at Windscale in 1962 (subsequently renamed Sellafield in 1981), and it has since become the UK's largest nuclear-reprocessing plant, as well as a huge local employer. There have been constant mutterings about radioactive pollution around Sellafield ever since the Windscale disaster, and although it is scheduled for decommissioning over the next decade, the plant's future still hangs in the balance; many local people are lobbying for one of the country's new nuclear plants to be constructed on the site to safeguard local employment, while environmental campaigners are adamant that it should close down once and for all.

And while Sellafield continues to stir up powerful feelings, even the national park hasn't always been an unmitigated force for good. The ever-increasing numbers of people on the fells, coupled with the ongoing need for new car parks, roads and facilities to cater for growing visitor numbers, and the conflicting demands of environmental protection and local industry, continue to present a non-stop headache for park authorities. It's a difficult balance to strike. On the one hand, tourist numbers are vital to the long-term survival of the park and the people who live and work within its boundaries, but increased visitor numbers inevitably come at a cost to the fragile environment. The park now employs a team of professional wardens and conservation staff to try to offset the inevitable damage caused by rising visitor numbers, and has implemented a host of schemes to encourage people to visit the area in a more environmentally conscious and sustainable way.

A new campaign to protect more than 39 threatened species including the red squirrel, great crested newt, marsh fritillary and song thrush has recently been established – find out about specific wildlife action plans at www .wildlifeincumbria.org.uk.

The Cumbria Wildlife Trust is one of the county's leading environmental campaign groups, and often runs voluntary programs that allow you to get involved with conservation projects in a hands-on way – learn more at www.cumbria wildlifetrust.org.uk.

The well-known local writer and photographer Bill Birkett has published a series of lavish photographic books detailing a year in the life of several Lakeland valleys, including Borrowdale, Langdale and the Duddon Valley.

Windermere & Around

Tracing a glassy 10.5-mile curve from Newby Bridge in the south to Ambleside's Waterhead jetties in the north, hemmed in by fields and fells, the stately lake of Windermere makes an unforgettable introduction to the charms of Lakeland scenery. In his 1810 *Guide to the Lakes,* Wordsworth mused on 'the splendour, the stillness and the solemnity' of a trip across Windermere's waters, and it's surely no coincidence that it was here, gazing across the point-to-point panorama from Orrest Head, that Alfred Wainwright cooked up his plan to document all the great Lakeland fells in his landmark *Pictorial Guides.*

These days, stillness and solemnity might not immediately spring to mind when thinking about the nation's most visited lake. Practically every last one of the national park's 15.5 million annual visitors make the pilgrimage to Windermere's shores at least once during their stay, and in peak season it can feel weirdly akin to an outing to the British seaside, with throngs of crimson-faced trippers strolling the tightly packed streets of Windermere town, or lining up along the lakeside jetties of Bowness-on-Windermere for a vintage cruise experience.

Thankfully, once you get beyond the hectic quays of Bowness, the lake rediscovers an air of tranquillity. At the lake's southern end stretch the grounds of Fell Foot Park. Nearby at Lakeside the puffing carriages of the Lakeside and Haverthwaite Railway steam south towards Ulverston, while the beautifully restored Arts and Crafts mansion of Blackwell House looks out over the lake's eastern shoreline. At the northern end of the lake is the bustling grey-slate town of Ambleside, originally an industrial centre and now a haven for foodies and fell walkers, while beyond the fells southeast of Windermere are the quiet Lyth and Winster Valleys, home to a cluster of country pubs and some of Cumbria's few remaining damson farms.

HIGHLIGHTS

- Explore Windermere's wooded islands aboard a **lake cruise** (p62)
- Admire the artistry and architecture of **Blackwell House** (p71)
- Dine in serious style at the **Punch Bowl Inn** (p73) in Crosthwaite
- Pack your own picnic and head for the landscaped gardens of **Fell Foot Park** (p71) or **Holehird** (p75)
- Seek out the gourmet spoils around Mill Yard in **Staveley** (p73)
- Follow in the footsteps of Postman Pat around the **Kentmere Valley** (p74)

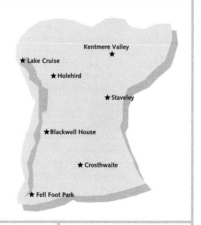

★ Lake Cruise
Kentmere Valley ★
★ Holehird
★ Staveley
★ Blackwell House
★ Crosthwaite
★ Fell Foot Park

| ■ Area of largest lake (Windermere): 5.7 sq miles | ■ Windermere Lake Cruises passengers in 2007: 1,274,976 | ■ Number of Michelin-starred restaurants: 2 |

ITINERARY 1
WANSFELL PIKE HIKE
6 miles/4 hours/Ambleside

This moderate hike from Ambleside takes in Wansfell Pike (1588ft), a lunchtime stop in Troutbeck and world-class views from Jenkin's Crag. It's fairly easy going, with only one tough climb up to the top of the pike.

The trail starts on Stock Ghyll Lane behind the Market Hall. Follow the path into **Stock Ghyll Park** and climb up through the woods to **Stock Ghyll Force**. Cross over the footbridge above the falls and follow the main path on to a Victorian turnstile. Turn left and follow the paved lane, then take the next right-hand path leading up the fell-side towards Wansfell Pike. Continue climbing before crossing over a drystone wall and making your final push towards the summit, from where you'll have grandstand views over Windermere, Ambleside and the distant Langdale range. The 'Pike' is actually one of two separate summits on Wansfell; Baystones (1601ft) to the northeast is higher, but Wansfell Pike is generally considered the superior summit thanks to its fine vistas.

From the fell-top, follow the marker cairns along the eastern path before connecting with Nanny Lane, which eventually winds down into **Troutbeck**. There's a choice of pubs to whet your whistle (a little to the north, the **Mortal Man**, p76, has the best views), or you can visit the yeoman's farmhouse at **Townend** (p75) if you have time.

Carry on south through the village past the post office, and look out for the right-hand turn onto Robin Lane (signed to Ambleside). Keep with the main track and follow the signs; after a while you'll pass by High Skelghyll Farm and into the NT-owned **Skelghyll Wood**, where a side-track leads up to the viewpoint at **Jenkin's Crag** – try to time your arrival for late afternoon, when the sinking sun lights up Windermere and the Langdale Pikes.

Return to the main path and follow the track downhill back towards Ambleside. You can either veer off to see the rhododendrons of **Stagshaw Gardens** (☎ 015394-46027; £2.50, payable at honesty box; ☯ 10am-6.30pm Apr-Jun) or continue along the trail to emerge near the Waterhead jetties.

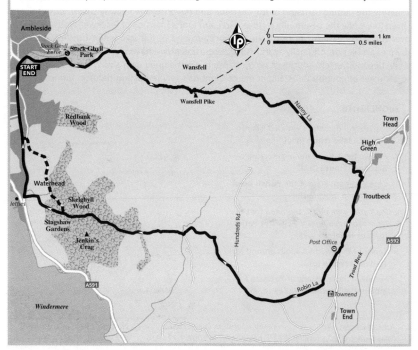

ITINERARY 2
UNDERLOUGHRIGG, THE STEPPING STONES & RYDAL MOUNT STROLL
2.5 miles/2 hours/Ambleside

If all you're looking for is a gentle, flat stroll through typical Lakeland countryside, then this walk around Underloughrigg and Rydal Park is ideal. This is part of the route Dorothy Wordsworth once used to follow when walking from Grasmere to Ambleside, and you can still spot a few places she mentions in her journals. It's flat and easy all the way, although, as always, you'll be wise to pack wet-weather gear and to pull on a decent pair of waterproof shoes.

Start out on Vicarage Rd in **Ambleside** and cut straight through the green lawns of **Rothay Park**, before crossing over Miller Bridge on the park's west side. Turn immediately right and follow Underloughrigg Lane past **Fox How**, once the home of the poet and pioneering educationalist Matthew Arnold. Follow the path onwards beneath the lower slopes of Loughrigg Fell; before long you'll come to the famous **Stepping Stones** over the River Rothay, mentioned by Dorothy Wordsworth in her diaries.

Straight on there's another crossing at **Pelter Bridge**; where you can link up with the walk around Rydal Water described on p85. Otherwise carry on over the bridge and turn left onto the main road. After around 200m you'll see the right-hand turning up towards Wordsworth's house at **Rydal Mount** (p91).

The route back to Ambleside continues through the grounds of **Rydal Hall** directly opposite Wordsworth's house; the hall was formerly the stately home of the Le Fleming family and the Diocese of Carlisle, but is now a busy conference centre. If you're feeling a little peckish you'll find sustenance and scones at the **Old School Room Tea Shop** (p91). Follow the trail past **Rydal Beck**, with its pretty waterfalls, to reach the tree-filled grounds of **Rydal Park**, best seen in early spring or late autumn, when the trees are a blaze of colour. After about 20 minutes the path links up at Scandale Bridge with the main A591, which you can follow back into central Ambleside.

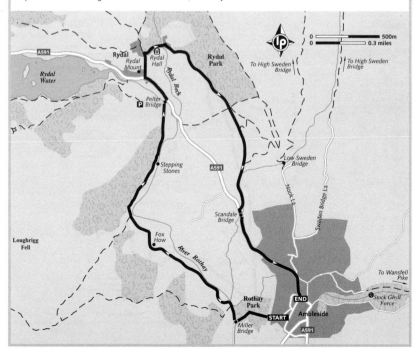

ITINERARY 3
EAST WINDERMERE DRIVE
25 miles/4 hours/Windermere

This picturesque drive takes in the quiet countryside to the east of Windermere and offers plenty of stops en route to revel in the scenery and visit the sites. Start off in Windermere (opposite) and head down through **Bowness** (p61) to **Blackwell House** (p71), one of the most elegant Arts and Crafts houses in England. If the weather is fine, indulge in elevenses on the terrace once you've looked round the house and explored the surrounding grounds. Then head southeast along the A5074 through Winster, pootling across the hilltops all the way to **Crosthwaite**, where a slap-up lunch at the award-winning **Punch Bowl Inn** (p73) awaits.

You could take an optional detour south via the **Whitbarrow National Nature Reserve** (p73), a beautiful limestone ridge populated by rare birds and butterflies, before backtracking to follow the road west past Strawberry Bank to the famous viewpoint of **Gummer's How** (p73). Park in the Astley's Plantation car park and stroll to the summit for one of the best all-round views over Windermere. From the top you'll be able to see the southern stretches of the lake as well as the densely forested expanse of Claife Heights on the lake's western shore. Look out for the tell-tale plume of steam from the Lakeside and Haverthwaite Steam Railway far below, not to mention the regular cruise boats beetling across the silver expanse of Windermere.

Once you've had your fill of the views, it's time for afternoon tea and a gentle stroll around the lakeside grounds of **Fell Foot Park** (p71) before returning back along the lake's eastern side.

Alternatively, you could extend the trip with a drive up Windermere's west side, stopping at either **Stott Park Bobbin Mill** (p72), the **Lakes Aquarium** (p72) or Beatrix Potter's house at **Hill Top** (p123) before catching the **Windermere Ferry** (p70) back to Bowness; this optional route is best reserved for the shoulder months, as the summer queues for the car ferry will probably have you weeping into your steering wheel.

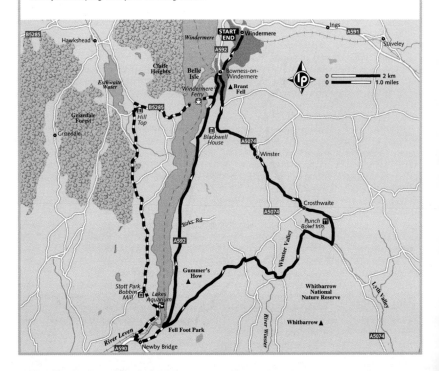

WINDERMERE TOWN & BOWNESS-ON-WINDERMERE

pop 8432

The largest natural body of water in England, Windermere has been a tourist magnet ever since the first steam trains chugged into town in 1847, and it still exerts an irresistible pull. It's a place where tradition and mass-market tourism meet head on; Victorian villas and smart slate-fronted hotels line up in ordered ranks along the streets of Windermere town, a mile inland from the lake proper, while down by the cluttered Bowness shoreline, historic cruise barges and wooden row boats bob alongside the higgledy-piggledy piers. It's brash, busy and the summertime traffic can certainly take the shine off things, but Windermere is still an essential stop on every Lake District itinerary.

HISTORY

Prior to the mid-19th century, the area around present-day Windermere was little more than a collection of cottages and tumbledown outbuildings making up the tiny farming hamlet of Birthwaite. The vast majority of people would have skirted past Birthwaite altogether, instead making a beeline for the passenger ferry at Bowness, which crossed over to the lake's western shore and the villages of Near Sawrey, Far Sawrey and nearby Hawkshead.

But this sleepy settlement was changed beyond recognition when the decision was made to extend the west coast railway towards Windermere in the 1840s, in order to open up the Lakes to tourism from the rapidly growing cities scattered across England's industrial north. The controversial plan met with vehement opposition from both residents (many of whom were forcefully required to sell parts of their land to the railway company) and local notables, including the newly appointed Poet Laureate William Wordsworth, who wrote a series of stinging letters to newspaper editors, the Board of Trade and the House of Commons, and even penned an anti-railway sonnet published in the *Morning Post* in 1844.

Despite the opposition, the plan received royal assent in 1845. The original intent had been to run the tracks right down to the lakeshore, but due to the enormous expense and considerable technical challenges presented by the downhill track into Bowness, it was subsequently decided to terminate the line near Birthwaite at a new station called Windermere, renamed in order to reinforce its connection with the lake (conveniently overlooking the fact that the station lies over a mile inland from the water's edge).

Construction was completed in double-quick time, and within a few years the little hamlets of Birthwaite and Bowness had been all but submerged by a swathe of new houses and villas that sprang up to cater for the tourist traffic; over 120,000 visitors arrived in the railway's first year. Horse-drawn coaches and charabancs ferried visitors up and down the hill from the station to the lakeshore, where steam-powered boats set out for jaunts around the lake, and well-to-do visitors were encouraged to stroll the promenades and jetties dotted around the lake's edge. By the early 20th century continued construction around Lake Rd meant that Windermere and Bowness had become all but indistinguishable from each other, although officially both still retain their status as separate towns.

ORIENTATION

The train and bus stations, as well as the main tourist office and big supermarkets, are all in Windermere town. Most hotels and B&Bs are dotted on or around Lake Rd, which leads downhill towards Bowness and the lakeshore. The main road to Windermere from eastern Cumbria is the A591, which skirts the lake's northeastern edge en route to Ambleside. The smaller A592 leads south through Bowness, tracking the eastern edge of the lake en route to Fell Foot Park and Newby Bridge.

INFORMATION

Emergency

Windermere Police Station (Map p62; ☎ 0845 33 00 247; Lake Rd; ⏰ 9am-5pm Mon-Fri)

Internet Access

Library (Map p62; ☎ 015394-62400; Broad St, Windermere town; per half hr £1; ⏰ 9.30am-5pm Mon-Tue & Thu-Fri, 10am-1pm Sat, closed Wed & Sun)

Purple Chilli Cafe (Map p66; ☎ 015394-45647; Lake Rd, Bowness-on-Windermere; per hr £3; ⏰ 10am-6pm Mon-Fri, 10am-4pm Sat)

WINDERMERE & AROUND

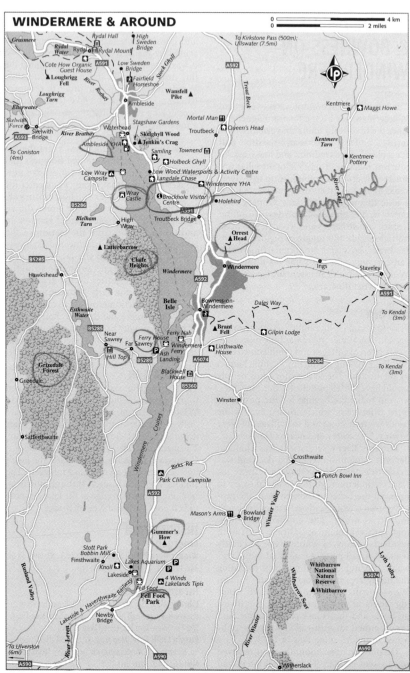

0 ————— 4 km
0 ————— 2 miles

Adventure playground

Grasmere

Rydal Hall
High Sweden Bridge

To Kirkstone Pass (500m);
Ullswater (7.5mi)

Rydal Water
Rydal
Rydal Mount
Cote How Organic Guest House
A591
Low Sweden Bridge

Stock Ghyll

A592

Loughrigg Fell
Fairfield Horseshoe

Loughrigg Tarn
River Rothay
Ambleside

Wansfell Pike

Kentmere
Maggs Howe

Ellterwater
Mortal Man
Queen's Head

Skelwith Force
Stagshaw Gardens
Troutbeck

Trout Beck

Skelwith Bridge
A593
Waterhead
River Brathay
Skelghyll Wood
Jenkin's Crag

Kentmere Tarn

To Coniston (4mi)
Ambleside YHA
Samling
Townend

River Kent

Kentmere Pottery

Holbeck Ghyll

Low Wray Campsite
Low Wood Watersports & Activity Centre
Langdale Chase

Wray Castle
Windermere YHA

Brockhole Visitor Centre
Holehird

B5286
Blelham Tarn
High Wray
Troutbeck Bridge

A591

Orrest Head

Latterbarrow

Claife Heights

B5285
Hawkshead
Windermere
A592
Windermere
Ings
Staveley
A591

Esthwaite Water
Belle Isle
Bowness-on-Windermere
Dales Way
To Kendal (3mi)

B5285
Near Sawrey
Ferry House
Ferry Nab
Brant Fell
Gilpin Lodge

Grizedale Forest
Hill Top
Far Sawrey
Windermere Ferry
Ash Landing
Linthwaite House
A5074
B5284
To Kendal (3mi)

Grizedale
B5285
Blackwell House
B5360

Satterthwaite
Winster
Crosthwaite
Punch Bowl Inn

Birks Rd
Park Cliffe Campsite
Windermere Cruises
A592

Mason's Arms
Bowland Bridge

Winster Valley

Gummer's How

Stott Park Bobbin Mill
Finsthwaite
Lakes Aquarium
Knoll
Lakeside
4 Winds Lakelands Tipis
Fell Foot

Rusland Valley
Whitbarrow National Nature Reserve
Whitbarrow
A5074
Lyth Valley

Fell Foot Park
Whitbarrow Scar

Lakeside & Haverthwaite Railway
Newby Bridge
River Leven

To Ulverston (6mi)
A590
A590
Witherslack
River Winster

BROCKHOLE VISITOR CENTRE

If you're a first-timer to the Lakes, it might be worth heading straight for the national park's main visitor centre at **Brockhole** (Map p60; ☎ 015394-46601; www.lake-district.gov.uk), which is crammed from floor to ceiling with details on sights, activities and background information on the Lake District and the surrounding area. The centre is lodged inside an elegant mansion built in 1895 for the wealthy Mancunian silk merchant William Henry Aldolphus Gaddum, but it's been a visitor centre since 1969. Alongside informative displays on the geology, environment and history of the national park, you'll also find a revolving program of film shows, talks and guided walks, as well as a wonderful kids' playground and lakeside gardens designed by the Victorian landscaper Thomas Mawson, who oversaw the garden design for other upper-crust homes, including Holker Hall (p183), Holehird (p75), and Rydal Hall (p91).

The visitor centre is about 3 miles from Windermere on the main A591. Entrance is free, but the large visitor car park is pay-and-display (£2.20/4/6 for two hours/four hours/all day). Buses 555 and 599 both make stops at the centre, as do the northern cruise boats run by Windermere Lake Cruises (p62).

Laundry

Windermere Laundrette (Map p62; 19 Main Rd; ☺ 8.30am-5.30pm Mon-Fri, 9am-5pm Sat)

Money

Most of the major banks have branches in Windermere town:

Barclays (Map p62; ☎ 08457 555 555; 3 Crescent Rd; ☺ 9.30am-4.30pm Mon-Fri)

HSBC (Map p62; ☎ 08457 404 404; 15 Crescent Rd; ☺ 9.30am-4.30pm Mon-Fri)

Natwest (Map p62; ☎ 0845 302 1609; 2 High St; ☺ 9am-4.30pm Mon-Fri)

Post

Bowness Post Office (Map p66; 2 St Martins Pde; ☺ 9am-12.30pm & 1-5.15pm Mon, Tue & Thu, 9am-12.30pm & 1-5pm Wed & Fri)

Windermere Post Office (Map p62; 21 Crescent Rd; ☺ 9am-5.30pm Mon-Fri, 9am-12.30pm Sat)

Tourist Information

Bowness Tourist Office (Map p66; ☎ 015394-42895; bownesstic@lake-district.gov.uk; Glebe Rd; ☺ 9.30am-5.30pm Easter-Oct, 10am-4pm Fri-Sun Nov-Mar) In a stand-alone building near the boat jetties.

Mountain Goat (Map p62; ☎ 015394-45161; Victoria St, Windermere town; ☺ 9am-5.30pm Mon-Sat) Organised minibus tours and general info on the Lake District and the Cross-Lakes Shuttle.

Windermere Tourist Office (Map p62; ☎ 015394-46499; windermeretic@southlakeland.gov.uk; Victoria St; ☺ 9am-5.30pm Mon-Sat, 9.30am-5.30pm Sun Apr-Oct, shorter hours in winter) In a chalet opposite Natwest bank. Offers accommodation booking service (£3) and internet access (£1 for 15 minutes).

SIGHTS & ACTIVITIES

Most people buzz straight through Windermere town in a headlong dash for the attractions of the Bowness shoreline. First call for Tiggywinkle fans is the **World of Beatrix Potter** (Map p66; ☎ 015394-88444; www.hop-skip-jump.com; adult/child £6/3; ☺ 10am-5.30pm Apr-Sep, 10am-4.30pm Oct-Mar), which brings to life scenes from practically all the author's books (including life-size versions of Peter Rabbit's garden and Mr McGregor's greenhouse). The displays are unashamedly aimed at the younger crowd; grown-ups can seek refuge in the Tailor of Gloucester tearoom if it all gets too button-cute, or mosey around the gift shop in search of those all-essential Squirrel Nutkin souvenirs. Queues can be long in the high season, so make sure you pitch up early.

A little further north along Rayrigg Rd is the **Windermere Steamboat Museum** (Map p62; ☎ 015394-45565; www.steamboat.co.uk; Rayrigg Rd), home to one of nation's most comprehensive collections of vintage steamers and lake-going vessels. Sadly, at the time of writing, the museum was closed for the foreseeable future while plans for a revamped national boating museum gather steam. All the latest news is detailed on the museum's website, so keep checking for the most up-to-date info.

When you've had enough of the hustle and hum of downtown Bowness, seek some solitude with a peaceful walk along the lakeshore past **Cockshott Point** (Map p66). The public footpath starts on Glebe Rd, winding through patches of woodland and pastureland along the lake's northeastern edge, and offering wonderful views of the water and the wooded

WINDERMERE & AROUND

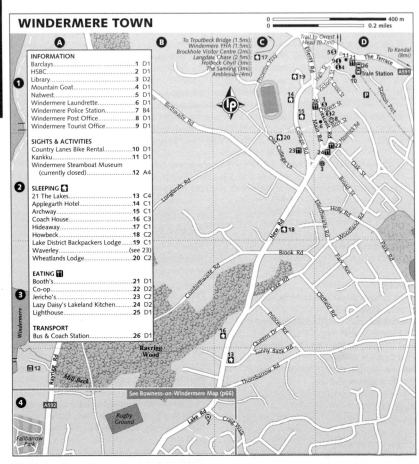

WINDERMERE TOWN

0 — 400 m
0 — 0.2 miles

INFORMATION
Barclays.................................1 D1
HSBC....................................2 D1
Library..................................3 D2
Mountain Goat.....................4 D1
Natwest...............................5 D1
Windermere Laundrette........6 D1
Windermere Police Station....7 B4
Windermere Post Office........8 D1
Windermere Tourist Office....9 D1

SIGHTS & ACTIVITIES
Country Lanes Bike Rental.....10 D1
Kankku.................................11 D1
Windermere Steamboat Museum
    (currently closed)..............12 A4

SLEEPING
21 The Lakes.........................13 C4
Applegarth Hotel...................14 C1
Archway...............................15 C1
Coach House.........................16 C3
Hideaway.............................17 C1
Howbeck..............................18 C2
Lake District Backpackers Lodge......19 C1
Waverley..............................(see 23)
Wheatlands Lodge.................20 C2

EATING
Booth's.................................21 D1
Co-op..................................22 D2
Jericho's...............................23 C2
Lazy Daisy's Lakeland Kitchen......24 D2
Lighthouse............................25 D1

TRANSPORT
Bus & Coach Station..............26 D1

islet of **Belle Isle** (p64). The path emerges at the southern end of Braithwaite Fold, near the Windermere Canoe and Kayak jetty and the Windermere Ferry.

Boat Trips

Somewhat bizarrely, Lake Windermere is officially designated as a public highway (effectively the same as a road or motorway), a hangover from the 19th century when the lake was an important industrial thoroughfare for barges ferrying coal, lumber, copper and slate from the nearby mines to the railways. It wasn't long, however, before the lake's potential as a tourist attraction took precedence over its commercial traffic. The first passenger ferry was launched in 1845 (see boxed text opposite), and these days **Windermere Lake Cruises** (Map p66; ☎ 015395-31188; www.windermere-lakecruises.co.uk) keeps the tradition alive with trips aboard a fleet of modern cruisers and a trio of period beauties. The company's most venerable vessel, *Tern,* was originally built as a private steamer in the 1890s, while *Swan* and *Teal* were both built in the 1930s.

There are several routes, all of which explore different sections of the lake and allow you to jump off at one of the ferry landings (Waterhead/Ambleside, Wray Castle, Brockhole, Bowness, Ferry House, Fell Foot and Lakeside) and to catch a later boat back. **Blue Cruise** (adult/child/family £6.20/3.10/17) Circular cruise around Windermere's shoreline and islands. Departs from Bowness with an optional stop at Ferry House.

Bowness to Ferry House (adult/child/family single £2.20/1.20/6.20) Ferry service which links up with the Cross-Lakes Shuttle (p70) to Hill Top and Hawkshead.
Green Cruise (adult/child/family £6.20/3.10/17) Forty-five minute cruise from Waterhead/Ambleside via Wray Castle and Brockhole Visitor Centre.
Red Cruise (adult/child/family £8.25/4.50/23) North lake cruise from Bowness to Ambleside.
Yellow Cruise (adult/child/family £8.50/4.70/24) South cruise from Bowness to Lakeside, stopping at the Lakes Aquarium.

A Freedom of the Lake ticket allows a day's unlimited travel and costs £15/7.50/40 per adult/child/family. Joint tickets are available with the **Lakeside and Haverthwaite Railway** (p71; ☎ 015395-31594; return from Bowness adult/5-15yr/family £13.50/7.20/37.20, from Ambleside £18.70/9.35/52; ☻ Apr-Oct) and the **Lakes Aquarium** (p72; return ferry & aquarium from Bowness adult/5-15yr/family £15.25/8.70/45.50, from Ambleside £21.75/11.50/61.50).

Boat & Bike Hire

If you'd prefer to explore under your own steam, boats can be hired from the **rental kiosk** (Map p66; summer ☎ 015394-88178, 015394-40347; ☻ 9am-5pm Apr-Oct; winter ☎ 015394-43360; ☻ Sat & Sun only) just to the right of the Bowness promenade. Row boats will set you back £5/2.50 per adult/child for an hour. Open-top motorboats cost £15 per hour for two adults, or there's a closed-cabin version for £18. Controversially there's now a 10mph speed limit on Windermere (dropping to 6mph in the busier areas), which came into force in 2000 – a bone of some contention among local power boaters and waterskiers, who are now effectively banned from all of the major lakes inside the national park.

Windermere Canoe & Kayak (Map p66; ☎ 015394-44451; www.windermerecanoeandkayak.co.uk; Ferry Nab Rd; ☻ 9am-5pm), based on Ferry Nab Rd near the Windermere Ferry, hires out 'sit on tops' (£25/35 per half/full day), as well as canoes (£30/40) and kayaks (£35/45). One-on-one hourly tuition is available from £50/35 per adult/child, although discounts are available for larger groups and longer sessions. Bikes can also be hired for a full day for £20/15 per adult/child.

Alternatively, try **Country Lanes** (Map p62; www.countrylaneslakedistrict.co.uk; train station ☎ 015394-44544; ☻ 9am-5pm Apr-Oct, 9am-5pm Wed-Sun Nov-Mar; Lakeside ☎ 07748-512286; ☻ 9.30am-5.30pm Easter-Oct), which has outlets beside the platform at Windermere train station and behind the Lakes Aquarium at Lakeside. Charges are £19/10 for an adult/child front-suspension bike, £24 for a model with disc brakes and £30 for a full-suspension set-up.

Lake & Islands

The largest lake in the national park, Windermere encompasses an area of 5.7 sq miles between Ambleside in the north and Newby Bridge in the south. The lake is fed from the rivers Brathay and Rothay to the north, outflowing to the south into the River Leven. The deepest section of water lies near its northern end, where the lake bed is around 220m below the surface, while at its widest point the lake measures about a mile across. Windermere supports a rich variety of underwater life, particularly pike, perch and a unique species of Arctic char, trapped here when the glaciers retreated at the end of the last ice age. It's also home to the largest population of goldeneye ducks in the Lake District.

ALL ABOARD!

The first passenger vessel launched on Windermere (or any English lake, for that matter) was the paddle steamer *Lady of the Lake*, built by Richard Ashburner of Greenodd for the Windermere Steam Yacht Co. The ship measured 80ft from bow to stern, carried up to 200 passengers and was luxuriously furnished with all the creature comforts expected by her well-to-do clientele, including a positively regal 1st-class saloon furnished with carpets, mirrors and cushioned seats.

All the great and the good of fashionable Lakeland society arrived to celebrate the ship's launch in 1845 (with the notable exception of William Wordsworth, who passionately opposed the idea of introducing pleasure vessels onto any of the lakes, and flatly refused to participate in the launch ceremony). To the sound of polite applause from the jetties and assorted parps, toots and cymbal clashes from the onboard brass band (borrowed for the occasion from the Kendal Cavalry), the ship set off on its maiden voyage from Newby Bridge to Ambleside; she continued in service for the next 20 years before finally being decommissioned in 1865.

The name of the lake derives from Old Norse *Vinandr mere,* meaning 'Vinandr's lake'.

Various stretches of the shoreline are in the hands of private landholders, the national park or the National Trust (which owns the southern end around Fell Foot Park, p71, and much of the western side). Intriguingly, the lake bed (and effectively the lake itself) is commonly owned by the people of Windermere; the local philanthropist Henry Leigh Groves donated the sum of £6000 in 1938 in order to purchase the lake on behalf of local residents. Since then the South Lakeland District Council has acted as landlord on their behalf, administering and maintaining its moorings and jetties.

Officially speaking there are 14 islands on Windermere, although some of the smaller ones amount to little more than a cluster of stones, foliage and shrubs (tiny **Maiden Holme**, the lake's smallest island, isn't attached to anything, and park authorities are currently pondering whether they should try to preserve it or abandon it to the whims of mother nature).

Largest of all is **Belle Isle** (Map p66), the densely wooded island visible from the Bowness promenade and Cockshott Point. The island was originally home to a Roman villa occupied by the commander of the Roman garrison stationed nearby; during the Civil War it was occupied by the aristocratic Phillipson family, who were staunch supporters of the Royalist cause (legend has it that the island was shelled by Parliamentarian artillery from nearby Cockshott Point).

Known then as Long Holme, the island was purchased by the Nottingham merchant Thomas English in 1774, who constructed the island's distinctive Italianate roundhouse and classical portico at a cost of around £6000 (Wordsworth subsequently lambasted it as a glorified 'pepper pot' in the *Prelude*). In 1781 English sold the island at a considerable loss to local mine owner (and MP for Carlisle) John Christian Curwen, who embellished the landscaped grounds, planted an arboretum of rare trees, and renamed the island 'Belle Isle' in honour of his wife Isabella. The island is still privately owned and is the only one inhabited year-round; it's currently off-limits to the general public.

Some of the other islands to look out for on the lake include the twin **Lilies of the Valley** (East and West), named after the prodigious blossoms that once grew here (and which featured, again, in the *Prelude*); **Lady Holme** (owned by the National Trust), formerly occupied by a pair of priests who lodged their brood of chickens on nearby **Hen Holme**; and **Crowe Holme**, which once served as a convenient kennel for the hunting dogs belonging to the aristocratic owner of Ferry House.

The wooded island of **Thompson Holme** (known locally as Tommy Holme) has recently become a kind of miniature nature reserve, with a series of nesting boxes and conservation programs designed to study the local wildlife, while **Silver Holme** is rumoured to have been the inspiration for 'Cormorant Island' in Arthur Ransome's *Swallows and Amazons*. Holme, incidentally, derives from another Norse word meaning island.

Walking
ORREST HEAD
The most popular walk near Windermere is the bracing hour's stroll up to Orrest Head (Map p60). At 784ft, the peak is famous for its 360-degree panorama encompassing Windermere, the Langdale Pikes and the Troutbeck Valley, as well as for being the first fell walk undertaken by Alfred Wainwright in 1930. The trail starts opposite Windermere Train Station near the Windermere Hotel (look out for the signpost for Orrest Head, and take care crossing the busy main road).

BRANT FELL
There's another wonderful outlook from the summit of Brant Fell (Map p60), whose trail starts near the end of Brantfell Rd in Bowness, winding up the public path past Brantfell Farm, and hooking up with the Dales Way (the long-distance trail that travels 80 miles east all the way to Ilkley in Yorkshire). If you're just after an afternoon stroll, follow the hillside up towards the rocky summit (629ft) and drink in the views all the way to Morecambe Bay when the weather's particularly fine. It's an hour's stroll of about 2.5 miles there and back from Bowness, or you can follow the Dales Way north towards Windermere if you prefer (an extra 3 miles/two hours).

WINDERMERE WAY
For something more challenging, the **Windermere Way** (www.windermere-way.co.uk) is a 45-mile circular route around the lake split into four stages, each encompassing a day's

WEIRD WINDERMERE

A strange menagerie of ghoulies, ghosties and fantastical creatures are said to stalk Windermere's shores. One of the oldest legends is the **Crier of Claife**, whose ghostly voice could often be heard calling across the water to the boatmen at Ferry Nab. According to the legend, one young boatman decided to investigate, but was so terrified by what he saw across the lake, he was immediately struck dumb and perished the following day. The spirit was eventually exorcised by a monk who lived on one of the Windermere islands, but it's said that a phantom figure still occasionally appears to walkers in the woods around Claife Heights on the lake's western shore.

The lake shore is also said to be frequented by a **phantom white horse** who appears during times of trouble, as well as a weird creature known as the **tizzie-wizzie**, said to have the body of a hedgehog, the tail of a squirrel and the wings of a bee. Even more mysteriously, there have been several sightings of an unidentified underwater creature in Windermere, dubbed (predictably enough) **Bownessie** – you can see some rather fuzzy photographic evidence at the **Lakes Aquarium** (p72).

walk. Anticlockwise, the first half of the route follows the western lakeshore from Ambleside to Lakeside, taking in Loughrigg, Wray Castle, Ferry House and Finsthwaite en route; the second half hooks round through Newby Bridge before climbing up past Gummer's How (p73) and the wooded slopes all the way back to Bowness. A fold-out route map is available for £2.47, either from the website or the Windermere or Bowness tourist offices.

SLEEPING
Windermere Town

Windermere has more accommodation than practically anywhere else in the Lakes. Lake Rd, New Rd and the surrounding streets are chock-a-block with B&Bs and guesthouses, but it's worth booking well ahead for the choicer sleeps.

BUDGET

Lake District Backpackers Lodge (Map p62; ☎ 015394-46374; www.lakedistrictbackpackers.co.uk; High St; dm £10-12.50; ▯) The titchy dorms at this slate-roofed cottage get sardine-can full in summer (largely thanks to its cheap rates and proximity to the station). It's rather threadbare compared to the top-notch Lakeland hostels, and there's hardly any kitchen space, but there's a cosy lounge (with Sky TV), organised hiking trips, and Windermere town on your doorstep.

MIDRANGE

Waverley (Map p62; ☎ 015394-42522; www.jerichos.co.uk; College Rd; s £35-45, d £66-90, f £120-140; 🛜) The accommodation plays second fiddle to the food at this 'restaurant with rooms', but it's definitely a cut above the crowd. Tangled ivy

cloaks the outside, while inside cool creams and off-whites predominate. A chef-cooked breakfast and fell views from the top floor top off the classy package.

Archway (Map p62; ☎ 015394-45613; www.the-archway.com; 13 College Rd; d £46-60) Small but perfectly formed, this traditional terraced house serves up one of the top brekkies in town, bursting with fresh eggs, home-made muesli, buttery pancakes and dry-cured bacon. The rooms are none too shabby, either – cool and uncluttered in white and pine, with hill views to the Langdale Pikes from the front.

Applegarth Hotel (Map p62; ☎ 015394-43206; www.lakesapplegarth.co.uk; College Rd; s £55-60, d £96-156; Ⓟ) This stately mansion was built by the 19th-century industrialist John Riggs, and it's now one of Windermere's most dashing guest houses. Polished panels, antique lamps and stained-glass windows conjure a Victorian vibe, and the downstairs restaurant, JR's, serves supper in similarly ornate surroundings.

our pick Coach House (Map p62; ☎ 015394-44494; www.lakedistrictbandb.com; Lake Rd; d £60-80; Ⓟ) Chuck out the chintz – this zesty number sizzles in candy pinks, sky blues and lime greens. Originally a stable-block, it's been converted to provide five snug rooms with cast-iron beds and black-and-white en suite showers, and there's a cosy sitting room where you can kick back with magazines and books. Packed lunches and continental brekkies on request.

Wheatlands Lodge (Map p62; ☎ 015394-43789; www.wheatlandslodge-windermere.co.uk; Old Lake Lane; d £70-150; Ⓟ) The guest-house equivalent of a gentleman's waistcoat: outside solidly staid, but with a dash of colour to the inner liner. Scarlet walls and polished floors in the

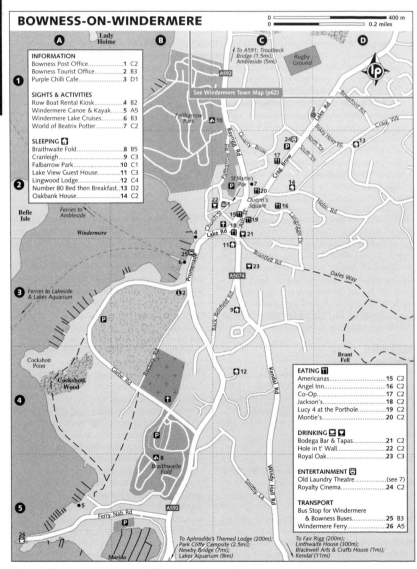

BOWNESS-ON-WINDERMERE

INFORMATION
Bowness Post Office...............1 C2
Bowness Tourist Office............2 B3
Purple Chilli Cafe..................3 D1

SIGHTS & ACTIVITIES
Row Boat Rental Kiosk...........4 B2
Windermere Canoe & Kayak......5 A5
Windermere Lake Cruises.........6 B3
World of Beatrix Potter..........7 C2

SLEEPING
Braithwaite Fold.................8 B5
Cranleigh........................9 C3
Falbarrow Park..................10 C1
Lake View Guest House..........11 C3
Lingwood Lodge................12 C4
Number 80 Bed then Breakfast...13 D2
Oakbank House.................14 C2

EATING
Americanas......................15 C2
Angel Inn.......................16 C2
Co-Op...........................17 C2
Jackson's.......................18 C2
Lucy 4 at the Porthole...........19 C2
Montie's........................20 C2

DRINKING
Bodega Bar & Tapas.............21 C2
Hole in t' Wall.................22 C2
Royal Oak......................23 C3

ENTERTAINMENT
Old Laundry Theatre..........(see 7)
Royalty Cinema.................24 C2

TRANSPORT
Bus Stop for Windermere
 & Bowness Buses...............25 B3
Windermere Ferry..............26 A5

lobby, with rooms offering LCD TVs, modern furnishings and either walk-in shower or sexy free-standing bubble-tub. Choice.

21 The Lakes (Map p62; ☎ 015394-45052; www.21thelakes.co.uk; Lake Rd; d £70-180; [P]) Glitzy bolthole or daft design project? Love it or hate it, this camped-up guest house makes Barbara Cartland's wardrobe look positively understated. Some rooms are classic, others more up-to-date: Grasmere has a flouncy four-poster and outdoor hot tub, the Regal Mini Suite boasts a scarlet chaise longue and gilded pelmets, and the Contemporary boasts wacky furniture including a 'floating' bed. Not as swish or sexy as it thinks, perhaps, but good gaudy fun.

SOMETHING FOR THE WEEKEND

We've gone the whole hog on this luxury weekend getaway in Windermere. For the first night treat yourself to a room and dinner at the Michelin-starred **Gilpin Lodge** (p68). Then on Saturday have a wander into Windermere and indulge in a leisurely brunch at **Lazy Daisy's Lakeland Kitchen** (p69) before driving over to the inspiring country house of **Blackwell** (p71). Choice options for room and board are the gorgeous **Punch Bowl Inn** (p73) in Crosthwaite or the **Swan Hotel** (p72) down by Newby Bridge. On Sunday it's up to **Ambleside** (p76) and lunch at **Lucy's** (p82) followed by a leisurely walk around town and a lake cruise from the **Waterhead jetties** (p77). Check into the deluxe **Waterhead Hotel** (p81) and try out the **Glass House** (p82) for a first-class end to your luxury break.

Howbeck (Map p62; ☎ 015394-44739; www .howbeck.co.uk; New Rd; d £91-109; **P** 📶) The 'luxury' rooms are worth the outlay at this stone-fronted villa between Bowness and Windermere. Extra cash buys smarter furnishings, plusher beds, slate-floored bathrooms and complimentary fruit and sherry (although you can't escape the road noise). Think traditional if you opt for the cheaper rooms; for a flasher finish, ask for Windergill or Glenridding, or splash out on the fancy 'Retreat' (with stripped-oak floor, private patio and super-minimal bathroom).

TOP END

Hideaway (Map p62; ☎ 015394-43070; www.the hideawayatwindermere.co.uk; Phoenix Way; £90-190; **P**) Victorian features rub shoulders with a style mag refit at this mini-hotel. The cheaper rooms are disappointingly bland; plump instead for the 'Super' or 'Ultra Comfy' doubles, all with spa baths and luxury furnishings. The best is the split-level number 12, offering oak furniture and a palatial bed on the top floor, with a spiral staircase down to the bathroom boasting his-and-hers sinks, roll-top tub and under-floor heating.

Bowness-on-Windermere

CAMPING

Braithwaite Fold (Map p66; ☎ 01539-442177; adult £4.60-6, child £1.50-2.50, site £4.80-7.60; 🌣 mid-Mar–Nov) You couldn't ask for a handier lakeside spot, but sadly for campers this place is caravan-only. It's a stone's throw from the marina, but space is tight so your manoeuvring skills will need to be up to scratch.

Fallbarrow Park (Map p66; ☎ 015394-44422; www .southlakelandparks.co.uk; Rayrigg Rd; site for 4 adults, caravan & car £18.50-30) Huge caravan and chalet site scattered among trees just off Rayrigg Rd. The facilities are first-rate and include a spanking new timber-slatted cafe, bike hire, laundry, play area and even a private lake jetty, but it's aimed squarely at the family crowd. Fixed chalets and timber lodges are also available, but no tents are allowed.

BUDGET & MIDRANGE

Lake View Guest House (Map p66; ☎ 01539-447098; www.lakeview-guesthouse.co.uk; 2 Belsfield Tce; d £44-70; **P**) If you're counting the pennies, you could do worse than this bare-bones B&B above a busy coffee shop. The decor's plain to the point of spartan, but the rooms are clean, en suite, and you're right in the Bowness action.

Lingwood Lodge (Map p66; ☎ 015394-44680; Birkett Hill; www.lingwoodlodge.co.uk; s £50, d £76-80; **P** 📶) Simple, efficient and reassuringly unpretentious, the six rooms at this detached house are pleasantly understated in creams and whites, with pine-effect furniture and pocket-sized digital TVs. There's plenty of parking, free wi-fi and Bowness is a short walk away.

Number 80 Bed then Breakfast (Map p66; ☎ 015394-43584; www.number80bed.co.uk; 80 Craig Walk; d £60-75) Despite the clever-clever name, this intimate place is the very picture of a 21st century B&B. Sleek greys, crimsons and sandy browns are offset by chocolate throws, twisted willow and leather tub chairs in the four rooms; all the bathrooms sparkle, too.

Fair Rigg (☎ 015394-43941; www.fairrigg.co.uk; Ferry View, d £66-84; **P**) Expect pastel blues, country creams and checked duvets at this rather conventional house, set back from the touristy fizz of Bowness. Ground breaking it ain't, but a decent option for simple, spick-and-span rooms.

Aphrodite's Themed Lodge (☎ 015394-45052; www.aphroditeslodge.co.uk; Longtail Hill, d £70-110; **P**) Another wildly kitsch offering from the proud owners of 21 The Lakes, showcasing the same histrionic approach to interior design. Here the choices include a 'log cabin' room with wood burner, a 'Flintstone' hideaway draped in faux-fur furnishings, a 'Tarzan and Jane' room with jungle plants and bamboo walls, and even an 'Austin Powers' suite with teardrop bed and pop-art colours.

Cranleigh (Map p66; ☎ 015394-43293; www.thecran leigh.com; Kendal Rd; r £80-160) This up-and-coming B&B has something of a split personality thanks to an ongoing overhaul. The older bedrooms are decidedly dowdy, but the newer ones have been reinvented with a keen designer eye: goose-down bedding, iPod docks and ultra-futuristic bathrooms, some with flat-screen TVs set into the tiles. Lashings of leather, wood and bespoke wallpaper keep the metro-vibe ticking.

Oakbank House (Map p66; ☎ 015394-43386; www .oakbankhousehotel.co.uk; Helm Rd; d £82-88; P) Reliable Bowness B&B in a slate-topped house along Helm Rd. Rich reds and regal blues meet hefty wardrobes and plush rugs; the four superior rooms offer a smidgen more comfort. Lake views throughout, plus access to a nearby country club.

Around Town
CAMPING

Park Cliffe Campsite (Map p60; ☎ 015395-31344; www .parkcliffe.co.uk; Birks Rd; site for 2 adults incl car & tent £19-25, caravans £23-25) Award-winning 10-hectare campsite between Windermere and Newby Bridge along the A592, with a choice of fields (fell-side for lake views, ghyll-side for electrical hook-ups, or Moor How views for tourers). There's plenty of space, so things don't seem too overcrowded even in midsummer, and there are lots of facilities, including a grocery shop, laundrette and restaurant. You can even bag your own private bathroom for an extra £12.50.

TOP END

Gilpin Lodge (Map p60; ☎ 015394-88818; www.gilpin lodge.co.uk; Crook Rd; r £135-155, ste £170-195; P) One of the cosiest country house hotels within easy reach of Windermere. The feel is formal (plenty of Audis and Mercedes in the driveway), but it's far from snooty. Rooms are classic, all with fine views, Molton Brown bath goodies and upmarket furniture. Top of the heap are the garden suites, with cedar-wood hot tubs and glass-fronted lounges overlooking private gardens.

Langdale Chase (Map p60; ☎ 015394-32201; www .langdalechase.co.uk; r £150-290; P) Historic oils and burnished panelling set the aristocratic tone for this grand old girl, one of Windermere's most venerable country retreats (which starred in Hitchcock's *The Paradine Case*). Steer clear if you like things minimal; puffy pelmets, country prints and old-fashioned furniture are the order of the day.

Holbeck Ghyll (Map p60; ☎ 015394-34743; www .holbeckghyll.com; s £175, d £210-330; P) An old Windermere favourite which toes the traditional country house line. The big, comfy rooms are decked out in appropriately genteel fashion, and nearly all have stunning views over parkland and the lake. Sherry decanters await on the bedside table, and the Michelin-starred restaurant serves up classic Brit *haute cuisine*.

our pick Linthwaite House (Map p60; ☎ 015394-88600; www.linthwaite.com; Crook Rd; r £188-380; P) This ivy-clad pamper-pad mixes vintage Lakeland architecture with the best of contemporary design. Wooded walks, a croquet lawn and a private tarn encircle the house, which boasts luxury spoils including a cinema, a conservatory and a choice of three bars. Rooms are sleek, chic and soothingly beige, with minimal decorative clutter (although they're small considering the price).

Samling (Map p60; ☎ 015394-31922; www.the samling.com; Dove Nest; r weekdays £200-490, weekends £230-520; P) If money's no object, this luxe getaway 3 miles north of Windermere is the choice for style gurus and sojourning celebs. Ten rustic-chic rooms and self-contained cottages drip with designer trappings: split-level mezzanines and slate bathrooms in some, clawfoot tubs, rain showers and private lounges in others.

EATING
Cafes & Quick Eats

Montie's (Map p66; ☎ 015394-42723; Crag Brow; lunch £2.75-5.50; ☺ 9am-5.30pm Mon-Sat, plus 7-10pm Fri & Sat) Cute Bowness cafe that's top for all-day brekkies, toasted sandwiches and hot jacket spuds. For liquid refreshment, try one of the creamy milkshakes or the lip-puckering lemon refresher (made with lemon sorbet and lemonade). On Fridays and Saturdays there's a fab value two-course dinner for £9.95.

Lucy 4 at the Porthole (Map p66; ☎ 015394-42793; 3 Ash St; tapas £4.95-7.50; ☺ dinner Wed-Mon) The Lake District's current culinary trendsetter,

Lucy Nicholson, has brought her tapas-to-share ethos to Bowness in the renovated Porthole Restaurant. Expect the same cosy lighting and wine-bar feel as the original Lucy's in Ambleside, along with a tempting chalkboard of lamb koftas, Italian figs and coconut mussels.

Lighthouse (Map p62; ☎ 015394-88260; Main Rd; mains £8-20; ☻ breakfast, lunch & dinner) Continental cafe-bar at the top of Windermere, ideal for pastries and coffee, or something more substantial at lunchtime. Plate-glass windows keep things light and bright; opt for a streetside table if the outlook is sunny.

Restaurants

our pick **Lazy Daisy's Lakeland Kitchen** (Map p62; ☎ 015394-43877; 31-33 Crescent Rd; lunch £3.50-9.95, dinner £8.75-11.95; ☻ Mon-Sat) Cosier than your grandma's kitchen, this welcoming little place serves up the most comforting (and best-value) grub in Windermere. Tuck into soup and a sarnie (£6.50) for lunch, followed by fresh-made cakes for teatime; after dark try the steak-and-merlot pie, trout in caper butter or lamb shank in minted gravy. Sweet tooths should pitch up for the weekly 'pudding club', where £4.95 buys you a slice of chocolate lumpy-bumpy or apple pie accompanied by a steaming mug of hot chocolate.

Angel Inn (Map p66; ☎ 015394-44080; www.the-angelinn.com; Helm Rd; lunch mains £4.95-12, dinner mains £13-22) Pining for your friendly neighbourhood gastropub? Then you're in luck – Bowness' Angel is definitely the place. The menu is stuffed with superior fare – beer-battered cod, Goosnargh chicken, Grizedale venison – and the atmosphere is sleek and cityish, with the requisite glossy wood and sofas to sink into. There's also a lovely front terrace for sunny days.

Jackson's (Map p66; ☎ 015394-46264; St Martin's Sq; mains £12-18; ☻ dinner Mon-Sat) This straightforward bistro has been filling Bowness bellies for donkey's years, and it's still a reliable staple for simple and unpretentious food – duck, pan-fried fish, risotto – served up among pine tables and potted plants.

Americanas (Map p66; ☎ 015394-88700; Ash St; mains £12.95-19.95, steaks £15.95-39; ☻ lunch & dinner Mon-Sat) Dine like a New Yorker at this Manhattan-style bistro in Bowness, which specialises in stonking great slabs of beef (including a monstrous 16oz Chateaubriand) served in jazzy surroundings.

Jericho's (Map p62; ☎ 015394-42522; College Rd; mains £14-18; ☻ dinner Tue-Sun) Windermere's original fine-diner has recently upped sticks and moved in house at the Waverley Hotel. The food is as complex and satisfying as ever, as you'd expect from a former chef at Miller Howe – baby brill on potato cake, or Lune Valley lamb with Provençal veg.

Self-Catering

Booth's (Map p62; ☎ 01539-446114; ☻ 8am-8pm Mon-Sat, 10am-4pm Sun) is the main supermarket in Windermere, next door to the train station, or there are two branches of **Co-op** (Oak St; Map p62; ☻ 8am-10pm Mon-Sat, 9am-10pm Sun; Crag Brow; Map p66; ☻ 8am-9pm daily).

DRINKING

Bodega Bar & Tapas (Map p66; ☎ 015394-46825; Ash St; tapas £1.95-6.75; ☻ noon-midnight) They mix the meanest margaritas in town at this spicy Hispanic-themed joint, a popular meeting spot for Bowness boozers. There's also decent tapas on offer for when you get the munchies.

Hole in t' Wall (Map p66; ☎ 015394-43488; Fallbarrow Rd; mains £5-9) Polish off an ale or two at this venerable boozer (built in 1612), with the all-essential flagstones and fireplaces, plus a beer patio in case the Lakeland weather behaves.

Royal Oak (Map p66; ☎ 015394-43970; Brantfell Rd; mains £8.25-8.95) Attractive pub with a good selection of Lakeland ales (including Coniston Bluebird and Hawkshead Bitter). The grub's not bad – mainly of the lasagne and cottage pie variety – and there's a pool room with a retro juke box where you can choose your own tunes.

ENTERTAINMENT

For recent flicks, head for the **Royalty Cinema** (Map p66; ☎ 015394-43364; Lake Rd), or for live entertainment and touring theatre and dance productions, check out what's on at the **Old Laundry Theatre** (Map p66; ☎ 01539-488444; www.oldlaundrytheatre.co.uk; Crag Brow).

GETTING THERE & AROUND
Bus

There's a daily National Express coach from London (£33, 8½ hours) via Lancaster and Kendal.

The Lakeslink Bus (Bus 555/556, hourly Monday to Saturday, 10 on Sunday) runs to Kendal (30 minutes) and on to Lancaster (one hour 40 minutes), and in the opposite

---

CROSS-LAKES SHUTTLE

To help cut down on the hideous summer traffic jams, the **Cross-Lakes Shuttle** (mid-Mar–Oct) network has been designed to allow you to travel from Windermere to Coniston using several different transport operators, without ever needing to get behind the wheel.

Windermere Lake cruise boats travel from Bowness to Ferry House, from where a minibus travels on to Hill Top and Hawkshead. From Hawkshead, you can catch the X30 bus to Moor Top, Grizedale Forest and Haverthwaite, or catch the 505 Stagecoach bus to High Cross and Coniston Water, where you can hop aboard the Coniston Launch.

At the time of writing, single prices from Bowness: to Ferry House (adult/child £2.20/1.70), to Hill Top (£4.70/2.50), to Hawkshead (£5.60/2.90), to Coniston (£9.70/5.10) and to Grizedale (£7/3.80). A return from Bowness to Coniston and back costs £16.60/9.

The route operates 10 times daily from Bowness to Coniston, and nine times in the opposite direction (roughly hourly from 10am to 5pm) from mid-March to October.

The only drawback is that the buses get very crowded in summer, and if they're all full you'll have no choice but to wait for the next one (as currently you can't pre-book). Cyclists should note there's very limited space for bike carriage on the buses (usually no more than two) so if the bike rack's full you'll just have to rely on pedal power.

For info and timetables, contact **Mountain Goat** (Map p62; 015394-45161; www.mountain -goat.com).

---

direction to Troutbeck Bridge (five minutes), Brockhole Visitor Centre (seven minutes), Ambleside (15 minutes), Grasmere (30 minutes) and Keswick (50 minutes). Three buses run daily from Keswick on to Mirehouse (10 minutes) and Carlisle (one hour 10 minutes).

The Coniston Rambler (Bus 505) travels from Windermere to Coniston (50 minutes, eight times daily Monday to Saturday, six on Sunday) via Brockhole (seven minutes), Ambleside (15 minutes) and Hawkshead (35 minutes).

The open-topped Lakes Rider (Bus 599) travels between Bowness, Windermere, Troutbeck, Brockhole, Rydal Church (for Rydal Mount) and Grasmere between March and August. There are up to three buses every hour from Monday to Saturday, and half-hourly buses on Sunday, with a reduced service between September and November.

Ferry

The **Windermere Ferry** (01228-227653) has been transporting passengers for over 500 years, although the old row boats that once plied the waters have thankfully been replaced by a modern diesel-powered vessel capable of carrying 18 cars and 100 passengers.

The ferry runs roughly every 20 minutes year-round from Ferry Nab, just south of Bowness, over to Ferry House on the lake's western side. The service runs from 6.50am to 9.50pm Monday to Saturday and 9.10am to 9.50pm on Sunday from March to October, and from 6.50am to 8.50pm Monday to Saturday and 9.50am to 8.50pm on Sunday during winter. Current fares are 50p for foot passengers, £1 for bicycles, £1.50 for mopeds and motorbikes, and £3.50 for cars and caravans, but be prepared for seriously nasty queues in high season when waits of up to an hour are not uncommon; services can also be cancelled at short notice during bad weather. For further information visit www.cumbria.gov.uk/roads-transport and click on the Windermere Ferry link.

Train

Windermere is the only town inside the national park accessible by train. It's on the branch line via Kendal to Oxenholme (£4, 14 to 16 daily Monday to Saturday, 10 on Sunday, 30 minutes). From here there are hourly connections south to Manchester (£25.50, two hours) and London Euston (off-peak £77.60, anytime £123.50, four hours), and north to Glasgow (£39, 2½ to 3½ hours).

Taxi

For a cab, call:
Bowness Taxis (015394-46664)
Lakes Taxis (015394-46777)
Windermere Taxi Services (015394-45282)

AROUND WINDERMERE & BOWNESS

BLACKWELL HOUSE

Situated 1.5 miles south of Bowness on the B5360, **Blackwell House** (Map p60; ☎ 015394-46139; www.blackwell.org.uk; adult/child £6.60/3.85; ☼ 10.30am-5pm Apr-Oct, 10am-4pm Feb-Mar, Nov-Dec) is one of the finest examples of the 19th-century Arts and Crafts movement. Inspired by the aesthetic principles of John Ruskin and William Morris, Arts and Crafts was a reaction against the machine-driven mentality of the Industrial Revolution, placing emphasis on simple architecture, high-quality craftsmanship and natural light. Designed by Mackay Hugh Baillie Scott, the house has all the hallmarks of classic Arts and Crafts design: light, airy rooms; a serene, symmetrical layout; natural motifs; and plenty of bespoke craftwork created by local Lakeland artisans.

Just off the wood-panelled entrance corridor is the Great Hall, undoubtedly the most impressive room of the house, blending the stately atmosphere of a medieval baronial hall with some gloriously detailed decorative touches (look out for the delft-tiled inglenook fireplace, a handmade wooden 'Manxman' piano and some sumptuous peacock-frieze wallpaper). At the far end of the entrance corridor is the famous White Drawing Room, which makes a striking contrast to the stern, masculine symmetry of the rest of the house; even on the gloomiest of days it is flooded with light through the floor-to-ceiling windows and offers stunning views down to Windermere. Again, look out for the natural motifs favoured by the Arts and Crafts designers, such as the slender branch-like pillars and the fire dogs decorated with rowan berries.

Upstairs most of the bedrooms have been converted into exhibition spaces, although a few have been refurbished in period style. One room collects together a series of vintage photos detailing the history of the house, from its early days as the family home of the wealthy brewing magnate Sir Edward Holt, through to subsequent stints as a refuge for wartime evacuees and later as a girl's prep school. Having been purchased by English Nature in 1997, the house was almost totally renovated using Heritage Lottery funding, and was reopened to the public in 2001.

Once you've finished moseying around the house, there's an excellent arts bookshop that also sells work by local craftspeople, or you can grab a bite to eat at the cafe next door before strolling the grassy grounds.

LAKESIDE, NEWBY BRIDGE & THE SOUTHERN SHORE

South of Bowness, the A592 skirts along the tree-lined eastern edge of the lake for around 8 miles en route to **Fell Foot Park** (Map p60; NT; ☎ 015394-31273; www.nationaltrust.org.uk/main/w-fell footpark; ☼ 9am-5pm), a magnificent Victorian country park, whose manicured lawns and flower-filled grounds sweep down to the lake's southeastern edge. Originally the gardens formed part of the Fell Foot estate; the original 17th-century manor house was subsequently revamped by a string of owners (including the notoriously unpopular Robinson brothers, known locally as Terrible Dick and Black Jack) before being demolished by its last owner, Oswald Henley, in around 1910. Henley intended to rebuild the house but never got around to it, and the site remained in ruins until it passed into the hands of the National Trust after the end of WWII. These days the gardens make a luxurious spot for a picnic, especially if you time your visit to coincide with the annual displays of daffodils and rhododendrons. If you just can't resist a bit of messing about on the lake, vintage row boats are available to hire from the old Victorian boathouses, and there's also a fancy tearoom selling sandwiches, cream teas and cakes.

A couple of miles further round from Fell Foot and Newby Bridge is the small bustling landing-station of Lakeside, the southerly terminus for the Windermere cruise boats from Bowness and Fell Foot Park, and the end of the line for the chuffing steam trains of the vintage **Lakeside and Haverthwaite Railway** (Map p60; ☎ 015395-31594; www.lakesiderailway.co.uk; Haverthwaite Station, nr Ulverston; standard return adult/5-15yr/family £5.40/2.70/14.80, joint ticket with aquarium £11.95/6.60/35.50; ☼ mid-Mar–Oct). This wonderful 19th-century standard-gauge railway was originally built to ferry materials south from the Lakeland mines and timber plantations to Ulverston and Barrow, but it's now one of northern England's most popular vintage railways. Classic steam carriages rattle down the line via Newby Bridge to Haverthwaite, near Ulverston; there are five to seven daily trains in season, timed to correspond with the Windermere cruise boats.

Bang next door to the station platform is the **Lakes Aquarium** (☎ 015395-30153; www.aquarium ofthelakes.co.uk; Lakeside, Newby Bridge; adult/3-15yr/family £8.50/5.50/45.50; 9am-6pm Apr-Oct, 9am-5pm Nov-Mar), which explores a variety of watery habitats ranging from tropical Africa through to Morecambe Bay. Alongside the usual fishy inhabitants, the aquarium is also home to a boa constrictor, a family of marmosets and a pair of Asian short-clawed otters (feeding time is at 10.30am and 3pm daily), but the highlight is the underwater tunnel which simulates a trip beneath Windermere's surface, complete with carp, char and diving ducks. Joint tickets can be purchased to include a Windermere cruise or the Lakeside and Haverthwaite Railway.

Half a mile north from Lakeside is **Stott Park Bobbin Mill** (Map p60; EH; ☎ 015395-31087; adult/ child £4.20/2.10; 10am-5pm Mon-Fri Easter-Oct), built in 1835 to manufacture the wooden bobbins (thread-spools) that fed the industrial looms of nearby Lancashire and other northern counties. When the textile trade faltered at the end of the 19th century, the mill branched out into making other wooden items such as pick-axe handles, hammer shafts and even yo-yos. Although the factory closed down in 1971, much of the original machinery is still in place, and admission includes a guided tour and a demonstration of the bobbin-making process (you might even take one home as a souvenir).

Sleeping & Eating

Knoll (Map p60; ☎ 015395-31347; www.theknoll-lakeside .co.uk; s £60-95, d £84-150;) Tucked away in a secluded spot on Windermere's quiet southwestern side, this lovely country B&B is the place if you want to dodge the crowds. There are just eight rooms, so the feel is intimate and exclusive; posh cotton linen, country-style furnishings and a choice of four-poster or sleigh beds ratchet up the charm.

Swan Hotel (☎ 015395-31681; www.swanhotel.com; Newby Bridge; r £99-250;) Plonked beside the humpbacked crossing at Newby Bridge overlooking the lake, the old Swan has been a staple stopoff for travellers for centuries. The whitewashed facade looks olde worlde, but the interior is modern through and through: tasteful rooms are divided into standard,

deluxe and suite classes, with extra cash buying luxuries such as in-room espresso machines, iPod docks and lake views. The rest of the hotel has been refitted in smart style; musty carpets and wood beams have been stripped out in favour of boutique wallpapers, mood lighting and exposed stone. The old inn serves beers, light bites and lunches; for sit-down dinners try the upmarket River Room.

our pick 4 Winds Lakeland Tipis (Map p60; ☎ 01539-823755; www.4windslakelandtipis.co.uk; Fell Foot Woods, Newby Bridge) Ever wanted to do like the Sioux and live in a real-life wigwam? Well this is your lucky day, – 4 Winds offers seven authentic Native American tipis (admittedly made in Scotland) sleeping two to six, supplied complete with cushions, cutlery, gas cooker and, yes, your very own medicine blanket. The only disappointment? You're not allowed to light a fire inside due to insurance regulations. Tipis cost £120/250 for two people per weekend/week or £240/450 for four people. From Newby Bridge head up the A592 towards Bowness and take the right-hand turn to Gummer's How. Look out for another right-hand turn into Lakeland Forest Fuels, and park in the car park.

Lakeside Hotel (☎ 015395-30001; www.lakesidehotel .co.uk; Lakeside, Newby Bridge; r £305-455;) This stately stone-fronted Victorian hotel next to the Lakeside car park is the traditional choice for well-heeled trippers, with 70-odd rooms kitted out in old-fashioned four-star style (upholstered armchairs, padded quilts, marbled bathrooms). Naturally, you'll have to pay through the nose for a lake view. For dining, there's John Ruskin's Bar for brasserie food (£39 for three courses), or the upmarket Lakeview Restaurant (£49 for six courses), but you'll need to bring your piggy bank – even afternoon tea costs £16 a head.

Getting There & Away

If you're not arriving aboard a Windermere lake cruise or via the steam railway, the main public transport to Newby Bridge is the 618 bus (six daily Monday to Saturday, four on Sunday), which travels north to Bowness Pier, Windermere Station, Troutbeck Bridge and Ambleside, and in the opposite direction to Haverthwaite (five minutes), Ulverston (20 minutes) and Barrow-in-Furness (45 minutes). The X35 bus also stops at Newby Bridge en route from Barrow (40 minutes) to Kendal (40 minutes).

DAMSON COUNTRY

Westmorland damsons (sometimes known locally as Witherslack damsons) are a soft, delicate fruit related to the plum. They've been thriving around the Lyth and Winster Valleys for centuries, but are thought to have been introduced to England during the Roman occupation, and were later cultivated by monks at Furness Abbey. Bright white damson blossoms fill the surrounding hedgerows from early April, and the fruit harvest usually takes place in late August or early September. The fruits are traditionally used to make **damson jam**, but these days their delicate flavour is used in everything from ice cream and chocolates to wine, beer and even damson gin; in days gone by the skins were used to make a purple dye for colouring wool and cloth.

Visit www.lythdamsons.org.uk for details of local growers and a handy downloadable map; as long as there's been a decent harvest, many growers put out little roadside stalls where you can pick up some fruit or buy some home-made damson jam.

LYTH & WINSTER VALLEYS

To the east of Fell Foot Park a twisting road leads northeast into the little-explored countryside around the Winster and Lyth Valleys, both renowned growing areas for the Westmorland damson (see boxed text above). En route, the road passes the 1054ft **Gummer's How** (Map p60), a well-known local viewpoint with fantastic views over rolling fields and woodland around the southern section of Windermere. There's a small car park nearby at Astley's Plantation, from where it's a half-hour stroll to the summit (you'll know when you've reached the top thanks to the stone trig point).

Further east is the start of the Winster Valley and the Mason's Arms (below), a fine little watering hole much favoured by Arthur Ransome, who lived nearby at Low Ludderburn while penning his classic children's tale *Swallows and Amazons*. From here, the road rolls on to Bowlands Bridge and the junction with the A5074 back to Bowness, but it's worth pressing on to the sweet little hamlet of **Crosthwaite** (Map p60), home to a small church, a scattering of cottages and a fantastic pub managed by the owners of the Drunken Duck (p121).

Southeast of Crosthwaite, the A5074 runs along the Lyth Valley past the low limestone ridge of Whitbarrow Scar, home to the **Whitbarrow National Nature Reserve** (Map p60) and a resident population of rare birds and butterflies. If you've never seen a great spotted woodpecker, sparrowhawk or meadow pipit, this might well be the place to try.

Sleeping & Eating

Mason's Arms (Map p60; ☎ 015395-68486; www .masonsarmsstrawberrybank.co.uk; r £65-145, cottages £130- 175; Ⓟ) Much of the old country clutter's been ditched at this overhauled inn, but thankfully plenty of original character survives. Rough bench seats, hefty rafters, quirky furniture and the odd farming curio dot the bar, which is as well known for its quality grub as for its local ales. If you fancy staying, there are pleasant rooms and some impressive self-contained cottages on offer.

our pick **Punch Bowl Inn** (☎ 015395-68237; www.the -punchbowl.co.uk; Crosthwaite; r £160-310; Ⓟ) Recently picked by the Michelin head honchos as their 'pub of the year', this gorgeous hideaway boasts the same blend of rustic sophistication and top-class food (mains £13 to £17) as its sister establishment over on Hawkshead Hill. Reclaimed beams and Roberts radios grace the nine rooms, all named after Crosthwaite vicars: top spot goes to 'Noble', with its twin roll-top baths, plasma screen and wonky eaves. As you'd expect, the pub-restaurant is an utter treat, with slate floors and crackling fires, home-brewed ales from the Barngates Brewery and chalkboards stuffed with the pick of seasonal produce. Mmmmm.

STAVELEY

Four miles east of Windermere off the A591 is the stout village of Staveley, hunkered down on the banks of the River Kent. The town was originally settled by Iron Age Celts and Norse Vikings, and later became the site of a busy medieval market and 17th-century timber and bobbin mill (the tradition of Staveley woodworking remains strong to this day). These days the village is better known for its foodie credentials, with an enticing helping of artisan bakeries, wholefood cafes and cake shops dotted around the redeveloped Mill Yard.

DETOUR – FOULSHAW MOSS

Along with neighbouring Meathrop Moss and Nichols Moss, Foulshaw Moss, near Witherslack, is one of the largest areas of **peat bog** left in Cumbria. Peat bogs were once widespread throughout much of the county, but have reduced in number thanks to environmental damage, water extraction and pollution. Up to 6m deep in places, the bog is a fantastic spot for wildlife, with regular visitors including red deer, dragonflies, butterflies, moths and lots of birds. The reserve is about half a mile east of the Witherslack junction on the A590; look out for the small track leaving the road near a signed lay-by that leads past a gate to the car park. A boardwalk circles the reserve and is dotted with a few explanatory panels on the flora and fauna of the area. Watch out for ticks in summer. Find out more at www.cumbriawildlifetrust.org.uk.

It's a real feast for gourmets: organic chutneys and preserves are available from **Friendly Food & Drink** (☎ 01539-822326; www.friendlyfoodand drink.co.uk), while neighbouring **Fairground** (☎ 01539-822823; www.fairgroundcoffee.co.uk) sells fair trade coffee and teas, and **Scoop Ice Cream** (☎ 01539-822866; www.windermereicecream .co.uk; ☒ Easter-Oct) sells deluxe ice cream and chocolates courtesy of the Windermere Ice Cream Co, whose adventurous flavours include hazelnut and stracciatelli, melon and ginger, and Granny's apple crumble.

Across the yard, **Organico** (☎ 01539-822200; www.organi.co.uk; ☒ 10am-6pm) sells organic wines (the original shop is in Ambleside), and nearby **Munx** (☎ 01539-822102; www.munx .co.uk) turns out gorgeous speciality breads, as well as locally sourced flours and yeasts (you can even watch the bakers at work on the top floor). **Lucy's Cookery School** (☎ 015394-32288; www.lucycooks.co.uk) runs cookery courses covering everything from baking your own bread to handling a halibut throughout the year, starting at around £100; contact them to see what's on offer.

For many people, however, Staveley's main attraction is the home base of the **Hawkshead Brewery** (☎ 01539-822644; www.hawksheadbrewery .co.uk), the celebrated ale manufacturer that has been whetting Lakeland whistles since 2002. Tours of the brewery take place at 1pm, 2pm or 3pm on Saturdays or by arrangement, and you can sample a few brews at the in-house **beer hall** (☒ noon-5pm Mon-Tue, noon-6pm Wed-Sun), including the original Hawkshead Bitter that started it all.

Having worked up an appetite, round things off with a well-earned visit to the much-loved **Wilf's Cafe** (☎ 01539-822329; www .wilfs-cafe.co.uk; mains £3-10; ☒ 10am-5pm), which specialises in filling fare such as crumpets, casseroles, jacket spuds, huge sandwiches and a smorgasbord of tasty rarebits (toasted bread topped with grilled cheese and a choice of toppings, £4.30 to £5.75). The cafe is occasionally open for 'speciality' nights, each exploring a different national cuisine – six courses cost £19.95, but you'll need to book ahead and bring your own wine.

Getting There & Around

Staveley is on the branch railway between Windermere and Oxenholme. The hourly 555 Lakeslink bus stops en route from Kendal (20 minutes) to Windermere (10 minutes), Grasmere (40 minutes) and Keswick (one hour). The 519 Kentmere Rambler bus also travels north into the Kentmere Valley eight times on Sundays and Bank Holidays between late May and September.

For two-wheeled transport, Staveley is home to the UK's biggest bike emporium, **Wheelbase** (☎ 0870 600 3435; www.wheelbase.co.uk; ☒ 9am-5.30pm Mon-Sat, 10am-4pm Sun). Bike hire is available for £16/12 per full/half day, and the shop produces custom trail maps to some of the area's most popular rides.

KENTMERE VALLEY

Directly to the north of Staveley beyond the gushing weir at Barley Bridge runs the remote valley of Kentmere, a rural patchwork of isolated houses, criss-crossing bridleways and emerald fields much favoured by walkers looking to escape the throngs on the better-known fells.

During the 19th century Kentmere was a hub of industrial activity; 15 mills were dotted along this isolated valley, drawing power from a series of waterwheels turned by the clattering waters of the River Kent. The capriciousness of the river power supply led to the construction of a large reservoir at the head of the valley in 1848; the classic **Kentmere Round** (12 miles, seven hours) takes in most of the surrounding summits, including Yoke, Ill Bell, Froswick, Thornthwaite Crag, Mardale Ill Bell, Harter Fell, Kentmere Pike and Shipman Knotts. There are less strenuous routes around the valley bottom; the NPA organises **guided walks** throughout the summer starting at Wilf's Cafe in Staveley at around 10.30am. Call ☎ 015394-40808 for more information.

The little village of **Kentmere** (Map p60) itself is huddled on the fell-side about half-way along the valley. The village church dates back to at least Norman times, and possibly marks the site of an earlier Saxon chapel; nearby Kentmere Hall has an impressive pele tower, although the house is on private land so you'll have to make do with the view from the public footpath.

Halfway along the valley between Staveley and Kentmere is **Kentmere Pottery** (☎ 01539-821621; gordon.fox4@btinternet.com), where you can pick up handmade ceramics by local potter Gordon Fox.

Sleeping & Eating

Maggs Howe (Map p60; ☎ 01539-821689; www.maggs howe.co.uk; Lowfield Lane; dm £10, s £25-27, d £50-54) Pretty much the only accommodation option in the valley is this rural farmhouse, which offers simple B&B rooms in the main house, and bunk beds, showers and cooking facilities in the nearby camping barn (handy for hikers setting out early on the Kentmere Round). Hearty cooked breakfasts and cream teas are available in season; large groups can hire out the whole bunkhouse for £90 per night.

Getting There & Away

Parking in the valley is very limited; you're better off walking from Staveley, or catching the 519 Kentmere Rambler, which runs eight times daily on Sundays and Bank Holidays between late May and September.

TROUTBECK

A mile north of Windermere, two minor roads turn off the main A591, travelling along either side of Trout Beck. The right fork (A592) passes the impeccably groomed gardens of **Holehird** (Map p60; ☎ 015394-46008; www.holehirdgardens.org.auk; admission free, but donations welcome; ☻ 10am-5pm Apr-Oct), home of the Lakeland Horticultural Society and three national collections of hydrangeas, astilbe and ferns, while the left-hand branch (Bridge Lane) travels past the beautifully preserved farmhouse of **Townend** (NT; ☎ 015394-32628; Troutbeck; adult/child £3.80/1.90; ☻ 1-5pm Wed-Sun Mar-Oct, 1-4pm Wed-Sun Nov & late Mar), built for a wealthy yeoman farmer in the 17th century. Topped by pepper-pot chimneys and grey-slate tiles, the house contains rustic artefacts, books and vintage farming tools, plus original wood panelling and furniture carved by the Browne family, who owned the house until 1943.

At the head of the valley, past the small hamlet of Troutbeck, the two roads join forces again and continue the precipitous climb up towards **Kirkstone Pass** (p174), which cuts between the windswept hilltops of Raven Crag and Hart Crag before plunging down the valley towards Ullswater.

Sleeping & Eating

Windermere YHA (☎ 0845 371 9352; windermere@yha.org.uk; Bridge Lane, Troutbeck; dm £11.95-16.95; ☻ mid-Feb–Nov; ☻ reception 7.30-11.30am & 1-11pm; [P] [□]) The nearest YHA to Windermere is a wonder; a converted manor house with extensive grounds and a breathtaking lake outlook. The house has been divided into a series of shipshape modern dorms (mostly four-

POSTMAN PAT'S PATCH

Along with the nearby valley of Longsleddale, Kentmere's main claim to fame is as the onscreen double for the valley of Greendale in John Cunliffe's landmark children's BBC series *Postman Pat*. The adventures of the bumbling, big-nosed postman and his black-and-white cat, Jess, delighted an entire generation of British kids throughout the 1980s. However, much to the fury of Postman Pat purists, the series has recently been given a 21st-century update, with Pat upping sticks from Greendale to the nearby sorting office in Pencaster and swapping his trademark little red van for a GPS receiver, motorbike and even a high-tech helicopter. Predictably enough, the update has caused a flurry of protests among local residents and Pat enthusiasts, but for the moment it looks like the BBC is sticking to its decision, so there's no sign that Pat will be ditching his gadgets and returning to Greendale anytime soon…

berth or smaller), plus a well-stocked shop, a canteen, a kitchen, a gear-drying room and a brand new bar. Buses stop at Troutbeck Bridge, a mile from the hostel; minibus pickups can be arranged from Windermere between April and October.

ourpick Queen's Head (☎ 015394-32174; www .queensheadhotel.com; Troutbeck; d £95-120; **P**) This place is like a Lakeland Tardis. Outside, a solid old coaching inn; inside a bang up-to-date gastropub, where cool slate and flickering fires combine with the crest of modern Brit cooking (braised lamb shank, celeriac pork, pan-fried pigeon). The upstairs rooms mix checks, stripes and flowery prints; space is tight in the 'La'al Doubles', while the 'Reet Grand' bedrooms and Four Poster suites offer more elbow room.

Mortal Man (☎ 015394-33193; www.themortalman.co .uk; Troutbeck; mains £8-14; r weekdays £95-145, weekends £120-170; **P**) Another well-seasoned choice overlooking the Troutbeck Valley, especially popular for a Sunday roast or an afternoon pint on the fell-view terrace. The gabled, whitewashed building dates back to 1689, and its rooms have a flavour of a bygone era; nearly all have top-drawer views, and one has a stonking great four-poster. In case you're wondering about the curious name, have a look at the pub sign on your way in – it's taken from an old Lakeland rhyme.

Getting There & Away

The Kirkstone Rambler (No 517; three daily mid-July to August, weekends only mid-March to July and September to November) travels through Troutbeck south to Windermere and Bowness (20 minutes) and north to Kirkstone Pass (10 minutes) and Glenridding (35 minutes).

AMBLESIDE

pop 3382

Gathered along the steep banks of Stock Ghyll, Ambleside was by far and away the busiest town in central Lakeland before the arrival of the Windermere railway in the late 1940s. Tanning, brewing, milling, smithing and bobbin making were all important local trades, but these days most of the heavy industry has long gone and the town is better known as a walking base and commercial centre. Handily plonked between Grasmere, Windermere, Ullswater and the Langdale

Valley, within easy reach of many of the classic Lakeland fells, Ambleside makes an attractive launch-pad for exploring the central sights of the national park.

INFORMATION
Bookshops

Wearings Bookshop (Map pp78-9; ☎ 015394-32312; Lake Rd) Good all-round bookseller, with lots of maps, guides and local-interest titles.

Emergency

Ambleside Police Station (Map pp78-9; ☎ 0845 33 00 247; Rydal Rd)

Langdale and Ambleside Mountain Rescue Team (Map pp78-9; www.lamrt.org.uk; Lowfold, Lake Rd)

Internet Access

Ambleside Library (Map pp78-9; ☎ 015394-32507; Kelsick Rd; per hr £3; ☺ 10am-5pm Mon & Wed, 10am-7pm Tue & Fri, 10am-1pm Sat)

Laundry

Ambleside Laundry Services (Map pp78-9; ☎ 015394-32231; Kelsick Rd; ☺ 10am-6pm)

Money

Barclays (Map pp78-9; Market Pl; ☺ 9am-4.30pm Mon-Fri)

HSBC (Map pp78-9; Market Pl; ☺ 9am-4.30pm Mon-Fri)

Natwest (Map pp78-9; Cheapside; ☺ 9am-4.30pm Mon-Fri)

Post

Post office (Map pp78-9; Market Cross; ☺ 9am-5.30pm Mon-Fri, 9am-12.30pm Sat) In the tourist office building.

Tourist Information

Ambleside Tourist Office (Map pp78-9; ☎ 015394-32582; tic@thehubofambleside.com; Market Cross; ☺ 9am-5pm) Sells fishing permits, guidebooks and bus passes.

www.amblesideonline.co.uk Online access to all things Ambleside.

SIGHTS

The site of present-day Ambleside was first earmarked by the Romans, who constructed a fort known as **Galava** in around AD 79 just west of the modern jetties at Waterhead. You can still (just about) make out the foundations of the fort including the gates, officer's lodgings and granary stores. The land is now owned by the National Trust and is free to visit.

Norse-Irish settlers followed in the wake of the Romans. The oldest area of town is situated around the warren of streets above Stock High Bridge; the sprawling stone farmhouse of **How Head** is the oldest inhabited building in Ambleside, dating back to the early 16th century. Directly opposite is **St Anne's Chapel**, built in 1812 on the site of a much earlier village church. The area 'Above Stock' officially lay in the parish of Grasmere, so until the 19th century deceased parishioners had to be lugged down Nook Lane onto the old Corpse Rd, which meanders behind Rydal Mount to St Oswald's Church in Grasmere.

In their 19th century heyday, Ambleside's pounding mills and clacking waterwheels must have made an almighty racket (which explains Bridge St's former nickname of Rattle Ghyll). Little of the town's industrial architecture now remains, although you can still view one of the old town waterwheels on the side of the Old Mill Tea Room, while the Glass House Restaurant (p82) has left much of its 19th-century machinery in place.

Ambleside's best-known (and certainly most photographed) landmark is **Bridge House**, which spans Stock Ghyll a little way downhill from Market Cross. The building is now occupied by a National Trust shop, but was originally used as an apple store for the nearby orchard belonging to the (demolished) Ambleside Hall; constructing it above the river was a clever wheeze to avoid incurring any land tax.

Further along Rydal Rd is the **Armitt Museum** (☎ 015394-31212; www.thearmittcollection.com; Rydal Rd; adult £2.50; ◷ 10am-5pm), which contains an intriguing collection of local artefacts including a lock of John Ruskin's hair, a collection of fascinating prints by the pharmacist-turned-photographer Herbert Bell, and a moving series of botanical sketches and watercolours by Beatrix Potter.

South of Market Cross on Church St is the **Old Stamp House**, where William Wordsworth worked following his appointment as Distributor of Stamps for Westmorland in 1813 (a position that earned him the considerable annual salary of £500, and helped fund his move from Dove Cottage). Footy fans should also take a peek inside **Homes of Football** (☎ 015394-34440; 100 Lake Rd; admission free; ◷ 10am-5pm Wed-Sun), which displays football-themed photos amassed over two decades by the local photographer Stuart Clarke.

West along Kelsick Rd, past the White Platts Recreation Ground and town bowling green, is Ambleside's most prominent landmark – **St Mary's Church**, with its distinctive skyscraper steeple, constructed by the architect George Gilbert Scott (who also designed London's St Pancras Station and the Foreign and Commonwealth Office in Whitehall). Inside the structure is a mural depicting Ambleside's annual rushbearing ceremony, painted by the artist Gordon Ransom in 1944, while behind the church stretch the glossy green fields of Rothay Park, backed by the River Rothay and the stern 1101ft heap of **Loughrigg Fell** (p92).

ACTIVITIES
Lake Cruises & Boat Hire
Down towards the lakeshore, cruise boats (see p62) set out from the Waterhead jetties for Bowness and the other landing stations around the lake.

Self-powered vessels can be hired from **Low Wood Watersports & Activity Centre** (Map p60; ☎ 015394-39441; watersports@elhmail.co.uk), including row boats (one/four hours £10/25), kayaks (two/four hours £14/21), canoes (two/four hours £20/26), dinghies (two/four hours £35/53) and motor boats (one/four hours £18/45).

Walking
STOCK GHYLL FORCE
There are some great walks all starting from the centre of Ambleside. The most popular is the walk up to Stock Ghyll Force, which we've detailed as part of our Wansfell Pike walk at the start of this chapter on p56. It's an easy stroll up from Cheapside starting behind the old Ambleside Market Hall and following the trail through Stock Ghyll Park, which leads straight up to the falls.

SWEDEN BRIDGES
For a slightly longer walk, you could follow the trail up to the packhorse bridges at Low Sweden Bridge and High Sweden Bridge. The route starts at the end of Nook Lane, climbing steadily through open countryside past Nook End Farm to the bridges, a round trip of about 4 miles or two hours. An alternative route starts on Sweden Bridge Lane. Whichever one you take, it's quite steep on the way up and can be a bit muddy in wet weather.

AMBLESIDE

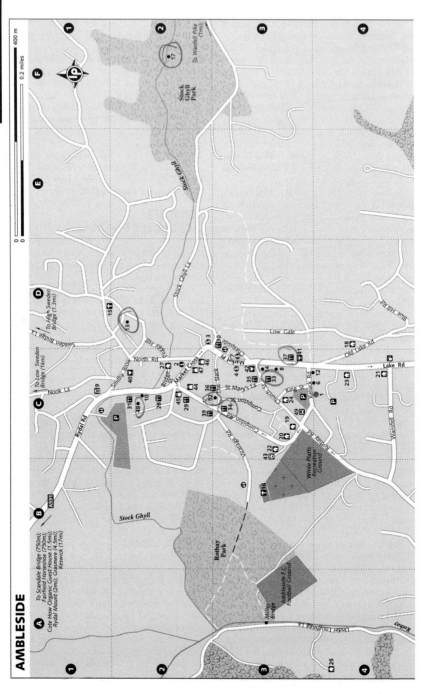

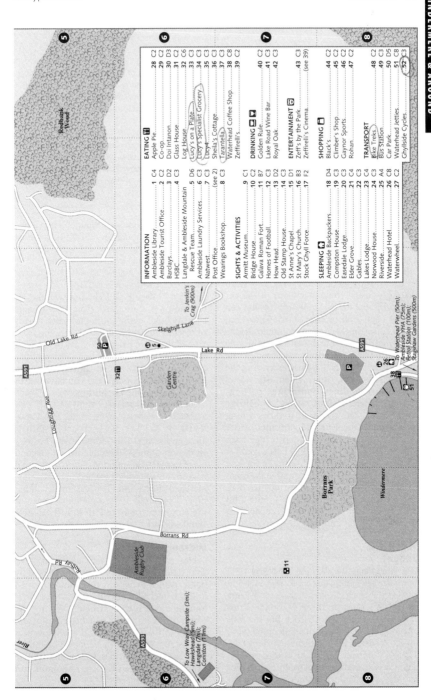

INFORMATION
Ambleside Library...1 C4
Ambleside Tourist Office...2 C3
Barclays...3 D2
HSBC...4 C3
Langdale & Ambleside Mountain Rescue Team...5 D6
Ambleside Laundry Services...6 C3
Natwest...(see 2)
Post Office...7 C3
Wearings Bookshop...8 C3

SIGHTS & ACTIVITIES
Armitt Museum...9 C1
Bridge House...10 C2
Galava Roman Fort...11 B7
Homes of Football...12 C3
How Head...13 D2
Old Stamp House...14 C3
St Anne's Chapel...15 D1
St Mary's Church...16 B3
Stock Ghyll Force...17 F2

SLEEPING
Ambleside Backpackers...18 D4
Compston House...19 C3
Easedale Lodge...20 C3
Elder Grove...21 C4
Gables...22 C3
Lakes Lodge...23 C4
Norwood House...24 C3
Riverside...25 A4
Waterhead Hotel...26 C8
Waterwheel...27 C2

EATING
Apple Pie...28 C2
Co-op...29 C2
Doi Intanon...30 D3
Glass House...31 C6
Log House...32 C6
Lucy's on a Plate...33 C3
Lucy's Specialist Grocery...34 C3
Lucy4...35 C3
Sheila's Cottage...36 C3
Tarantella...37 C3
Waterhead Coffee Shop...38 C8
Zeffirelli's...39 C2

DRINKING
Golden Rule...40 C2
Lake Road Wine Bar...41 C3
Royal Oak...42 C3

ENTERTAINMENT
Zeff's by the Park...43 C3
Zeffirelli's Cinema...(see 39)

SHOPPING
Black's...44 C2
Climber's Shop...45 C3
Gaynor Sports...46 C2
Rohan...47 C2

TRANSPORT
Bike Treks...48 C2
Bus Station...49 C3
Car Park...50 D5
Waterhead Jetties...51 C8
Chylside Cycles...52 C3

RUSHBEARING

One of Ambleside's oldest annual festivals is the yearly rushbearing ceremony, which sees local parishioners parading around the town's streets carrying big bundles of rushes, reeds and fragrant grasses, harvested from nearby lakeshores and either carried in tightly tied sheafs or arranged into ornamental shapes. The tradition dates back to the days when local churches had mud rather than slate floors, and rushes were laid underfoot to keep the church interior dry (and also to mask any unpleasant smells associated with the nearby graveyard).

The rushes were changed with great pageantry once a year, but the ceremony died out in many areas following the introduction of stone floors to many Cumbrian churches during the 19th century. The tradition lives on in Ambleside, where the annual procession takes place on the first Saturday of July; nearby Grasmere has its own rushbearing ceremony on the third Saturday in July, and you'll also still find rushbearing processions in the villages of Warcop, Great Musgrave and Urswick.

FAIRFIELD HORSESHOE

The main object for long-distance hikers is the 10.5-mile Fairfield Horseshoe (Map p60), a strenuous full-day walk taking in the summits of Nab Scar, Heron Pike, Great Rigg, Fairfield, Hart Crag, Dove Crag and High Pike. The usual route starts out in the car park on Rydal Rd in Ambleside, or you can cut off a half-mile or so by starting nearer to Rydal. Pick up the trail at Scandale Bridge about half a mile northwest of Ambleside and follow it as it winds up through the grounds of Rydal Hall before ascending the high fells behind, offering fantastic views of the surrounding countryside, particularly Grasmere, Helm Crag and Loughrigg to the west. The trail then follows a long loop around the Fairfield summits before descending past High Sweden Bridge back into Ambleside. This walk is best saved for a settled, clear day, as high-altitude fog and cloud will obscure the views and make navigation difficult (bring a good quality map and a compass in case). There's quite a bit of elevation involved, too, so be prepared for some stiff climbs and lofty drops.

SLEEPING
Budget

Low Wray Campsite (Map p60; ☎ 015394-32810; lowwraycampsite@nationaltrust.org.uk; adult £4.50-5.50, 5-15yr £2-2.50, car £3-3.50, premium pitches £5; ☷ Easter-Oct; Ⓟ ♿) One of three National Trust campsites in the Lake District, but the only one lodged by the lakeshore with grand views up to Wansfell Pike and the Fairfield fells. There's waterside access for canoes or lake-going vessels, and the usual facilities including laundry, shop and wheelchair-accessible loo.

There are no bookings though. The campsite is 3 miles along the B5286; turn left at Clappersgate and follow the signs. Bus 505 stops about a mile from the campsite.

Ambleside YHA (Map p60; ☎ 0845 371 9620; ambleside@yha.org.uk; Windermere Rd; dm £13.95-17.95; ☷ reception 7.15am-11.45pm; Ⓟ 🖳) This massive lakeside mansion has more space than your average country hotel, with facilities to match. Loads of recently refurbished rooms, ranging from 10-bed dorms to private doubles (some with waterfront views); throw in a local-produce cafe-bar, wi-fi, bike hire and organised activity trips on your doorstep, and you have one of the YHA's flagship establishments.

Ambleside Backpackers (☎ 015394-32340; www.englishlakesbackpackers.co.uk; Old Lake Rd; dm incl breakfast £16; Ⓟ 🖳) The old backpacker spirit is alive and well at this indie cottage-hostel a short walk from Ambleside town. It's a good place to meet like-minded chums, but you'll have to contend with crammed-in bunks, mismatched cutlery and the occasional clanking pipe. Thankfully there's plenty of space in the common room and an industrial-style stainless-steel kitchen.

Midrange

Gables (☎ 015394-33272; www.thegables-ambleside.co.uk; Church Walk; s £40-50, d £60-80; Ⓟ) Gabled by name, gabled by nature, this double-fronted house is tucked away on a side street overlooking the recreation ground. Offering big, comfy beds with colour-matched curtains and throws in the 14 rooms, and a window seat downstairs stocked with *National Geographic* and Lakeland magazines. Guests also receive a discount at Sheila's Cottage restaurant, run by the B&B's owners.

Compston House (☎ 015394-32305; www.comp stonhouse.co.uk; Compston Rd; d £56-68) Saddle up, pardners – this dandy little Yankee-themed B&B is run by ex–New Yorkers, and all the rooms have their own Stateside touch. Maine has a stripy-topped four-poster and Cape Cod bedspread, New York has Manhattan maps and Big Apple posters on the walls, and Arizona has mountain views and sun-baked decor. Best of all, even the breakfasts have an American flavour, including fresh-baked blueberry muffins and pancakes with maple syrup.

Easedale Lodge (☎ 015394-32112; www.easedale ambleside.co.uk; Compston Rd; d £70-96) Twisted willow, zingy cushions and wrought-iron bed frames decorate this immaculate guesthouse on the corner of Compston Rd. Some rooms are finished in cappuccino and creams, others in stripes, florals or cool greys; all have private bathrooms, although not necessarily en suite.

Riverside (☎ 015394-32395; www.riverside-at-amble side.co.uk; Under Loughrigg; d £82-98; P) Ambleside can feel hectic in high season, which makes this detached Victorian villa down by the River Rothay a welcome retreat. The rooms are light and airy, but it's the extra spoils that really sell the place: Pure Lakes bath products in the bathrooms, Hawkshead relishes and local bacon on the breakfast table, and a little wooden sun deck out back where you can soak up the rays. Ask for a spa-bath room for maximum luxury.

Waterwheel (☎ 015394-33286; www.waterwheel ambleside.co.uk; 3 Bridge St; r £85-100) Fall asleep to the sound of the rushing river at the dinky Waterwheel, a lovingly converted cottage with three small but perfectly formed rooms. Top choice is Stockghyll, finished with brass bed knobs, china-blue wallpaper and claw-foot bath; Rattleghyll is cosily Victorian; while Loughrigg is squeezed up on the 2nd floor with views over Ambleside's rooftops. Complimentary port and Kendal mintcake in every room.

Lakes Lodge (☎ 015394-33240; www.lakeslodge.co .uk; Lake Rd; r from £90; 💻) City types will feel at home at this stripped-back, stylish mini-hotel. Slate-floored bathrooms mix with stark white walls in the rooms, all with flat-screen TVs and DVD players (a library of films is available at reception). Local bangers and fresh fruit salad are served up for breakfast in the puce-and-lilac dining room.

ourpick Cote How Organic Guest House (Map p60; ☎ 015394-32765; www.bedbreakfastlakedistrict.com; Rydal, near Ambleside; s £98-£108, d £110-120; P 🛜) Kip with a clear conscience at this charmingly eco-conscious cottage 1½ miles north of Ambleside, which bends over backwards to do its bit for the planet (it's one of only three B&Bs certified by the Soil Association). The food is all organic, while mini-kettles, a green power supplier and low-energy light bulbs keep the carbon footprint to a minimum (wind-up torches are available on request, and there's a 5% discount if you hand in your car keys during your stay). Rugs, chaise longues, roll-top baths and original fireplaces create an upmarket Edwardian atmosphere; ex-president Woodrow Wilson once bunked in the Rydal Suite.

Also recommended:

Norwood House (☎ 015394-33349; www.norwood house.net; Church St; d £60-96; 🛜) Eight plain, attractive rooms (all with en suite bathrooms, complimentary corkscrews and teddy bears), with free hiking advice from a member of the Langdale and Ambleside Mountain Rescue Team.

Elder Grove (☎ 015394-32504; www.eldergrove.co.uk; Lake Rd; d £70-90; P 🛜) Basic but cosy B&B, worth considering for its fab breakfast of Manx kippers, free-range farm eggs, Cumberland sausage and handmade jams.

Top End

ourpick Waterhead Hotel (☎ 08458 504503; water head@elhmail.co.uk; r £106-256; P 🛜) The architecture might be classic Lakeland, but the interior is undeniably urban at this stunning lakeside town house, decked out with all the boutique credentials you'd expect from a luxury four-star hotel. Huge, ice-white rooms are stripped of unnecessary clutter; wood, slate, and chrome dominate the decor, with the odd piece of contemporary art or bay window thrown in to break up the minimalist lines. Flat-screen TVs are huge and wall-mounted, bathrooms glitter in marble and slate, and there's a choice of two fantastic restaurants. Sexy.

EATING
Cafes & Quick Eats

Waterhead Coffee Shop (☎ 015394-32028; lunches £3-10) The chunkiest ciabattas and frothiest cappuccinos in town are served up at the Waterhead Hotel's lakeside coffee shop, but the house speciality is the super-indulgent 'hot choc dip' ice cream – definitely one to avoid if you're on a diet. Call before noon and they'll pack you a takeaway picnic for the following day.

Apple Pie (☎ 015394-33679; Rydal Rd; lunches £4-12) Sticky cakes, sandwiches and salads are the mainstay at this sunny lunch spot on the main street, but for something more satisfying plump for one of the trademark pies, which come in tempting concoctions including broccoli, stilton and mushroom; potato and cheddar; and Cumberland sausage.

Restaurants

Lucy4 (☎ 015394-34666; 2 St Mary's Lane; tapas £4-8; ☯ 5-11pm Mon-Sat, 5-10.30pm Sun) Can't find a table at the original Lucy's? Don't panic – there's nearly always room at this nifty wine bar just down the street, where you can sample Lucy's take on traditional tapas accompanied by beers and wines from across the globe.

Zeffirelli's (☎ 015394-33845; Compston Rd; pizza £5.50-7.45; ☯ cafe from 10am, restaurant 5.30-11pm) This funky brasserie/cinema/jazz bar (known just as Zeff's to Amblesiders) is a fine place for schmoozing and boozing over pizza and Med-inspired food. Moody lighting and a frozen glass waterfall create a cosmopolitan atmosphere, and at weekends there's live music in the upstairs jazz bar. Light bites are served at the cafe throughout the day. The owners also run Ambleside's cinema; the popular £16.95 Movie Deal includes dinner and a ticket to the flicks.

our pick Lucy's on a Plate (☎ 015394-31191; www .lucysofambleside.co.uk; Church St; lunch £6-12, dinner £15-25; ☯ 10am-9pm) The Lake District's current culinary celebrity, Lucy Nicholson, started her gastronomic adventure with a specialist grocery on Church St back in 1989 (now transplanted to Compston Rd, see right). These days she's the owner of a string of businesses around Ambleside, as well as an outpost in Bowness (p68) and a cookery school in Staveley (p74), but this buzzing little bistro is still the best place to sample her unique approach to cooking. The menu is crammed with eclectic dishes such as 'Pruned Piggy Wig' and 'Give Us A Strog' (often accompanied by a self-penned missal from Lucy herself), and the atmosphere is deliberately informal. Daily specials are chalked up on boards, and there's a plant-strewn conservatory that floods with light on sunny days. A word of warning though – Lucy's secret is well

and truly out, and many people think it's lost a bit of its old insider charm.

Glass House (☎ 015394-32137; Rydal Rd; lunch £8-14, dinner £12.95-19; ☯ lunch & dinner) Having received a thorough roasting a few years back on Gordon Ramsay's *Kitchen Nightmares*, the Glass House has since turned things around and now serves some of the town's classiest food. First-rate local ingredients – Herdwick lamb, Lakeland chicken, and fish from the North coast ports – form the backbone of the menu, while the split-level dining room still features vintage machinery left over from the building's former incarnation as a fulling mill.

Doi Intanon (☎ 015394-32119; Market Pl; mains £8.50-15.50; ☯ dinner) Inside Ambleside's old Market Hall, this longstanding Thai restaurant specialises in all things hot and spicy, which makes it a favourite with hikers looking to banish the chill from those post-hike bones. Red, green and yellow curries feature alongside tempting regional specialities.

Sheila's Cottage (☎ 015394-33079; The Slack; £9.50-19.95; ☯ noon-5pm & 6-9pm) This cute cottage restaurant sets out to warm your innermost cockles. Hefty plates of lamb's liver and bacon, crunchy pork and roasted veg, and Cumberland sausage with champ mash are dished up beneath beams, brass knick-knacks and rough stone ceilings.

Tarantella (☎ 015394-31338; 10 Lake Rd; mains £9.95-15.95; ☯ noon-2pm & 5.30-11pm, also 8.30am-noon Sat & Sun) Authentic Italian served in stylish surrounds. Alongside the usual risottos, pastas and 12in pizzas, you'll find more unusual mains including duck-and-chilli sausage and roast tuna.

Log House (☎ 015394-31077; Lake Rd; mains £14.95-19.95, 2-/3-course menu £15/17.50; ☯ dinner Tue-Sat) This extraordinary clapboard building looks like it's fallen from the pages of *Heidi*, but it was actually shipped over from Norway by the Lakeland artist Alfred Heaton Cooper. Nowadays it's a solid bet for traditional British cooking from the old school – Berkshire black pork, sea bass and chips, Vale of Lune lamb. If you fancy staying, there are a few atmospheric rooms squeezed in among the rafters (£80 to £90).

Self-Catering

Lucy's Specialist Grocery (☎ 015394-32223; Compston Rd) may have new premises on Compston Rd, but it still offers the same irresistible selection of local goodies, including crusty breads, relishes, chutneys, biscuits, rum butter and Lucy's very own version of sticky toffee pudding. Several chiller counters are stocked with local meats and cheeses – ideal for self-creating picnics.

For basic supplies, there's a **Co-op** (☎ 01539-433124; Compston Rd; ⏱ 8.30am-8pm Mon-Fri, 10am-6pm Sun) up the road.

DRINKING & ENTERTAINMENT

Royal Oak (☎ 015394-33382; Market Pl) The town's most central pub packs in the punters, with bench seats outside for warmer days and plenty of cosy nooks and crannies inside where you can snuggle down with a lukewarm ale.

Golden Rule (☎ 015394-33363; Smithy Brow) Country prints and the odd brass horseshoe dot the walls at this ale-drinkers' haven, with a line-up of brews including Old Stockport Bitter, Robinson's Hatters Mild and Hartleys XB, plus pork pies and scotch eggs for the peckish.

Lake Road Wine Bar (☎ 01539-433175; 10-14 Lake Rd; ⏱ 10am-midnight) Ambleside's trendy set strut their stuff at this designer den, equipped with the essential DJ decks, plasma TV, pop-art prints and chocolate-coloured sofas. Hot drinks are served till 7pm, with DJs and cocktails taking centre stage after 9pm.

Zeffirelli's Cinema (☎ 015394-33100; Compston Rd) Ambleside's two-screen cinema is next to Zeff's (known as Zeff's by the Park), with extra screens in a converted church down the road.

SHOPPING

If those tired old trail boots have seen better days, don't worry – Ambleside has more outdoors suppliers than any other town in the central lakes.

For all-round gear, the best places are **Black's** (☎ 015394-33197; 42 Compston Rd) or **Gaynor Sports** (☎ 015394-33305; Market Cross), one of the UK's biggest outdoors stores. Rock-climbers can get specialist advice and equipment at the **Climber's Shop** (☎ 015394-32297; Compston Rd), while fashion-conscious fell walkers will probably prefer **Rohan** (☎ 015394-32946; Market Cross).

GETTING THERE & AROUND
Bus
Lots of buses run through Ambleside, including the 555 to Grasmere and Windermere (hourly, 10 on Sunday), the 505 to Hawkshead and Coniston (10 Monday to Saturday, six on Sunday mid-March to October) and in the opposite direction to Windermere (eight daily Monday to Saturday, six on Sunday), and the 516 (six daily Monday to Saturday, five on Sunday) to Elterwater and Langdale. The main bus stop is on Kelsick Rd.

Bike Hire
Ghyllside Cycles (☎ 015394-33592; www.ghyllside.co.uk; The Slack; per day £16) and **Bike Treks** (☎ 015394-31505; www.biketreks.net; Rydal Rd; per half/full day £14/18) both rent mountain bikes including maps, pump, helmet and lock.

Grasmere & the Central Lake District

The broad green bowl of Grasmere acts as a kind of geographical junction for the Lake District, sandwiched between the rumpled peaks of the Langdale Pikes to the west and the gentle hummocks and open dales of the eastern fells. But Grasmere is more than just a geological centre – it's a literary one too thanks to the poetic efforts of William Wordsworth and chums, who collectively set up home in Grasmere during the late 18th century and transformed the valley into the spiritual hub of the Romantic movement.

It's not too hard to see what drew so many poets, painters and thinkers to this idyllic corner of England. Grasmere is one of the most naturally alluring of the Lakeland valleys, studded with oak woods and glittering lakes, carpeted with flower-filled meadows, and ringed by a stunning circlet of fells including Loughrigg, Silver Howe and the sculptured summit of Helm Crag. Wordsworth spent countless hours wandering the hills and trails around the valley, and the area is dotted with literary landmarks connected to the poet and his contemporaries, as well as boasting the nation's foremost museum devoted to the Romantic movement. But it's not solely a place for bookworms: Grasmere is also the gateway to the hallowed hiking valleys of Great and Little Langdale, home to some of the cut-and-dried classics of Lakeland walking as well as one of the country's most historic hiking inns.

HIGHLIGHTS

■ Get up close and personal with the Wordsworths at **Dove Cottage** (p87) and **Rydal Mount** (p91)

■ Bone up on the Romantics' backstory at Grasmere's fascinating **Wordsworth Museum** (p89)

■ Banish those camping blues by snuggling down in a luxurious **yurt** (p96) in the grounds of Rydal Hall

■ Sink your teeth into a stonking Sunday lunch at Elterwater's **Britannia Inn** (p97) or **Chesters Cafe by the River** (p96) in Skelwith Bridge

■ Tackle the stunning ascents of **Helm Crag** (p92) or the **Langdale Pikes** (p86)

■ Stop off for a slab of Britain's best gingerbread at **Sarah Nelson's Gingerbread Shop** (p89) in Grasmere

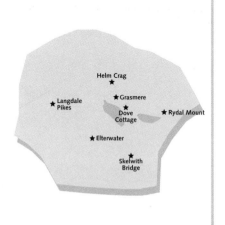

| ■ Area of largest lake (Grasmere): 0.24 sq miles | ■ Number of visitors to Dove Cottage in 2007: 61,870 | ■ Highest fell in Great Langdale (High Raise): 2500ft |

ITINERARY 1
GRASMERE LOOP & OLD COFFIN TRAIL WALK　　3.5 miles/2 hours/Grasmere centre

You don't always have to slog your guts out for scenic views. This popular lakeside trail tracks the shores of Grasmere Lake and Rydal Water, before making an easy loop back behind Rydal Mount along the old pallbearer's route to St Oswald's Church.

Start out in Grasmere, and follow Red Bank Rd past the tea garden. Look out for a left-hand turn over a stile and onto a bridleway about 10 minutes' walk from Grasmere, and follow the trail down to the lakeshore, from where there are fantastic views up to Helm Crag and Dunmail Raise. Keep heading east to the far shore of the lake, past a weir and a small footbridge. At the next junction you could backtrack west along the upper trail to the viewpoint from Loughrigg Terrace. Alternatively follow the trail east along the shores of **Rydal Water**, or plump for the higher trail that leads up to the disused slate quarries and the gaping maw of **Rydal Cave**.

Continue walking east towards Pelter Bridge, from where, if you wish, you can link up with the Underloughrigg trail (p57) into Ambleside; otherwise, stick to the path, cross over a small footbridge onto the main A591 and then take the left-hand turn up to **Rydal Mount** (p91).

Up behind the house is a path (signed 'Public Bridleway Grasmere') that leads into open fields. This is the beginning of the old coffin trail that leads all the way to **St Oswald's Church** (p89) back in Grasmere; look out for the stone slabs along the route that once allowed coffin carriers to rest their burdens without having to lay them on the ground. The path offers lovely views over Rydal Water and **Nab Cottage** (p93), passing beneath the face of Nab Scar on your right-hand side. Carry on past **White Moss Common** on your left; eventually you'll reach a paved road where you can turn right back towards Dove Cottage and Grasmere.

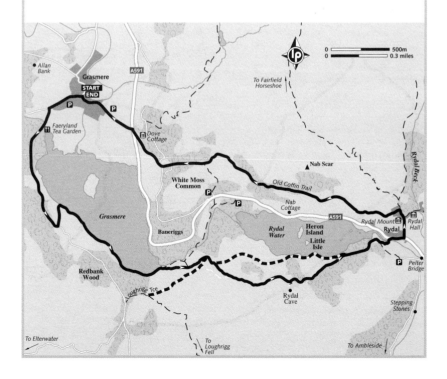

ITINERARY 2
LANGDALE PIKES HIKE
7 miles/6 to 7 hours/New Dungeon Ghyll Hotel to
Old Dungeon Ghyll Hotel

This strenuous high-level walk is a favourite target for people looking to tick off a handful of Wainwright summits in a day – although you'll have to work for the rewards, as there are some steep climbs and dizzying drops along the way.

The trail starts out behind the **New Dungeon Ghyll Hotel** (p100), leading steeply north up the ravine of **Stickle Ghyll**. There are two possible paths up the valley; the easier one tracks the left-hand side of the beck, pushing straight up the slope all the way to **Stickle Tarn**.

Take a breather and admire the craggy views of your next target, **Pavey Ark** (2297ft), officially an outlying peak of the nearby fell of **Thunacar Knott** (2372ft). There are several routes to the fell summit, including the notoriously stomach-churning scramble up **Jack's Rake**. A marginally easier route leads up **Easy Gully**, but the most achievable ascent is the route dubbed by Wainwright as **North Rake**. The trail veers away from the tarn up **Bright Beck**, passing through a short scree gully onto grassy slopes that ascend all the way to the summit cairn. From here, the plunging views are some of the loftiest in the entire Lake District, but steer well clear of the edge.

Peak-bagging purists will want to make the short detour via the top of Thunacar Knott, before trudging south along the ridge to the unmistakeable lion's-head hump of **Harrison Stickle** (2415ft). A stony path leads west to the foot of **Pike O' Stickle** (2326ft), once the centre of the prehistoric Langdale axe industry, as well as the westerly outpost of a string of impressive crags including Loft Crag, Gimmer Crag and Thorn Crag. If you want to bag the peak, you can scramble west to the summit, before clambering back to the path leading west across the grassy slopes of **Martcrag Moor** to the junction of Stakes Pass. From here the trail winds down for around 3 miles through **Langdale Combe** into the **Mickleden Valley** and back across the fields of Great Langdale to the **Old Dungeon Ghyll Hotel** (p100).

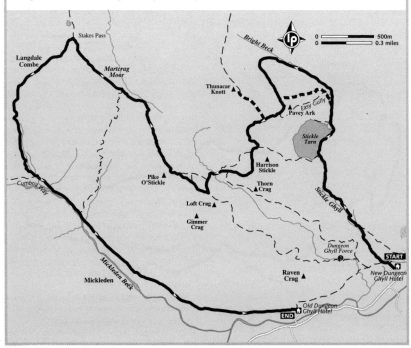

GRASMERE & AROUND

pop 1458

If it's Romantic connections you're searching for, then look no further than the gorgeous village of Grasmere – home for nigh-on 50 years to the grand old daddy of the Lakeland Romantics himself, William Wordsworth. After his long-awaited return to the Lake District in the early 1790s, William never felt too much desire to stray from his adopted home in Grasmere, and two centuries after his death, his spirit still looms large over the village. The poet's former houses at Dove Cottage and Rydal Mount are both open to the public (another, at Allan Bank, is sadly off-limits), and you can also visit the village school where he taught (now a celebrated gingerbread shop) as well as his family tombs sheltered under the spreading yew trees of St Oswald's Churchyard. Unfortunately Grasmere's literary cachet has its drawbacks: the village's narrow slate streets are crammed to bursting throughout the summer months, and the modern-day rash of gift shops, tearooms and coach-tour hotels has done little to preserve the quiet country charm that drew Wordsworth here in the first place. Still, the setting is stunning, and if it all gets a bit too frantic you can seek refuge around the quiet shores of Grasmere Lake or out on the airy summits of nearby Helm Crag and Loughrigg Fell.

ORIENTATION

The main A591 between Ambleside and Keswick runs along the east side of the village. The main car park is just off Stock Lane, which leads straight into the centre of Grasmere past St Oswald's Church to Red Lion Sq. Grasmere Lake is a short walk south of the village along Redbank Rd, while to the north of the village Easedale Rd leads up to the youth hostels and the climb to Helm Crag.

INFORMATION

There's no library, laundrette, bank or tourist office in Grasmere.

Grasmere Post Office (Map p90; ☎ 015394-35261; Red Lion Sq; ◷ 9am-5pm Mon-Wed & Fri, 9am-12.30pm Thu & Sat) Tiny village post office, which has the village's only ATM.

Sam Read Booksellers (Map p90; ☎ 015394-35374; Broadgate; ◷ 9am-5.30pm Mon-Sat) General bookshop with good selection of hiking maps and guides.

SIGHTS

Dove Cottage

Covered with climbing roses, honeysuckle and tiny latticed windows, the whitewashed **Dove Cottage** (Map p88; ☎ 015394-35544; www .wordsworth.org.uk; adult/child £7.50/4.50; ◷ 9.30am-5.30pm) seems hardly to have changed since the days when William Wordsworth and his beloved sister Dorothy first clapped eyes on it in the early 1790s. In those days it was still an old coaching inn called the Dove and Olive, which lay on the main packhorse road through Cumberland en route to Keswick and the north. On 20 December 1799, the small inn became William and Dorothy's first permanent Lake District home since their childhood in Cockermouth. In 1802 they were joined by William's new wife (and former childhood sweetheart) Mary Hutchinson, followed in swift succession by the births of the three eldest Wordsworth children – John, Dora and Thomas – in 1803, 1804 and 1806.

The tiny house became a cramped but happy home for the growing family and a seemingly never-ending stream of literary visitors. Samuel Taylor Coleridge, William Hazlitt, Robert Southey, Walter Scott, Thomas de Quincey and Wordsworth's older brother John all spent considerable periods of time at Dove Cottage during the Wordsworths' tenure – a period memorably recounted in Dorothy's wonderful diary, later published as the *Grasmere Journal*. William subsequently came to describe his period at Dove Cottage as his 'golden decade', and he wrote some of his finest poems during his time there, including 'Ode: Intimations of Immortality', several sections of the *Prelude* and, famously, 'I Wandered Lonely as a Cloud', which came to him during an afternoon ramble along the shores of Ullswater.

Now owned and lovingly restored by the Wordsworth Trust, the tiny cottage provides a fascinating window into the daily lives of the Wordsworth family. Entry is via timed ticket to avoid overcrowding, and includes an absorbing guided tour with one of the cottage curators.

On the ground floor is the wood-panelled entry hall, known to the Wordsworths as 'the houseplace'; look out for a portrait of one of the Wordsworths' favourite dogs, Pepper, a pooch given to them by Sir Walter Scott.

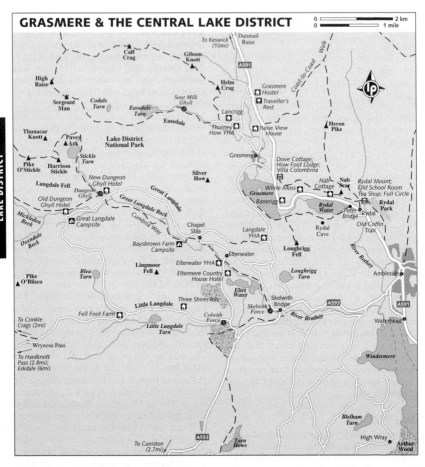

GRASMERE & THE CENTRAL LAKE DISTRICT

Beyond the hall is a little dining room (used by the Wordsworths as Dorothy's bedroom), and beyond a gloomy kitchen and larder. The only illumination at the time would have come from smoky tallow candles that, combined with all the open fireplaces, had the inconvenient side effect of staining the walls black, so whitewashing the walls would have been a laborious and frustratingly frequent domestic chore. At the back of the house is the magical little cottage garden, described by Wordsworth as his 'domestic slip of mountain', where the family spent many happy hours declaiming William's latest poetry in the summer house or planting blooms, shrubs and vegetables.

Upstairs are the family bedrooms and Wordsworth's little writing study. There are lots of fascinating artefacts dotted all over the place, so keep your eyes peeled: Wordsworth's paper passport hangs on one of the bedroom walls, portraits of the poet line the walls of his study and a cabinet displays items including his spectacles, shaving case and razor, Dorothy's needlework box, and a set of scales reputedly used by de Quincey to weigh out his opium. Perhaps most interesting of all is the little room used as a bedroom for the Wordsworth children, which Dorothy insulated with pages from the daily newspapers – another episode recounted in the pages of her journal.

Eventually the Wordsworths were forced to leave Dove Cottage to find more space at the nearby house of Allan Bank in 1808, but the family (and perhaps more strongly Wordsworth himself) never truly felt settled until they moved into Rydal Mount (p91) in 1813, where they remained until William's death in 1850. After the Wordsworths' departure, Dove Cottage was leased by Wordsworth's awestruck young friend Thomas de Quincey, who remained at the house on and off for the next 20-odd years.

Wordsworth Museum & Art Gallery

Admission to Dove Cottage also includes entry to the **Wordsworth Museum and Art Gallery** (Map p90; ☎ 015394-35544; www.wordsworth.org.uk; ⏱ 9.30am-5.30pm), which houses the nation's largest archive relating to the Romantic movement. The museum moves through the lives and work of most of the great figures of British Romanticism in roughly chronological order; among the intriguing items on display are Thomas de Quincey's beloved blackthorn walking stick (the subject of a recent BBC Radio 4 documentary) and a glass cabinet containing Wordsworth's court suit, cloak, umbrella and his favourite panama hat. Eeriest of all are the haunting life masks of Wordsworth and John Keats, which bring you literally face to face with two of England's most illustrious poets – guaranteed to send a shiver down your spine. The collection changes throughout the year, and the museum also hosts regular poetry readings and literary seminars.

St Oswald's Church

Sheltering under the spreading boughs of several great yew trees at the centre of Grasmere is St Oswald's Church (Map p90), parts of which date back to the 13th century. For hundreds of years this was the main parish church for the district; deceased parishioners from outlying areas, including Ambleside, Elterwater and the Langdale Valley had to be carried along a series of 'coffin trails' or 'corpse roads' in order to be buried at Grasmere. The church interior is worth a look for its interweaving oak rafters, a marble memor-ial to Wordsworth and the poet's own well-thumbed prayer book, but most visitors make the pilgrimage straight out

to the **Wordsworth graves**, hidden away in a quiet corner of the churchyard. Protected behind low iron railings are the tombstones of William, Mary and Dorothy, as well as the Wordsworth children Dora, Catherine and Thomas; Coleridge's carousing son Hartley; and several members of the Quillinan family (related to the Wordsworths by marriage).

Sarah Nelson's Gingerbread Shop

Beside the church in the village's former schoolhouse is **Sarah Nelson's Gingerbread Shop** (Map p90; ☎ 015394-35428; www.grasmeregingerbread.co.uk; Church Stile; ⏱ 9.15am-5.30pm Mon-Sat, 12.30pm-5pm Sun), where ladies in frilly pinnies and starched bonnets have been cooking traditional gingerbread to the same secret recipe for the last 150 years. Part sticky cake, part crumbly biscuit, Sarah's unique gingerbread was an instant bestseller when it was first developed in the mid 1850s, and the village shop is still the only place in the world where you can buy the real McCoy (the original formula is still top secret and is safely locked away inside the vault of a bank in Ambleside). The gingerbread comes in greaseproof packets of six or twelve slabs (£3.50 for 12). You can also pick up jars of Sarah Nelson's delicious home-made rum butter, along with other Lakeland specialities including Penrith fudge and toffee, Cartmel sticky toffee sauce and Kendal mintcake.

More recently, Sarah Nelson's shop hit the national headlines over an application to trademark the name of 'Grasmere Gingerbread'. The current owners of Sarah Nelson's have alleged that only their gingerbread has a real right to use the term, a claim hotly contested by many other local businesses, who believe that the recipe dates back to at least the mid-18th century when spices, rum and sugar first arrived in Cumbrian ports (meaning traditional gingerbread existed long before Sarah Nelson cooked up her first batch).

Heaton Cooper Studio

Few artists sum up the spirit of Lakeland painting better than the Heaton Cooper family, arguably the Lake District's best-known artistic dynasty. Alfred Heaton Cooper (1864–1929), a Manchester-born artist who was heavily influenced by Turner and Constable, became one of the most

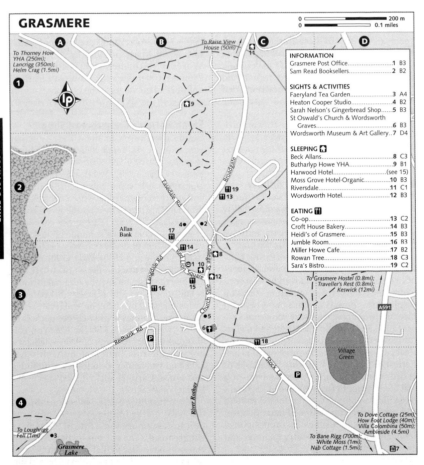

GRASMERE

0 ———— 200 m
0 ———— 0.1 miles

To Thorney How
YHA (250m);
Lancrigg (350m);
Helm Crag (1.5mi)

To Raise View
House (50m)

Fisdale Rd

Broadgate

Allan
Bank

Langdale Rd

Red Lion Square

College St

Church Stile

Redbank Rd

River Rothay

Stock La

To Loughrigg
Fell (1mi)

Grasmere
Lake

To Grasmere Hostel (0.8mi);
Traveller's Rest (0.8mi);
Keswick (12mi)

A591

Village
Green

To Dove Cottage (25m);
How Foot Lodge (40m);
Villa Colombina (50m);
Ambleside (4.5mi)

To Bane Rigg (700m);
White Moss (1mi);
Nab Cottage (1.5mi);

INFORMATION
Grasmere Post Office...................**1** B3
Sam Read Booksellers..................**2** B2

SIGHTS & ACTIVITIES
Faeryland Tea Garden...................**3** A4
Heaton Cooper Studio..................**4** B2
Sarah Nelson's Gingerbread Shop.....**5** B3
St Oswald's Church & Wordsworth
Graves..............................**6** B3
Wordsworth Museum & Art Gallery..**7** D4

SLEEPING
Beck Allans..............................**8** C3
Butharlyp Howe YHA....................**9** B1
Harwood Hotel.........................(see 15)
Moss Grove Hotel-Organic.............**10** B3
Riversdale...............................**11** C1
Wordsworth Hotel.......................**12** B3

EATING
Co-op......................................**13** C2
Croft House Bakery......................**14** B3
Heidi's of Grasmere.....................**15** B3
Jumble Room............................**16** B3
Miller Howe Cafe.......................**17** B2
Rowan Tree..............................**18** C3
Sara's Bistro.............................**19** C2

celebrated painters of Lakeland landscapes during the late 19th century, and established a studio in Grasmere to display his work. The artistic tradition was later continued by his son William (1903–1995), another fine landscapist as well as a pioneering rock climber, and his wife, the talented sculptor Ophelia Gordon Bell (1915–1975). Various other members of the Heaton Cooper family are still exhibiting at the gallery, including William's son Julian (born 1947), who has ranged across the globe from Cumbria to Kathmandu in search of wild vistas to capture in paint.

The **Heaton Cooper Studio** (Map p90; ☎ 015394-35280; www.heatoncooper.co.uk; ⊙ 9am-5.30pm Mon-

Sat, 11am-5.30pm Sun) sells prints, postcards and original canvases from all of the Heaton Cooper artists, as well as books and art materials.

Grasmere Lake & Rydal Water

From the centre of the village, Redbank Rd leads southwest towards the lakeshore and the **Faeryland Tea Garden** (Map p90; ☎ 015394-35060; ⊙ 10am-6pm Mar-Oct), where you can hire a row boat and scull out to the tree-covered island at the centre of the lake (a favourite early evening pastime for Wordsworth and his companions).

We've detailed the walk around Grasmere Lake on p85.

Rydal Mount

Though tiny Dove Cottage receives all the plaudits (and most of the visitors), for a more revealing glimpse into Wordsworth's life, head for **Rydal Mount** (Map p88; ☎ 015394-33002; www.rydalmount.co.uk; adult/concession/5-15yr £5.50/4.75/2, gardens only £3; ☾ 9.30am-5pm Mar-Oct, 10am-4pm Wed-Mon Nov & Feb), which is still owned and run by the poet's descendants.

Thanks to a new-found financial security provided by his appointment as the Distributor of Stamps for Westmorland in 1813, coupled with the steady proceeds stemming from his poetry, writing and lecturing, Wordsworth rather unexpectedly found himself in a position to afford a larger and more prestigious home. Sadly this comfortable economic situation could do nothing to prevent the sudden deaths of two of his children, Catherine and Thomas, within six months of each other in 1812 (Catherine died of convulsions just before her 4th birthday in June, and Thomas died of measles aged six in December of the same year). This tragic turn of events undoubtedly contributed to the poet's desire to make a new start for himself and what remained of his young family.

In 1813 William moved his unhappy brood – including wife Mary, sister Dorothy, and his three surviving children, John, Dora and William – into a spacious country house at Rydal Mount halfway between Grasmere and Ambleside, rented at some expense from the wealthy owners of nearby Rydal Hall. Fortunately Rydal Mount seems to have provided the happy family home the Wordsworths had been searching for so desperately since their departure from Dove Cottage; both William and Mary lived out the rest of their lives at the house, until their respective deaths in 1850 and 1859.

In contrast to the poky charm of Dove Cottage, Rydal Mount still feels very much like a family home, and the house is packed with original furniture, manuscripts and possessions relating to the poet's life and work. The heart of the house is the grand book-lined library and smart dining room, where Wordsworth liked to entertain his many literary and political visitors. Much of the room's furniture dates from Wordsworth's residency, and the glass display cases contain some fascinating artefacts including the poet's own pen, inkstand, picnic box and ice skates. The large portrait of Wordsworth above the fire is by the American painter Henry Inman, who stayed at Rydal Mount in 1844; the picture is reputed to have been one of Mary's favourite paintings of her husband.

Upstairs you can nose around the family bedrooms (including Mr and Mrs Wordsworth's boudoir and the room belonging to Wordsworth's sister Dorothy, who never married and remained with the family until her death in 1855, after a long bout of mental illness). On the top floor is Wordsworth's study, containing his encyclopaedia and a sword belonging to his younger brother John, who was killed in the shipwreck of the *Earl of Abergavenny* in 1805.

But perhaps the most revealing insight into the poet's character lies outside, in the hectare of gardens surrounding the main house. Wordsworth often joked that if he hadn't been a poet he would have been a landscape gardener, and most of the formal terraces and winding pathways around Rydal Mount were laid out according to his designs. You can even rest your legs in the little summer house where the poet liked to sound out his latest verses.

Below the house is **St Mary's Church** (built in 1824) and the wooded walk through **Dora's Field**, now owned by the National Trust. Wordsworth originally bought the site with the intention of building a home for his daughter Dora and her husband Edward Quillinan; the house never materialised, and following Dora's death from tuberculosis in 1847, William and Mary planted the field with daffodil bulbs in memory of their eldest daughter.

Across the lane from Rydal Mount is Rydal Hall, the family seat of the le Fleming family since 1576, and the home of Wordsworth's erstwhile landlords. It's now a business conference centre, but it's worth investigating for the excellent **Old School Room Tea Shop** (Map p88; ☎ 01539-432050; soup £2.95, cream tea £3.30, sandwiches £2.95-3.50; ☾ 10am-5pm, shorter hours in winter), which sources its organic milk and cheese from Low Sizergh Barn (p214) and its relishes from the Hawkshead Relish Co (p121). The grounds of the hall are now also home to one of the Lake District's fanciest campsites, Full Circle (see p96).

Across the main A591 you can pick up the trail along the small lake of **Rydal Water** back to Grasmere Lake and Grasmere Village; alternatively you could stroll back to Grasmere along the old coffin trail (p85), which starts behind the main house, or follow the walk through Rydal Park to Ambleside.

Rydal Mount is a mile southeast of Grasmere, off the A591. Bus 555 (and 599 from April to October), between Grasmere, Ambleside, Windermere and Kendal, stops at the end of the drive.

WALKING
Loughrigg Fell

An optional add-on to the Grasmere Loop and Coffin Trail (p85) is the short, steep hike up to the summit of Loughrigg Fell (1099ft), from where there are wonderful views across the Grasmere Valley, stretching south to Windermere and west to the Langdale Pikes. The paved path veers off the main trail past Grasmere Lake – it's a steep up-and-down hike of about an hour and a half, but the views are definitely worth the effort.

Silver Howe

Another fell that packs in superstar views despite its diminutive height is Silver Howe (1292ft). The traditional route from Grasmere travels past Allan Bank, winding along rural lanes and through woodland before cutting south over Wray Gill to the summit and circling back down to the village near the Faeryland Tea Garden. This route will take two hours or so and covers around 3 miles.

Helm Crag & Easedale Round

Another must-do ascent for nearly every visitor is the summit of Helm Crag (1328ft), which looms over the north side of Grasmere. Sometimes referred to as the 'Lion and the Lamb', after the twin crags that sit atop its summit, this is another sharp but rewarding two-hour climb with predictably impressive views south over Grasmere and north towards Dunmail Raise. Another rocky outcrop at the top of the fell is known as the 'Howitzer' thanks to its distinctive cannon-shaped profile.

The trail starts on Easedale Rd and climbs quickly up over White Crag to the summit; it's fairly well signposted from the main road, but as always a map will come in handy. Wainwright described Helm Crag as 'the best known hill in the country' and you can download an MP3 version of his original guide to the route from www.golakes .co.uk/downloads/podcasts/wainwright .aspx, read by the narrator of the BBC series *Wainwright Walks*.

An optional add-on is the Easedale Round (8.5 miles), a tough six- to seven-hour circuit around the valley via the ridge to **Gibson Knott**, followed by **Calf Crag**, **High Raise**, **Sergeant Man** and down to **Easedale Tarn**, which Thomas de Quincey considered one of the district's most 'gloomily sublime' lakes. A little further east from the tarn is the clashing waterfall of **Sour Milk Ghyll**, from where it's a 1.5 mile stroll back down the valley into Grasmere. If you're only looking for a short walk, the falls make a pleasant and not too taxing objective in their own right.

SLEEPING
BUDGET

Thorney How YHA Hostel (Map p88; ☎ 0870 770 5836; Easedale Rd; dm £13; ☺ Apr-Oct) There's a slice of bona fide hostelling history up the lane at Thorney How, the ramshackle farmhouse which became the YHA's first ever hostel in 1931. The house has obviously been updated, but it's still dotted with original beams, fireplaces and wonky chimney pots. Dorms are roomy, and there's an evening meal served in the cosy communal dining area. It's a walkers' favourite; the Coast-to-Coast trail and the Helm Crag route run right past the front gate.

Butharlyp Howe YHA (Map p90; ☎ 0845 371 9319; grasmere@yha.org.uk; dm £15.50; ☺ daily Feb-Nov, weekends Dec-Jan, reception 7am-11pm; Ⓟ 🖳) Grasmere's biggest YHA is housed in another fantastic Victorian mansion, bucolically situated off Easedale Rd overlooking woodland and trimmed lawns. Bright, modernish dorms (including plenty of private doubles and quads) and a decent cafe (serving everything from puddings to Perry cider) make this another superior YHA.

our pick **Grasmere Hostel** (Map p88; ☎ 015394-35055; www.grasmerehostel.co.uk; Broadrayne Farm; dm £17.50; Ⓟ) Forget institutional dorms and saggy bunk beds – this brilliant indie hostel does backpacking in style. Lodged inside a converted farmhouse off the A591 near the Traveller's Rest pub, you'll find five small three- to six-bedded rooms, all with private

---

GRASMERE SPORTS

Like many villages across England, Grasmere is fiercely proud of its annual **sports day**, when local lads and lasses get the chance to test their mettle against each other at a selection of traditional sports on the village green.

Grasmere Sports usually takes place on the Sunday of the August Bank Holiday, and has been held practically every year since 1852. In its heyday over 50,000 spectators flocked to the village to enjoy the show; these days audience figures are a more modest 10,000, but the event remains one of the highlights of the Grasmere calendar. Among the more unusual events on display are **hound trailing**, in which dogs race each other along a pre-marked scented trail; **guides racing**, the Grasmere equivalent of fell running, in which super-fit runners slog up and down a selection of fells in pursuit of the fastest time; and **Cumberland and Westmorland wrestling**, which shares many similarities with traditional forms of wrestling practised in Celtic areas such as Cornwall and Brittany. Dressed in the traditional wrestler's garb of white long johns, patterned trunks and a white vest, contestants aim to unbalance their opponent over a series of three bouts.

Grasmere also has its own annual **rushbearing ceremony**, similar to the one held every year in Ambleside (p80). The procession takes place on the Saturday nearest to St Oswald's Day (5 August), in honour of the patron saint of the village church.

---

bathrooms and fell views, as well as two stainless steel kitchens, a comfy lounge and a Nordic sauna for soothing those aching bones. They'll even look after your luggage while you're on the trail. Bus 555 stops nearby.

Nab Cottage (Map p88; ☎ 015394-35311; www .nabcottage.com; Rydal) Few houses in Grasmere have such cast-iron Romantic credentials as Nab Cottage – Coleridge, his son Hartley, and Thomas de Quincey all lived here at various times, and the house's linguistic history continues on to this day (it's now an English-language school). Rooms are sometimes rented out to non-students outside the summer – phone ahead for prices and details.

MIDRANGE

Raise View House (Map p88; ☎ 015394-35215; www .raiseviewhouse.co.uk; White Bridge; s/d £48/96; P ⚏) Looking for that all-essential room with a view? Raise View is definitely the place – four of the rooms have stunning fell outlooks, best seen from 'Helm Crag' and the double-aspect 'Stone Arthur', while others have panoramas of gardens and green fields. Indulgent spoils keep this place streets ahead of the competition – Farrow & Ball paints, Gilchrist & Soames bath products and fresh Farrers coffee on the breakfast table.

Harwood Hotel (Map p90; ☎ 015394-35248; www .harwoodhotel.co.uk; Red Lion Sq; d £60-80; P) Heart-shaped scatter cushions, floral wallpapers, and a palette of pinks, peaches and creams define this intimate hotel, plum in the centre

of Grasmere village. The (smallish) rooms feature luxurious touches including underfloor heating and 'splash TVs' in the bathrooms, allowing you to watch your favourite soap while you scrub. Room 1 has floor-to-ceiling windows and a private patio, while Room 3 has a shower straight out of *Doctor Who*.

Beck Allans (Map p90; ☎ 015394-35563; www.beck allans.com; College St; d £62-81; P) Plain, unpretentious B&B digs and self-catering apartments in a modern slate house near the village centre. No great surprises in the rooms, but nearly all have grassy garden views and en suite bathrooms (2nd-floor rooms have power showers, and superior rooms have a bit more space).

Banerigg (Map p90; ☎ 015394-35204; www.guest house-cumbria.co.uk; Lake Rd; d from £66; P) The only drawback to staying in central Grasmere is the lack of a lake outlook. Thankfully five out of the six rooms at Banerigg, situated on the village outskirts, boast fine watery views, although you'll just have to try and ignore the main road outside. The owners are full of local knowledge, and there's a cosy fire-lit lounge in case the weather turns sour. A recommended refuge from the Grasmere buzz.

How Foot Lodge (Map p88; ☎ 015394-35366; www .howfoot.co.uk; Town End; d £66-76; P) Wordsworth groupies will adore this stone house just a stroll from William's digs at Dove Cottage. The six rooms are light and contemporary, finished in fawns and beiges; ask for the one with the private sun lounge for that indulgent edge.

GRASMERE & THE CENTRAL LAKE DISTRICT

Riversdale (Map p90; ☎ 015394-35619; www.rivers dalegrasmere.co.uk; White Bridge; d £72-82; P 🛜) Nicely set back on the edge of Grasmere, this three-roomer ticks all the modern B&B boxes: unfussy decor, satellite-equipped LCD TVs, and mini-fridges with fresh milk and bottled water.

White Moss (Map p88; ☎ 015394-35295; www.white moss.com; Rydal Water; d £84-104; P) Owned and run by the congenial Dixons, this welcoming lake-view house feels like a real home away from home. Ticking grandfather clocks, soft sofas and lashings of flowery furnishings might not be everyone's cup of tea, but the country location is hard to quibble with and the breakfast is an absolute beauty – Slacks bacon, Fleetwood kippers, homemade marmalades and hot aga-cooked porridge.

TOP END

our pick **Lancrigg** (Map p88; ☎ 015394-35317; www .lancrigg.co.uk; Easedale; r £140-210; P) Originally the home of Arctic adventurer John Richardson, Lancrigg now touts itself as the Lakes' only 100% vegetarian hotel. All the rooms have individual quirks: Whittington is lodged in the attic and reached via a private staircase, Franklin has Middle Eastern rugs and a four-poster, while Richardson has a plasterwork ceiling and claw-foot bath screened by lace cur-tains. It's half a mile along Easedale Rd down a private track; afternoon tea is often served to passing hikers heading for Helm Crag.

Wordsworth Hotel (Map p90; ☎ 015394-35592; www .grasmere-hotels.co.uk; d £190-270; P ♿ 🛜) The pick of the large chain-owned hotels in central Grasmere offers 30-odd elegantly decked-out rooms (traditional furniture, country-chic furnishings, hefty drapes) and a couple of super suites (oak beams, four-posters, whirl-pool baths). As you'd expect, the service is first-rate, but it feels a tad soulless.

EATING
Cafes & Quick Eats

Heidi's of Grasmere (Map p90; ☎ 015394-35248; Red Lion Sq; lunch mains £3-8; 🕙 9am-5.30pm) Pretty little pine-and-stone cafe tucked in underneath the Harwood Hotel on Red Lion Sq. Chutneys, cakes and deli sandwiches fill the chilled dis-play counter, and there's heaps of hot food on offer too – including a daily home-made soup and the house special 'cheese smokey', served with tomato salsa.

Rowan Tree (Map p90; ☎ 015394-435528; Stock Lane; mains £3-10, pizzas £6-9; 🕙 lunch & dinner) Grasmere's cutest patio is perched above the brook at the back of the Rowan Tree, another sunny cafe-cum-bistro that's especially popular with veggie diners. Lunch is mainly sandwiches, salads and baguettes, with pizzas and pastas taking over after dark.

Miller Howe Cafe (Map p90; ☎ 015394-35234; Red Lion Sq; mains £5-12; 🕙 breakfast & lunch) If Heidi's is too down to earth, try the chrome-tinged Miller Howe across the square for more up-market fare – smoked salmon muffins, toasted sandwiches, generous salads and the best nuttycinos and toffeecinos for miles around.

Restaurants

Villa Colombina (Map p88; ☎ 015394-35268; Townend; lunch mains £4-10, dinner mains £8-16) The old Dove Cottage tearooms have had a refit. Sandwiches, teas, pies and cakes are still served throughout the day, but after dark things turn elegantly Italian, with risottos and rich Italian dishes served in Tuscan-themed surroundings.

Sara's Bistro (Map p90; ☎ 015394-35266; Broadgate; mains £9.95-15.95) Hearty homespun cook-ing is Sara's raison d'être, so you can forget about silver cutlery and snooty service – fresh local produce, unpretentious cooking and generous grub are the only things that matter here. Count on roast chicken breast,

---

SOMETHING FOR THE WEEKEND

Check into the fabulously indulgent **Moss Grove Hotel · Organic** (opposite) and pop out for supper at the **Jumble Room** (opposite). Saturday is all about Wordsworth – start out with **Dove Cottage** (p87), then follow up with the essential companion piece of **Rydal Mount** (p91) and a quick lunch at the **Old School Room Tea Shop** (p91). If the weather is nice, a stroll around Rydal Water and Grasmere Lake is a must-do, followed by afternoon tea at **Heidi's** (above) and supper at the hearty old **Traveller's Rest** (opposite) or **Sara's Bistro** (above). Sunday is reserved for the **Langdale Valley** (opposite), with time set aside for a great pub lunch at the **Britannia Inn (p97)** and a stroll round **Elterwater** (p97). Round things off with a night at the original Lakeland inn, the **Old Dungeon Ghyll Hotel** (p100).

> **SOMEWHERE SPECIAL**
>
> `our pick` **Moss Grove Hotel · Organic** (Map p90; ☎ 015394-35251; www.mossgrove.com; ste depending on season £125-325; P ⊛) Eco-conscious principles and a razor-sharp approach to design combine at one of Grasmere's trendiest hideaways. All 11 rooms dazzle – glossy wood floors, custom fabrics, Bose hi-fis, and magnificently minimal bathrooms with double sinks and underfloor heating – but the environmental credentials are just as crucial as the wow-factor. Water is filtered to remove chlorine and pesticides; wall paints are organic and clay-based; insulation is made from sheep's wool; and beds are crafted from reclaimed wood. Even the buffet breakfast is chock-a-block with fair trade, locally sourced goodness. Hard to fault.

hot goat's cheese soufflé or braised lamb shanks, served in a snug dining room full of down-home charm.

`our pick` **Jumble Room** (Map p90; ☎ 015394-35188; Langdale Rd; mains £13-23; ☺ lunch & dinner Wed-Sun) There's a distinct hint of hippie chic hanging around this well-loved local's bistro off the main square. Moody blues and smoky jazz drifts out from the stereo, and the dining room is a riot of kitsch cushions, country furniture, psychedelic colours and quirky artwork. The same offbeat aesthetic runs into the menu, which gives a fusion spin to old favourites such as game pie, halibut fillet, seafood curry and cullen skink (haddock-and-veg soup). Friendly, fun and fab.

Self-Catering

Self-caterers in Grasmere are limited to a **Co-op** (Map p90; ☎ 015394-35229; Broadgate; ☺ 8.30am-8pm Mon-Sat, 10am-6pm Sun) and the **Croft House Bakery** (Map p90; ☎ 015394-35555; Red Lion Sq), which sells fresh-baked pasties, pastries, cookies and flans, as well as energy-packed fudge, chocolate and cheesecake to keep you fuelled up on the fells.

DRINKING

Traveller's Rest (Map p88; ☎ 015394-35604; on the A591, Grasmere; ☺ noon-11pm Mon-Sat, noon-10.30pm Sun) Nearly all the big village hotels have public bars, but they're decidedly short on charm. For proper pub atmosphere you'll have to head outside the village to the Traveller's Rest, a smashing whitewashed coaching inn hunkering under slate roofs and low ceilings, offering good country nosh (stews, steak pies, pork medallions) and a choice of Jennings beers.

GETTING THERE & AWAY

The main bus for Grasmere is the hourly 555, which takes about 20 minutes to travel north

from Windermere (stopping at Ambleside, Rydal Church and Dove Cottage on the way) and another 20 minutes to complete the journey north to Keswick.

The open-top 599 runs from Grasmere south via Ambleside, Troutbeck Bridge, Windermere and Bowness. There are two or three buses every hour from mid-March to August, but from September onwards the service drops to around 10 daily buses from Monday to Saturday, and around four on Sundays.

LANGDALE VALLEY

Beyond the southern reaches of Silver Howe and Loughrigg Fell stretches the dramatic valley of Langdale, home to some of the Lake District's most majestic peaks.

From Ambleside, the A593 cuts west across the River Brathay at **Skelwith Bridge**, where it splits into two, with one branch leading west into the quiet valley of **Little Langdale** and a second heading northwest past the quiet village of **Elterwater** en route to the panoramic peaks of **Great Langdale**, overlooked by the brooding summits of the Langdale Pikes.

Langdale's name derives from the Old Norse for 'long valley', although the area was settled long before the Vikings arrived. During Neolithic times the area served as a centre for stone quarrying and tool making, and around two-fifths of the Stone Age axes found in Britain are thought to have been fashioned from Langdale stone.

Bus 516 (the Langdale Rambler, six Monday to Saturday, five on Sunday) is the only scheduled bus service to the valley, with stops at Ambleside, Skelwith Bridge, Elterwater, and the Old Dungeon Ghyll Hotel in Great Langdale.

YURTS RULE OK

Your tent's drenched, your sleeping bag's soaked and your guy ropes have gone AWOL. Let's face it – camping in Britain can sometimes be a soggy, saggy and altogether rather dispiriting experience. But tents don't necessarily have to equal torture thanks to **Full Circle** (Map p88; ☎ 07975 671928; www.lake-district-yurts.co.uk; yurts per week £340-410), based at the former stately home of Rydal Hall just outside Grasmere. Forget flyaway tents and squelchy groundsheets – here you'll be nuzzling down in a handmade Mongolian yurt, complete with wooden floors, colourful rugs and even a cast-iron wood-burning stove (free firewood supplied, of course). All the yurts come with a springy double bed and a couple of singles for the kids (furnished with proper mattresses and sheets), and there's even a gas hob complete with all the pots, pans and kitchen paraphernalia you could need. Quite simply, the sexiest, swankiest camping experience you will ever have. Tents are toast – long live the yurt…

SKELWITH BRIDGE

Three miles south of Grasmere, Skelwith Bridge itself is little more than a knot of cottages lined up along the banks of the unruly River Brathay. Since the 19th century this small village has been an important hub for the local slate-quarrying industry, and you can still view examples of local slate craft at the **Kirkstone Slate Gallery** (☎ 015394-33296; ⏰ 9am-5pm Mon-Sat, 10am-4pm Sun).

For most people, the main reason for stopping at Skelwith is to view the **Skelwith Force**, a modest 15ft tumble of water about 10 minutes' walk from the village. This little waterfall inevitably looks more impressive after a bout of heavy rain; for something more spectacular, it might be worth heading instead for **Colwith Force**, which plunges down a series of 40m rock steps about a mile west of the village in the woods of the Tongue Intake Plantation. It's possible to link the two falls together with a circular loop via the lake at Elterwater, a start-to-finish stroll of around 2½ hours; you'll need a decent walking map as the signposts leave a lot to be desired.

If you're in need of sustenance after the stroll, the **Skelwith Bridge Hotel** (☎ 015394-32115; www.skelwithbridgehotel.co.uk; s £45-60, d £80-144; Ⓟ) serves good pub food in the wood-panelled Talbots Bar or four-course meals in its more upmarket bistro-style restaurant. The rather corporate-style bedrooms aren't bad value either, especially if you bag one of the more expensive rooms with an always-welcome jacuzzi bath.

Better still, head for **Chesters Cafe by the River** (☎ 015394-32553; lunch mains £7.50-12; ⏰ 10am-5pm), a sister establishment to the Drunken Duck (p121) and the Punch Bowl Inn (p73), and

run along the same gastro-gourmet lines (think onion-and-gruyère tart rather than steak-and-ale pie). A wood-burning stove ticks away in one corner, while vintage pictures and clocks adorn the walls, and a sextet of French windows swing out onto a grassy river terrace.

LITTLE LANGDALE

Separated from Great Langdale by the summit of Lingmoor Fell (1540ft), the valley of Little Langdale traditionally marks the juncture between the old counties of Cumberland, Westmorland and Lancashire – a point officially marked by the **Three Shire Stone**, plonked near the steep summit of Wrynose Pass. The stone was broken into bits when it was hit by a wayward motorist in 1997; it was restored the following year by a local stonemason thanks to the generous donations of Langdale residents and the National Trust.

The valley is a popular hiking base, with nearby destinations including **Blea Tarn**, **Little Langdale Tarn** and **Lingmoor Fell**. The tortuous climb up to Wrynose and Hardknott Pass (p135) begins to the west of the valley, from where the road drops down again into the former mining valley of Eskdale before dribbling out towards the Cumbrian Coast.

About the only place to stay nearby is the **Three Shires Inn** (☎ 015394-37215; www.threeshires inn.co.uk; Little Langdale; d £76-106; Ⓟ 🛜), a pleasant country inn dating from the late 19th century, originally built to accommodate travellers toing and froing from Wrynose Pass. The 10 rooms are comfy, if a little olde worlde (flowery drapes, 80s tea trays), but nearly all have views of the Tilberthwaite Fells. Ales from Coniston, Hawkshead and

Jennings are on tap in the Slaters Bar, accompanied by generous slabs of game, lamb and mutton in the next-door dining room (mains from £14).

Fell Foot Farm (☎ 015394-37149; www.fellfootfarm .co.uk; s £40-48, d £50-58; **P**), a National Trust–owned farm with Beatrix Potter connections, also has its very own flock of prize-winning Herdwick sheep. The two rooms are farmhouse fresh, although the layouts are a bit quirky – one is en suite, the other has a private bathroom. Brekkie is cooked on an aga using produce straight from the farm, and the rural views are divine (fields, fells and sheep). The farm is about a mile west of the Three Shires Inn.

ELTERWATER

Named by Norse settlers after the colonies of whooper swans that still swoop across its surface every winter, Elterwater (literally, 'swan lake') presents the picture-postcard image of a traditional Lakeland village, with its tree-fringed lake and clump of slate-roofed cottages gathered around a maple-shaded village green. Somewhat bizarrely for such a tranquil spot, Elterwater originally grew up around the industries of slate quarrying, farming and gunpowder manufacture, but these days the main trade is in tourism – only around a quarter of the village houses are occupied year-round, with the rest converted for use as holiday homes.

The quiet country setting is definitely the main draw, although the Britannia Inn (see right) draws its fair share of Sunday lunchers and post-hike punters. If you have time, it's worth making the half-mile trek up to **Chapel Stile**, northwest of the village, where you'll find a collection of quarrymen's cottages constructed from the area's distinctive green slate, and a sturdy mid-19th–century church, notable for its delicate Victorian stained glass.

Sleeping & Eating

Langdale YHA (☎ 0845 371 9748; langdale@yha.org.uk; High Close, Loughrigg; dm from £11.95; ☽ Mar-Oct; **P** 🖳) Halfway between Grasmere and Elterwater, this huge Victorian hostel (officially owned by the National Trust) is a favourite for activity groups, so you'll need to book well ahead. Extensive grounds and period features are the selling points, but the dorms are bog-standard YHA.

Elterwater YHA (☎ 0845 371 9017; elterwater@yha.org .uk; Elterwater; dm from £13.95; ☽ Easter-Oct; ☽ reception 7.30am-10am, 5-10.30pm; 🖳) One of the village's most venerable farmhouses now serves as Elterwater's youth hostel, much favoured by walkers setting out on the Langdale trails. As you'd expect, it's more boarding school than boutique, but the rural location is a treat. Accommodation is in two-, four- or six-bed dorms, and amenities include bike hire, basic kitchen and an evening meal. Parking is very limited.

Eltermere Country House Hotel (☎ 015394-37207; www.eltermere.co.uk; Elterwater; d from £90; **P**) This 18th-century manor is just about the only country hotel in Elterwater, and makes a homely enough base so long as you're not expecting designer lines. Rooms are spacious and vintage – with patterned quilts and wood furniture – and the lake-view restaurant revolves around meaty staples such as haunch of venison and poached bream. There's a private jetty onto the water, and you're welcome to borrow the hotel row boat if you fancy trying to land your own supper.

Brambles Cafe (☎ 015394-37500; Chapel Stile; mains £3-10; ☽ 9am-5pm summer, 9.30am-4pm winter) On the first floor of the Langdale Co-op, this little locals' cafe is well known for its tiffin cake and orange and lemon sponge, but walkers should plump for the Brambles Picnic Pack (butty, salad and cake for £5.50). They'll even refill your Thermos (tea £1.50, coffee £2.50).

Wainwrights' Inn (☎ 015394-38088; Chapel Stile; mains £7.95-10.25) Chapel Stile's only pub is a regular in the good beer guides, and it's no wonder – it's got beam, slate and country charm aplenty, as well as a line-up of local ales and gourmet burgers (our tip's the Wainwrights' burger with bacon and blue cheese).

our pick Britannia Inn (☎ 015394-37210; www .britinn.net; Elterwater; mains £8-16; **P**) This hugger-mugger hiker's inn has been in business for five centuries, and it's still the hub of social activity in Elterwater. The rooms have been redone with fresh fabrics and shiny en suites (doubles from £94 to £114) but, unsurprisingly for such an old establishment, they're on the poky side. Hearty plates of lamb henry, Flookburgh shrimps and Cartmel duck are served in the beamed restaurant, and the front terrace makes a tempting place for a pint or three of Coniston Bluebird (pitch up in mid-November for the pub's very own beer festival).

Langdale Co-op (☎ 015394-37260; Chapel Stile; ☯ 9am-5pm) This local emporium in Chapel Stile was originally founded way back in 1884 to provide goods and groceries to local slate miners; it's still the only place nearby for supplies. Tinned goods, food, and fruit and veg are sold downstairs, while upstairs there is outdoors gear, camping supplies and all manner of hiking hardware.

GREAT LANGDALE

West of Elterwater, the sky opens out and the mountain tops stack up along the horizon as you move ever deeper into the broodily breathtaking valley of Great Langdale, one of the Lake District's most naturally dramatic (and photogenic) spots. Isolated farmsteads, snaking drystone walls and the occasional pocket-sized cottage dot the broad valley floor, while in the far distance rise some of the true giants of the Lakeland fell roster – **Pike O' Blisco** (2313ft), the five summits of the **Crinkle Crags** and the sawtooth chain of summits known as the **Langdale Pikes**: Pike O' Stickle (2326ft), Loft Crag (2270ft), Harrison Stickle (2415ft) and the nearby peak of Pavey Ark (2297ft).

Walking

Unsurprisingly hiking is very much the main attraction in Great Langdale, and it's a notoriously popular spot with Lakeland walkers – during the summer you might well find that all the parking spaces at the two official car parks (at Stickle Ghyll and the Old Dungeon Ghyll Hotel) are full up by 9am, so it's worth setting out as early as possible. Many people prefer to follow in Wainwright's footsteps and clamber aboard the Langdale Rambler bus instead, which trundles up and down the valley three or four times a day during the high season.

On the southern side of the valley, the little road through Great Langdale switchbacks up over Side Pike, passing east of Blea Tarn before dropping back down to the valley floor of Little Langdale (p96).

LANGDALE PIKES

The valley has an almost endless choice of seriously scenic routes for hikers. Several of Wainwright's favourite fells are dotted around the edges of Langdale, and the surrounding summits provide an irresistible attraction for dedicated peak baggers. The arduous circuit around the Langdale Pikes (see p86) is probably the valley's most popular hike, allowing you to tick off between three and five Wainwrights depending on your chosen route.

If you're after something more modest, try the half-hour climb up to the 60m waterfall of **Dungeon Ghyll** from the car park, or the more challenging hour's slog up to the shores of **Stickle Tarn**.

SCAFELL PIKE

We've detailed the classic route up to Scafell Pike from Wasdale on p127, but there's an alternative route up the mountain's western approach from Langdale, ascending via Angle Tarn, Esk Hause and Great End (2984ft), before following the dramatic path between Ill and Broad Crags to the summit. It's a longer proposition than the ascent from Wasdale (count on around 11 miles and seven hours on the mountain), but this route allows you to explore the remote western section of Langdale, and offers stunning views of the surrounding valleys.

CRINKLE CRAGS & BOWFELL

Perhaps the most rewarding Langdale fell walk – among the very best in the park, according to AW – is the trek along the rumpled series of five peaks known as the Crinkle Crags, followed by the ascent of nearby Bowfell. The classic route climbs up via Oxendale and Red Tarn, before winding out over a ridge trail across the jagged 'crinkles', providing a fantastic outlook over the valley. The only real challenge (apart from the steep ascent) is a section of scrambling over the rocky obstacle of the 'Bad Step' – not quite full-blown rock climbing, but still a considerable challenge for many hikers.

Further north beyond the Crinkles looms the distinctive dome-shaped summit of Bowfell (2959ft), from where the trail runs back down to Angle Tarn and Langdale. All told, count on a walk of around 9 miles and six hours depending on your route.

Sleeping & Eating

ourpick Great Langdale Campsite (☎ 015394-37668; langdalecamp@nationaltrust.org.uk; adult £4.50-5.50, child £2-2.50, car £3-3.50, camping pods £20-35, yurts per week £250-410; Ⓟ ⓖ) This gloriously remote National Trust campsite unsurprisingly fills up quickly and is located about a mile up the

ASHLEY COOPER

How did you get involved with mountain rescue? I've been involved with the mountains all my life – ever since I was a young lad. Obviously I've climbed nearly all the hills there are to climb in the Lakes, and I'm a keen mountaineer as well. So it seemed like a natural step for me to get involved in the hills in some kind of professional capacity. It gives me plenty of opportunity to spend time doing what I love, as well as helping people who are in trouble.

Unlike many other parts of the world, mountain rescue teams in the Lake District are composed entirely of volunteers. That's right – the Lake District is unusual in that sense. It's a tradition that can be traced back to the very early days of hill walking, when local farmers and villagers often banded together to search for people who disappeared out on the fells. There's also an obvious difference between most of the Lakeland fells and somewhere like the Alps, where there's a clear need for a full-time, professional mountain rescue team thanks to the year-round season. But just because we're not full-time doesn't mean we're not professionals – all our members are fully qualified and are required to train at least two or three times a week. And despite the relatively low altitude of the fells, we're still kept remarkably busy – we respond to around 100 to 110 call outs every year, of which, sadly, around 10% are fatalities.

Why do you think the Lake District still has such a special place in the hearts of British hikers? It's just a unique landscape. There's nowhere else in the world like it. Canada, the US and Europe may have bigger mountains, but they're just not the same as the Lakeland fells. In many ways, this is the birthplace of British hiking, and I think people still value that sense of tradition and history. It's also really accessible – we're within an hour's drive of most of the major northern conurbations, and most of the fells can be tackled by toddlers and grannies alike. You don't have to be Joe Simpson or Chris Bonington to have an exhilarating day out.

What are the main difficulties people get into out on the fells? Basically, the number one problem is people not being prepared. The weather changes so fast in the Lake District – hot sun can turn to thick cloud in the click of your fingers, so it's absolutely vital that you have the proper equipment and know how to use it. People getting lost on the trail is obviously a very common problem, and we also quite often get called out to cases of exposure and exhaustion, or common injuries such as sprained ankles or limb breaks. But we've had some really strange call outs over the years too – one of the weirdest was trying to coax down a crag-fast sheep.

What does the future hold for mountain rescue in the Lakes? Obviously we're a volunteer service funded by charitable donations, so money is always an issue. But to be honest one of the major problems we face is getting young people involved with the service. It's very definitely a young person's game, this, but thanks to the huge rise in second homes and the massive growth in house prices over the last decade, it's really difficult for young local people to be able to afford to live and work in the area. That has very real consequences not just for the local community, but for vital services such as our mountain rescue team, too.

Ashley Cooper is the team chairman of the Langdale and Ambleside Mountain Rescue Team

valley from the Old Dungeon Ghyll Hotel. Facilities include a small shop and laundry (£3 per load) and a wheelchair-friendly loo, and upmarket campers can choose between either a luxurious Mongolian yurt, complete with wood-burning stove and Moroccan rugs, or a wooden 'camping pod', with its own lockable front door and super-cosy sheep-wool insulation.

Baysbrown Farm Campsite (☎ 015394-37300; sites from £8) Simple but undeniably stunning campsite on an 320-hectare Herdwick sheep farm offering wonderful views of the Pikes, Bowfell and Crinkle Crags.

Stickle Barn (☎ 015394-37356; Great Langdale; dm £10-12) If the campsites are full, the bunkhouse at the Stickle Barn is a useful fall back (as always, you'll need your own sleeping bag and camping supplies). Breakfast is served at the main inn, which doubles as a lively posthike hangout. There are local ales on draught and a hearty menu of casseroles, stews and curries to warm those weary bones (mains £5 to £10).

Old Dungeon Ghyll Hotel (☎ 015394-37272; www
.odg.co.uk; d £100-110; P) Lakeland hotels don't
come any more classic than the ODG, still the
getaway of choice for many a devoted hiker.
Huddled under rocky fells, with jaw-dropping
views unfurling from every window, it's a
hotchpotch of old-fashioned charm. Old oak
beams, sputtering fires, chintzy wallpapers and
scruffy armchairs to sink into, with a choice of
shared or en suite rooms (some with rickety
brass bedsteads, others fancy four-posters).
Downstairs, hikers congregate in the Walkers'
Bar to swap tall tales and Lakeland ales.

New Dungeon Ghyll Hotel (☎ 015394-37213; www
.dungeon-ghyll.co.uk; d £108-120; P) Next door to
the ODG, this slate hotel feels more up to
date than its well-worn neighbour, although
it's still a long way from luxury. Cream walls
and country patterns define the rooms, and
there's good pub food in the bar (mains £9 to
£14) or more sophisticated meals in the sit-
down restaurant (set menu £27.50).

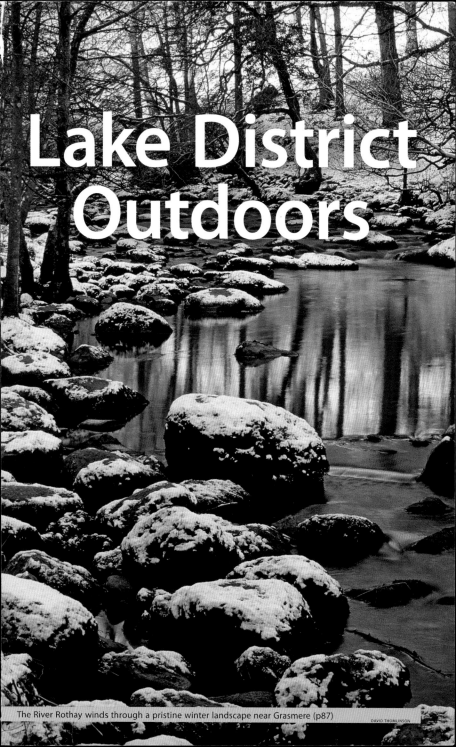

Lake District Outdoors

The River Rothay winds through a pristine winter landscape near Grasmere (p87)

DAVID THOMLINSON

HIKING

If there's one activity that sums up the spirit of the Lake District, it's hiking. Ever since the Romantics first strode out across the fells in the early 19th century, millions of visitors have been flocking to the Lakes every year to indulge in a spot of high-level walking. The Lake District has some of the most stunning mountain scenery anywhere in England – perhaps not quite on an Alpine scale, but darn impressive nonetheless. There are walks to suit every age and ability, ranging from relaxed valley rambles to full-blown multi-peak circuits (dubbed 'horseshoes' or 'rounds' in this part of the world). Even on a short walk, you'll be treated to some of England's most unforgettable scenery, from tinkling streams and forest-fringed lakes to thundering waterfalls and razor-blade crags. Arguably the most spectacular peaks are Scafell Pike (p127), England's highest summit, and Helvellyn (p165) with its famous ridge walk via Striding Edge.

We've included a selection of our favourite walks throughout this guide, ranging from easy to challenging, but there are enough routes in the county to fill several lifetimes of walking. Long-distance trails include the 190-mile **Coast-to-Coast Walk** (www.coast2coast.co.uk)

WAINWRIGHT'S FAVOURITE FELLS

In his seventh and last *Pictorial Guide*, Alfred Wainwright chose his top six fells based on a complex system that included height, views, difficulty, steepness and general good looks. The fells he picked were Scafell Pike (3209ft), Bowfell (2959ft), Pillar (2926ft), Great Gable (2949ft), Blencathra (2848ft) and the Crinkle Crags, with special favour also given to the Langdale Pikes and, of course, Haystacks, where his ashes were finally scattered.

Wainwright's final place of rest: Innominate Tarn nestled on the slopes of Haystacks (p163)

MICHAEL ARTHUR THOMPSON/ALA

from St Bees to Robin Hood's Bay devised by none other than Alfred Wainwright, the 84-mile **Dales Way** (www.dalesway.org.uk) from Ilkley in Yorkshire to Windermere and the 70-mile **Cumbria Way** (www.thecumbriaway .info) from Ulverston to Carlisle. Other options include the Allerdale Ramble (54 miles) via Borrowdale, Keswick, Skiddaw, Cockermouth and the Solway Firth, and the Cumbria Coastal Way (150 miles) from Silverdale to the Scottish border. There are also annual walking festivals in Ullswater, Coniston and Ulverston.

BOATING

Any national park that goes by the name of the Lake District is likely to have one or two watery activities on offer. Top of the aquatic list here in Cumbria has to be a lake cruise, which is tantamount to a Lakeland rite of passage for any tourist: you can make an excursion to the shores and islands of Windermere, hop on and off the hikers' launch around Derwent Water, steam over Ullswater or jump aboard a solar-powered launch on Coniston Water.

Since the introduction of 10mph speed limits on four of the lakes, waterskiing and power-boating are pretty much off-limits, but that doesn't mean there aren't other ways to get your feet wet. Canoes, kayaks, dinghies and sailing boats are available from the marinas at Low Wood on Windermere (p63), Nichol End (p149) and Platty+ (p160) on Derwent Water, the Glenridding Sailing Centre on Ullswater (p172), and by the ferry jetty on Coniston Water (p115), while row boats can be hired on Windermere, Grasmere Lake and Derwent Water.

Handy with an oar? Windermere awaits (p63)
DAVID ELSE

Swimming might look tempting, but you might think twice once you've tested the water, which remains icy-cold in many of the lakes for much of the year. Some lakes are off-limits to bathers since they're water reservoirs; contact the National Parks Association (NPA) before diving in.

PEAK BAGGING

Everyone knows the English have an obsessive habit for collecting things, but there are few more obsessive pastimes than the sport of peak bagging. Alfred Wainwright listed 214 official fells over 1000ft in his *Pictorial Guides*, and dedicated peak baggers set out to conquer every single one, registering their success with the Wainwright Society, which holds an official register of all its members who have completed the 214-fell circuit.

Once finished, peak baggers will have covered a total distance of around 391 miles and around 121,900ft of ascent. Many people take an entire lifetime to complete all the summits (Wainwright himself required 14 years), but somewhat unbelievably, in 1986 the veteran fell runner Joss Naylor completed all the official Wainwright fells in a total time of seven days, one hour and 25 minutes – a record that remains unbeaten to this day. The youngest ever person to complete all 214 fells is Tom Fryers, who completed the round at the tender age of just six years and four months in August, 2008.

CLIMBING & SCRAMBLING

The Lake District's plentiful peaks and craggy faces are an irresistible magnet for rock climbers, and there are certainly few more spectacular places to test your mountaineering mettle. Classic ascents up Dow Crag, Gimmer, Esk Buttress or Broad Stand have been a proving ground for budding rock-bunnies for decades, and many Lakeland climbers have gone on to scale some of the globe's most challenging mountains (notably Sir Chris Bonington, perhaps Britain's best-known mountaineer and a long-time resident of Caldbeck). A less extreme version of the sport is scrambling, pitched somewhere between a strenuous hike and a full-blown rock climb; it might be worth getting some practice in on the climbing walls in Keswick (p149) and Kendal before you tackle the real thing.

CYCLING

If you prefer seeing the countryside from the (relative) comfort of the saddle, Cumbria has some fantastic cycling, although, let's be honest, in this neck of the woods you're not going to get away without tackling the odd hill or six. There are dedicated mountain-bike parks at Grizedale Forest (p122) and Whinlatter Forest Park (p156), and endless bridleways, quiet roads and back lanes to explore around the rest of the national park. The comprehensive website www.cyclingincumbria.co.uk has suggestions for routes whether you're a family

Almost there... A climber tackles Pavey Ark (p86) high above the obsidian expanse of Stickle Tarn

ASHLEY COOPER/ALA

Stopping for a breather: a group of cyclists enjoy the views from Ashley Bridge near Keswick (p145)
INGOLF POMPE 28/ALAMY

cyclist or a hardcore downhiller; mountain bikers should check out www.mountain-bike
-cumbria.co.uk. Tourist offices and bike shops can help with other route ideas, and we've
detailed our own rides in the individual chapters.

If you're after a long-distance spin, there's the **Sea to Sea Cycle Route** (C2C; www.c2c-guide.co.uk)
from Whitehaven or Workington to Sunderland or Tynemouth, or if you're feeling super-
man fit you could enter the Helvellyn Triathlon in September or the 112-mile Fred Whitton
Challenge, taking in six (count 'em) of the Lake District's highest passes.

TEST YOUR METTLE

Hiking and biking too humdrum? Don't fret – there are endless other ways to risk your neck in
pursuit of the next adrenaline rush.

Petrol heads could try some off-road driving with **Kankku** (☎ 015394-47414; www.kankku.co.uk;
Windermere) or quad biking at the **Holmescales Activity Centre** (☎ 01539-722147; www.holmescales
.com; Old Hutton, Kendal), but for real daredevils, soaring through the air on a glorified kite provides
the ultimate high. Look out for the colourful canopies of local paragliders and hang-gliders wheel-
ing around the summits in summer; if you fancy having a go, contact the **Cumbria Soaring Club**
(www.cumbriasoaringclub.co.uk), which also organises the new X-Lakes challenge, a 44-mile run-cum-
paraglide race held in July.

If you'd rather get your kicks closer to the ground, a network of zip wires and rope bridges
swing through the trees at the Go Ape parks in Grizedale (p122) and Whinlatter (p156), while the
UK's first Via Ferrata traverses the cliff tops at the Honister Slate Mine (p163) using a system of
fixed ropes and ladders (vertigo sufferers need not apply).

But for traditionalists there's really only one extreme sport worth its salt in the Lakes, and that's
fell running, in which competitors run pell-mell up and down a predetermined set of fells in an
attempt to record the quickest time. There are lots of different races, but the toughest has to
be the Bob Graham Round, which involves conquering 42 peaks (yes, 42) in under 24 hours. For
details of this insane activity contact the **Fell Runner's Association** (www.fellrunner.org.uk) or check
out the boxed text on p161.

There are lots more ideas for adrenaline-driven activities at www.lakedistrictoutdoors.co.uk.

NATURAL ATTRACTIONS

Nowhere in England is more renowned for its natural wonders than the Lake District, and with good reason. The national park packs an astonishing variety of landscapes into a relatively tiny space, and a single day's journey can carry you through varied vistas of forest, valley, lake, mountain and moor. Up on the fell tops, hardy sheep roam the heaths, while down in the valleys, ancient drystone walls divide a chequerboard of fields, pastures and meadows. Standout scenic valleys include Grasmere, Great and Little Langdale, Buttermere and Borrowdale, and the Duddon Valley.

The Lake District is one of the most forested corners of England, and the plentiful rainfall and sheltered valleys favour a wide variety of plant species, making the region an ideal location for Victorian landscape gardeners. Muncaster Castle (p130) is renowned for its rhododendron collection (one of Europe's oldest), while hydrangeas and ferns take centre stage at Holehird (p75), completely over-the-top topiary fills the grounds of Levens Hall (p214), and roses and flowering shrubs ripple with colour around Dalemain

> 'The national park packs a variety of landscapes into a relatively tiny space'

(p167). But for our money you can't top the landscaped splendours of Holker Hall (p183), Fell Foot Park (p71) and John Ruskin's gardens at Brantwood (p112).

Obviously the lakes themselves are another highlight. Everyone has their favourite: Wast Water (p137) for wildness, Derwent Water (p147) and Coniston Water (p114) for views, Bassenthwaite (p153) for wildlife, and Ullswater (p167) and Windermere (p63) for all-round scenic grandeur. It's also certainly worth seeking out the lesser-known lakes, especially if you're averse to crowds. Ennerdale (p139), for instance, has a serene splendour of its own, while Haweswater (p175) is one of the least accessible of all the lakes.

And don't forget about the park's mountain pools – Easedale Tarn (p92), Stickle Tarn (p86), Tarn Hows (p121) and Blea Tarn (p96) are all worth visiting in their own right, and there are hundreds more to discover.

Pause to reflect: craggy Langdale Pike (p86) peaks above, mirror-still Blea Tarn (p96) below

DAVID THOMLIN

A blaze of autumn colour frames Stock Ghyll Force
DAVID THOMLINSON

top five
LAKELAND WATERFALLS

Aira Force (p170)

Dungeon Ghyll (p98)

Stock Ghyll Force (p77)

Stanley Ghyll Force (p134)

Taylor Ghyll Force (p162)

The mainstay of Cumbrian hill farmers for generations: Herdwicks in the valley of Buttermere (p160)

SHANNON BRUCE N/

WILDLIFE SPOTTING

Along with the Lake District's two million sheep, you might be lucky enough to spot some other furred and feathered beasties around the national park. The most exciting residents are undoubtedly the ospreys at Bassenthwaite Lake (p153), the first-known pair to breed in England for over 150 years. Two viewpoints have been established around the lake, with live webcams at the Whinlatter Visitor Centre.

You'll be even more fortunate to spot England's sole remaining golden eagle at Haweswater (p176). Birds have been nesting here since the 1970s, but no fledglings have been reared since the mid-1990s. For more reliable aerial displays, head for the Lakeland Birds of Prey Centre (p175), the World Owl Centre at Muncaster Castle (p132), or the bird-rich coastal areas around Morecambe Bay (p182) and St Bees Head (p191).

Red squirrels are another elusive resident of the Lake District; there's no telling where

> 'For aerial displays head for the Birds of Prey Centre or the World Owl Centre'

you might spot them, although Dodd Wood, Ennerdale Forest and the shores of Derwent Water and Ullswater seem to be frequent hangouts. For a guaranteed sighting, head for the visitor centre at Whinlatter (p156), which has recently installed 'squirrel cams' at various dreys around the forest.

For more exotic beasties, the South Lakes Wild Animal Park (p188) is your best bet – lions, macaques, wallabies, baboons, lemurs, rhinos, spectacled bears and two types of tiger roam across the park, situated near Ulverston on the Cumbrian coast.

Coniston, Hawkshead & Around

She might not have the stature of Windermere or the comeliness of Derwent Water, but compared to her sister lakes Coniston Water somehow manages to retain an air of unruffled serenity even on the busiest of days. Stretching for five glassy miles and overlooked by the sombre granite stack known as the Old Man, the lake is still famous for the world-record speed attempts made here by Malcolm and Donald Campbell between the 1930s and 1960s. These days it's an altogether more tranquil place, and the only boats you'll see skimming across its surface are the solar-powered Coniston Launches and the puffing steam yacht *Gondola*, which glide out across the lake to John Ruskin's former home at Brantwood.

Out to the east, mountain bikers, walkers and art lovers congregate along the shady trails of Grizedale Forest, while a little to the north is the pretty whitewashed village of Hawkshead, where a young Willie Wordsworth received his elementary education. But if you can face the crowds, there's no doubting the top draw in this corner of the Lakes – the idyllic farmhouse of Hill Top in the village of Near Sawrey, where Beatrix Potter famously put pen to paper and dreamt up her anthropomorphic tales of mischievous kittens, house-proud hedgehogs and light-pawed bunny rabbits.

CONISTON, HAWKSHEAD & AROUND

HIGHLIGHTS

- Trace Beatrix Potter's biography at **Hill Top** (p123)
- Explore the outlandish outdoor artworks of **Grizedale Forest** (p122)
- Cruise a stretch of **Coniston Water** (p114) in a steam yacht or solar-powered launch
- Indulge in microbrewed beer and modern gastro-cooking at the **Drunken Duck** (p121)
- Keep your eyes peeled for Squirrel Nutkin around the shores of **Tarn Hows** (p121)
- Sit at William Wordsworth's very own desk at the **Hawkshead Grammar School** (p118)
- Browse around John Ruskin's elegant lakeside retreat at **Brantwood** (p112)

- Area of largest lake (Coniston Water): 1.84 sq miles
- Visitors to Grizedale Forest in 2007: 231,500
- Official number of tales penned by Beatrix Potter: 23

ITINERARY 1
CONQUERING THE OLD MAN WALK   6.5 miles/3 to 4 hours/Coniston

Hunkering above Coniston like a benevolent giant, the Old Man (2276ft) presents an irresistible challenge for hikers. There are endless ways to attack the summit – we've chosen a moderate route (although you'll still be tackling some steep ascents).

The trail starts beside Coniston's **Black Bull Inn** and heads uphill past the disused railway station to a drystone wall at the end of the paved road. Where the tarmac ends, the **Walna Scar Rd** continues across the open fell-side. Continue west along the trail past the small reed-covered pond of **Boo Tarn**, where a zigzagging path leads north to the summit via Bursting Stone Quarry. Carry on west instead, across the fell for another mile or so, until you reach a right-hand fork that leads north past the scree slopes of **Dow Crag** to **Goat's Water**.

Take a break at the tarn and fuel up – the climb up to **Goat's Hawse** is steep and can be slippery, so take things slow. Ascend via the east side of the lake and when you reach the saddle you'll need to turn sharp right; the hump of the Old Man is clearly visible to the southeast.

After the slog up Goat's Hawse, the final hike up Old Man feels like a breeze; at the top you'll be rewarded with a 360-degree panorama east over Coniston Water, north to the Langdale Pikes, northwest to the Scafell Range and west to Dow Crag.

From the summit you should be able to see a zigzag trail tracking down the peak's northern side. Follow the path down to the shores of **Low Water**, and then east past the old copper mines and stone works beneath **Colt Crag**. Continue along the old quarry road, and at the next junction take the left-hand fork, which skirts the banks of **Levers Water Beck** and **Church Beck** down to Coniston. If you have time, just before the junction turn-off a side trail leads north into the rock-strewn area known as Boulder Valley, with its famous 25ft-high 'Pudding Stone'; climbing this huge lump of rock is probably best left for experienced rock-bunnies.

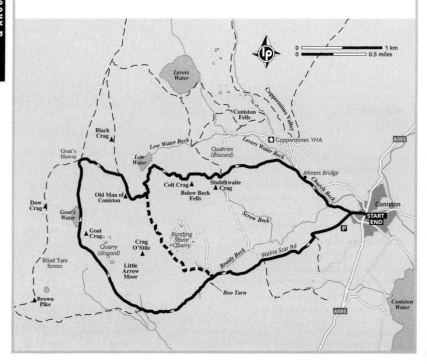

ITINERARY 2
CLAIFE HEIGHTS CYCLE　　　　　　　　　　　　　13 miles/3 hours/Hawkshead

This easy-to-moderate cycle route visits the west shore of Esthwaite Water, the wooded slopes of Claife Heights and the western banks of Windermere, with a couple of Beatrix Potter sights thrown in to break up the journey. It takes in several off-road and forest sections – nothing too tough, and well within the capabilities of even novice cyclists, but probably not something you'd want to tackle on a road rig.

The route starts in **Hawkshead** (p118) and follows the minor road south along the west side of **Esthwaite Water** (p120) into **Ridding Wood**. Pause for a breather at the car park at the southern end of the lake, then veer along the left-hand turn up to **Near Sawrey** (p123) where you can stop off for a look around Beatrix Potter's house at **Hill Top** (p123) if the crowds aren't too big, or have a hearty lunch at the delightful **Tower Bank Arms** (p124).

Once you've explored Near Sawrey, follow the road downhill through **Far Sawrey** (p123) to **Ferry House**, where the Cross-Lakes Ferry docks for Windermere. Just before the ferry landing, there's a little left-hand road leading north to the Station Scar car park, where you can hook up with a public bridleway that winds all the way along the wooded west side of Windermere to another car park near **Belle Grange Bay**. Be aware that the wooded section here can be *very* muddy in wet weather – if it's been raining heavily you might well have to hop off and walk through some of the worst sections. Despite the terrain, this is a gorgeous route to cycle, passing through gentle woodland and quiet glades.

After around 2.5 miles of pedalling, you'll reach **Red Nab**, where the path turns back into tarmac and joins up with the minor road past the hamlet of **High Wray**, skirting the west side of **Latterbarrow** en route to the **Colthouse Plantation**. Turn right at the next fork in the road and journey back into Hawkshead.

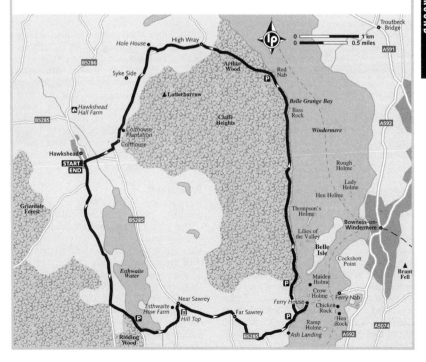

CONISTON

pop 1948

Hunched beneath the slate-domed summit of the Old Man of Coniston (2276ft), the workaday town of Coniston originally grew up as a booming centre for the local copper-mining industry, but nowadays the only obvious reminders of the town's industrial heyday are the abandoned quarries and mineshafts littering the surrounding hilltops. Modern-day Coniston revolves almost exclusively around the tourist trade, and while the town isn't the most immediately arresting in the Lakes, it makes a pleasant enough base for exploring the attractions of Grizedale, Hawkshead and the surrounding area.

HISTORY

Copper and slate have both been mined in Coniston since at least the Bronze Age, but it wasn't until the mid-17th century that the industry really kicked into full swing, when large numbers of German miners arrived in the area to exploit the rich mineral deposits (and to inadvertently introduce a tradition for making long sausages, which still endures in Cumbria to this day).

As ever, it was the uber-industrious Victorians who really maximised the potential of the local mining industry. A branch line was pushed through to Coniston from Furness in 1859 to speed up the transport of slate and ore to the west-coast ports, and terraced houses and ordered shop-fronts sprang up along Coniston's main street to cater for the mine employees. Unfortunately the arrival of the railway also coincided with a global crash in copper and mineral prices in the mid-1860s, leading to a widespread financial crisis that contributed directly to the closure of many of Britain's mineral mines – perhaps a blessing in disguise, since the rich seams of Coniston copper were already showing signs of drying up by the mid-19th century. Fortunately the new tourist trade stepped in to plug the gap, and like many other Lakeland towns Coniston switched its focus to catering for the influx of visitors who arrived to take a cruise across Coniston Water or to conquer the summit of the Old Man (both still must-do items for any self-respecting tripper).

INFORMATION

Barclays (Bridge End; 9am-4pm Mon, Wed, Fri) Coniston's only bank (bizarrely) has no ATM, but there are fee-charging Link machines at the post office and petrol station.

Coniston Tourist Office (☎ 015394-41533; www .conistontic.org; Ruskin Ave; 9.30am-5.30pm Easter-Oct, till 4pm Nov-Mar;) This super-efficient information centre (run entirely by local staff) sells walking leaflets (£1) and the Coniston Loyalty Card (£2), which offers local discounts. There's wi-fi for a small donation.

Hollands Cafe (☎ 015394-41303; Tilberthwaite Ave; internet per 15 min/hr £1/4; 9am-5pm Mon-Fri, 8am-5pm Sat & Sun)

Post office (Yewdale Rd; 9am-5.30pm Mon-Fri, 9am-12.30pm Sat)

SIGHTS
Ruskin Museum

Coniston's quirky little town **museum** (Map p116; ☎ 015394-41164; www.ruskinmuseum.com; Yewdale Rd; adult/child £4.25/2; 10am-5.30pm Easter–mid-Nov, 10.30am-3.30pm Wed-Sun mid-Nov–Easter) is a treasure trove for Lakeland history buffs. Founded at the turn of the century by Ruskin's long-time compatriot and amanuensis WG Collingwood, the museum houses displays of prehistoric and Bronze Age artefacts, and provides plenty of background on copper mining, drystone walling, sheep farming and local crafts such as linen and lace making. There's also an extensive section on John Ruskin, with displays of his writings, watercolours and sketchbooks. At the time of writing a new extension to the museum was being built to house Donald Campbell's *Bluebird* boat, following its painstaking restoration (see boxed text, p114). In the meantime you can view the boat's tail fin and air-intake, as well as a comprehensive archive exploring the Campbell story.

Brantwood

John Ruskin (1819–1900), the Victorian polymath, philosopher and critic, was one of the great thinkers of 19th-century society, expounding views on everything from Venetian architecture to the finer points of shell collecting and lace making. In 1871 he purchased **Brantwood** (Map p113; ☎ 015394-41396; www.brantwood.org.uk; adult/5-15yr £5.95/1.20, gardens only £4/1.20; 11am-5.30pm mid-Mar–mid-Nov, 11am-4.30pm Wed-Sun mid-Nov–mid-Mar) and spent the next 20 years expanding and modifying the house and grounds, championing his concept of 'organic architecture' and the value

CONISTON, HAWKSHEAD & AROUND

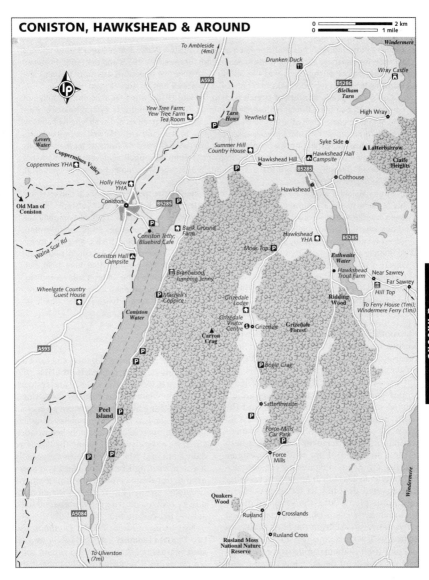

of traditional Arts and Crafts over soulless factory-made materials.

The result is a monument to Ruskin's aesthetic principles: every inch of the house, from the handmade furniture through to the formal gardens, was designed according to his painstaking instructions (he even dreamt up some of the wallpaper designs).

Highlights include the grand but surprisingly cosy drawing room and Ruskin's tome-filled study, both with wonderful views over Coniston Water, and the little upstairs bedroom decorated with some of Ruskin's favourite watercolours (mostly by JMW Turner, a favourite artist of Ruskin's, but sadly not the originals). In the corner of

---

THE CAMPBELL STORY

With its puttering launches and tree-lined shores, Coniston Water seems like a rather unlikely location for smashing a string of world speed records. Between the 1930s and the 1960s, however, this quiet corner of the Lakes was the setting for a series of audacious attempts to break the world water-speed record thanks to Sir Malcolm Campbell and his son, Donald.

Coniston's speed connections stretch back to the late 1930s, when Sir Malcolm – plainly not content with being a national motorcycle champion, Grand Prix motor racer and holder of nine land-speed records – chose the lake to try to regain the water-speed record, which he had already broken three times (on Lake Geneva, Lake Maggiore in Italy and Lake Halwell in Switzerland). On 19 August 1939, piloting the revolutionary powerboat *Bluebird K4* (with its jet-fuelled Rolls Royce engine and unique three-point hydroplane design), Campbell achieved a phenomenal speed of 141.74mph – a record that was still intact a decade later, when he died peacefully at home in Surrey in 1948.

But Sir Malcolm wasn't the only Campbell to be bitten by the speed bug. Donald had watched his father's speed attempts as a young boy and decided to follow in his footsteps. Having been honourably discharged from the RAF during WWII due to illness, Donald Campbell set about redesigning the original K4 powerboat to mount his own challenges on the world water-speed record, spurred on by the news that other racers were building their own crafts to try to snatch away his father's title. The record was finally broken by the American pilot Stan Sayers, who achieved a new speed of 160.32mph in his boat *Slo-mo-shun IV* in June 1950, but Campbell's own ambitions suffered a serious setback in 1951 when the K4 hit a submerged log at around 160mph and promptly sank. Undeterred, Donald commissioned a new version of the boat (renamed the *Bluebird K7*), and went on to break Sayers' record twice in 1955, firstly at

---

the room is the little circular turret where Ruskin whiled away many hours watching the waters of the lake and pondering the great issues of the day.

Outside the house, 100 hectares of landscaped gardens and formal terraces are arranged over the mountainside behind the main house (*brant* derives from the Old Norse for steep). Among Brantwood's botanical havens are the Hortus Inclusus, a herb garden modelled along medieval designs, and the Zig-Zaggy, inspired by the purgatorial mount in Dante's *Inferno*. Several other gardens are devoted to ferns, moorland, mountain plants and the delights of the Victorian herbaceous border. By far the best views, however, are from the High Walk, designed by Ruskin's cousin Joan Severn.

Brantwood is about 3 miles from Coniston on the east side of the lake; follow the B5285 east of town and look out for signs to the property. A more stylish way to arrive is aboard one of the Coniston cruise boats (right), which dock along the lake's shoreline below the main house. While you're waiting for the next connection, piping hot soups, cream teas and steak pies are served at the **Jumping Jenny** (☎ 015394-41715; lunches £4-8), housed in Ruskin's former coach house.

ACTIVITIES
Boat Trips

For a dash of Victorian elegance, you can't top the puffing steam yacht **Gondola** (☎ 015394-63850; adult/5-15yr £6.50/3.30), built in 1859 and restored to its former glory in the 1980s by the National Trust. Looking like a cross between a Venetian vaporetto and an English houseboat, complete with cushioned saloons and polished wooden seats, it's a stately way of seeing the lake (five daily from mid-March to October), especially if you're visiting Brantwood. And you don't need to fret about carbon emissions from the *Gondola*'s steam-plume; she's switched from mucky coal to eco-friendly waste-wood logs, cutting her carbon footprint by 90%.

Not to be outdone by the *Gondola*, the two **Coniston Launches** (☎ 015394-36216; www.conistonlaunch.co.uk) were converted to run on solar panels in 2005, making them just about the greenest ferries in England. The Northern service (adult/child return £6.20/3.10) calls at the Waterhead Hotel, Torver and Brantwood, while the Southern service (adult/child return £8.60/4.80) sails to the jetties at Torver, Water Park, Lake Bank, Sunny Bank and Brantwood via Peel Island. You can break your journey and walk to the next jetty – trail leaflets are sold on board for £1.80.

Ullswater with a new record of 202.32mph, followed by another record speed of 216.1mph at Lake Mead in the United States. Campbell broke the record four more times between 1956 and 1959 – this time on home water at Coniston, just as his father had done over a decade earlier – and again at Lake Dumbleyung in Western Australia in 1964, where he set a new water-speed record of 276.3mph, having already achieved the fastest ever speed achieved on land (403.1mph) just a year before.

Sadly, the Campbell story was to end in tragedy during another speed attempt at Coniston on 4 January 1967. Having already clocked a speed of 297mph, Donald decided to make another attempt on the record without allowing sufficient time for the wake from his previous run to subside. Near the end of her return run, at a speed of around 328mph, the *Bluebird*'s bow rose out of the water, flipped and struck the lake nose-first, killing Donald instantly. Thirty seconds later the boat had sunk without trace.

But the *Bluebird* story doesn't end there. Controversially the remains of the boat and its pilot were recovered from the bottom of the lake in March 2001, where they had lain undisturbed since the day of the fatal crash. Campbell finally received his long-awaited burial at the village church of **St Andrew's** (Map p116), and various parts of the boat were donated to the **Ruskin Museum** (p112) for display to the general public. In 2007 a local engineer and wreck diver, Bill Smith, announced an ambitious plan to restore the boat to its full (working) glory, and although the project has received the blessing of Campbell's own daughter, Gina, it has met with considerable opposition from many quarters. Eventually it's hoped the boat will be housed at the new purpose-built extension at the Ruskin Museum; you can find out all the latest news at the restoration project's website www.thebluebirdproject.com.

Arthur Ransome based parts of his most famous tale around Coniston Water – Peel Island, towards the southern end of Coniston Water, doubles in the book as 'Wild Cat Island', while the steam yacht *Gondola* allegedly gave Ransome the idea for Captain Flint's houseboat. The Coniston Launch runs a special tour (adult/child £9/5.50, 12.35pm Wednesday from mid-March to October) exploring sights from *Swallows and Amazons*, and another (adult/child £8/5, 1pm Tuesday from mid-March to October) detailing the history of the Campbells on Coniston.

For self-propelled exploration, the **Coniston Boating Centre** (Map p113; ☎ 015394-41366; Coniston Jetty) hires out row boats (£9 per hour for up to six people), Canadian canoes (£12 per hour) and electric motor boats (£18 per hour), plus wayfarers and toppers (£18 to £35 for two hours) for experienced sailors.

SLEEPING
Budget

Coniston Hall Campsite (Map p113; ☎ 015394-41223; sites for 2 adults & car £13; ✆ Easter-Oct) The only campsite within striking distance of Coniston is about a mile south of town, just off the A593. The site is spread out over 12-odd hec-

tares along the lakeside, with plenty of decent showers, an on-site laundry and a modest shop, but finding some peak-time summer space can be a challenge.

Coppermines YHA (Map p113; ☎ 0870 770 5772; dm £13.95; ✆ reception 7-11am & 5-10pm Easter-Oct) Hostels don't get much more remote than this former mine manager's cottage, hidden away in the hilltops 2 miles from Coniston on the way to the Old Man. The mountain views and tranquil location are superb, but the accommodation is on the rustic side, with clunky showers, a battered old kitchen, and bunks in three four-bed dorms and two larger dorms. The hostel is reached via a partly unsealed road that starts off Yewdale Rd just past the Black Bull Inn. Take extra care if you're driving, especially when it's wet.

Holly How YHA (Map p113; ☎ 0845 371 9511; conistonhh@yha.org.uk; Far End; dm £15.95; ✆ reception 7.30-10am & 5-10pm) Another fine gabled house turned smart YHA, along the road to Ambleside. The communal areas are particularly posh, and include a lovely lounge (with original plasterwork ceiling) and a bright, sunny cafe serving evening meals; the dorms, however, are rather bland. It's a school-trip and activity-group stalwart, so book ahead.

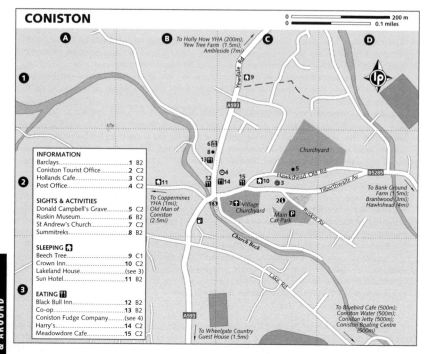

CONISTON

0   200 m
0   0.1 miles

INFORMATION
Barclays.................................1 B2
Coniston Tourist Office.............2 C2
Hollands Cafe.........................3 C2
Post Office.............................4 C2

SIGHTS & ACTIVITIES
Donald Campbell's Grave..........5 C2
Ruskin Museum.......................6 B2
St Andrew's Church.................7 C2
Summitreks............................8 B2

SLEEPING
Beech Tree............................9 C1
Crown Inn.............................10 C2
Lakeland House....................(see 3)
Sun Hotel.............................11 B2

EATING
Black Bull Inn.......................12 B2
Co-op..................................13 B2
Coniston Fudge Company......(see 4)
Harry's................................14 C2
Meadowore Cafe..................15 C2

Midrange

Lakeland House (Map p116; ☎ 015394-41303; Tilberthwaite Ave; s £35-40, d £60-70) Perched above Hollands Cafe, this no-nonsense B&B places the emphasis on function rather than form. The en suite rooms are clean but spartan – a bed, tea tray and shower is about all you'll get – but it's cheap and right in the heart of the village. Don't forget to choose your breakfast the night before.

Crown Inn (Map p116; ☎ 015394-41243; www.crowninn coniston.com; Tilberthwaite Ave; s £50, d £80-95; P) For plain pub accommodation, you can't argue with the old Crown, which offers 10 rooms decked out in comfy style. Big beds with tartan or patterned bedspreads, decent bathrooms and satellite TV make for a solid if unspectacular night's sleep.

Beech Tree (Map p116; ☎ 015394-41717; Yewdale Rd; d £50-60) Eight spick-and-span rooms (some en suite, some with private bathrooms across the corridor) in a 19th-century house a short walk from Coniston's centre. Decoratively, it's a bit generic, but the veggie-friendly breakfasts and handy location ensure it's worth a second look.

our pick Bank Ground Farm (Map p113; ☎ 015394-41264; www.bankground.com; East of the Lake; d £70-90; P) Antique sleigh beds, country-style fabrics and the fluffiest, plumpest pillows in Coniston fill the seven rooms of this idyllic farmhouse, parts of which date from the 15th century. It sits in 24-odd hectares of secluded grounds with its own private access to the lakeshore, and even boasts literary cachet – Arthur Ransome used it as the blueprint for 'Holly Howe Farm' in *Swallows and Amazons*. For longer stays, there are several self-catering cottages, including a huge three-floored converted barn.

Wheelgate Country Guest House (Map p113; ☎ 015394-41418; www.wheelgate.co.uk; Little Arrow; d £74-84) Climbing plants and colourful blooms run riot across this slate-roofed farmhouse, built in the 17th century, but the frilly decor might be a little too much for some. Rooms are named after local lakes: snuggle down in Derwent among oak beams, plump for the four-poster in Buttermere or choose Coniston for garden views.

Summer Hill Country House (Map p113; ☎ 01539-436180; www.summerhillcountryhouse.com; Hawkshead

Hill; d £76-110; (P) (💻)) Effortless elegance is the watchword at this 17th-century manor house halfway between Hawkshead and Coniston. Gilchrist & Soames bath goodies, fresh fruit and DAB radios feature in all five rooms, and there's even a net-connected Apple Mac mini for when you need to get online. Our favourite is Room Four, with its monochrome colour scheme and bay window overlooking the gardens.

Sun Hotel (Map p116; ☎ 015394-41248; www .thesunconiston.com; d £80-110) Campbell connections aplenty at this elderly coaching inn (Donald had his HQ here during his final fateful campaign). The 10 rooms hark back to decades past, with faded drapes, hefty furniture and the odd musty corner – modernists will want to look elsewhere, but if you can bag a room with a view, you should be happy enough.

EATING

Yew Tree Farm Tea Room (Map p113; ☎ 015394-41433; www.yewtree-farm.com; cakes £1-2.50, meals £3.50-7.70; (P)) You couldn't wish for a better cream tea or hot cheddar scone than the ones dished out at the Yew Tree Farm's rustic tea room, but for something more filling, there are hot Herdwick sandwiches (£5.95) and hearty mains such as Beltie beef in Bluebird beer (£7.95). Parking is fairly limited, but it makes an ideal place to reward yourself after a day on the fells.

Meadowdore Cafe (Map p116; ☎ 015394-41638; Hawkshead Old Rd; £3.95-6.50) The cafe-style menu at the Meadowdore dabbles mainly in chicken and chips, ploughman's lunches and filled baguettes, but it's filling and cheap, and there's a patio out front for when the sun peeps through the clouds.

Bluebird Cafe (Map p113; ☎ 015394-41649; Lake Rd; lunches £4-8; (☾) breakfast & lunch) Down by the Coniston jetty, this buzzy lakeside cafe was initially built as accommodation for workers employed by the Furness Railway Company, but it now makes an ideal place for a quick sandwich, spud or salad before you jump aboard the cross-lake launch.

Black Bull Inn (Map p116; ☎ 015394-41335; www .conistonbrewery.com; Yewdale Rd; mains £6-14; (☾) lunch & dinner) Coniston's best pub grub is served up at the Black Bull, which is also well known for brewing some of the best small-scale ales in the Lakes – the Bluebird and Old Man bitters have bagged awards from some of the nation's most distinguished real ale organisations.

Harry's (Map p116; ☎ 015394-41389; 4 Yewdale Rd; mains £6.95-11.90; (☾) 9am-11pm) Brown leather, chrome and moody lighting set the swish wine-bar tone at Harry's, which offers a menu of pasta standards, beer-battered cod, pizzas and Aberdeen Angus burgers, as well as plenty of global wines and beers to wash things down.

Self-Catering

Coniston has a **Co-op** (Map p116; Yewdale Rd; (☾) 9am-8pm Mon-Sat & 10am-7pm Sun), and you can pick up authentic butter fudge and biscuits across the road at the **Coniston Fudge Company** (Map p116; ☎ 015394-41259; Yewdale Rd; (☾) 9am-5pm Mon-Sat), in the same building as the post office.

GETTING THERE & AROUND

Bus 505 runs from Windermere (12 Monday to Saturday, six on Sunday mid-March to October), via Ambleside, Skelwith Fold and Hawkshead, with a couple of daily connections to Kendal (1¼ hours).

The Ruskin Explorer ticket (adult/child £14.95/6.50) includes the Windermere bus fare, a Coniston launch ticket and entrance to Brantwood; pick it up from the tourist office or the bus driver.

CONISTON, HAWKSHEAD & AROUND

SOMEWHERE SPECIAL

our pick **Yew Tree Farm** (Map p113; ☎ 015394-41433; www.yewtree-farm.com; r £100-124; (P)) Seen *Miss Potter*? Then you might find this gorgeous farmhouse in the Coniston countryside eerily familiar – it doubled in the film as Beatrix's house at Hill Top. It's still very much a working farm, so you'll fall asleep in one of the three luxuriously appointed rooms to a soundtrack of assorted moos and bleats. Cream of the crop is 'Tarn Hows' with its higgledy-piggledy rafters and king-size four-poster; 'Wetherlam' has an antique bed and double bath, and little 'Holme Fell' has original wood floors and valley views. The farm is about 1.5 miles north of Coniston along Yewdale Rd.

GILLIAN HODGSON

There are plenty of cruise operators in the Lake District – what makes the Coniston Launches special? Boat cruises have been a major part of the Lake District for decades, ever since the first Victorian tourists arrived in the mid-19th century. But for us, the major difference is that we've made the 21st-century transition from the old steam-powered boats or diesel engines to sustainable sources of energy. Both our launches run almost entirely on solar energy, which we soak up using solar panels on the top of the boats and store in electric batteries.

Obviously this is great for the environment, but it means our cruises are very special too – they're much, much less noisy than many other boats, and you're able to contemplate the scenery in relative peace and quiet. We're hoping to take part in the special Green Boat Show on the Coniston shoreline in 2009, where people can learn all about the different green energy technologies and how they can be applied to different transport systems – watch this space!

The Lakes are well known for the fickleness of their weather, so what happens to the launches when there's no sunshine? Well so far we haven't managed to get ourselves stranded out on the lake just yet! The panels are quite sensitive and will harness sunshine even when it's quite cloudy – normally there's enough energy available to top up the batteries over lunchtime. And if we get really stuck we have an electric motor for emergencies – we converted the boats to solar power in 2004, and so far no-one's had to swim back to shore! Cruising on the lake when it's raining can be a really special time, too. The lake has a completely different character depending on the different seasons and different weathers, so we just try to encourage people to get their wellies on, wrap up warm and get out there and enjoy it.

How many people have you got working on the boats? We've got a team of seven full-time people, five of whom are fully qualified 'boat masters'. It takes a massive investment of time and resources to train people up to the required standard – in excess of 60 hours crewing, as well as courses in fire safety, first aid, radio operating and navigation. We also give full commentaries on all our cruises, as well as special ones devoted to the Campbell story and *Swallows and Amazons* – so our guys definitely need to put in the hours!

Gillian Hodgson is the owner of the Coniston Launch

HAWKSHEAD

pop 1640

For many people the quaint hamlet of Hawkshead presents the picture-perfect image of a Lakeland village – a jumble of tiny cottages, cobbled alleys and criss-crossing lanes, huddled amid thick woods and dappled fields on the northern shores of Esthwaite Water. The village owes its existence to monks from Furness Abbey, who founded Hawkshead as a centre for the medieval wool trade. Following the dissolution of the abbey under Henry VIII, Hawkshead was granted its own market charter by James I, and became one of the main trading villages in the central Lakes.

Traffic is banned in the centre of the village, which makes Hawkshead a fine place for an afternoon wander. There are several tempting foodie shops to browse around, and some intriguing connections to both Wordsworth and Beatrix Potter, while to the south of the village Esthwaite Water boasts some of the best trout fishing in the national park.

INFORMATION

Hawkshead Post Office and Village Shop (Map p119; ☎ 015394-36911; Main St; ☼ 7.30am-5.30pm Mon-Sat, 8am-4pm Sun)

Hawkshead Tourist Office (Map p119; ☎ 015394-36946; www.hawksheadtouristinfo.org.uk; Main St; ☼ 9am-5.30pm Mon-Sat, 10am-4pm Sun) The village's unofficial tourist centre is on the corner of Main St near the car park, and has a Link ATM, as well as bike hire, books and tourist leaflets.

SIGHTS

Hawkshead Grammar School

First stop is the historic **Hawkshead Grammar School** (Map p119; admission £2; ☼ 10am-1pm & 2-5pm Mon-Sat & 1-5pm Sun Apr-Sep, 10-1pm & 2-3.30pm Mon-Sat & 1-3.30pm Sun Oct) on the edge of the village, where well-to-do young Lakeland gentlemen were sent to receive their educational foundations in Latin, Greek, mathematics, science and classical literature. Among the school's famous alumni were William Wordsworth and his older brother John, who arrived in Hawkshead following their mother's death in 1778; William remained in Hawkshead for the next nine years, before eventually leaving in 1787 to continue his education at Cambridge.

The schoolroom has been left largely unchanged since the school closed in 1909; in Wordsworth's day pupils would have sat here for up to 10 hours a day, covering such weighty subjects as Euclidean geometry, Pythagorean arithmetic, Platonic debate and Greek and Latin rhetoric – so it's little wonder that naughty young Willie felt the urge to scratch his name into one of the school desks (probably earning a birching for his trouble). Upstairs you can also view the headmaster's former study – one of the schoolmasters during Wordsworth's scholastic days was Edward Christian, the older brother of Fletcher Christian (of mutiny on the *Bounty* fame). Both the Christian brothers were born in nearby Cockermouth (p157).

Beatrix Potter Gallery

In the centre of the village are the former offices of Beatrix Potter's husband, the solicitor William Heelis, whose firm had been based in Hawkshead since the mid-19th century. The offices have now been converted into the **Beatrix Potter Gallery** (Map p119; NT; ☎ 015394-36355; Main St; adult/child £4/2; ☺ 10.30am-4.30pm Sat-Thu mid-Mar–Oct), displaying a collection of watercolours, sketchbooks and studies from the National Trust's Beatrix Potter archive.

While she is obviously best known for her children's books, Beatrix was also a perceptive student of nature and wildlife, and her botanical sketches of flowers, animals and fungi provide an intriguing counterpoint to her more famous work. There are also some informative displays on Beatrix' work as a conservationist and early environmentalist, especially her long campaign to protect the unique natural landscape of the Lakes from over-development by buying up local land and farms.

Tickets can also be purchased from the nearby **National Trust Shop** (☎ 015394-36471; ☺ 10am-5pm daily mid-Mar–Nov, 10am-4pm Wed-Sun Nov-Dec & late Feb–mid-Mar, 10am-4pm daily early Feb). There's a discount on the admission price for holders of a valid ticket to Hill Top.

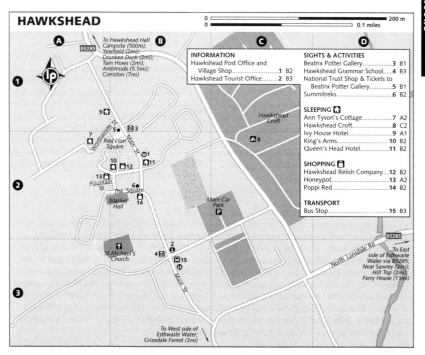

HAWKSHEAD

0   200 m
0   0.1 miles

To Hawkshead Hall
Campsite (500m);
Yewfield (2mi);
Drunken Duck (2mi);
Tarn Hows (2mi);
Ambleside (5.5mi);
Coniston (7mi)

Hawkshead Croft

Main Car Park

St Michael's Church

Market Hall

Fountain St

The Square

Red Lion Square

Wordsworth St

Main St

North Lonsdale Rd

B5285

To East side of Esthwaite Water via B5285; Near Sawrey (2mi); Hill Top (2mi); Ferry House (11mi)

To West side of Esthwaite Water; Grizedale Forest (3mi)

INFORMATION
Hawkshead Post Office and
  Village Shop..........................1 B2
Hawkshead Tourist Office..........2 B3

SIGHTS & ACTIVITIES
Beatrix Potter Gallery.................3 B1
Hawkshead Grammar School.....4 B3
National Trust Shop & Tickets to
  Beatrix Potter Gallery.............5 B1
Summitreks................................6 B2

SLEEPING
Ann Tyson's Cottage.................7 A2
Hawkshead Croft........................8 C2
Ivy House Hotel.........................9 A1
King's Arms.............................10 B2
Queen's Head Hotel................11 B2

SHOPPING
Hawkshead Relish Company....12 B2
Honeypot................................13 A2
Poppi Red...............................14 B2

TRANSPORT
Bus Stop................................15 B3

St Michael's Church

Lodged on a slight rise just behind the village, St Michael's largely dates from the 16th century, although parts of the building (including the eight-belled tower) are thought to be older. The church is notable for its elegant central nave, lined with circular pillars and decorative arches, as well as a striking war memorial designed by Ruskin's secretary, WG Collingwood (apparently inspired by his interest in Cumbria's pre-Norman crosses).

Esthwaite Water

The biggest **trout fishery** (Map p113; ☎ 015394-36541; www.hawksheadtrout.com) in northwest England is found at this small lake to the south of Hawkshead. Courses are available if you fancy learning the finer points of line casting and fly tying; tuition costs £90 for a full day including tackle hire and boat, plus £25 for every extra person. If you already know the drill, a daily shore permit costs £25 per day and includes a 'catch and release' limit of up to four fish. A boat permit costs £38/64 for one/two people and includes boat hire and four fish per person. Evening permits start at 4pm and cost £18 onshore or £28/44 on the water. Coarse fishing for pike, perch and roach is also offered between October and March.

SLEEPING & EATING
Budget

Hawkshead Hall Campsite (Map p113; ☎ 015394-36221; www.hawksheadhall-campsite.co.uk; 2 people, tent & car £13.50; ⊙ mid-Mar–mid-Oct) Basic tap-and-tent site in an open field about a quarter of a mile north of the village. It's mainly geared towards families and couples (ie no stag nights or hens parties), and facilities are limited to a portacabin shower block, but at least you're guaranteed a fairly quiet night.

Hawkshead Croft (Map p119; ☎ 015394-36374; www .hawkshead-croft.com; 2 people, tent & car £14-16.75; ⊙ mid-Mar–mid-Sep) Caravans rule the roost here, although there's a rather cramped field that's reserved solely for pitchers. Facilities include a coin-op laundry, games room and modern shower block.

Hawkshead YHA (Map p113; ☎ 0845 371 9321; hawks head@yha.org.uk; dm from £15.95; ⊙ reception 7.30am–10pm; ☐) Right on the shores of Esthwaite Water, Hawkshead's hostel is lodged inside a regal Regency house decked out with original cornicing, panelled doors and even a stately veranda. As usual the dorms are less fancy, but there's bike rental, a good restaurant (meals around £3 to £6) and buses stop outside the door.

Midrange

Ann Tyson's Cottage (Map p119; ☎ 015394-36405; www.anntysons.co.uk; Wordsworth St; s £29-55, d £58-78) Both the Wordsworth boys once lodged at this tiny cottage down one of Hawkshead's narrow backstreets, where they were looked after by the genial 'old dame' Ann Tyson. These days the house is a snug and chintzy hideaway crammed with padded bed heads, low ceilings and tiny windows, as well as an antique bed that once belonged to John Ruskin.

Queen's Head Hotel (Map p119; ☎ 015394-36271; www.queensheadhotel.co.uk; Main St; d £40-90; ☐) A vintage pub, packed with oak-panelled character and backed up by a hearty menu of Winster Valley pork and venison from Holker Hall (mains £14 to £22.50). Unsurprisingly the ancient building means the rooms are on the teeny side; most have been refurbished, but they're probably not going to win any interior design awards. More are available in an annexe next door.

SOMETHING FOR THE WEEKEND

You'll feel a whole world away snuggled down in the countryside around Coniston and Hawkshead. Begin with a night at the multi-award-winning **Drunken Duck** (opposite) on Hawkshead Hill, as notable for its puffy pillows as its belt-busting cuisine. On Saturday head down for a walk around **Tarn Hows** (opposite) before heading through **Hawkshead** (p118) and along **Esthwaite Water** (above) for lunch at the endearingly olde-worlde **Tower Bank Arms** (p124) and an afternoon at **Hill Top** (p123). Return along the east side of Esthwaite and check into upmarket **Yewfield** (opposite) before heading into Hawkshead for a posh pub supper at the **Queen's Head Hotel** (above).

Take a Sunday morning cruise on **Coniston Water** (p114) over to **Brantwood** (p112), with lunch at **Jumping Jenny** (p114). Spend the afternoon mooching around the forest trails of **Grizedale** (p122) before laying your head down at **Grizedale Lodge** (p122).

King's Arms (Map p119; ☎ 015394-36372; www.kings armshawkshead.co.uk; The Square; s £42-47, d £74-94) Nice pub nosh (dinner mains around £12) – steak pie with Hawkshead ale, trio of Cumberland bangers or bean chilli – dished up among beams and brass horseshoes in a 500-year-old inn. The rooms are well used – think wonky walls and scruffy furniture – but they're appropriately comfy considering the price.

our pick **Yewfield** (Map p113; ☎ 015394-36765; www.yewfield.co.uk; Hawkshead Hill; d £78-120; **P**) Zen aesthetics mingle with Victorian Gothic and veggie food at this swanky guest house on Hawkshead Hill, a couple of miles from the village. Oak panels meet Oriental bedspreads and sheep-shag carpets in the rooms, but there's a more austere feel to the tower suite, with views over the Esthwaite Valley. The vegetarian breakfast offers continental and cooked options, accompanied by home-baked bread, muesli and fresh fruit (occasionally sourced from the nearby orchards).

Ivy House Hotel (Map p119; ☎ 015394-36204; Main St; d £90-100; **P**) Kip amid swags, drapes and gilded fabrics at this Grade-II–listed B&B on the west side of Hawkshead. A circular staircase swirls up through the house to six prissy rooms stocked with four-poster beds and teddy bears; the ones in the rear annexe are less fancy. The restaurant is a find too, serving upper-crust food (dinner mains £13.50 to £17) amid ornate antiques; afternoon tea (£5.75) includes scones, sponge cakes and quartered sarnies, all served on a towering cake stand.

Top End

our pick **Drunken Duck** (Map p113; ☎ 015394-36347; www.drunkenduckinn.co.uk; Barngates; mains £17.95-24.95; **P**) The designer Duck is much, much more than a bog-standard gastropub – it's a brewery, boutique B&B, historic boozer and ultra-creative bistro rolled into one indulgent bundle. Inside the 400-year-old inn, vintage architecture marries up with modern touches. Slate fireplaces and old signs sit alongside leather chairs and neutral shades, and while the rooms (from £120 to £250) are small, they're all fresh and inviting with Roberts radios, enamel baths and rolling rural views. The real treat, though, is the pub itself, where home-brewed ales from the Barngates Brewery accompany a menu oozing with sophisticated flavours – crab-claw salad, venison loin or confit of duck with girolles mushrooms. A spoil from start to finish.

SHOPPING

Hawkshead has a couple of excellent delis where you can stock up on picnic supplies. Cumbrian cheeses, takeaway coffees, freshly made sandwiches and Lakeland honeys are sold at the **Honeypot** (Map p119; ☎ 015394-36267; The Square), while the **Hawkshead Relish Company** (Map p119; ☎ 015394-36614; www.hawk sheadrelish.com; The Square; ☷ 9.30am-5pm Mon-Sat, 10am-5pm Sun) sells award-winning chutneys, relishes and mustards, from the super-fruity Westmorland Chutney to classic piccalilli and damson jams.

Meanwhile **Poppi Red** (Map p119; ☎ 015394-36434; Main St; ☷ 9am-6pm) offers an eclectic range of gifts, home furnishings, pottery and craftwork, and also has a small tea room for when you've finished nosing around the shop.

GETTING THERE & AROUND

Hawkshead is linked with Windermere, Ambleside and Coniston by bus 505 (10 Monday to Saturday, six on Sunday mid-March to October), and to Hill Top and Coniston by the Cross-Lakes Shuttle (p70).

Bikes can be hired at a cost of £30/25/15 for a full-suspension/front-suspension/child model from the tourist office. Prices include helmets.

AROUND HAWKSHEAD

TARN HOWS

About 2 miles off the B5285 from Hawkshead, a twisting country lane wends its way to Tarn Hows, a picturesque man-made lake backed by pine and spruce, built on land donated to the National Trust by Beatrix Potter in 1930. It's now one of the area's most popular picnic spots, as well as a favourite hangout for Cumbria's endangered population of red squirrels. There's an easy circular stroll around the lake lasting about an hour, with plenty of places along the route where you can stop for a sandwich or a cup of tea from the thermos. Better still, pick up a cornet of award-winning Windermere Ice Cream Company ice cream from the Scoop van in the National Trust car park. There's also a newly built visitor centre, clad in locally sourced wood and decorated with ceramic tiles fashioned by local school kids, which explores the history of the lake and some of the notable people involved in its development.

Parking at Tarn Hows can be a headache on busy summer weekends, so you might find it easier to tackle the hill on foot from Hawkshead. It's a 5- to 6-mile round trip of around three hours.

GRIZEDALE FOREST

Stretching across the hills between Coniston Water and Esthwaite Water is Grizedale, a dense woodland of oak, larch and pine whose name derives from the Old Norse *griss-dale*, meaning 'valley of pigs'. Though it looks lush and unspoilt today, the forest has been largely replanted over the last 100 years; by the late 19th century, the original woodland had practically disappeared thanks to the demands of the local logging, mining and charcoal industries. Criss-crossed by hiking trails and mountain-bike routes, as well as a high-wire adventure park strung between the trees, the forest makes a fantastic all-day outing. But it's not just worth visiting for its natural attractions; since 1977 artists have created over 90 outdoor sculptures around the forest, including a wooden xylophone, a wave of carved ferns and a huge Tolkienesque 'man of the forest'. Many of the artworks nestle almost invisibly among the trees, so you'll have to keep your eyes peeled on your walk around.

There are eight marked trails through the forest, from the relatively short routes around **Ridding Wood** (1 mile/one hour; marked in blue) and **Machell's Coppice** (1.5 miles/one hour; marked in purple) through to the tough hike up to the forest's highest point at **Carron Crag** (3 miles/two hours; marked in red) and the long-distance **Silurian Way** (9 miles/five hours; marked in green).

There are also five different **bike routes** starting at various points around the park – some are easy family rides, while others, including the new **North Face Trail**, are meant for serious mountain bikers familiar with fast single-track, boards, steps and rock gardens.

At the time of writing the park's facilities were in the process of being completely upgraded, although there's a temporary **Visitor Centre** (Map p113; ☎ 01229-860010; www.forestry.gov .uk/grizedaleforestpark; ⏰ 10am-5pm summer, 11am-4pm winter) at the main Grizedale car park, as well as a small takeaway cafe. Maps of all the main forest trails are sold at the visitor's centre, while hire bikes, route guides and trail maps are available from **Grizedale Mountain Bike Hire** (☎ 01229-860369; www.grizedalemountainbikes.co.uk; per

day adult £20-30, child £15; ⏰ 9am-5.30pm Mar-Oct, last hire 2pm in winter, 3pm rest of year).

If you prefer exploring the forest on four legs rather than two wheels, **horse riding** is available from **Bowkerstead Farm** (☎ 01229-860208; Satterthwaite; 1/2/3-hr ride £30/38/45), about 1.5 miles from the Grizedale Visitor Centre.

Meanwhile, budding Tarzans and Janes can test their skills at the forest's latest attraction, **Go Ape** (Map p113; ☎ 0870 458 9189; www.goape.co.uk; adult/child £25/20; ⏰ 9-5pm Mar-Oct, plus winter weekends), a dizzying assault course through the Grizedale trees along rope ladders, bridges, platforms and hair-raising zip slides. The course takes about two hours to complete from end to end; there's a minimum age limit of 10 years, and you'll need to be more than 4ft 7in in height.

Sleeping

Bowkerstead Farm (☎ 01229 860208; www .grizedale-camping.co.uk; Satterthwaite) Just outside Satterthwaite, this farm campsite is one of the few places that accepts group campers, so things can get rowdy in high season. There's a big pitching field backed by woods and drystone walls, a twin his-and-hers shower block, and a smattering of camping pods hidden among the trees for that extra bit of shelter. The site can get a bit boggy during heavy periods of rain.

Pepper House (☎ 01229-860206; www.pepper-house .co.uk; Satterthwaite; s £35, d £60; P) Up on the slope above Satterthwaite, this cruck-framed farmhouse is one for the animal lovers; lambs graze in a nearby paddock while assorted cats and dogs range at will around the house. There are a couple of fire-warmed lounges for guest use, plus fresh bread for breakfast and views across the forest from the terrace.

Grizedale Lodge (Map p113; ☎ 015394-36532; www .grizedale-lodge.com; d £95-100; P) Budding babes in the wood should make a beeline for this seriously smart B&B, right in the middle of Grizedale Forest (if you're veeeery lucky, you might glimpse a red deer grazing on the lawn). There's space to spare in the rooms, the best of which boast canopy beds and puffy sofas, and for breakfast there's whisky-laced porridge and a full-on fry-up that'll keep you going till supper time.

Getting There & Away

The main car park at Grizedale, where you'll find the visitor centre and bike-hire centre, is

LADY OF THE LAKES

Of all the Lake District's literary luminaries, none commands a more fanatical following than Beatrix Potter (1866–1943). More than a century on from the publication of her first book, *The Tale of Peter Rabbit,* her anthropomorphic children's fables continue to sell by the bucket-load, and her former house at Hill Top remains one of the most visited tourist attractions in Northern England, receiving in excess of 65,000 visitors every year.

Born to a privileged family in South Kensington in 1866 (her father was a barrister, her mother the wealthy daughter of a cotton magnate), Beatrix Potter's connections with the Lake District date back to a family holiday to the region in 1882. A shy and lonely child (largely thanks to her strict governess-administered education and enforced isolation from other children), the young Beatrix was fascinated by animals, botany and nature, and she instantly felt an extraordinary kinship with the Lake District landscape. Over the course of several subsequent holidays in the Lakes, she whiled away countless hours sketching local flowers, trees, landscapes and endless varieties of fungi, not to mention her motley menagerie of frogs, newts, toads, ferrets and a pair of bunny rabbits named – as if you hadn't guessed – Peter and Benjamin Bouncer (whom she apparently liked to parade around on a lead). Some of her early work is displayed at the **Armitt Museum** (p77) in Ambleside and the **Beatrix Potter Gallery** (p119) in Hawkshead.

Though her parents often frowned on her creative leanings, Beatrix was encouraged to pursue her artistic ambitions by the local vicar and family friend Canon Hardwicke Rawnsley, who recognised her talent and encouraged her to complete her first book, *The Tale of Peter Rabbit.* Though initially rejected by several publishers, the book was eventually printed by the small firm Frederick Warne & Co in 1901, and was an almost instant smash hit, selling in excess of 25,000 copies in its first year. Its financial success enabled Potter to buy her farm at **Hill Top** (below) – the first of many property purchases in the Lakes – and spawned a series of 22 further books over the next 20 years, culminating with *The Tale of Little Pig Robinson* in 1930.

But while her literary life was an unquestionable success, she had her share of hardships. Her first engagement to her publisher, Norman Warne, ended tragically in 1905 when he died suddenly of anaemia, but she later married the local solicitor William Heelis in 1913, and increasingly moved away from her literary work to concentrate on her domestic life. During the 1920s and 30s, she established her own prize-winning flock of Herdwick sheep, became a respected agricultural judge and president of the Herdwick Sheep Breeders' Association, and worked tirelessly to champion the values of the Lakeland landscape and traditional Cumbrian customs. She died in 1943 at the age of 77, bequeathing her 1600-hectare estate to the National Trust.

about 3 miles south of Hawkshead along the minor road that travels through the centre of the forest. Other useful car parks include Moor Top, at the northern edge of the forest; Bogle Crag and Blind Lane to the south of the Grizedale Visitor Centre; and Machell's Coppice, on the forest's west side.

The X30 Grizedale Wanderer (four daily March to November) runs from Haverthwaite to Grizedale via Hawkshead and Moor Top, tying in with the Cross-Lakes Shuttle (p70) to Windermere.

HILL TOP & NEAR SAWREY

If there's anywhere in the Lakes where you can still discern the spirit of the real Beatrix Potter beneath all the kitschy clutter, it's **Hill Top** (NT; ☎ 015394-36269; Near Sawrey; adult/child £5.80/2.90; ⊙ 10.30am-4.30pm Sat-Thu, garden 10.30am-5pm mid-Mar–Oct, 10am-4pm Nov-Feb, Sat & Sun only early Mar). Beatrix purchased this picture-perfect farmhouse in the shady hamlet of Near Sawrey in 1905 (largely on the proceeds of her first book, *The Tale of Peter Rabbit*), and went on to write a string of bestsellers at the house, although after 1909 she mostly lived at nearby Castle Farm, and used Hill Top mainly as a base from which to administer her rapidly expanding property portfolio.

The house has hardly changed since Potter's death in 1943, and still contains much of her original pottery, china and furniture (as stipulated in her will). Dedicated Potterites will spot countless decorative details that Beatrix wove into her animal tales: the cast-iron kitchen range was a regular recurrence in many of her underground animal burrows, while the garden and vegetable patch appeared in *Peter*

CONISTON, HAWKSHEAD & AROUND

Rabbit, and you might recognise the Tower Bank Arms pub up the road from *The Tale of Jemima Puddleduck.*

As befits one of Lakeland's key visitor attractions, Hill Top can be a serious scrum in summer, especially since the success of the 2006 biopic *Miss Potter,* starring Renée Zellwegger. Entry is by timed ticket to avoid overcrowding, but the queues can still be horrendously long during the holiday seasons (tickets are often sold out by 2pm, and don't even think about trying to visit on a Bank Holiday).

About a mile west through the patchwork fields and coppices of Claife Heights is the neighbouring settlement of **Far Sawrey**. From here, the little road runs on downhill to Ash Landing and Ferry House, where Windermere's cross-lake ferry (p70) docks on the lake's western shore.

Sleeping & Eating

Sawrey House (☎ 015394-36387; www.sawreyhouse.com; Near Sawrey; s/d from £49.50/70; **P**) This splendid Victorian mansion is steps from Hill Top, so it's a great option if you want to beat the early-morning crowds. The building's a beauty, all tall chimneys, elegant gables and panoramic Windermere views, but the 70s-style rooms are smothered by a surfeit of ruffles, ruches and floral fabrics.

Tower Bank Arms (☎ 015394-36334; www.tower bankarms.co.uk; Near Sawrey; s/d £50/80) More Potter connections and a fine line up of ales from the Barngates and Hawkshead breweries make this bewitching little village pub tempting; chuck in cosy rooms (all christened after Cumbrian numbers) and a menu stocked with beef casserole and sticky toffee pudding (mains £8 to £14), and it's rather irresistible.

Sawrey Hotel (☎ 01539-443425; www.sawrey-hotel .co.uk; Far Sawrey; d £70; **P**) Just about the only place for a pint and a pie between Ferry House and Near Sawrey is the Sawrey Hotel, whose black-and-white bulk sits just behind the B5285 road. The rooms are a tad tired, but you'll find rich Brit standards (cod and chips, roast beef) in the attached restaurant, followed by pints at the Claife Crier bar next door (apparently built using wood from local shipwrecks).

Buckle Yeat (☎ 015394-3644; www.buckle-yeat .co.uk; Near Sawrey; d £80) You can actually sleep inside a Beatrix Potter tale at this gorgeous 17th-century cottage, which featured in *The*

DETOUR

During the Victorian era, several 'viewing stations' were established around Claife Heights to enable well-heeled visitors to admire the views without muddying up their bustles and britches. The only surviving example is at **Claife Station**, which is accessible along a (sometimes steep and slippery) public footpath between Ferry House and Far Sawrey, which starts near the National Trust car park at Ash Landing. In its heyday in the 1830s and 40s, this viewing station would have been appointed with fine furniture, fashionable fabrics and snappily dressed attendants serving afternoon tea; the windows of the drawing room would have been tinted in different colours to simulate the effect of changing light on the landscape (light blue for winter, green for spring, yellow for summer and dark blue for moonlight).

Tale of Tom Kitten. The six rooms don't quite match up to the Potter prestige, but they're snug in a country farmhouse kind of way, if a little overpriced.

Garth (☎ 015394-36346; www.thegarthcountryhouse .co.uk; Near Sawrey; d £95-105) Ornamental shrubs and ordered lawns make for a calming backdrop at this Victorian villa, while a couple of rooms also have views across the Esthwaite Valley; our favourite is the Balcony room, with its scarlet sofa and super-sized bed. Contemporary furnishings, CD players and zingy throws ensure the chintz factor is kept to a minimum.

Getting There & Away

Near Sawrey is 2 miles south of Hawkshead. Bus 505 travels through the village, or you can catch the Cross-Lakes Shuttle (p70) up from Ferry House.

WRAY CASTLE & CLAIFE HEIGHTS

Overlooking the northwest side of Windermere are the splendid turrets, gateways and battlements of Wray Castle, an imposing mansion built in typically ostentatious Victorian style during the heyday of the Gothic Revival in 1840. It was built for a retired Liverpudlian surgeon, Dr Dawson, partly by plundering funds from his wife's gin fortune, but sadly it proved an unhappy project – his wife apparently loathed the house so much she utterly refused to live there and the house almost immediately fell into disuse. Later the house served as a rather lavish holiday home for the young Beatrix Potter and her family, who rented the property during their first sojourn to the Lakes in 1882. Eventually Wray Castle and its 25-hectare estate were gifted to the National Trust in 1929, largely thanks to the persuasive powers of Canon Hardwicke Rawnsley, one of the trust's founder members.

The estate is still owned by the National Trust, and its lovely **grounds** are open to the public year-round – it's particularly notable for its varied tree population, filled with up-standing examples of sequoia, lime, redwood and beech (as well as a spreading mulberry allegedly planted by Wordsworth). The **house** (Map p113; ☎ 015394-47997; adult/child £3/1; ⌚ 11am-4pm August) is usually open to the public during late July and August – call ahead to make sure or ask at the Coniston tourist office (p112) or the Windermere Lake Cruises information office (p62).

South of Wray Castle stretch the thick woodlands of Claife Heights, criss-crossed by quiet paths and bridleways that make a delightful place for an afternoon stroll; hardier souls can stride out for the summit of **Latterbarrow** (803ft). During the 19th century, Claife Heights was one of the most popular spots for Victorian walkers, mainly thanks to the guidebook author Thomas West, who eulogised the area in his 1778 *Guide to the Lakes*.

Western Lake District

The lonely valleys and mist-shrouded fells of the western Lakes make up some of the last remaining pockets of wilderness in England. Home to the nation's smallest church (St Olaf's in Wasdale), highest peak (Scafell Pike) and deepest lake (Wast Water), not to mention two of its steepest roads (the side-by-side passes of Hardknott and Wrynose), it's a corner of England where the scenery outstrips the usual superlatives. Huge humps of land loom up along the horizon, capped by cloud and carpeted by snow throughout much of the year, while steep slopes tumble down from the summits into glacial valleys filled with dense forest and silent lakes, with nary a cruise boat, country teashop or Beatrix Potter trinket in sight.

For many people, this is the quintessential Lake District landscape, so it's perhaps unsurprising that one of its most famous panoramas, the view of Great Gable from Wasdale Head, topped a recent TV poll to find Britain's favourite view. Fittingly enough, the very same view has featured on the logo of the national park since its foundation in 1951, and for many fell walkers the summits of Great Gable, Red Pike and Scafell Pike still provide the nation's ultimate hiking challenge. But while the undeniably photogenic valley of Wasdale scoops the scenic awards, neighbouring Eskdale attracts its own flurry of visitors thanks to the pocket-sized choo-choos of the Ravenglass and Eskdale Railway, which steam along the valley between the coastal harbour of Ravenglass and the abandoned iron mines of Eskdale. To the northwest of Wasdale is Ennerdale Water, one of the least-developed of all the national park's major lakes, while to the southeast is the wonderfully remote Duddon Valley, where the Herdwicks still outnumber the humans by a considerable margin, and red squirrels, peregrine falcons and highland cattle roam freely across the fells.

HIGHLIGHTS

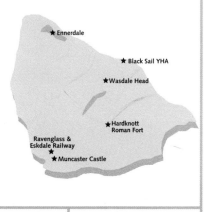

- Survey the scene from the ruined battlements of Mediobogdum, otherwise known as **Hardknott Roman Fort** (p135)
- Clamber aboard the miniature carriages of the **Ravenglass and Eskdale Railway** (p130)
- Explore the forest trails and quiet shores of **Ennerdale** (p139)
- Sleep amid mountain peaks at the fabulously remote **Black Sail YHA** (p140)
- Down some microbrewed beer at the classic hikers' haven of **Wasdale Head Inn** (p139)
- Spot the spooks at Cumbria's most haunted castle, **Muncaster** (p130)

★ Ennerdale

★ Black Sail YHA

★ Wasdale Head

★ Hardknott Roman Fort

Ravenglass & Eskdale Railway ★

★ Muncaster Castle

| ■ Area of largest lake (Wast Water): 1.09 sq miles | ■ Ravenglass & Eskdale Railway passengers in 2006: 118,517 | ■ Highest Wainwright peak (Scafell Pike): 3209ft |

ITINERARY 1
SCALING SCAFELL PIKE   **7 miles/5 hours/Wasdale Head**

Every year thousands of ambitious peak baggers set out to conquer England's rooftop and, despite its lofty height, this strenuous route is achievable as long as you're fit, properly equipped and prepared for a steep slog. Scafell Pike's exposed summit and considerable altitude makes this walk dangerous and difficult to navigate during bad weather, so it's best saved for a decent day. Needless to say, emergency supplies, compass and a detailed map are essential.

There are several routes to the top, but this classic ascent starts from the **Wasdale Head car park**. Head south over **Lingmell Beck** and follow the path up towards **Lingmell Gill**. Cross the stones over the beck (take extra care during wet weather) and continue climbing steeply up the track along **Brown Tongue**, overlooked to the south by the stern cliffs of Black and Scafell crags.

You'll soon reach a junction: the right fork leads to an alternative ascent of the peak via the scree-covered pass of Mickledore, as well as the vertiginous scramble to the top of Sca Fell via Lord's Rake (now made dangerous by recent rockfall, so best avoided). Take the left fork instead, traversing the boulder-strewn expanse of **Hollow Stones** onto a long zigzagging trail up to **Lingmell Col**, where the route ascends southeast over a shattered plain of rocks, scree and boulders all the way up to England's highest point.

A huge cairn marks the actual **summit** (3209ft), and you will almost certainly be sharing the mountain top with a smattering of fellow walkers. The views across the valley are astounding, especially the interlocking panorama of peaks to the north, including Great Gable, Kirk Fell, Green Gable and Pillar. Sca Fell looms to the southwest, connected to its neighbour via the narrow ridge of Mickledore; look out for rock climbers tackling the classic challenge of Broad Stand nearby.

Once you've basked in the views, retrace your steps from the summit plateau all the way back down to **Wasdale Head**. Pat yourself on the back – you're now officially a Scafell Piker.

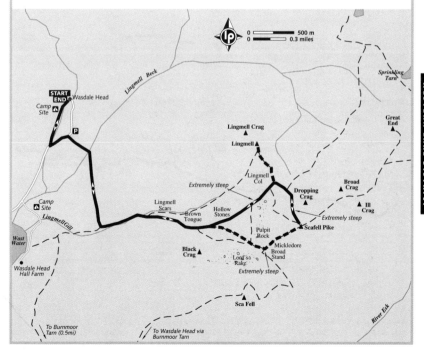

ITINERARY 2

WRYNOSE–HARDKNOTT DRIVE   39 miles/3 hours/Ambleside to Eskdale Green

Is this the nation's most spectacular road? Many seasoned drivers seem to think so. Traversing both of the steepest passes in England and reaching rubber-shredding 30% gradients in some places, it's a real roller-coaster of a drive; make sure your tyres are pumped up, your brakes are in good nick, and take it slow.

Start off in Ambleside with breakfast at **Apple Pie** (p82), and pick up some supplies for the road at **Lucy's Specialist Grocery** (p82). Then hop in the motor and spin west through **Skelwith Bridge** (p96), stopping for a stroll to the falls at **Skelwith Force** (p96). Then it's on into **Little Langdale** (p96), where the views get seriously grand and the road gets seriously steep. At the western end of the valley the road scrapes up the mountainside through a series of hairpins, overlooked to the north by the summits of Pike O' Blisco, Wrynose Fell and Cold Pike, before reaching a small car park next to the **Three Shire Stone** (p96), where the counties of Cumberland, Westmorland and Lancashire historically met. It's a good point to fortify yourself with a bite to eat before tackling the final push up to **Wrynose Pass**.

From Wrynose, the road plunges down into the hollowed-out bottom of Cockley Beck, which sits at the northern end of the **Duddon Valley** (p135). A branch road travels south towards Ulpha and Broughton-in-Furness, but you'll be taking the right-hand fork back into the hills along the edge of Hardknott Gill, where the road traverses its steepest, twistiest and hairiest section up to the high point of the pass, cutting between the summits of Hard Knott (1801ft) and Harter Fell (2142ft). Take a break to steady your nerves and admire the views at **Hardknott Roman Fort** (p135); on a clear day you'll be able to see all the way to Cumbria's west coast.

From the pass follow the long plunge west into the green stretch of Eskdale, rewarding yourself with a well-earned pint at the **Woolpack Inn** (p135) or the **Boot Inn** (p135). What a ride...

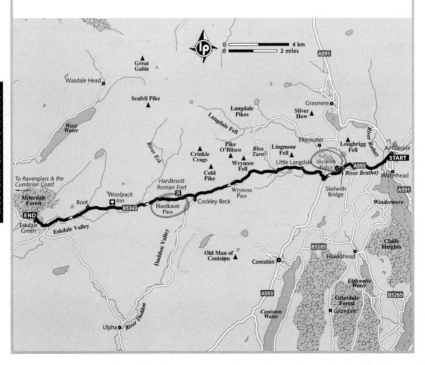

ITINERARY 3
ENNERDALE CIRCUIT CYCLE
17 miles/3 to 4 hours/Cleator Moor

Tracing sections of the Sea to Sea Cycle Route (C2C) across west Cumbria, this is an easy spin along mixed-use trails, disused railway lines and rural lanes through the charming Ennerdale Valley. It's much quieter than many areas of the Lakes and fairly flat the whole way, so it's excellent cycling country, and there are some handy pubs in Ennerdale Bridge, roughly halfway along the circuit, where you can slake your thirst and stock up with calories for the return journey.

Start in **Cleator Moor** at the car park at Phoenix Bridge, from where the marked cycle trail heads east towards the little village of **Parkside**. The first section is a treat, travelling through flower-filled hedgerows and rolling countryside all the way to Rowrah. The route then crosses the **High Leys Nature Reserve**, a gorgeous site reclaimed from five fields that have remained deliberately unplughed since the 1940s, and are now a haven for wildflowers including marsh marigolds, ox-eye daisies, willowherbs and rare orchids.

At the end of the trail, turn left onto the minor road and then right through the village of Kirkland until you reach a T-junction; turn right and travel into **Croasdale**. At this point you can either head west to Ennerdale Bridge, or continue southeast to the shores of **Ennerdale Water** and the viewpoint at **Bowness Knott**, where mountain bikers can tackle the off-road trails around **Ennerdale Forest**. Despite the extra mileage, this detour is well worth it; few areas in the Lake District feel as remote and unspoilt as Ennerdale Water. If you make the Bowness Knott side trip, you'll have to backtrack 1.5 miles to Croasdale to join up with the return loop.

If you haven't brought along your own supplies, the Shepherd's Arms (p140) in **Ennerdale Bridge** makes an ideal place to break the return journey – ale aficionados will approve of the local brews, and the grub's not bad either. From here the route follows the meandering course of the **River Ehen**, passing along quiet roads all the way back to Cleator Moor.

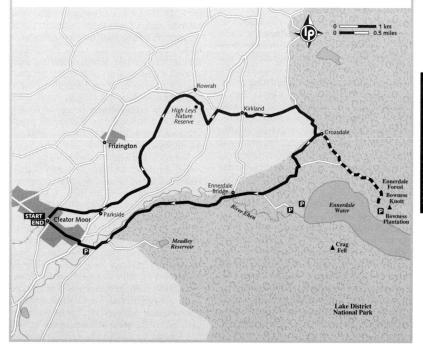

RAVENGLASS & AROUND

Flung out on the western border of the national park, the compact coastal harbour of Ravenglass is pretty quiet these days, but spin the clock back a couple of millennia and you'd discover the thriving naval base of Glannaventa, one of the most important Roman ports in northwest England. Few traces of the occupation now remain, save for the ruins of a Roman bathhouse just behind the harbour; most of present-day Ravenglass dates back to the 19th century, when the harbour was redeveloped as a vital link between northern England's thriving industrial ports and the iron-rich Eskdale mines to the east, accessed via the miniature trains of the Ravenglass and Eskdale Railway. Apart from a trip on the railway, there's not a great deal to keep you in Ravenglass overnight; you'll find more attractive accommodation options further inland at Eskdale or Wasdale.

SIGHTS

Ravenglass & Eskdale Railway

Steam junkies will be in seventh heaven at the **Ravenglass and Eskdale Railway** (☎ 01229-717171; www.ravenglass-railway.co.uk), built to ferry iron ore from the Eskdale mines to the coast. Affectionately known as La'al Ratty (a Cumbrian term roughly translating as 'little passage'), the teeny steam trains chug for 7 miles along a gloriously scenic track into Eskdale and the Lake District foothills, making several stops en route at Muncaster Mill, Irton Rd (for Eskdale Green), Fisherground and Beckfoot before terminating at Dalegarth Station, near Boot (p134) – the traditional starting point for local hikes and bike rides. There are up to 17 trips daily in summer, dropping to two in midwinter; single fares are £6/3 per adult/child; family tickets for two adults and two children cost £26. Day tickets allow unlimited travel on the railway for £10.20/5.10 per adult/child; if you're planning on bringing your own bike, you'll need to pre-book by calling the railway – each bike costs an extra £3 on top of the standard fare. While you wait for your train, there's a small museum exploring the railway's history across the car park from the La'al Ratty platform, next to the Ratty Arms pub.

Roman Bathhouse

About 500m inland from the harbour along a signposted track off the main road, Ravenglass' **Roman bathhouse** (also known as Walls Castle, EH; admission free) is one of the largest surviving Roman structures in England. Over a thousand soldiers were once stationed at the coastal fort of **Glannaventa**, which provided a crucial link along the supply chain from the coast to Hardknott Fort (p135) and the garrisons positioned further inland around the tempestuous trouble spots along Hadrian's Wall. No self-respecting Roman settlement would be complete without its communal bath tub, and Glannaventa's was a doozy; a series of hot and cold plunge pools, steam rooms and saunas were once housed within the building, and although the underfloor heating system (known as the 'hypocaust') hasn't survived, many of the original walls are still standing and you can just about make out the bathhouse's essential footprint. One thing's for sure – those Romans definitely knew how to take a dip.

Muncaster Castle

A mile east of Ravenglass is **Muncaster Castle** (☎ 01229-717614; www.muncaster.co.uk; adult/5-15yr incl owl centre, gardens & maze £5.50/3, castle extra £3/2.50; ☼ gardens 10.30am-6pm/dusk, castle noon-4.30pm Sun-Fri Feb-Nov), the ancestral seat of the Pennington family for the last seven centuries, built around a 14th-century pele tower designed to resist raids from across the Scottish border. Highlights include the dining room, great hall and an extraordinary octagonal library, as well as a collection of historic oil paintings by artists including Joshua Reynolds and Thomas Gainsborough.

But while the house is undoubtedly worth a visit for its art and architecture, it's most renowned for its spooks, spirits and spectres. Countless phantoms are said to stalk the castle's corridors, including the Muncaster Boggle, thought to be the spirit of a young girl murdered outside the castle gate in the 1800s. The castle's most famous ghost is the malevolent jester Tom Skelton (sometimes known as just Tom Fool, hence the word 'tomfoolery'), who was purportedly chums with William Shakespeare and is often cited as the last official jester in England. Budding ghost hunters can even arrange for their very own overnight **ghost sit** (per group Mon-Thu £405, Fri & Sun £440, Sat £475) in the castle's Tapestry

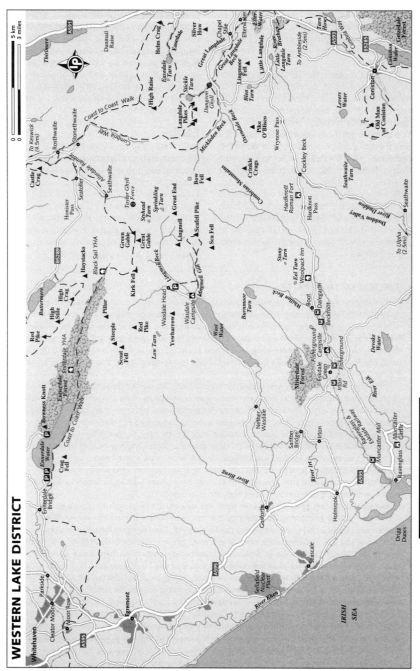

Room, supposedly the most haunted in the castle; even if you don't spot a spook, you can console yourself over a full English fry-up the following morning at **Creeping Kate's Kitchen**.

Outside the castle, the 28-hectare grounds are populated by an exotic range of plants, trees and shrubs, many brought here by pioneering Victorian landscapers from distant climes such as Nepal, Vietnam and China. You can also get thoroughly lost in the castle's ornamental maze, or swoop by the **World Owl Centre** (see p130 for ticket prices and opening times), home to one of the planet's largest captive owl populations. Pygmy owls, barn owls, eagle owls, and a range of other winged beasties, including herons, waders and birds of prey, all spread their wings at the centre; there's a daily talk and aerial display at 2.30pm, and you can watch the heron feeding at 3.30pm.

In winter, the castle itself is generally closed, although the gardens and owl centre remain open. There's a special spooky twilight tour around the grounds called **Darkest Muncaster** (included in day-ticket price, otherwise per adult/child after 4.30pm £5.50/3), and the house is open most Sundays in December for Victorian Christmas–themed displays – call for details or check out the website.

EATING

Ratty Arms (☎ 01229-717676; mains £8-15) Next to the main station platform in Ravenglass, this extraordinary little pub feels like it's tumbled straight from the set of *Brief Encounter*. Its tobacco-tinted walls are covered with train memorabilia, sepia-tinted photos and faded adverts plucked from the railway's heyday, and there's a dining room that has the unmistakeable air of a 1950s train carriage overlooking the station platform.

THE TALE OF LA'AL RATTY

The chequered history of the Ravenglass and Eskdale Railway began on 20 November 1876, when it received its official opening as England's very first narrow-gauge railway. The railway was built as a transport link to the Nab Gill iron mine, situated on the steep fells north of the village of Boot; the huge boom in Victorian construction during the late 1800s meant there was a massive demand for cheap, readily available iron ore, and at two-thirds the width and one-third the cost of an equivalent standard-gauge railway, the Eskdale line seemed like a foolproof money spinner for canny industrial investors.

Unfortunately, the railway was a disaster almost from the outset. Huge extraction costs, difficult working conditions and the enormous expense of transporting the ore down the valley meant that barely any of the Eskdale mines turned a profit, and within six months the railway had been put into receivership. Despite its problems the line struggled on, diversifying into carrying slate, granite and agricultural goods alongside iron ore. Rather unexpectedly, the pocket-sized choo-choos also proved a hit with tourists, who arrived in increasing numbers to take the scenic 7-mile trip through the Eskdale countryside. Several hotels and guest houses sprang up along the valley to cater for the trippers, but the relatively short summer season and the slow decline in demand for industrial iron and slate meant that the railway was again facing closure at the outbreak of WWI. It closed down, seemingly for good, in 1913.

But La'al Ratty was saved at the 11th hour, not by industrial investors but by steam enthusiasts. A pair of well-known model makers by the names of Wynne Bassett-Lowke and RP Mitchell reopened the line in 1915, reinvigorating the tourist and slate-transport business, relaying many sections of the line and eventually extending it to its present-day terminus at Dalegarth Station by the mid 1920s. But despite its temporary reprieve, the railway hit hard times again during WWII, and its future looked bleak following the closure of the Eskdale quarries in the mid-1950s. But once again a dedicated bunch of steam enthusiasts stepped in at the last minute to prevent the railway's closure – this time the Ravenglass and Eskdale Railway Preservation Society, which still owns and operates the railway to this day. Under its careful stewardship the line has gone from strength to strength: it's now one of Cumbria's top 10 tourist attractions, with just under 120,000 passengers taking a trip on its trains every year. You can find out more about the society's work at www.rerps.co.uk; membership costs £16/8 per adult/child, and entitles you to a year's free travel on La'al Ratty. All aboard...

SOMETHING FOR THE WEEKEND

Start out with a pub supper and a night at the **Shepherd's Arms Hotel** (p140) in Ennerdale. On Saturday morning explore the forest trails and walks around the wonderfully peaceful **Ennerdale Valley** (p139) before heading down to **Ravenglass** (p130) for lunch at the **Ratty Arms** (opposite) and an afternoon spin along the **Ravenglass and Eskdale Railway** (p130). Stop off for a pint at the **Woolpack Inn** (p135) before catching the return train to Ravenglass, or stop overnight at the **Stanley Ghyll** (p135). Sunday is set for exploring one of the wildest Lakeland valleys, **Wasdale** (p136). Consider tackling one of the nearby **peaks** (p137) if you're feeling energetic, or just take a leisurely stroll along the lake before finishing up with a night at the utterly fabulous **Wasdale Head Inn** (p139).

GETTING THERE & AWAY

Next to the pub is the platform for the main Ravenglass station, which has frequent links north to Whitehaven (£3.80, 30 minutes), Maryport (£6.40, 50 minutes) and Carlisle (£12, one hour 40 minutes), and in the other direction to Ulverston (£7, one hour 20 minutes), Grange-over-Sands (£11.10, 1½ hours) and Arnside (£14.30, 1¾ hours). The **Cumbrian Coast Day Ranger** (adult/child/railcard holder £15/7.50/9.90) is valid for all stations along the Cumbrian Coast line.

Bus 6 from Whitehaven stops at Ravenglass and terminates at Muncaster (70 minutes, five daily). Bus X6 travels the same route on Sunday (four daily).

ESKDALE

Inland from Ravenglass, the chugging engines of La'al Ratty chunter along the base of the Eskdale Valley before reaching journey's end at Dalegarth Station, a stone's throw from the scattered houses and whitewashed inns of Boot. Further east along the valley, the road snakes up into the hilltops before reaching the high mountain pass of Hardknott, home to Cumbria's most spectacularly sited Roman fort. Out to the east, the road continues over Wrynose Pass into the valley of Little Langdale (p96).

ESKDALE GREEN

Whether you're arriving by road or rail, the first village you'll reach from the west is Eskdale Green, a teeny farming hamlet that marks the junction of the minor roads from Wasdale, Santon Bridge and the coast. There's been some kind of settlement here since at least Roman times, and possibly long before, and the village became an important gateway into the Eskdale Valley following the arrival of the La'al Ratty railway, which stops on the edge of the village at the station at Irton Rd. There's another request stop on the east side of the village near the Fisherground campsite.

In the 1890s the village formed part of the Gatehouse estate, founded as a country retreat by the Liverpudlian coal merchant James Rea. The house itself has been an Outward Bound centre since the 1950s, but the bamboo plantations, maple trees, azaleas and ornamental pools of its formal **Japanese garden**, designed by the renowned Victorian landscaper Thomas Mawson, are slowly being restored to their former glory by the Forestry Commission after decades of neglect. The gardens can be reached via a public footpath through Giggle Alley Forest, near the car park beside the little chapel of St Bega, which has been recently redeveloped as an unmanned visitor centre for the valley, with displays on the history and geography of the area.

High above the village, the tall oaks and birch trees of **Miterdale Forest** fan out across the granite hilltops, and make an excellent place to stretch your legs, especially in early spring or late autumn. There's a car park beside Miterdale Beck, and another just below Irton Pike on the road from Santon Bridge.

The village is at its liveliest in late summer for the **Eskdale Fete**, a family-friendly knees-up held in the grounds of the Outward Bound Centre on the Sunday of the August Bank Holiday. Even more important is the historic **Eskdale Show**, held on the last Saturday in September in a field near the King George IV pub. This traditional country gathering is the largest Herdwick sheep show in the whole of Cumbria, and attracts breeders from all over northern England; there are also displays of hound trailing, fell running and local craftwork.

WESTERN LAKE DISTRICT

DETOUR – ESKDALE MILL

Just behind Boot village, across the 17th-century humpback bridge over Whillans Beck, is the **Eskdale Mill** (☎ 019467-23335; admission £1.50; ✆ 11am-5.30pm Tue-Sun Apr-Sep, sometimes closed Sat Apr & Sep), built in 1578 and one of the oldest working mills left in England. The mill's twin waterwheels were once employed to grind flour and grain, and were still in use well into the 1920s; they were later used to generate electricity until the valley was eventually hooked up to the national grid in the mid-1950s. Admission includes a guided tour around the mill and its wooden machinery in the company of Dave King, the genial miller who's been in charge of the site for the last 17 years.

Sleeping & Eating

Fisherground Farm Camping (☎ 019467-23349; www .fishergroundcampsite.co.uk; Eskdale Green; adult/child/car £5/2.50/2.50; ✆ Mar-Oct) This convivial family-orientated campsite is popular with hikers and overnighters on La'al Ratty, with lots of space spread out over a couple of farm fields, and separate his-and-hers bathroom blocks with coin-op showers and a nearby laundry. There's even a little adventure playground for the kids, but space is tight in summer.

King George IV (☎ 019467-23262; www.kinggeorge -eskdale.co.uk; Eskdale Green; r £60-72; (P)) History lurks in every cranny at the village's main drinking hole, clad in beams, flagstones and climbing ivy, and surrounded by rolling countryside. Expect countrified wallpapers and satin bedspreads in the rooms, an impressive line-up of 200 whiskies behind the bar, and a pub-standard menu stocked with sarnies and steaks (mains £4 to £12).

Bower House Inn (☎ 01946-723244; www.bower houseinn.co.uk; Eskdale Green; d £78; (P)) Sunny colours and polished pine ensure the rooms feel smarter up at the Bower House, plonked beside the local cricket pitch. Downstairs the beamed bar centres around a big log fire, with plenty of alcoves to shelter in. There's Theakston's and local bitters on tap, and a surprisingly adventurous bistro menu (£22.50) that dabbles in cider and apple soup and duck breast with roasted fruits.

DALEGARTH & BOOT

East of Eskdale Green the railway winds through the ever-emptier valley for another 2 miles before reaching the end of the line at Dalegarth Station, set against the moody backdrop of hills around Hardknott Pass. If you're feeling peckish there's a decent cafe inside the station, as well as a small gift shop and **visitor centre** (☎ 019467-23226; ✆ when trains are running) that also rents out mountain bikes (half/full day £8/14).

Dalegarth is the starting point for several easy cycling routes including the 8.5-mile Eskdale Trail: you can pick up route cards from the visitor centre. There's also a short trail opposite the station leading to the 60ft **Stanley Ghyll Force** and the nearby chapel of **St Catherine's**, overlooked by the menacing lump of Scafell Pike. Parts of the church date back to the 12th century, although the delicate stained glass and simple wooden pews are much more recent. In the churchyard, you can't fail to spot the florid tombstone belonging to Thomas Dobson, former master of the Ennerdale and Eskdale Hunt. Fittingly enough, his graven image is flanked by carvings of both quarry (fox) and companion (hound).

Half a mile further east from Dalegarth is the shoebox-sized village of Boot, which marks the last sign of human habitation before the tortuous slog up to Hardknott. This area was at the clanking heart of the Eskdale iron-mining boom in the 19th century, and the surrounding hilltops are pock-marked with abandoned quarries, shafts and mine works.

Back in the village, Boot's twin inns make a useful stop off where you can slake your thirst before tackling the Hardknott road; pitch up in mid-June and you'll find yourself in the middle of the annual **Boot Beer Festival** (www .bootbeer.co.uk). There's also the small **Fold End Gallery** (☎ 019467-23335; ✆ phone for times) displaying local sculptures, ceramics, paintings and hand-blown glass.

Sleeping & Eating

Hollins Farm Campsite (☎ 019467-23253; www.hollins farmcampsite.co.uk; Boot; adult £6.60-7.60, child £2.25-2.35; (P)) Another quiet farm site aimed squarely at family campers, with a strict no-music, no-fires and no-rowdiness policy. The camping field is spacious and sheltered by tall pines, the shower blocks sparkle, and the Brook House Inn is within stumbling distance.

Eskdale YHA (☎ 0870 770 5824; eskdale@yha.org.uk; Boot; dm £15.95; ☯ Easter–Oct) Hunkering under the hills, this purpose-built hostel is a favourite way station for walkers and Ravenglass railway travellers. Zingy pinks, yellows and tangerines liven up the dorms and TV lounge, there's bike hire and a decent kitchen, and countless walks start right outside the front door.

Stanley Ghyll (☎ 019467-23327; www.stanleyghyll -eskdale.co.uk; near Boot; s/d/f £48/70/90; ℗) This gabled Victorian hotel turned thoroughly snug B&B boasts some of the best bedroom views in the valley. Tiled fireplaces, lofty ceilings and a smart stripped-wood breakfast room make for cosy lounging, and the rooms are unfussily decorated, with white walls and a choice of bold primary colours.

Boot Inn (☎ 0845 130 6224; www.bootinn.co.uk; Boot; s/d £50/100; ℗) Boot's most popular boozer is another beauty, offering hale and hearty Lakeland food (mains £7 to £12) and local ales served at the green-slate bar. The beer garden's particularly nice, with great views and play areas to keep the nippers happy.

Brook House Inn (☎ 019467-23288; www.brook houseinn.co.uk; Boot; s/d £55/79; ℗) Broad green fields and tumbledown walls make for divine views at this old Eskdale inn. The rooms are fairly ordinary in magnolia and pine, but the pub's a peach, with a carefully chosen ale list (including brews from the Barngates, Hawkshead and Coniston breweries) and blackboard menus (mains £8 to £15) making the most of fresh produce from nearby suppliers.

Woolpack Inn (☎ 019467-23230; Boot; r £65-120; ℗) Just east of Boot, the Woolpack has its own microbrewery concocting home-made ales for the two hugger-mugger 'baas', both covered in country memorabilia and sporting prints. There's often live music (think fiddles and guitars), but the upstairs rooms are a bit overpriced.

HARDKNOTT & WRYNOSE

Belt up: the hair-raising road up to the packhorse pass of Hardknott (p128) is one of the most spectacular (not to mention steepest) in England. From the valley floor the road rapidly gains almost 800m in altitude before it finally tops out beside the ruins of **Hardknott Roman Fort**. Known to the Romans as Mediobogdum, the fort was built between AD 120 and AD 138 to guard the vital supply route between the harbour at Ravenglass and the inland forts at Galava and around Hadrian's Wall. Though the building itself has been almost entirely dismantled over the last couple of millennia (largely by local farmers, for whom the ruins provided a handy source of building materials) you can still make out its essential foundations, including the parade ground, watchtowers, baths and commandant's house. The views down the Eskdale Valley and to the distant Cumbrian coastline are simply stunning, but you can't help feeling a little sympathy for the legionaries stationed here – it must have been a pretty tough posting for soldiers raised on Mediterranean climes, and it's hard to think of a lonelier spot in the entire Roman Empire.

From the high point at Hardknott, the road plummets down into the neighbouring valley of Cockley Beck (from where a branch road cuts south through the Duddon Valley) before

---

DETOUR – DUDDON VALLEY

If you really want to leave the outside world behind, the **Duddon Valley** (www.duddonvalley.co.uk) is a perfect spot. Stretching from the tip of Cockley Beck, halfway between Hardknott and Wrynose, down to the little village of Ulpha near the edge of the Duddon Sands, this remote valley is still traditional farming country: sheep and cattle outnumber the people by a considerable margin, and the fells and valley slopes are home to just a few farmhouses, tumbledown barns and crumbling walls. There are several uncrowded walks, including the stroll up **Wallowbarrow Crag** and **Harter Fell** (2142ft), and picnic spots aplenty, as well as a wonderful little inn in the village of Seathwaite, the **Newfield** (☎ 01229-716208; mains £6-14), which cooks up the meanest Sunday lunch for miles around.

Accommodation is thin on the ground: campers can head for **Turner Hall Farm** (☎ 01229-716420; sites from £8) near Seathwaite or the **High Wallabarrow Camping Barn** (☎ 01229-715011; www .wallabarrow.co.uk; dm £8.50) near Ulpha, while there's simple B&B digs at **Troutal Farm** (☎ 01229-716235; www.troutalfarm.co.uk; Seathwaite; s/d £35/70; ℗) or in the converted barn at **Seathwaite Lodge** (☎ 01229-716840; www.seathwaitelodge.co.uk; Seathwaite; d £50-60; ℗).

soaring back up the opposite side to the pass of Wrynose – at gradients of 25%, a marginally less taxing proposition than Hardknott, but not by much. From Wrynose the road drops down into the gentle valley of Little Langdale (p96), which makes a reassuringly level sight after the automotive challenges of the Hardknott–Wrynose road.

WASDALE

If it's a hardcore wilderness hit you're after, few places in the Lakes can match up to the unruly emptiness of the Wasdale valley. Closer to the wide-open vistas of the Scottish highlands than the gentle dales of the eastern Lakes, Wasdale (pronounced 'woz', rather than 'waz') still feels thrillingly remote: the only signs of human habitation are a historic hiker's inn, a web of drystone walls and a handful of slate-roofed farm cottages, all dwarfed by the backdrop of scree-scattered peaks and the inky black expanse of Wast Water, England's deepest lake. The views become increasingly dazzling as you venture into the valley from the western gateway at **Nether Wasdale**; the road tracks the west shore of the lake all the way to **Wasdale Head**, overlooked by a moody cluster of some of the national park's highest mountains, including Great Gable, Lingmell and England's tallest, Scafell Pike.

Shops are few and far between in the valley – the only place for supplies once you get beyond Nether Wasdale is the **Barn Door Shop** (☎ 019467-26384; Wasdale Head), which sells food, outdoors gear and hiking supplies, and also runs the useful community website www.wasdaleweb.com.

The only public transport to the valley is the **Wasdale Taxibus** (☎ 019467-25308), which runs between Gosforth and Wasdale Head twice daily on Thursday, Saturday and Sunday – ring to book a seat.

GOSFORTH & SANTON BRIDGE

Other than a smattering of pubs, shops and B&Bs, there's not too much to keep you in either of the villages at the western end of Wasdale – but it's worth finding the time to visit the 14ft **Gosforth cross** in the churchyard of St Mary's, one of the earliest (and tallest) 10th-century stone crosses to survive in mainland England. Its four carved faces

are renowned for their mix of pagan and Christian influences, intermingling elements of the Norse sagas with Biblical imagery – the lower parts of the cross are decorated with interlocking foliage, thought to represent *Yggdrasil*, the Norse tree of life, while the upper surfaces depict various warriors and figures (including one said to be either a depiction of Christ on the cross or the resurrection of the Viking god Baldur). A rather less impressive cross, also dating from the 10th century, can be seen in the churchyard at **Irton** nearby.

Sleeping & Eating

Rainors Farm (☎ 019467-25934; www.rainorsfarm.co.uk; Gosforth; s £30-40, d £55-65) Three sweet rooms in a whitewashed farmhouse cottage, prettied up with crimson spreads and country views. There's a choice of traditional or veggie breakfasts, and campers can bunk down in a back-garden yurt (£550 per week).

Lutwidge Arms Hotel (☎ 019467-24230; www.lutwidgearms.co.uk; Holmrook, Santon Bridge; s £40-55, d £65-90; **P**) Luxury it ain't, but the Lutwidge is a reasonable fall back so long as you're a sucker for spartan decor. Off-white walls and flower-or-check fabrics keep things stolidly traditional, and the family rooms have sofa beds for the kids. The brook-side location beside the River Irt is a selling point, too.

Bridge Inn (☎ 019467-26221; www.santonbridgeinn.com; Santon Bridge; mains £8.95-14.50; 🛜) Near the junction of the road between Santon Bridge and Nether Wasdale, this black-and-white coach stop packs in the punters thanks to its fibbing competition (see boxed text, opposite), but it's also a good bet for lamb in Jennings bitter or battered haddock, served amid wood stanchions and country trinkets. The rather tired upstairs rooms will do in a pinch (single/double £85/95), but you could do better.

Gosforth Hall Hotel (☎ 019467-25322; www.gosforthhallhotel.co.uk; Gosforth; mains £8.95-15.95; **P**) Off-kilter floors, spiralling staircases and even an original 'priest's hole' built to shelter clandestine Catholics hint at the age of this 17th-century manor. The old kitchen has been turned into a cosy pub (complete with brick-surround hearth), and the restaurant dabbles in rump steaks and a 'hunger annihilation' pie. The rooms (doubles £70 to £120) are less stellar, although the four-poster suite has some historic cachet.

FIBBING & FACE PULLING

Cumbrians are well known for their propensity for telling tall tales, but Will Ritson, a 19th-century landlord at the Wasdale Head Inn, took the tradition to an entirely different level. Will was known throughout the region for his outlandish stories; one of his most famous tales concerned a Wasdale turnip that was so large that local residents burrowed into it for their Sunday lunch, and later used it as a shelter for their sheep. He also claimed to own a cross between a foxhound and a golden eagle that could leap over drystone walls. In honour of Will's mendacious tradition, the Santon Bridge Inn holds the **Biggest Liar in the World** competition every November; Cumbrian dialect is allowed, but lawyers and politicians are barred from entering. One of the competition's recent winners was the TV comedian Sue Perkins, who scooped the top prize with a tale about sheep in the valley breaking wind and causing a hole in the ozone layer.

Alternatively, you could head for the **World Gurning Competition**, held in mid-September in Egremont, near St Bees. To gurn is to pull an ugly face; the challenge is believed to stem from the 12th century, when the lord of the manor handed out sour crab apples to his workers. Locally born Anne Wood won the trophy 24 years running till she was finally beaten in 2001.

WASDALE HEAD

Half a mile on from West Water's northern tip is Wasdale Head, the valley's only settlement. There's a public car park next door to the Wasdale Inn, which affords a barnstorming view of the rest of the valley: great green-brown humps and scree-covered slopes recede into the far distance, clearly marking the course of the long-extinct glacier that carved through the surrounding mountains. There's a real edge of untamed – and rather un-English – wilderness around Wasdale Head, so unsurprisingly it's an irresistible target for fell walkers; classic ascents of Great Gable, Great End, Sca Fell and Scafell Pike all start within easy reach of the village car park, while the old packhorse trail over Styhead Pass into Borrowdale (p160) begins to the northeast.

Other than the fells, the only real sight in the village is the minuscule church of **St Olaf's**, reputed to be the smallest in England. Though the foundations of the church date back to at least the 16th century, it's probably much older – many of the surrounding place names have their origins in Old Norse, indicating that the valley was almost certainly first settled by Vikings, and the central roof beam is rumoured to have been fashioned from the hull of a Viking longboat. Despite its age, the churchyard was officially unconsecrated until 1901, meaning that the dead had to be carried along the old coffin route over Eskdale Moor and Burnmoor Tarn to be buried at the church in Boot.

In his *Guide to the Lakes,* Wordsworth described **Wast Water** as 'long, narrow, stern and desolate', and seen on a cold, wintry day shrouded by spidery mist and low cloud, it's a description that still seems apt. The lake itself is owned by the National Trust, and is the deepest body of water in the national park at a maximum depth of around 258ft. It's also one of the coldest and clearest; very little life can survive in its inhospitable waters (apart from the hardy Arctic char), and the clarity of the water makes it a popular location with local lake divers. The lake's best-known feature are the screes that cover the fell slopes along its eastern edge; some reach a height of around 2000ft in places, and were formed over several millennia by the combined effects of ice, wind and rain on the rocks of the nearby mountains of the Borrowdale Group.

Walking

Walkers have endless options in the Wasdale Valley, with well-trodden routes up all the nearby peaks including **Great Gable** (2949ft), **Scoat Fell** (2759ft) and **Lingmell** (2624ft). **Sca Fell** (3163ft), England's second-highest peak, is almost as popular a target as its neighbour, **Scafell Pike** (3209ft); the two summits are connected by the Mickledore pass, but the old scramble up Lord's Rake is now considered unsafe due to unstable rockfall. Instead you'll have to follow the long roundabout loop via Burnmoor Tarn.

One of the quintessential long-distance walks is the **Mosedale Horseshoe** (10.2 miles) a tough but fantastically rewarding circuit starting at Wasdale Head and ascending towards the Black Sail Pass and the rocky Pillar (a favourite target for Lakeland rock climbers)

WESTERN LAKE DISTRICT

before continuing on via Scoat Fell, Steeple, Red Pike and Yewbarrow. It's a tough full-day proposition, but well worth the lactic acid.

Sleeping & Eating

BUDGET

Wasdale Campsite (☎ 019467-26220; www.wasdale campsite.org.uk; adult £4.50-5.50, child £2-2.50, car £3-3.50) This National Trust campsite is in a fantastically wild spot, nestled beneath the Scafell range a mile from Wast Water. Facilities are basic (laundry room, showers and not much else), but the views are, needless to say, rather fine.

Barn Door Campsite (☎ 019467-26384; Wasdale Head; per person £2.50) Wasdale's other campsite is next door to the Barn Door Shop, opposite the Wasdale Head Inn. It's strictly for campers who like their sites rudimentary (the on-site luxuries are limited to a cold tap and a toilet), but there's nearly always space. The site doesn't take reservations – just pay at the shop when you arrive.

Murt Camping Barn (☎ 01946-758198; philsgrant@ btinternet.com; Nether Wasdale; dm £7) About 250m from Nether Wasdale, this simple stone barn sleeps around eight people in chilly but dry surroundings. There's a single loo and shower, and hot water on tap, but you'll need bedding and camping supplies. If you're feeling peckish, the farm also makes four types of cheese named after local fells – you can either buy on-site or check out the cheeseboards at the Wasdale Head Inn or Low Wood Hall.

Wast Water YHA (☎ 0845 371 9350; wastwater@yha .org.uk; Wasdale Hall, Nether Wasdale; dm £11.95; ⊙ reception 8am-10am & 5-10.30pm, open year round by advance booking) Another stunning Lakeland hostel in a half-timbered 19th-century Gothic mansion in Nether Wasdale. Originally the country manor of Wasdale Hall, the house still bears many of its original features – wood panelling, gabled roof and cornicing – and there's a great restaurant serving Cumbrian nosh. Some dorms have the kind of lake outlooks you'd normally have to pay through the nose for.

MIDRANGE

Burnthwaite Farm (☎ 019467-26242; www.burnthwaite farm.co.uk; Wasdale Head; d without bathroom £50, with bathroom £60; Ⓟ) Down-to-earth farmhouse-style lodgings with the usual low ceilings, flower-print duvets, and cholesterol-heavy brekkie – two rooms are en suite, others share facilities. It's one of the last remaining sheep farms in the valley, so if you ever wanted to get up close and personal with a fellbred, now's your chance.

Strands Inn (☎ 019467-26237; www.strandshotel .com; Nether Wasdale; s/d £50/75; Ⓟ) Built around 1800 as a post house and coaching inn, the Strands offers a few more creature comforts – cosy rooms finished in sunny pastels and pine bed frames, a convivial beamed bar warmed by a crackling fire, and a restaurant dishing up stonking portions of lamb shank and cod loin (mains £7.50 to £11.50).

THREE PEAKS CHALLENGE

Most people struggle to get to the top of Scafell Pike in a single day, but for a select bunch of souls scaling England's highest summit just isn't enough – so how about tackling Britain's two other highest summits for good measure? The gruelling Three Peaks Challenge is one of the toughest tests any British hill walker can tackle, and involves reaching the three highest points of the British mainland – Ben Nevis (4408ft) in Scotland, Snowdon (3560ft) in Wales and, the baby of the bunch, Scafell Pike (3209ft) in England – all in under 24 hours.

Thousands of hopefuls attempt the route every year, but unsurprisingly only a hardy few ever make it across the finishing line. A few hardcore purists have even tried to complete the challenge without the use of motorised vehicles, using relay teams of cyclists and runners.

The customary summertime route starts in the late afternoon with the ascent of Ben Nevis, followed by a six-hour overnight dash to scale Scafell Pike before breakfast, topped off by another three-hour drive and then the climb up to the top of Snowdon. To successfully complete the challenge, participants have to make it back to the bottom of Snowdon before the clock ticks round to the 24-hour mark.

The generally accepted record is held by the heroic fell runner Joss Naylor, who completed the challenge in just under 12 hours in the early 1970s. Increased traffic on the motorways means his record is unlikely to be broken in the foreseeable future.

The pub brews its own beer, too – ask the barman for the story behind the curiously named 'Errmmm…' ale.

Low Wood Hall (☎ 019467-26111; www.lowwoodhall .co.uk; Nether Wasdale; s £55-85, tw £80-90, d £75-120; Ⓟ) The valley's only real hotel offers two categories of room – the cheaper annexe ones are dowdy, but the superior rooms in the main building have LCD TVs, comfy sofas and prissy Laura Ashley–style fabrics. The restaurant (mains £14 to £20) is about the area's best for bistro food – mainly steak, game and fish – and the valley views from the conservatory are to die for.

Lingmell House (☎ 019467-26261; www.lingmell house.co.uk; Wasdale Head; d £60; Ⓟ) Squatting at the head of the valley surrounded by majestic peaks, this bare-bones B&B is the place if you're desperate to dodge the madding crowds. A former vicarage, it still feels austere – rooms are simply furnished with beds, battered TVs and not a great deal else, but the setting is inescapably grand.

our pick **Wasdale Head Inn** (☎ 019467-26229; www .wasdale.com; Wasdale Head; d £108-118; Ⓟ) This gloriously atmospheric inn is inextricably linked with the history of British mountaineering – one of its former owners, Will Ritson, helped pioneer the sport in the late 19th century, and vintage climbing memorabilia and dog-eared photos of Victorian gents in tweed britches and hobnailed boots decorate the interior bars. It's long been a hiker's favourite; the snug rooms are crammed with charm, but there are no TVs, so you'll just have to make do with the world-class view (for more space ask for one of the self-catering flats in the converted barn). Hikers congregate in the hugger-mugger bars for home-brewed ales and plates of chicken curry and stew (bar menu £8 to £11), or retire to the wood-panelled restaurant for filo parcels, baked salmon and venison haunch (four courses £28). Reet grand.

ENNERDALE

Over the windswept fell-tops to the north of Wasdale is the neighbouring valley of Ennerdale, often cited by seasoned lakelanders as the most scenic corner of the entire national park. In many ways it feels even more remote than Wasdale – there's just a single village at **Ennerdale Bridge**, and the rest of the valley is taken up by the blue-green 2.5-mile arc of **Ennerdale Water**, encircled by fields, crags, rocky peaks and thick woodland, overlooked by the high points of **Pillar** (2927ft) and **Scoat Fell** (2759ft).

Ennerdale Water is one of the most westerly lakes in the national park, and the only one not ringed by an access road – there's a car park at Bleach Green at the lake's western tip, and another on its northern shore beneath Bowness Knott, ensuring the eastern end of Ennerdale remains entirely free of the traffic jams, cruise boats and heaving crowds you'll find at many of the region's other beauty spots. If the view looks spookily familiar, don't be surprised – Ennerdale provided the suitably remote backdrop for the closing scenes of Danny Boyle's British zombie flick *28 Days Later*.

Ennerdale is also home to one of the largest areas of managed forest in Cumbria – the barren eastern end of the lake was heavily replanted with pine, spruce and conifer in the 1930s (a highly controversial decision at the time and one which Wainwright later lambasted at considerable length), and today provides one of the county's main commercial lumber plantations. But in partnership with the National Trust and United Utilities, the Forestry Commission has recently committed to returning large parts of the valley to their wild origins as part of the Wild Ennerdale Project. Timber felling is being scaled back and wild cattle have been reintroduced to the area. Walking leaflets describing the many trails through the Ennerdale Forest are available from the shops in Ennerdale Bridge, or can be downloaded from the excellent project website at www.wildennerdale.co.uk.

Obviously, tackling the nearby fells is one of the main draws of the Ennerdale Valley, and the area is often much quieter than the better-known peaks around Wasdale. Several walks start from Bowness Knott car park: the easy **Smithy Beck Trail** (one hour, 2 miles) runs along the lakeshore into the Ennerdale Forest, or there's a more taxing **Round-the-Lake route** (four hours, 7 miles) via the high point of Angler's Crag on the lake's southern side. The valley is also on the long-distance Coast-to-Coast Walk from Whitehaven, which cuts through Ennerdale Bridge before climbing over Black Sail Pass into Borrowdale and Seatoller.

WESTERN LAKE DISTRICT

For a truly challenging walk, the **Ennerdale Round** tracks a 22.4-mile course around all the major peaks overlooking Ennerdale, including Red Pike, Haystacks, Green Gable, Kirk Fell, Pillar and Steeple. Most hikers opt to break the hike into two days, overnighting at the fantastically remote Black Sail YHA, but some steel-legged fell runners opt to tackle it in a single leg-jellying day. Definitely not for the faint-hearted.

SLEEPING & EATING

our pick **Black Sail YHA** (☎ 07711-108450; dm £13.95; ⏱ Apr–mid-Oct, by arrangement at other times) Views, views and more views – this high-mountain refuge is a legend among Lakeland walkers (so bookings are essential), nestled at the top of the Black Sail Pass 6 miles east of Bowness Knott, and only accessible on foot. Converted from an old shepherds' bothy, the facilities make most prison blocks look luxurious: the dorms are cramped, the lounge doubles as a drying room for wet boots and smelly socks, and there's no phone reception, no TV and no electric power, but hearty three-course meals (including wine and beer) are cooked up by the hostel manager, and there's no better place to swap stories with like-minded walkers. Oh – and did we mention the views?

Ennerdale YHA (☎ 0845 371 9116; ennerdale@yha.org.uk; Cat Crag, Ennerdale; dm £13.95; ⏱ reception 8am-10am & 5-8pm, Apr-Aug; Ⓟ) Purpose-built hostel converted from forestry cottages, tucked away in green woodland at the eastern end of the lake. Power is supplied by the hostel's own hydroelectric generator, so it's as green as hostels come; the decor is fairly modern throughout and the dorms are limited to two six-bed and three four-bed configurations. It's a popular first-night stay for people tackling the Ennerdale round, so booking ahead is sensible.

Shepherd's Arms Hotel (☎ 01946-861249; www.shepherdsarmshotel.co.uk; s/d/f £49.50/79/99; Ⓟ 📶) Terrific village pub that doubles as Ennerdale's handiest stopover on the C2C route, offering smartly refurbished rooms decked out with hefty wooden sideboards, thick throws and big digital TVs. There's a stripy-walled lounge for guest use complete with magazines and original fireplace, a line-up of beers certified by the Campaign for Real Ale (CAMRA) behind the bar, and the usual pub standards on the blackboard menu (mains £8 to £16).

GETTING THERE & AWAY

There's no scheduled public transport into Ennerdale itself, although in summer the 263 'Ennerdale Rambler' travels three times on Sunday from Bowness Knott car park via Ennerdale Bridge (seven minutes), Loweswater (25 minutes) and Buttermere (50 minutes); one daily bus also continues to Cockermouth (70 minutes), Workington (one hour 50 minutes) and Maryport (two hours).

Keswick & Derwent Water

Pocked with islands, fringed by pebbled shores and overarching trees, and overlooked by the hulking dome of Skiddaw, there are few lakes with such an immediate wow factor as Derwent Water. Neither as touristy as Windermere or as wild as Wast Water, it's a place that sums up all that's green and good about the Lakeland landscape, and if you like nothing more than cruising the waters or wandering the hilltops, there are few corners of the Lakes where you'll be better served.

The attractive market town of Keswick makes the best base, handily plonked within reach of all the area's major sights. To the south and southwest of town are the twin valleys of Borrowdale and Buttermere, connected by the slate-strewn pass of Honister, while to the west are the towering conifer forests and mountain-bike trails of Whinlatter. The peaceful lake of Bassenthwaite, famous for the wild ospreys that have been soaring across its summer skies since 2001, lies a few miles to the north. Bookworms can check out Tennyson connections at the stately home of Mirehouse on the lake's eastern shore, while Wordsworth devotees can wander the halls of his childhood home in Cockermouth, lovingly restored by the National Trust after decades of neglect.

HIGHLIGHTS

- Feel the call of the wild watching the **Bassenthwaite ospreys** (p153)
- Test your nerve on the **Via Ferrata** (p163) at the Honister Slate Mine
- Trundle through the little-visited **Lorton Valley** (p156)
- Trace William's literary beginnings at **Wordsworth House** (p157) in Cockermouth
- Wander the gardens of marvellous **Mirehouse** (p153)
- Hop on the 77 bus into the **Buttermere Valley** (p163)

★ Cockermouth
★ Bassenthwaite Lake
Lorton Valley ★
★ Mirehouse
★ Buttermere Valley
★ Via Ferrata

Area of largest lake (Derwent Water): 2.05 sq miles	Cumberland Pencil Museum visitors in 2007: 85,000	Batmobiles at the Cars of the Stars Motor Museum: 3

ITINERARY 1
CATBELLS WALK

3.5 miles/3 hours/Hawes End

The miniature mountain of **Catbells** (1481ft) packs an impressive punch considering its modest height. The fell is well known as one of the most family-friendly Lakeland summits, but that doesn't mean it's without its challenges – the trail is steep and rocky in places and follows a lofty ridge, but once you're at the top you'll be treated to a stupendous outlook across **Derwent Water**.

The traditional starting point up Catbells (thought to be a corruption of the Old Norse *cat bield*, or wild cat's lair) is at **Hawes End** on the lake's west side. Parking is problematic, so the easiest way to get there is aboard the Keswick Launch or the 77 bus; alternatively you can walk from Keswick through **Portinscale** and the Lingholm Estate.

From Hawes End the path crosses a **cattle grid** and then offers a choice of two trails: the standard path leads straight on or there's an alternative trail a little further along the old 'green road', which traces a zigzagging course up the fell-side. This second path – engineered by Sir John Woodford, a local resident and much-decorated veteran of the Battle of Waterloo – eventually joins the first before the final ascent.

The trail runs over a false summit and a series of small depressions before climbing along the spectacular **ridge** to Catbells' true peak. The **summit** is a fell-spotter's dream; the northern aspect is the most impressive, with views of Skiddaw's twin peaks, flanked by Carl Side and Ullock Pike to the west and Lonscale Fell to the east. Over on the lake's eastern side, you can spot Walla Crag, Bleaberry Fell and High Seat; to the west is the Newlands Valley; while far off to the south is the Borrowdale Valley and the distinctive point of Castle Crag.

From the summit, you can continue the ridge walk southwest to Maiden Moor. Alternatively, follow the trail downhill, turning back towards the lake via **Hause Gate** and on to the main road. A right-hand trail leads down through the woods past **Brandlehow Bay** and back to Hawes End.

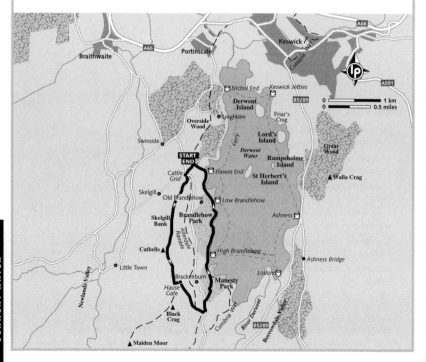

ITINERARY 2
SKIDDAW HIKE
8 miles/4 to 5 hours/Keswick

Cumbria has four mountains that top 3000ft – Scafell Pike, Sca Fell, Helvellyn, and **Skiddaw** (3054ft), which dominates Keswick's northern skyline. The chosen ascent is moderately challenging – it's a long puff to the top, but the track is clearly defined and the drops aren't too stomach churning. As with all high-altitude peaks, it's important to be prepared – 'Keswick's Matterhorn' is not just high and steep, it's also very exposed, and fog and cloud can make navigation tricky.

The walk initially follows the Latrigg route detailed on p148. Start on Brundholme Rd and follow Spooney Green Lane. You'll reach the Underscar car park at the end of Gale Rd after about an hour. If you're feeling lively you could add an ascent up Latrigg, otherwise stick to the trail and take the next left-hand fork, which begins the long plod to the fell-top. Look out for a ruined building known as the 'Halfway House' on your right as you ascend past **Lonscale Fell** (2344ft). Victorian and Edwardian tourists would once have paused here for refreshments (although you'll have to bring your own).

After another long climb you'll reach a left-hand detour to **Skiddaw Little Man** (2838ft), but this mini-summit is better left for the descent. Stick to the main trail and carry on up the steep path for around half a mile over a series of 'tops'; you'll know you've reached the true summit when you're standing next to the Ordnance Survey trig-point.

Standing proud of the surrounding fells, and covered with a shattered expanse of slate and rock, Skiddaw's peak is a dramatic place to be. If the weather's clear, there are unforgettable views in all directions; you should be able to glimpse all the great Lakeland ranges, including the Helvellyns, Scafells and, on a really good day, the Scottish peaks.

There are several possible descents, including the ridge trail over Carl Side and various routes down to Bassenthwaite Lake, but retracing your steps allows you to take in the summit of Skiddaw Little Man on the way down.

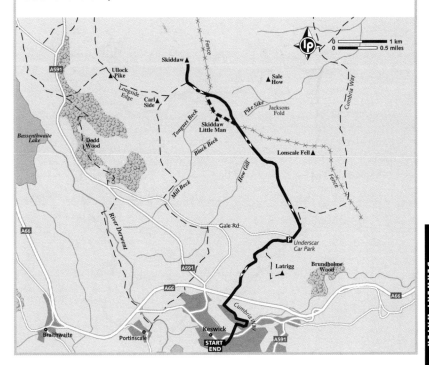

ITINERARY 3
BORROWDALE & BUTTERMERE DRIVE   28 miles/4 to 5 hours/Keswick

Buckle up – this is one of the Lakes' most beautiful road trips, taking in the unspoilt scenery of the Borrowdale, Buttermere and Lorton valleys. The roads are surprisingly good, although obviously they're on the narrow and winding side. The only really tricky section, however, is the steep ascent of Honister Pass.

Begin the day in **Keswick** (opposite). Pick up some goodies for the road from **Good Taste** (p151), not forgetting a few sticky spoils from **Bryson's** (p151), then head along the B5289 into the Borrowdale Valley. First stop is the lovely **Lodore Falls** (p160), followed by a detour to the little hamlet of **Grange** (p160). If your legs are feeling lively the village is a great place from which to tackle Castle Crag, one of Borrowdale's best-known summits. Otherwise carry on down the road and stop off at the great lump of rock known as the **Bowder Stone** (p160), before pootling along the valley to **Seatoller** (p161), where another scenic walk awaits up to **Taylor Ghyll Force** (p162).

Break for lunch at **Yew Tree Inn** (p162) and then tackle the steep crawl over **Honister Pass** (p163), where you can pick up some slatey souvenirs or take an underground mine tour.

From here the road swings and veers down into the beautiful valley of Buttermere; spot the zigzag peaks of High Stile, Haystacks and Red Pike looming on your left-hand side over the lake. Stop for afternoon tea at the **Bridge Hotel** (p163), or the **Fish Hotel** (p163), once famous as the home of the Maid of Buttermere, before paying your Wainwright respects inside **St James' Church** (p163). Continue along the shore of **Crummock Water** to **Low Lorton**, where a right-hand turn carries you through the **Lorton Valley** (p156) to the spectacular pass of Whinlatter and the nearby **Whinlatter Forest** (p156). The forest park makes a good spot for a late afternoon stop; there's a pleasant cafe at the **visitor centre**, as well as nature-themed displays on the local red squirrel and osprey populations.

From Whinlatter, it's a twisty drive downhill to the A66 junction at Braithwaite back to Keswick.

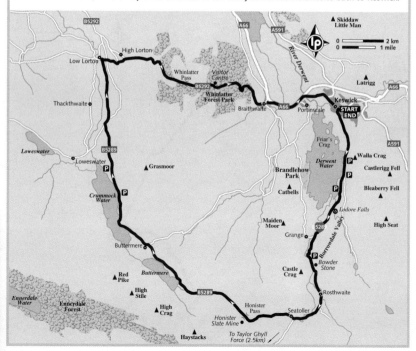

KESWICK

pop 5257

Nestled at the head of Derwent Water among a thicket of towering fells, Keswick is one of the handsomest of the Lake District's market towns. Centred on a cobbled marketplace crammed with bakeries, cafes and enough outdoors stores to launch an assault on Everest, the town is the northern Lakes' main commercial centre. Classic fell walks criss-cross the encircling hilltops, while barges and row boats scull out from the northern shores of the lake near Crow Park, and if the weather turns wet you can head indoors to discover Robert Southey's clogs, a 667-year-old mummified cat, the A-Team van and the world's largest pencil.

HISTORY

Keswick's name derives from the Old Norse *cese-wic* (cheese farm), and agriculture remained an important industry throughout the Middle Ages, following the endowment of the town's market charter in 1276. Wool, leather, charcoal and agricultural goods provided the main revenue, supplemented by slate, stone, and graphite (then known as plumbago, or black lead), which was discovered at Seathwaite in 1555.

In 1864 a railway between Cockermouth, Keswick and Penrith opened up the area to tourists and industrialists, leading to a building boom around Keswick and the creation of elegant mansions overlooking Hope Park and Fitz Park. The line was closed during the 1960s and '70s and now forms a section of the Sea to Sea Cycle Route (C2C).

ORIENTATION

Keswick's main thoroughfares are the pedestrianised Market Pl and Main St, which run parallel to the River Greta to the northeast. The tourist office is in the town's former moot hall at the head of Market Pl. Derwent Water is to the southwest of town along Lake Rd, overlooked by the green expanse of Crow Park.

INFORMATION

Branches of Natwest, Lloyds, Barclays and HSBC are located on Market Pl.

Bookends (☎ 017687-75277; 66 Main St; 9.30am-6pm Mon-Fri, 9am-6pm Sat, 10am-6pm Sun) Excellent local bookshop with walking guides and maps.

Keswick Laundrette (☎ 017687-75448; Main St; ☽ 8am-7pm Mon-Sat, 9am-7pm Sun)

Keswick Library (☎ 017687-72656; Heads Rd; internet per half hr £1; ☽ 10am-7pm Mon & Wed, 10am-5pm Tue & Fri, 10am-12.30pm Thu & Sat)

Police Station (Bank St; ☽ 9am-5pm Mon-Wed & Fri)

Post Office (☎ 017687-72269; 48 Main St; ☽ 9am-5.30pm Mon-Fri, 9am-12.30pm Sat)

Tourist Office (☎ 017687-72645; keswicktic@lake-district.gov.uk; Moot Hall, Market Pl; ☽ 9.30am-5.30pm Apr-Oct, 9.30am-4.30pm Nov-Mar) In the old Moot Hall at the top of Market Pl. Organises guided walks (see p148) and sells discount launch tickets.

U-Compute (☎ 017687-72269; 48 Main St; per half hr/hr £2/3; ☽ 9am-5.30pm) Internet cafe above the post office.

www.keswick.org Comprehensive guide to all things Keswickian.

SIGHTS
Keswick Museum

Tucked along Station Rd overlooking the orderly lawns of Fitz Park is the endearingly oddball **Keswick Museum and Art Gallery** (☎ 017687-73263; Station Rd; admission free; ☽ 10am-4pm Tue-Sat Feb-Oct), which has hardly changed since its opening in 1898. Glass display cabinets house a hotchpotch of exhibits including a Napoleonic teacup, a penny farthing bicycle, a man trap, a mounted golden eagle, a spoon made from a sheep's leg bone and a cluster of letters from Southey, Wordsworth, de Quincey and Ruskin. But the museum's most famous exhibits are its mummified cat (allegedly 667 years old) and the famous Musical Stones of Skiddaw, created from regional hornsfel rock in 1827 by the local stonemason Joseph Richardson. The stones' plink-plonk melody was a famous 19th-century tourist attraction, and even featured in a gala performance for Queen Victoria.

Cars of the Stars Motor Museum

Keswick's weirdometer moves up another notch at the **Cars of the Stars Motor Museum** (☎ 017687-73757; www.carsofthestars.com; Standish St; adult/child £5/3; ☽ 10am-5pm), an astonishing collection of celebrity vehicles amassed over 25 years by petrolhead Peter Nelson.

The line-up of eminent motors includes Chitty Chitty Bang Bang, Mr Bean's Mini, KITT from *Knightrider*, the A-Team van, Herbie the Love Bug, Mad Max's Interceptor and the Delorean from *Back to the Future*. Not impressed? Then look out for a trio of

KESWICK & DERWENT WATER

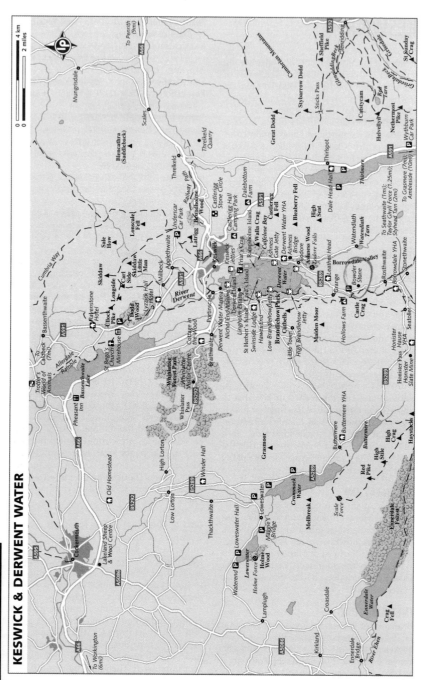

Batmobiles (including models from *Batman Forever*, Tim Burton's *Batman* and the original TV series starring Adam Faith) and an entire fleet of Bond cars, including an Aston Martin DB5 from *Goldfinger*, the Lotus Esprit from *For Your Eyes Only* and the tuk-tuk taxis from *Octopussy*.

Cumberland Pencil Museum

Plumbago, or graphite, has been an important export for Keswick since the 16th century. Local shepherds used graphite for years as a sheep marker, and the mineral was later used as a rust proofer, metal lubricant and even as a cure for stomach ailments, but it was only when some bright spark in Florence stuck it into a wooden holder that the graphite industry in Keswick really took off.

The first industrially produced pencil was made here in 1832, and you can explore a host of graphite-themed exhibits at the **Cumberland Pencil Museum** (☎ 017687-73626; www.pencilmuseum .co.uk; Southey Works; adult/child £3/1.50; ☯ 9.30am-5pm), including a reconstruction of the Seathwaite slate mine and the world's longest pencil (measuring an impressive 26ft tip to top). The museum is next door to the Cumberland Pencil Factory, which still manufactures luxury Derwent colouring pencils.

Derwent Water

Three miles long, a mile wide and 72ft from surface to lake bed, Derwent Water is a gem. Stretching from the tip of Crow Park and ringed on all sides by scowling fells, the lake's most famous features are its tree-covered islands. The largest is **St Herbert's**, named after the 'hermit of Derwent Water', a disciple of St Cuthbert who lived on the island in the 7th century, while the smallest is **Rampsholme Island**, which often gets completely swamped during periods of heavy rainfall.

In the northeastern corner is **Lord's Island**, formerly the property of local earls, while nearby **Derwent Island** was owned by Yorkshire monks and German miners before it was purchased by the eccentric aristocrat Joseph Pocklington, who built the island's wonderful Italianate house (Wordsworth thought it was an abominable eyesore and tried to get it pulled down). The National Trust now owns the island and rents it to long-term tenants, who have to open the house to the public for five days every year. Phone ☎ 017687-73780 for details.

One of the most renowned viewpoints is from the promontory known as **Friar's Crag**, reached via a 15-minute stroll along the shoreline from Lake Rd. With sweeping vistas of the southern lake to Castle Crag, it's a favourite spot for photographers and birdwatchers, and provided a memorable childhood visit for the young John Ruskin. The land is now owned by the National Trust and is dedicated to the environmentalist Canon Hardwicke Rawnsley, one of the organisation's co-founders.

Other intriguing sights dotted around the lakeshore include **Ashness Bridge**, a famously photogenic bridge about half a mile inland from the Ashness Gate pier, and the modest 90ft tumble of **Lodore Falls** (p160) at the lake's southern end. To the west is the woodland of **Brandlehow Park**, the first patch of land ever purchased by the National Trust, and to the northwest are the landscaped gardens of Lingholm, now unfortunately closed to the public.

The **Keswick Launch** (p148) runs a ferry service around the lake.

DETOUR – CASTLERIGG STONE CIRCLE

Of all the Lake District's stone circles, none has the dumbfounding drama of Castlerigg, perched on a lonely hilltop a mile above Keswick. Constructed between 3000 and 4000 years ago, the circle contains between 38 and 42 stones (depending on which ones you count), with a further rectangle of stones set inside the main ring; the tallest is around 8ft high, and the largest weighs over 16 tons. Quite how the ancient Britons dragged these massive lumps of rock to this isolated spot remains a total mystery, and archaeologists are still divided over its purpose – some think it's a prehistoric market place or communal monument, while others believe it's a celestial calendar that marked the passing seasons. One thing's for certain – those prehistoric builders certainly understood location, location, location.

The circle is signposted off the A66 and A591, or you can walk via the Threlkeld railway line (p148) or Springs Wood and the Castlerigg campsite.

ACTIVITIES
Walking
Keswick has enough hikes to fill a lifetime of tramping. The Cumbria Way and the Allerdale Ramble both pass through town along the lake's western shore, and you'll find lots of suggestions for short walks (with downloadable walk guides) at www.keswick.o rg/walks.asp.

Keswick Rambles (www.keswickrambles.org.uk) organises a daily guided walk from the tourist office from Easter to October. Hikes (adult/child £10/4) start at 10am returning around 4pm or 5pm, and cover distances of 8 to 10 miles; longer 'classic' routes (adult/child £12/5) run in summer.

WALLA CRAG
The easterly lookout at Walla Crag (1243ft) is easily reached from the town centre. Start on Ambleside Rd and follow the trail through Springs Wood up to Castlerigg Hall and Camping Park. Head south past Rakefoot to the crag, before descending via Falcon Crag to the lakeshore at Ashness Bridge. On the walk back, look out for the spiral-marked stone at **Calfclose Bay**, laid to commemorate the National Trust's centenary, and the famous promontory at **Friar's Crag** (p147). In all the there-and-back walk covers around 6.5 miles.

LATRIGG
A low hump just behind Keswick, utterly dominated by nearby Skiddaw, Latrigg (1203ft) is another easy summit with top-drawer views. It's an hour's walk from town: follow Station Rd past the museum onto Brundholme Rd, and turn right onto Spoonygreen Lane (part

---

of the Cumbria Way). You'll reach the right-hand trail up to the summit after about a mile; once you've reached the top, you can either retrace your steps or continue east via Brundholme Wood and the Threlkeld railway path. If you want, you can get a head start from the Underscar car park, off the A591 near Dodd Wood.

BLENCATHRA
Sometimes known by its alternative name of Saddleback, Blencathra (2848ft) looms up on the skyline northeast of Keswick, and (alongside Skiddaw) represents the toughest hiking challenge in the area. There are lots and lots of routes to the top; most start from either Scales or Threlkeld, the two villages within closest striking distance of the mountain. Whichever you choose, it's a notoriously difficult and unforgiving climb. Perhaps the most famous route is the hair-raising rock scramble along Sharp Edge, which manages to make even Helvellyn's ridges look tame by comparison.

RAILWAY PATH TO THRELKELD
The disused railway path belonging to the old Cockermouth, Keswick and Penrith railway (see p145) runs for around 3 miles from Keswick to Threlkeld via a series of tunnels, embankments and bridges; it makes a great walk and also forms part of the Sea to Sea (C2C) Cycle Route. You can pick up the trail on Station Ave near the Keswick Leisure Pool and Fitness Centre.

Lake Cruises
Boats run by the **Keswick Launch Company** (☎ 017687-72263; www.keswick-launch.co.uk) call at seven landing stages around the lake: Ashness Gate (near Derwent Water YHA), Lodore Falls, High Brandlehow, Low Brandlehow, Hawse End, Nichol End and back to Keswick. A circular trip costs £8.50/4.25 per adult/child, and allows you to hop on and off the boats and walk to the next jetty; single fares to each landing stage are also available.

There are eight daily boats from mid-March to mid-November, dropping to three a day from mid-November to mid-March. There's also a romantic twilight cruise at 7.30pm (adult/child £9/4.50, one hour, mid-July to August), and special yuletide cruises (conducted by Father Christmas himself) in December.

DETOUR – THRELKELD QUARRY

A century ago Threlkeld was a hive of industrial activity thanks to some of the region's richest granite, lead and copper mines. The remains of these old mine workings now make up the **Threlkeld Quarry and Mining Museum** (☎ 01768-779747; www.threlkeld miningmuseum.co.uk; Threlkeld; mine tour adult/child £5/2.50, museum £2/1.50; ☺ 10am-5pm Mar-Oct) where you can take a fascinating underground mine tour and browse vintage machinery and mining memorabilia including 'Sir Tom', a restored narrow-gauge locomotive built in 1926.

KESWICK

0 _____ 300 m
0 _____ 0.2 miles

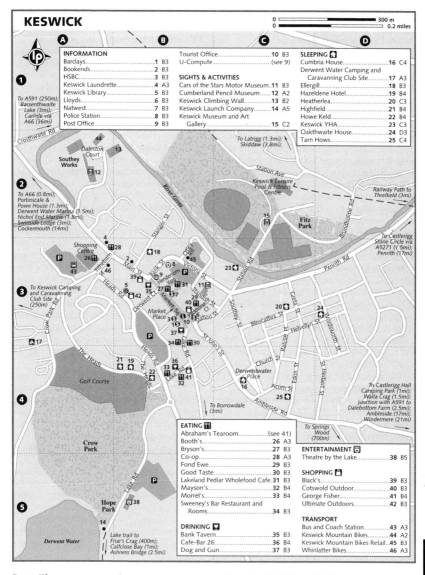

INFORMATION
Barclays...**1** B3
Bookends..**2** B3
HSBC..**3** B3
Keswick Laundrette........................**4** A3
Keswick Library..............................**5** B3
Lloyds..**6** B3
Natwest...**7** B3
Police Station.................................**8** B3
Post Office......................................**9** B3
Tourist Office...............................**10** B3
U-Compute..............................(see 9)

SIGHTS & ACTIVITIES
Cars of the Stars Motor Museum.**11** B3
Cumberland Pencil Museum......**12** A2
Keswick Climbing Wall...............**13** B2
Keswick Launch Company..........**14** A5
Keswick Museum and Art
    Gallery......................................**15** C2

SLEEPING 🏠
Cumbria House..............................**16** C4
Derwent Water Camping and
    Caravanning Club Site............**17** A3
Ellergill...**18** B3
Hazeldene Hotel............................**19** B4
Heatherlea......................................**20** C3
Highfield...**21** B4
Howe Keld......................................**22** B4
Keswick YHA..................................**23** C3
Oakthwaite House.........................**24** D3
Tarn Hows......................................**25** C4

Boat Hire

Row boats can be hired beside the Keswick Launch, or you can rent canoes, kayaks and dinghies from **Nichol End Marine** (Map p146; ☎ 017687-73082; Nichol End) or **Derwent Water Marina** (Map p146; ☎ 017687-72912; derwentwater marina.co.uk).

Keswick Climbing Wall

Keswick's **climbing wall** (☎ 017687-72000; www .keswickclimbingwall.co.uk; Southey Hill; 🕙 10am-9pm Tue & Fri, 10am-5pm Sat-Mon) is one of the northwest's largest indoor rock-climbing centres, and makes an ideal place to polish your skills before tackling the real thing. At the time of

EATING 🍴
Abraham's Tearoom...............(see 41)
Booth's...**26** A3
Bryson's..**27** B3
Co-op..**28** A3
Fond Ewe......................................**29** B3
Good Taste....................................**30** B3
Lakeland Pedlar Wholefood Cafe.**31** B3
Mayson's.......................................**32** B3
Morrel's...**33** B4
Sweeney's Bar Restaurant and
    Rooms.......................................**34** B3

DRINKING 🍷
Bank Tavern..................................**35** B3
Cafe-Bar 26..................................**36** B3
Dog and Gun.................................**37** B3

ENTERTAINMENT 🎭
Theatre by the Lake.....................**38** B5

SHOPPING 🛍
Black's...**39** B3
Cotswold Outdoor.........................**40** B3
George Fisher................................**41** B4
Ultimate Outdoors........................**42** B3

TRANSPORT
Bus and Coach Station................**43** A3
Keswick Mountain Bikes..............**44** A2
Keswick Mountain Bikes Retail...**45** B3
Whinlatter Bikes...........................**46** A3

KESWICK &
DERWENT WATER

writing, plans were afoot to move the wall to a new location at Goosewell Farm – contact the centre for the latest news.

SLEEPING
Budget

Castlerigg Hall Camping Park (Map p146; ☎ 017687-74499; www.castlerigg.co.uk; Rakefoot Lane; adult £5.50-6.75, car £2-2.50) Keswick's main campsite is on a hilltop off the A591, with separate fields for caravans and campers. Facilities are good – there's a fully stocked shop and a kitchen where you can whip up meals – but no reservations are taken, so you'll need to pitch early to bag a view.

Dalebottom Farm (Map p146; ☎ 017687-72176; www.dalebottomfarm.co.uk; Naddle, Keswick; sites from £10; ☺ Mar-Nov) On the A591 in the Naddle Valley, 2.5 miles south of Keswick, this campsite on a working hill farm is a useful fall back if the other sites are crammed, but it's rudimentary (basic showers, old toilet blocks).

Keswick Camping and Caravanning Club Site (☎ 017687-72392; www.campingandcaravanningclub.co.uk/keswick; Crow Park Rd; sites for 2 adults & car £14.80-23.20; ☺ Feb–mid-Nov) Great choice for lakeside camping, spread out across a 5-hectare field at the north end of Derwent Water.

Derwent Water Camping and Caravanning Club Site (☎ 01687-72578; www.campingandcaravanningclub.co.uk/derwentwater; sites for 2 adults & car £14.80-23.20; ☺ Mar–mid-Nov). Extra space is available at this sister-site nearby.

Keswick YHA (☎ 0870 770 5894; keswick@yha.org.uk; Station Rd; dm £17.95-20.95; ▢) You can almost smell the paint job at this newly refurbished YHA, housed in a former woollen mill. The facilities are brand spanking new – including an impressive kitchen and the lovely in-house cafe – and some dorms, doubles and triples have river balconies overlooking Fitz Park.

Midrange

Powe House (☎ 017687-73611; www.powehouse.com; Portinscale; s £40-50, d £76-84; ℗) Space to spare, chic surroundings and a wonderfully rural location a mile from Keswick make this guest house sparkle. All six rooms are fab value: the roomiest are 3 and 5, both with double sash windows overlooking trimmed gardens, but they all brim with little luxuries (DVD player, Freeview, herbal teas).

our pick **Howe Keld** (☎ 017687-72417; www.howekeld.co.uk; 5-7 The Heads; s £45, d £80-90) This revamped Crow Park B&B pulls out all the stops. The kitsch clutter has been jettisoned for goose-

down duvets, slate-floored bathrooms and handmade furniture courtesy of a local joiner; TVs are flat-screen, the decor is sleek, and the key-fobs are fashioned from local slate. The breakfast is even up for a national award: home-made smoothies, vegetarian rissoles, French pancakes and a smorgasbord of nuts, seeds and grains. Mmmmm.

Cumbria House (☎ 017687-73171; www.cumbriahouse.co.uk; 1 Derwentwater Pl; r £52-64) Spread over four floors, this amber-stoned Georgian house is geared towards eco-conscious types: fair trade, local grub and low-energy light bulbs feature, and there's a 5% discount for car-free guests. Families can rent the top rooms as a single suite, with views up to Blencathra.

Heatherlea (☎ 017687-72430; www.heatherlea-keswick.co.uk; 26 Blencathra St; d £54) One of the best choices in the B&B-heavy area around Blencathra St. Tasteful decor (pine beds, crimson-striped cushions, beige throws) distinguish the rooms; it's worth bumping up to superior for the sparkling shower and huge flat-screen TV.

Ellergill (☎ 017687-73347; www.ellergill.co.uk; 22 Stanger St; d £58-66) Rich crimson bedspreads and burgundy throws lend the four lovely rooms at this B&B a luxurious edge, while the rest of the house makes the most of its Victorian trappings (tiled hallways, hearths and cornicing).

Oakthwaite House (☎ 017687-72398; www.oakthwaite-keswick.com; 35 Helvellyn St; d £58-68) Another impeccably finished B&B with nary a floral or frill. Expect instead a preponderance of pale blues, creams and stone-greys, married with power showers, crisp linen and digital TVs. Plump for the compact and bijou dormer room or a roomy double with views of Castlerigg Fell.

Swinside Lodge (Map p146; ☎ 017687-72948; www.swinsidelodge-hotel.co.uk; Newlands; d incl dinner £98-118; ℗) Tucked below Catbells, this fancy number has scooped awards for its gourmet food and Georgian finery. It's classy without being chi-chi; rooms are furnished in countrified style, and the house is a reassuring mix of creaky floorboards, cosy lounges and book-stocked shelves. Supper at the bistro is included and at this price it's a steal.

Tarn Hows (☎ 017687-73217; www.tarnhows.co.uk; 3-5 Eskin St; s £33, d £58-70) Cast-iron bedsteads and fancy quilts in a traditional guest house.

Hazeldene Hotel (☎ 017687-72106; www.hazeldene-hotel.co.uk; The Heads; d £75-95) Crow Park view without the punishing price, although you'll have to sacrifice decorative pizzazz.

Top End

Highfield (☎ 017687-72508; www.highfieldkeswick .co.uk; The Heads; d £130-170; P) This Victorian mansion, covered with turrets, is the poshest of The Heads guest houses. The feel is formal: the best rooms boast Crow Park views, but many are surprisingly squashed considering the price tag. Go for room 5 for double-aspect views, rooms 9 and 15 for elbow room, or the Woodford for a regal rococo bed.

EATING
Cafes & Quick Eats

Bryson's (☎ 017687-72257; 42 Main St; cakes £2-5) For authentic Lakeland breads, buns and biscuits, Bryson's is still the best place in town – the Borrowdale Teabread and Cumbrian Fruit Cake are irresistible. Stop for afternoon tea at the upstairs cafe, or take your treats home to savour in secret.

ourpick **Good Taste** (☎ 01768-775973; 19 Lake Rd; lunches £3-6) Run by renowned chef Peter Sidwell, Good Taste does what it says on the tin: fresh food with first-class flavours. Savour marinated olives, Mediterranean veg or breakfast frittatas; tuck into posh fish-finger sandwiches and chicken flatbreads; stuff yourself silly with cakes, tarts and the frothiest of Italian lattes. Is there a better lunch spot in the Lakes? If so, we haven't found it.

Lakeland Pedlar Wholefood Cafe (☎ 017687-74492; www.lakelandpedlar.co.uk; Hendersons Yard; mains £3-10; 9am-5pm) Wholesome by name, wholesome by nature, this veggie cafe-cum–bike shop is an old fave among cyclists and hungry walkers, with a daily pot of home-made soup, plus burritos, stews, casseroles and chunky doorstep sandwiches.

Restaurants

Sweeney's Bar Restaurant and Rooms (☎ 017687-772990; www.sweeneysbar.co.uk; 18-20 Lake Rd; sandwiches £3.50-6.50, mains £8.95-14) Half wine bar, half restaurant-with-rooms, sophisticated Sweeney's is as good for lunch as it is for late-night tipples. Deep chocolate-leather sofas and gleaming wood floors conjure a relaxed metropolitan vibe; there are smoked mackerel muffins for lunch, and heartier portions of sea bream and Waberthwaite sausage for supper.

Mayson's (☎ 01768-774104; 33 Lake Rd; mains £7.95-9.95; dinner) Keswick's cheery answer to a fast-food diner: choose chow mein, Cajun chicken or beef stir-fry from one of the counter-top woks, plump for rice or noodles, and wait for your feast to be delivered to your table in double-quick time.

Morrel's (☎ 017687-72666; Lake Rd; mains £10.95-17.95; dinner Tue-Sun) The swankiest table in town, stylishly furnished in just-so tones of cream, chocolate and cappuccino offset by pop-art movie prints. The food has been praised by the Michelin crew: think chicken in prosciutto, wild boar bangers or Cumbrian pork served 'three ways'. Swish self-catering apartments are available upstairs (£320 to £600 per week).

Self-Catering

Keswick's big supermarket is **Booth's** (☎ 017687-73518; Tithebarn St; 8am-6pm Mon-Sat, 11am-4pm Sun), or there's a small **Co-op** (☎ 017687-72688) next to the laundrette. For local cheeses, try **Fond Ewe** (☎ 017687-73377; 9 Packhorse Ct; 9.15am-5pm Mon-Sat, 10am-4pm Sun) tucked away in the little shopping arcade of Packhorse Ct.

DRINKING

Dog and Gun (☎ 017687-73463; 2 Lake Rd) Keswick's drinking hole of choice, packed with sporting prints, scruffy bench seats and russet-faced punters. The food is decent, but the ales are the draw, and 10p from every pint of 'Thirst Rescue' goes into the coffers of the Keswick Mountain Rescue Team.

Cafe-Bar 26 (☎ 017687-80863; 26 Lake Rd; mains £3.25-7.50) Cosy street-side bar dressed in urban-chic togs: loads of leather, wood and shiny chrome, with bruschetta, burgers and ciabattas washed down with global beers.

Bank Tavern (☎ 017687-72663; 45-47 Main St) Jennings ales, an L-shaped bar and plenty of hidey-holes make this another decent place for an evening pint.

ENTERTAINMENT

Theatre by the Lake (☎ 017687-74411; www.theatre bythelake.com; Lakeside) This smart venue hosts new and classic drama, as well as touring bands and musical acts. It's also the main venue for the literature, theatre and mountain festivals (p22).

Alhambra Cinema (☎ 017687-72195; www.keswick -alhambra.co.uk; St Johns St). Keswick's local film hub is a rather lovely space where indie and art-house films are screened by the Keswick Film Club on Sunday nights from October to March.

SOMETHING FOR THE WEEKEND

Keswick makes the handiest base for a weekend getaway. On the first night check into the sleek **Howe Keld** (p150) or chic **Powe House** (p150), and enjoy a relaxed dinner at **Sweeney's** (p151) or the good old **Dog and Gun** (p151).

On Saturday morning, have a wander around the market town of **Keswick** (p145), taking in the offbeat **Keswick Museum** (p145) and the equally odd **Cars of the Stars Motor Museum** (p145). Pick up a gourmet picnic at **Good Taste** (p151) before wandering down via Crow Park to the shores of **Derwent Water** (p147) for a leisurely lake cruise, followed by an afternoon hike up to the top of **Catbells** (p142). Head back to town for early evening and treat yourself to supper at marvellous **Morrel's** (p151).

On Sunday you could head up to explore the shores of **Bassenthwaite Lake** (opposite), factoring in lunch at the **Pheasant Inn** (p155), a visit to the **osprey hides** (opposite) and **Whinlatter Forest Park** (p156), and a romantic night at **Lyzzick Hall** (p155) or the **Cottage in the Wood** (p156). Alternatively, venture south into the delightful valleys of **Borrowdale and Buttermere** (p160), stopping at the **Honister Slate Mine** (p163) before lunching at the historic **Fish Hotel** (p163) and overnighting in serious country style at **Winder Hall** (p157).

SHOPPING

Keswick has some of the best gear shops in the Lakes. The oldest establishment is **George Fisher** (☎ 017687-72178; 2 Borrowdale Rd; ☺ 10am-5pm Mon-Fri, 9am-5pm Sat, 10.30am-4.30pm Sun), spread out over three levels, with well-stocked departments devoted to camping, climbing, footwear and clothing, and a nice little attic cafe, **Abraham's Tearoom**, on the top floor.

For general kit, try **Cotswold Outdoor** (☎ 017687-81030; 16 Main St). **Black's** (☎ 017687-73309; 53-57 Main St; ☺ 9am-6pm Mon-Sat, 11am-5pm Sun) specialises in rucksacks and clothing, and **Ultimate Outdoors** (☎ 017687-74422; Heads Rd; ☺ 9am-5.30pm Mon-Thu, 9am-6.30pm Fri & Sat, 11am-5pm Sun) is often a good bet for cheaper brands.

GETTING THERE & AROUND
Bike Hire

Keswick Mountain Bikes (☎ 017687-75202; www .keswickbikes.co.uk; ☺ 9am-5.30pm Mon-Sat, 10am-5.30pm Sun) has three outlets: a workshop and hire centre near the Climbing Wall, a retail shop on Otley Rd, and another shop above the Lakeland Pedlar Wholefood Cafe. Bike hire costs £15 to £20 per day.

Alternatively, **Whinlatter Bikes** (☎ 017687-74412; Tithebarn St; ☺ 9am-5.30pm Mon-Sat) hires rigs for £10/15 per half/full day.

Bus

The Lakeslink bus (555/556) runs hourly to Ambleside (40 minutes), Windermere (50 minutes) and Kendal (1½ hours) from Keswick's bus station; the hourly X4/X5 travels from Penrith to Workington via Keswick (eight on Sunday).

The circular 77 travels four times daily to Portinscale and Catbells (10 minutes), Seatoller (30 minutes), Buttermere (40 minutes), Lorton (one hour 10 minutes) and Whinlatter (one hour 20 minutes); the bus also runs four times daily in the opposite direction. For Borrowdale, catch the 79 (twice-hourly Monday to Saturday, eight on Sunday) to Lodore Falls (10 minutes), Grange (15 minutes), Rosthwaite (20 minutes) and Seatoller (25 minutes).

Taxi

For personally tailored transport, who you gonna call? How about **KLM Taxis** (☎ 017687-75337), **Davies Taxis** (☎ 017687-72676) or **Derwent Taxis** (☎ 017687-75585).

AROUND KESWICK

Keswick is handily positioned for exploring the surrounding countryside, including the wooded reservoir of Thirlmere, the shining stretch of Bassenthwaite Lake, the rural haven of Back O' Skiddaw and the secluded valley of Lorton.

THIRLMERE

A couple of miles southeast of Keswick is Thirlmere, one of the Lake District's main water reservoirs, created from two separate lakes at the end of the 19th century to supply drinking water to the rapidly growing industrial city of Manchester. The project was passionately opposed by environmental campaigners including John Ruskin, who felt the new reservoir would irrevocably alter the local landscape. Looking at Thirlmere's tree-fringed shores these days, you'd be hard put to see what the fuss was all about, but the project certainly wasn't without its costs. Beneath the lake's waters are the drowned hamlets of Armboth and Wythburn, which were submerged after the construction of the reservoir dam at the lake's northern end.

The main reason for visiting the valley is to wander the area's lovely wooded trails or to tackle the alternative route up **Helvellyn** (p165) from Wythburn car park, which climbs up via Birkside under the shadow of **Nethermost Pike** (2920ft).

If you fancy staying, you've got a couple of options. In Thirlspot, on the lake's eastern side, there's the **King's Head** (☎ 017687-72393; www .lakedistrictinns.co.uk/kingshead_welcome.cfm; Thirlspot; d £100-120; P), a thoroughly refurbished 17th-century inn with a choice of meals (mains £6 to £18) either in the snug bar (warmed by a black-stone hearth) or the fancier St Johns Restaurant (with all-round views taking in St Johns in the Vale, Blencathra and Skiddaw).

Alternatively you could plump for pricey country-house surroundings at nearby **Dale Head Hall** (☎ 017687-72478; www.daleheadhall.co.uk; d £130-280; P), a sprawling lakeside manor partly dating back to the Elizabethan era. Choices range from standard through to four-poster and suite rooms, but you're certainly paying a premium for the lakeside location.

The only bus to the valley is the 555/556, which stops at Thirlspot and Wythburn en route from Keswick to Windermere.

BASSENTHWAITE LAKE

Here's a question: how many lakes are there in the Lake District? Loads, right? Wrong. In fact, there's only one, and that's Bassenthwaite (the others are actually all meres, waters or tarns). Three miles north of Keswick, nestling in the shadow of the Skiddaw range, Bassenthwaite is one of the few lakes that preserves its natural character; undisturbed by cruise boats and pleasure vessels, and surrounded by dense pine and beech forest, it's become an important haven for Lakeland wildlife, including red squirrels, wintering water birds and, of course, England's only pair of breeding ospreys. The wild show continues

under the water, too: Bassenthwaite is one of only two English lakes (along with Derwent Water) that harbours wild vendace, a highly endangered whitefish that became stranded here at the end of the last ice age.

Orientation & Information

The main A66 road to Cockermouth runs along the lake's western shore, while the minor A591 runs along the east side via Dodd Wood, where there's a car park for the Osprey Project and Mirehouse. The only village worth its salt is Bassenthwaite, nestled at the lake's northeastern corner.

Sights

DODD WOOD & THE BASSENTHWAITE OSPREYS

In 2001 the first ospreys to breed in England for 150 years set up home at Bassenthwaite. These magnificent birds of prey were once widespread, but were driven to extinction by hunting, environmental degradation and egg collectors. The last wild breeding pair was destroyed in Scotland in 1916, but following years of careful conservation, the ospreys have slowly recolonised several areas of the British Isles.

Over the last few years, the birds have returned to Bassenthwaite every April, spending the summer at the lake before heading for Africa in late August or early September. There are two official viewpoints, both in Dodd Wood, about 3 miles north of Keswick on the A591.

The **lower hide** (☼ 10am-5pm Easter-Oct) is 15 minutes' walk from the car park at Mirehouse (below), and the new **upper hide** (☼ 10.30am-4.30pm Easter-Oct) is another half an hour further through the forest (the walk is steep, so hiking boots are a good idea). Telescopes are provided at both viewpoints, but your own pair of binoculars will come in handy. If you don't spot the birds, there's an osprey display and video feed at the **Whinlatter Visitor Centre** (p156), or you can check out the webcam at www.ospreywatch.co.uk. Disabled visitors can arrange for access to the lower hide by calling the Whinlatter Visitor Centre.

MIREHOUSE

Built in 1666, the lakeside manor of **Mirehouse** (☎ 017687-72287; www.mirehouse.com; house & gardens adult/child £6/3, gardens only £3/1.50; ☼ gardens 10am-5.30pm Apr-Oct, house 2-5pm Sun & Wed Apr-Oct, plus 2-5pm Fri Aug) has been occupied since 1802 by the Spedding clan, and in many ways still feels

NATHAN FOX

Can you explain why the ospreys have returned to Bassenthwaite but not to other parts of England? Well, it's a combination of good luck and old-fashioned hard graft! We've had substantial success with the reintroduction of ospreys to Scotland – there are now over 150 breeding pairs north of the border – and in the late 1990s we noticed some birds were using Bassenthwaite as a migratory stopover. But the birds are quite choosy about their nest sites – they prefer to nest in tall, dead Caledonian pines, but the trees around Bassenthwaite are quite young, so the birds couldn't find anywhere they really liked. But Bassenthwaite is otherwise an ideal osprey environment: there's a high-quality habitat, relatively little competition from other species, and plenty of fish, so there was no reason they shouldn't stay if they could find a suitable site.

So we constructed a purpose-built nest platform to try to encourage them to stick around, similar to those previously used to good effect in Scotland and other parts of England. We even splattered white paint over it to simulate bird droppings! Luckily, they seemed to like what we'd done, and they've returned every year since 2001.

So how did the Osprey Project come about? Obviously once we had attracted birds back to the lake, it was important that we encouraged them, if possible, to stay and breed. So the three partner organisations – the Lake District National Park Authority, the Forestry Commission and the RSPB – created a special partnership organisation dedicated to the osprey's welfare. The Lake District Osprey Project achieved over £750,000 in external funding to help construct the two visitor viewpoints, redevelop the visitor facilities at Whinlatter, create a special project website and, most importantly, protect the birds. Sadly, even in the 21st century, the main threat the birds face is still from egg collectors, so one of our major investments was the installation of nest cameras and 24-hour surveillance to ensure the nests were 100% safe. It's a mammoth job, and we're enormously grateful to the staff and volunteers who have helped make it happen.

The original plan was to have just one viewpoint, rather than two, wasn't it? Yes, that's right – in 2008, the very first weekend we opened, the birds rather unsportingly decided to move nests! So we had to build an additional viewpoint higher in the forest to provide a better vantage point. Luckily, that also means we now have two available nest sites, so hopefully we'll be able to attract another pair of breeding birds in the very near future.

Nathan Fox is a Forest Ranger and the Lake District Osprey Watch Manager

more like a family residence than a stuffy museum piece.

A tinkling piano provides the soundtrack as you wander the hallways, stuffed to the rafters with furniture, literary memorabilia and quirky antiques. Among the items on display are vintage rocking chairs, a collection of clay pipes and an array of letters from eminent writers including Robert Southey, Thomas Carlyle, John Constable and Wordsworth, as well as Alfred Tennyson, who stayed at the house while writing his epic poem *Morte d'Arthur* in the company of his friend James Spedding (the first biographer of Francis Bacon). Outside, azaleas, roses, a rhododendron tunnel, a collection of Cumbrian fruit trees and adventure playgrounds are dotted around the grounds, and you can detour through a wildflower meadow planted to attract honey bees. A lakeshore path leads through Catstocks Wood to the tiny church of **St Bega**.

The nearest car park is at Dodd Wood, 10 minutes' walk from the house. Tickets are sold at the Old Sawmill Tearoom next to the car park; an admission discount of £3 is refundable against the car-parking fee.

TROTTERS WORLD OF ANIMALS

You'll meet everything from a Canadian lynx to Asian fishing cats and the world's titchiest otters at this **animal park** (☎ 017687-76239; www .trottersworld.com; adult/3-14yr £6.95/4.95; ☒ 10.30am-5.30pm), at the northern end of Bassenthwaite Lake. Unlike most zoos, here handling the animals is positively encouraged through animal interaction sessions – if you're feeling brave you could get hands-on with a boa constrictor or a red-kneed tarantula, although more cautious types will probably prefer to stick to stroking the billy goats and Shetland ponies. Regular flying demonstrations with the park's collection of owls, vultures, hawks and falcons are held throughout the day.

Sleeping & Eating

Lyzzick Hall Hotel (☎ 017687-72277; www.lyzzickhall .co.uk; Underskiddaw; r £120-144; P ▧) Lyzzick (meaning 'little oak') is pricey, but you're paying for the setting, wedged on the Skiddaw slopes with Eden Valley views. Rooms are a smidgen old fashioned (the Garden and Derwent suites are the most spacious), but the panoramic patio and indoor pool are tailormade for lounging.

Ravenstone Hotel (☎ 0800 163983; www.ravenstone -hotel.co.uk; A591; Bassenthwaite Lake; d £120-135; P) Another Edwardian pamper-pad boasting gables, porticoes and colonnades, as well as 19 restrained rooms – sandy-grey walls and icy whites mix with starchy sheets and *Homes & Gardens* fabrics. For a more up-to-date finish, ask for the Osprey Rooms, and for all-out luxury, plump for the Spa Room with its own jacuzzi.

Pheasant Inn (☎ 017687-76234; www.the-pheasant .co.uk; near Dubwath; lunch mains £6-14; dinner mains £14-25; P) The florid rooms are way overpriced (doubles from £160), but there's no quibbling with the top-notch nosh at Bassenthwaite's inn. Plates of Lakeland lamb, Old Spot pork or pan-fried pigeon are dished up amid wood-panelled finery, sporting prints and hunting trophies. Afternoon tea is lovely too – hot scones with rum butter, cucumber sandwiches, and lapsang souchong served in bone-china cups.

Getting There & Away

The 555 from Keswick runs up the lake's eastern side, stopping at Mirehouse (10 minutes, three daily March to November) and the Castle Inn (20 minutes). The 73/73A (Caldbeck Rambler) runs twice daily via Mirehouse, Bassenthwaite Village and the Castle Inn, and the 74/74A (the Osprey Bus, six on weekends April to mid-July, daily mid-July to August) makes a circular trip via Whinlatter, Trotters World of Animals, Mirehouse and Keswick.

BACK O' SKIDDAW

Tucked away beyond the northern edge of Skiddaw along the uppermost border of the national park is the area known as Back O' Skiddaw, a little-explored region that's still largely dominated by farming and agriculture. Patchwork fields and quiet villages are dotted around the countryside, including the solid little farming hamlets of **Uldale** and **Ireby**,

and the quaint village of **Hesket Newmarket**, arranged around a grassy green.

The most attractive of all is **Caldbeck** (www .caldbeckvillage.co.uk), whose name derives from the Norse for 'cold stream' and which is now best known as the home of the famous British mountaineer Chris Bonington. Notable landmarks include **St Kentigern's Church**, dedicated to the 6th-century saint who purportedly first preached the Christian gospel in this corner of England, and the **Priest's Mill**, which began life as a corn mill and has now reinvented itself as a thriving arts and community centre.

Elsewhere around the village you can browse for handmade jewellery at **Caldbeck Jewellers** (☎ 016974-78422; ☉ 11am-5pm mid-Feb–Oct, 11am-4pm Nov-Dec), and for gifts and toys at the **Hayloft Gift Shop** (☎ 016974-78237; ☉ 9am-5pm Mon-Sat). An eclectic mix of plants and garden knick-knacks can be found at the **Potting Shed** (☎ 016974-78404; ☉ 10am-3pm Mon, Thu & Fri, 10am-4pm Sat & Sun), while tempting lunches and cream teas are available at the **Old Smithy Cafe** (☎ 016974-78246; ☉ 9.30am-6pm) or the **Watermill Cafe** (☎ 016974-78267; ☉ 9am-5pm mid-Feb–Oct, 9am-4.30pm Nov-Jan).

Sleeping & Eating

Oddfellows Arms (☎ 016974-78227; www.oddfellows -caldbeck.co.uk; s/d £33/74; P) Friendly Jennings-owned pub in the centre of Caldbeck, much favoured by village drinkers.

High Houses (☎ 016973-71549; www.highhouses .co.uk; d £80-90; P) Converted farmhouse in Ireby, whose attractive features include three lovely rooms, a sitting room with an inglenook fireplace and a breakfast room converted from a former dairy.

Boltongate Old Rectory (☎ 016973-71647; www .boltongateoldrectory.com; d £98-120; P) If you're after somewhere to stay, the best place by far is this sparkling little number in nearby Boltongate. It has scooped a bevy of awards, and justly so; bedrooms and bathrooms glimmer with brass beds and soothing shades, while sophisticated food is on offer in the restaurant.

our pick **Old Crown** (☎ 016974-78288; www.theold crownpub.co.uk; mains £7-16; P) Fab little village pub in Hesket Newmarket, the first co-op–owned pub in Britain. The hotel brews a formidable line-up of beers including Blencathra Bitter, Old Carrock Ale and Great Cockup Porter, and you'll find solid pub mains (casseroles, pies, curries) to accompany the brews. Prince Charles has even stopped by on occasion.

KESWICK & DERWENT WATER

Getting There & Away

Public transport is frustratingly limited. The 620 bus shuttles between Hesket Newmarket, Caldbeck (four minutes) and Carlisle (40 minutes) once daily on Wednesday, while the 961 runs once on Tuesday between Penrith and Caldbeck (35 minutes). The 73/73A (Caldbeck Rambler) runs on Saturday year round (more frequently in summer) between Keswick, Hesket Newmarket (40 minutes), Caldbeck (44 minutes), Ireby (52 minutes) and Uldale (56 minutes) before running along Bassenthwaite's east side back to Keswick.

WHINLATTER, LORTON & LOWESWATER

West of the lake, the twisting B5292 veers sharply off the A66 near Braithwaite, and begins a long, snaking climb through thick conifer forests en route to Whinlatter Pass, perched 1043ft above sea level. Before the construction of the A66, the steep Whinlatter road was the primary coach route through the surrounding mountains; carriages and wagons would clatter up and over the pass into Lorton Vale en route to Cockermouth and the Cumbrian Coast. The outstanding valley views as you descend towards the tiny sheltered lake of Loweswater are well worth the detour, but take care during winter, as the pass is quite often snowbound during the colder months.

Whinlatter Forest Park

Encompassing 1200 hectares of pine, larch and spruce, Whinlatter is England's only true area of mountain forest, rising sharply from 330ft above sea level up to 2590ft around the Whinlatter Pass. The forest is a well-known sanctuary for local wildlife, and has recently become a designated red squirrel reserve; you can check out live video feeds from squirrel-cams dotted around the forest at the **Whinlatter Visitor Centre** (☎ 017687-78469; Whinlatter Forest Park; ☷ 10am-5pm), which also houses information panels and video displays for the Bassenthwaite ospreys.

Several marked walking trails wind through the forest, while thrill junkies can monkey about in the trees at **Go Ape** (☎ 017687-78469; Whinlatter Forest Park; adult/10-17yr £25/20; ☷ 9am-5pm mid-Mar–Oct, closed Mon in term-time, also open Sat & Sun Nov) or tackle the new **Altura Trail**, which provides some of the national park's most challenging mountain biking. You can hire bikes, pick up trail maps and get technique tips at **Cyclewise Training** (☎ 017687-78711; www.cyclewisetraining.co.uk; Whinlatter Forest Park).

For buses to Whinlatter, see p155.

SLEEPING & EATING

Cottage in the Wood (☎ 017687-78409; www.thecottageinthewood.co.uk; Whinlatter Forest, Braithwaite; d £90-120; **P**) Live out those *Little Red Riding Hood* daydreams at this bewitching retreat in Whinlatter Forest, surrounded by lofty conifers and tended gardens. The deluxe rooms are worth the splurge, with Freeview TVs and whirlpool tubs, but for true class you'll want the attic suite, with Velux skylights and claw-foot tub. Even the smart restaurant has panoramic forest views.

Siskins Cafe (☎ 017687-78469; lunches £3-8; ☷ 10am-5pm) Cosy tearoom tucked away next to the Whinlatter Visitor Centre, offering the usual line-up of jacket potatoes, cakes and sarnies.

Lorton & Loweswater

From the high point of the Whinlatter Pass, the B5292 traces a long, lolloping course down the fell-side into the jade-green Vale of Lorton, scattered with farmhouses, beech copses and rickety barns. After 3 miles the road passes through the twin hamlets of **Low Lorton** and **High Lorton**, where you can stop off for a wander around the 19th-century church of **St Cuthbert's** and pay a visit to the famous **Lorton Yew** (see boxed text, below).

THE LORTON YEW

'There is a Yew-tree, pride of Lorton Vale…' So begins Wordsworth's famous 1803 poem about the mighty Lorton Yew, which is still standing behind the village hall in Low Lorton. This mighty 1000-year-old tree once measured 27ft around, and the Methodist preacher John Wesley and the founder of the Quaker movement, George Fox, are both thought to have preached under its boughs. Unfortunately shortly after William had finished his ditty, a violent storm swept through the valley and split the tree's majestic trunk in half. It's still there two centuries on, albeit in rather slimmed-down form; the wood from the fallen half was used to fashion the mayor's chair in Cockermouth.

Four miles to the southwest is the tiny National Trust–owned lake of Loweswater, one of the smallest, shallowest and most secluded of all the Lakeland lakes. Barely a mile across and averaging just 60ft deep, it's a supremely peaceful spot, unsullied by the traffic, crowds and touristy razzmatazz of many other lakes. It's a 4-mile walk from Lorton, or there are car parks at Waterend, Loweswater Hall and Maggie's Bridge. The distinctive rocket-shaped summit looming on the lake's southern side is **Mellbreak** (1676ft), a popular fell-walkers' target; alternatively, follow the peaceful trail around the wooded lakeshore, and keep your eyes peeled for woodpeckers and red squirrels around **Holme Wood** and the tinkling tumble of **Holme Force**.

SLEEPING & EATING

Kirkstile Inn (☎ 01900-85219; www.kirkstile.com; Loweswater; s £59.50, d £87-97; P) Recently awarded top honours by the beer-quaffing gentlefolk from the Campaign for Real Ale (CAMRA), this Tudor inn prides itself on honest food and home-brewed ales (including Melbreak Bitter, Grasmoor Dark Ale and Kirkstile Gold). Upstairs rooms are tasteful, and some have views onto Lorton Vale.

Old Vicarage (☎ 01900-85656; www.oldvicarage.co.uk; Church Lane, Lorton; s £68-75, d £96-110; P) This is a quietly understated establishment straddling the boundary between Low and High Lorton; brass table lamps, framed watercolours and wooden headboards adorn the rooms, most of which overlook gardens and fields.

Winder Hall (☎ 01900-85107; www.winderhall.co.uk; Low Lorton; d £105-185; P) There's certainly no doubting the provenance of this Jacobean manor, and there are architectural quirks wherever you look (latticed windows, date stones and hefty lintels), but it's essentially just a warm and welcoming family-run hotel – the kind of place that lays on packed lunches, walking guides and wet-weather games just to make you feel good. Rooms are plain but pretty. Our faves are stylish Fellbarrow, Georgian Greystone and four-postered Hobcarton. There's even a Nordic sauna in the garden to sooth any aching muscles.

Wheatsheaf Inn (☎ 01900-85199; Low Lorton; mains £8.75-12.95) Lorton's whitewashed local is well loved and a touch scruffy around the edges. There are Jennings ales on tap, Cumberland sausage and Borrowdale trout on the menu,

and of course an open fire to warm your toes by. Camping is available in summer.

GETTING THERE & AWAY

The 77/77A bus trundles four times daily from Keswick via Whinlatter, Lorton and Buttermere, before travelling over Honister Pass and tracking Derwent Water's west shore, with stops including Seatoller, Catbells and Portinscale, before terminating again at Keswick.

COCKERMOUTH

pop 8225

Teetering on the far reaches of the northerly fells, the Georgian town of Cockermouth has two main selling points: it's the home town of the Lake District's grand old poet, William Wordsworth, as well as its best-loved brewery, Jennings. It's a good deal less polished and prettified than many of the other Lakeland towns, but it feels more authentic as a result: old coaching inns and whitewashed houses line either side of its arrow-straight main street, set back from the rattling waters of the River Cocker.

INFORMATION

Library (☎ 01900-325990; Main St; internet per half hr £1; ☼ 10am-7pm Mon & Wed, 10am-5pm Tue & Fri, 10am-12.30pm Thu, 10am-1pm Sat)
Police station (Main St; ☼ 8.30am-12.30pm & 1.30-4.30pm Mon-Thu, 8.30am-12.30pm & 1.30-4pm Fri)
Post office (Station St; ☼ 9am-5.30pm Mon-Fri & 9.30am-12.30pm Sat) Next to the Co-op.
Tourist office (☎ 01900-822634; cockermouthtic@co-net.com; ☼ 9.30am-5pm Mon-Sat & 10am-2pm Sun Jul-Aug, 9.30am-4.30pm Mon-Sat Apr-Jun & Sep-Oct, 9.30am-4pm Mon-Fri & 10-2pm Sat Nov-Mar) Inside the town hall.
www.cockermouth.org.uk Useful town guide.

SIGHTS
Wordsworth House

The elegant Georgian facade of **Wordsworth House** (NT; ☎ 01900-824805; Main St; adult/child £5.60/2.80; ☼ 11am-4.30pm Mon-Sat mid-Mar–Oct) dominates the southern end of Main St. Built around 1745, the house was leased to Wordsworth's father John, who was employed as an estate agent for the wealthy landowner Sir James Lowther (p175). All five Wordsworth children were born here – William was the second to arrive, born on

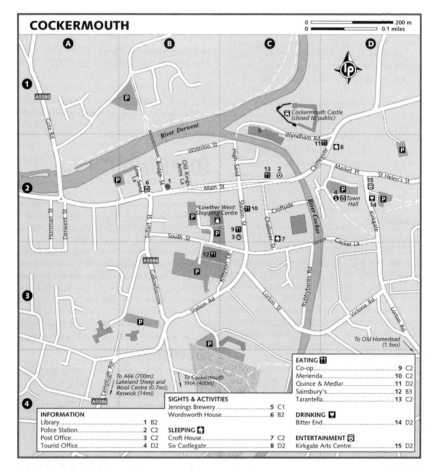

COCKERMOUTH

7 April 1770. Despite its literary importance, the house narrowly escaped demolition in the early 20th century; having fallen into disrepair, it was earmarked to make way for a new Cockermouth bus station, and was only saved at the last minute by a dedicated bunch of Wordsworth enthusiasts.

Now in the hands of the National Trust, the house has been beautifully restored based on family accounts from the Wordsworth archive. Highlights include the flag-stoned kitchen, the grand 1st-floor drawing room and the beautiful walled garden, name-checked in Wordsworth's autobiographical poem *The Prelude*; you can also wander around John Wordsworth's study, visit William's boyhood bedroom and browse Wordsworthian texts in an upstairs parlour. You're encouraged to get hands-on with the objects in many areas of the house, and costumed guides bring the whole experience to life – you might bump into a bonneted cook baking bread in the kitchen or a gardener planting vegetables in the kitchen garden.

Jennings Brewery

For something less cerebral, head for **Jennings Brewery** (☎ 01900-821011; www.jenningsbrewery.co.uk; adult/over 12yr £5.50/2.50), which has been plying Cumbria's pubs with traditional ales and bitters since 1874. Tours of the brewery include a tasting session in the Old Cooperage bar – try golden Cocker Hoop, malty Cumberland Ale or the spicy Sneck Lifter.

Lakeland Sheep & Wool Centre

More countrified pursuits take top billing at the **Lakeland Sheep and Wool Centre** (Map p146; ☎ 01900-822673; www.shepherdshotel.co.uk/sheep WoolCentre; entry to visitor centre free; ☺ 10am-5pm), a mile from town along the A66. There are displays on sheep breeds, farm architecture and the history of hill farming, but the main reason to visit is to watch some country folk in agrarian action – shearing sheep, handling Herdwicks or rounding up some Swaledales (or a flock of geese) with a well-trained sheepdog. There are four daily shows at 10.30am, noon, 2pm and 3.30pm from Sunday to Thursday March to October; tickets cost £5/4 per adult/child.

SLEEPING

Cockermouth YHA (Map p146; ☎ 0845 371 9313; cocker mouth@yha.org.uk; Double Mills; dm £16.95; ☺ reception 7am-10am & 5-10.30pm Apr-Oct) There are just two large dorms and a quad at this basic hostel in a converted watermill 10 minutes' walk from the town centre. It's not as glitzy as some other Lakeland hostels, so it's often pretty quiet; there's a pleasant A-framed lounge, bike storage and kitchen.

Six Castlegate (☎ 01900-826749; www.six castlegate.co.uk; 6 Castlegate; s £35-45, d £60-75; ☎) Gorgeously Georgian town house, where neutral colours and pared-back furnishings are offset by chandeliers and cornicing, and all the rooms boast Freeview TVs and the fluffiest of feather pillows. Fresh fruit juice, yoghurts and locally sourced bacon in the morning, too.

Croft House (☎ 01900-827533; www.croft-guest house.com; 6/8 Challoner St; s £38, d £65; P ☎) Reclaimed timber floors, funky blinds, sparkling bathrooms and the odd spot of exposed stone give this swanky guest house the air of a metropolitan crash-pad, and there are breakfast choices for veggies and carnivores.

our pick **Old Homestead** (Map p146; ☎ 01900-822223; www.byresteads.co.uk; Byresteads Farm; d £70-90; P) Not exactly your average farmhouse conversion. The clutter's been stripped out in favour of light, space and lofty ceilings, although the odd A-frame rafter or brick lintel adds rustic charm. If you're a sucker for space, go for the soaring ceilings of the two Cruck rooms, or for romantic character try the rough beams and handmade bed in the Master's Room.

EATING & DRINKING

Merienda (☎ 01900-822790; 7a Station St; mains £4-8) Cafe culture comes to Cockermouth – create pick-and-mix sandwiches, tuck into meze and tapas, or savour the town's best cappuccinos surrounded by stripped wood and chunky leather sofas.

Tarantella (☎ 01900-822109; 22 Main St; mains £8.95-15.95; ☺ dinner Tue-Sat) Sister restaurant to the Ambleside original, serving the same high-quality Italian food: fresh pastas and risottos, hand-thrown pizzas, as well as more adventurous choices such as roast quail and mullet with basil mash.

Quince & Medlar (☎ 01900-823579; www.quince andmedlar.co.uk; 13 Castlegate; mains from around £14; ☺ dinner Tue-Sat) An object lesson in why carnivores don't deserve all the culinary spoils. Gleaming wood, rich fabrics and moody lighting create the atmosphere of a Mayfair gentleman's club, but there's nary a steak or pork chop in sight. Instead you'll be treated to cream cheese and Wensleydale gateau, red pepper rotolo or port-poached pear. An education.

Bitter End (☎ 01900-828993; www.bitterend.co.uk; Kirkgate) From the sublime to the ridiculous; king-size Jennings is joined in Cockermouth by this miniature microbrewery, where the beers are brewed in the old-fashioned way using barley, wheat, hops and 100% Cumbrian spring water. Pint o' Cuddy Lugs, Grasp the Nettle or Cockermouth Pride, anyone?

Self-Catering

Cockermouth has a big **Sainsbury's** (☎ 01900-825694; 43 Station St; ☺ 8am-8pm Mon-Sat, 10am-4pm Sun) and a **Co-op** (☎ 01900-823137; 12 Station St; ☺ 7am-10pm), both near the town centre.

ENTERTAINMENT

Housed in a converted school, the **Kirkgate Arts Centre** (☎ 01900-826448; www.thekirkgate .com; Kirkgate) is the main venue for touring bands, art-house flicks and Cockermouth's annual pantomime.

GETTING THERE & AWAY

The X4/X5 (13 Monday to Saturday, six on Sunday) travels from Workington via Cockermouth on to Keswick (35 minutes) and Penrith (1¼ hours).

KESWICK & DERWENT WATER

BORROWDALE & BUTTERMERE

Ask many people for their quintessential image of a Lakeland dale, and chances are they'll come up with something close to the valleys of Borrowdale and Buttermere. Framed by fells, dotted with chimney-topped cottages and stitched with groves of yew and oak, in previous centuries these side-by-side valleys were dominated by two local industries – farming and slate mining – and much of the forest cover was cleared to make way for grazing cattle and agricultural land. Norse farmers, Furness Abbey monks and Honister quarrymen all left their mark on the landscape, but these days the valleys are mainly favoured by hikers striking out for the fell-tops piled along Buttermere and Crummock Water.

Orientation

The narrow B5289 winds its way through Borrowdale before veering over Honister Pass into Buttermere en route to Lorton and Cockermouth. The 77/77A (Honister Rambler) bus travels four times daily from March to November into Buttermere, either coming from Lorton to the north or from the Borrowdale Valley in the east, while the 79 (Borrowdale Rambler; hourly Monday to Saturday, eight on Sunday) travels from Keswick via Lodore, Grange, Rosthwaite and Seatoller.

LODORE, GRANGE & ROSTHWAITE

First stop on the wonderfully scenic 79 bus route is Lodore and its famous **waterfalls**, nestled at the southern end of Derwent Water. The waterfall was the subject of a splendidly verbose 1820 poem by Robert Southey, *The Cataract of Lodore*, but it dries up to a dribble in dry weather and is really only worth a visit after a good spell of rain. Lodore is a great spot to get out on the lake, with kayaks, Canadian canoes and dinghies available for hire from **Platty+** (☎ 017687-76572; www.plattyplus .co.uk; Lodore); if you've got a few friends, you can even paddle out on a Chinese dragon boat or a Viking longboat.

Beyond Lodore the main road winds past the tiny hamlet of Grange and its beautiful double-arched bridge, spanning the flood-prone River Derwent. The village makes a popular starting point for trails into the jagged gorge known as the Jaws of Borrowdale, whose most famous peak is the rugged **Castle Crag** (985ft), once used as a stone quarry.

A mile further south from Grange is another geological oddity, the house-sized lump of volcanic rock known as the **Bowder Stone**. Looming up above the forest trail and weighing a mighty 1870 tons, this massive boulder is thought to have been dumped here by an ancient glacier at the end of the last ice age; a set of steep wooden stairs takes you up to the top for views down the valley. Look out for the small National Trust car park on the left-hand side when travelling from Grange.

Beyond the Bowder Stone car park, the road curls into the small farming hamlet of Rosthwaite, which marks the starting point for the annual **Borrowdale Fell Race**. Held on the first Saturday in August, this muscle-shredding 17-mile slog makes the Iron Man Challenge look like child's play; you can see a list of previous winners in the bar at the Scafell Hotel (opposite).

Sleeping & Eating

BUDGET

Hollows Farm (☎ 017687-77298; www.hollowsfarm.co.uk; Grange; adult/child £6/3; P) Basic tap-and-toilet farm site near Grange; the views are fine and the field is spacious, but you'll be light on luxuries. B&B rooms are available in the farmhouse (double from £54).

Derwent Water YHA (☎ 0845 371 9314; derwent water@yha.org.uk; Lodore; dm £18.95; ⏰ reception 8.30am-10pm; P ⌨) Lakeland mansion turned tip-top hostel, originally built for the eccentric aristocrat Joseph Pocklington (who also created the man-made waterfall behind the house, which now powers a hydroelectric generator). It's a backpacker's treat – huge high-ceilinged rooms, sweeping grounds, a pool room and, of course, amazing lake views.

MIDRANGE

Yew Tree Farm (☎ 017687-77675; www.borrowdale herdwick.co.uk; Rosthwaite; d from £60; P) Not to be confused with the *other* Yew Tree Farm (p117), this fine farmhouse is a sanctuary of chintz. Floral motifs snuggle under low ceilings; bathrooms are titchy, and there are no TVs, so the views take precedence. For breakfast, there's Cumbrian bacon and bangers, and home-baked cakes across the road at the Flock Inn Tearoom.

FELL RUNNING

Forget marathons, triathlons and pentathlons – the ultimate British endurance sport has to be the lung-busting, leg-shredding, foot-blistering, ankle-cracking event known as fell running. The rules are simple enough – competitors battle it out over a series of fells in a bid for the fastest possible time – but give little idea of the truly gruelling nature of the sport. Races routinely take in some of the most challenging and treacherous peaks in the Lake District, and freezing rain and gale-force winds, not to mention broken limbs and shattered ankles, are all considered run-of-the-mill hazards for the average fell runner.

No one knows quite how this extraordinary pastime first started, but it was already a well-established Lakeland event by the early 19th century, when fell races regularly featured in traditional sports days (see p93). Wasdale, Ennerdale and Borrowdale all hold their own fell-running challenges, but perhaps the most famous race Is the Bob Graham Round (BGR), a gruelling event that involves completing a circuit of 42 peaks in under 24 hours (covering a total distance of around 42 miles, 28,500ft of ascent, and the summits of Scafell Pike, Helvellyn and Skiddaw). The event is named after Bob Graham, a local gardener and guest-house owner, who first completed the 'round' in 1932; his feat has since been duplicated by more than 1300 people (including a 66-year-old by the name of Brian Leathley). The current record held for the official BGR is held by the legendary fell runner Billy Bland, who completed the circuit in a mind-blowing 13 hours and 53 minutes in 1982.

The challenge has since been extended to include the highest number of peaks climbed in 24 hours; Alan Heaton notched up 54 peaks in 24 hours in 1962, while the famous Wasdale fell runner Joss Naylor managed a scarcely believable 72 peaks in 24 hours in 1975. Mark McDermott added another four peaks in 1988, but the current record is held by Mark Hartell, who conquered an astonishing 77 summits in 1997, an achievement so far unmatched by any other runner. The women's record is held by Anne Stentiford, who conquered 62 peaks in 1994.

For more information on the sport and to find out how to get involved, jog past the website for the official Fell Runners Association at www.fellrunner.org.uk.

Mary Mount Hotel (☎ 017687-77223; www.mary mounthotel.co.uk; Lodore; d £70-104; **P**) Borrowdale has plenty of big hotels, but for something more down to earth try this family-run number near the Lodore Falls. Rooms are in the main house or a detached bungalow, but they're more modest B&B than country hotel; some are fiercely floral, although the pricier ones have bay windows over the lake.

TOP END
Scafell Hotel (☎ 017687-77208; www.scafell.co.uk; Rosthwaite; d £123.90-175; **P**) Traditional black-and-white coaching inn in Rosthwaite with rooms overlooking fields or the river; ask for the more modern annexe if you're allergic to flower-print bedspreads and magnolia walls. Borrowdale punters cram into the Riverside Bar (the valley's only real pub) for pints of Theakston's, and there's solid food in the restaurant (mains £8 to £16).

Leathes Head (☎ 017686-77247; www.leatheshead .co.uk; Grange; d £165; **P** 🛜) Resolutely olde-worlde rooms at a smart detached house a mile from Grange. It's geared towards older travellers: the feel is straight from the country hotel textbook, with the emphasis firmly on comfort rather than style. Top rooms have double-aspect views of gardens and fells.

Hazel Bank (☎ 017687-77248; www.hazelbankhotel .co.uk; Rosthwaite; r £170-190; **P**) The pick of the Borrowdale digs, a neo-Gothic manor languishing in private grounds reached via its own humpbacked bridge. Drapes, swags and mahogany wardrobes ooze English luxury – Bowfell glitters in green and gold, while Great Gable boasts a king-sized four-poster that even Henry VIII would have envied. Afternoon tea is served on the lawn in view of the Borrowdale fells.

STONETHWAITE, SEATOLLER & SEATHWAITE
Beyond Rosthwaite, the road trundles on past a series of tiny settlements. First port of call is Stonethwaite, little more than a cluster of cottages arranged along a country track, which leads west towards the remote fell-walking country of the Langstrath Valley. A mile further on is Seatoller, huddled beneath the arduous

KESWICK & DERWENT WATER

climb up to Honister Pass; the village originally grew up as a settlement for workers employed in the local slate quarries, and still feels one step removed from the outside world.

From Seatoller, a road runs southwest to Seathwaite, which holds the dubious honour of being the wettest inhabited place in Britain – around 140in of rain falls in the village every year, topped only by nearby **Styhead Tarn**, which receives an astonishing 172in (just over 14ft). Thankfully there is a positive note to this prodigious precipitation; **Taylor Ghyll Force** is one of the Lakes' most impressive waterfalls, tumbling down 82ft through a series of clashing cascades about a mile from Seathwaite village.

Seathwaite's groves of yew trees famously featured in another memorable Wordsworth ditty as the 'fraternal Four of Borrowdale/ Joined in one solemn and capacious grove', and the village later became a mining centre following the discovery of local graphite. It's a popular starting point for alternative routes up to Great Gable and Scafell Pike, but more sedentary pleasures can be found on the peaceful waters of **Borrowdale Trout Farm** (☎ 017687-77293; Seathwaite; ⊙ 10am-6.30pm Easter-Oct).

Sleeping & Eating

Seatoller Farm (☎ 017687-77232; www.seatollerfarm .co.uk; Seatoller; camping adult/child £5.50/2.50, s £45-59, d £50-64; P) Lovely campsite with a choice of fields (riverside or woodside) on a 500-year-old farm in Seatoller. It's super-secluded, but you'll need to be prepared for damp camping (not to mention a few midges). Backup B&B rooms are available in the farmhouse if the weather turns intolerable.

Honister Hause YHA (☎ 0870 770 5870; Seatoller; dm £16.95; ⊙ daily Easter-Oct, Sat & Sun Nov) Next to Honister, these former quarry-workers' lodgings have been turned into another bare-bones walkers' hostel, with functional cooking facilities and a lounge that doubles as a drying room (beware stinky socks).

Borrowdale YHA (☎ 0870 770 5706; borrowdale@yha .org.uk; Longthwaite; dm £18; ⊙ reception 7.30am-10pm) Modern cedar-clad hostel, set back from the Rosthwaite road and heavily geared towards outdoorsy types. It's bright and cheery, with a fire-warmed lounge and loads of doubles and triples alongside the dorms; there's also a groovy cafe serving hot nosh and Cumbrian ales. It's popular with activity groups and long-distance hikers, so book ahead.

Seatoller House (☎ 017687-77218; www.seatoller house.co.uk; Seatoller; s/d £55/110; P) All the rooms at this Potteresque hidey-hole beneath Honister Pass have off-kilter touches – ground-floor Badger has a hearth and garden views, Rabbit has pine wardrobes and a window overlooking Glaramara, and Osprey boasts rafters and skylight. Rates include a four-course dinner and hearty breakfast.

our pick **Langstrath Inn** (☎ 017687-77239; www .thelangstrath.com; Stonethwaite; d £95-99; ⊙ closed Sun & Mon; P ⊙) Stonethwaite's solitary inn is a find: behind its sturdy whitewashed exterior you'll discover smart, stripped-back rooms in sleek whites and neutral tones, offset by original beams, slate-tiled bathrooms and Africanesque knick-knacks. Downstairs in the snug bar, the excellent food (mains £10.75 to £15.50) comes from local suppliers (Yew Tree lamb, Newlands beef) and there's heaps of stout stone character.

Yew Tree Inn (☎ 017687-77634; Seatoller; mains £8-18; ⊙ Tue-Sun) Seatoller's dinky little restaurant dishes up ploughman's and gravy-filled pies

---

MAID OF BUTTERMERE

The Fish Hotel (opposite) in Buttermere is famous as the home of the legendary beauty Mary Robinson, the so-called Maid of Buttermere. A visiting hiker named Joseph Palmer spied this 15-year-old glamour puss during a stopover in 1792, and later lionised her in his memoir *A Fortnight's Ramble in the Lake District*. Soon visitors were trekking from across the Lakes to see if Mary's beauty lived up to its reputation. Wordsworth was impressed, devoting several lines to her in *The Prelude*, although the rakish Coleridge was rather less dazzled.

Mary later became notorious for being duped by the unscrupulous con man John Hatfield, who passed himself off as an army colonel and MP in order to win her hand; within a year Hatfield had been exposed as a bankrupt and a bigamist, arrested by the Bow Street Runners in Swansea, and sentenced to death by hanging. Despite her terribly public embarrassment, Mary soldiered on and married a more reliable farmer-type from Caldbeck; together they ran the inn until Mary's death in 1837. The tale frames the central plot of Melvyn Bragg's novel *The Maid of Buttermere*.

by day, but after dark moves over to African-influenced flavours – ostrich steak, anyone?

HONISTER PASS

From Seatoller, the road crawls up the switch-backing road to the bleak, wind-lashed Honister Pass. This was once one of the most productive quarrying areas in the Lake District, and still produces much of the region's grey-green slate. Guided tours venture into the bowels of the 'Edge' and 'Kimberley' mines at the **Honister Slate Mine** (☎ 017687-77230; www.honister-slate-mine.co.uk; adult/child £9.75/4.75; ◷ tours 10.30am, 12.30pm & 3.30pm Mar-Oct); a tour into the 'Cathedral' mine runs on Friday by request, but you'll need eight people. Either way, it's cold and wet underground, so come suitably dressed. Slate goodies (signs, clocks, coffee tables) are on sale, and for £10 you can fill up your car boot with cast-off slate.

Honister's latest attraction is the UK's first **Via Ferrata** (Iron Way; adult/under 16yr/16-18yr £19.50/9.50/15). Modelled on the century-old routes across the Italian Dolomites, this vertiginous clamber follows the cliff trail once used by the Honister slate miners, using a system of fixed ropes and iron ladders. It's exhilarating and great fun, but unsurprisingly you'll need a head for heights.

BUTTERMERE & CRUMMOCK WATER

Up and over the pass, the road drops sharply into the deep bowl of Buttermere, gouged out by a steamroller glacier and backed by a string of impressive peaks and pea-green hills. The valley's twin lakes, Buttermere and Crummock Water, were once joined, but became separated by glacial silt and rockfall; the little village of Buttermere sits halfway between the two, and provides a wonderfully cosy base for exploring the rest of the valley.

Buttermere's jagged skyline occupies a special place in the hearts of many hill walkers, since it was one of Wainwright's favourite walking destinations. The classic circuit is via **Red Pike** (2479ft), **High Stile** (2644ft), **High Crag** (2443ft) and **Haystacks** (1958ft), a fantastic ridge walk of around 8.5 miles, lasting about seven hours. At the walk's northern end, near Buttermere village, you'll pass the plunge of **Scale Force** (at 170ft it's one of the highest waterfalls in the Lake District), while on the summit of nearby Haystacks you'll be literally walking in Wainwright's footsteps – as requested in his will his ashes were scattered here by his

second wife, Betty. A window plaque inside **St James' Church**, above Buttermere village, commemorates the great man and looks out over the summit of his favourite fell.

Sleeping & Eating

Syke Farm (☎ 01768-770222; Buttermere; adult/child £6/3; ◷ Feb-Nov) As simple as campsites come, but with undeniably grand vistas. Facilities are limited to basic showers and loos, but pick your spot and you'll wake up to views of Red Pike, High Stile and Haystacks. There's a river to chill your booze in and the farmer makes ice cream with milk straight from his dairy herd (the marzipan is to die for).

Buttermere YHA (☎ 0870 770 5736; buttermere@yha.org.uk; dm £20.95; ◷ reception 8.30am-10am & 5.30-10.30pm; ℗) Halfway along the Honister–Buttermere road, this perfectly positioned hostel has the kind of mountain views you'd normally expect to pay through the nose for. Period slate and stone grace the outside, but inside it's smart, colourful and modern; there's a great cafe-kitchen and a lounge overlooking the lake, and lots of quads and six-bed dorms.

Wood House (☎ 017687-70208; www.wdhse.co.uk; Buttermere; d £100; ℗) B&Bs are rare in Buttermere, which makes this prim and proper retreat even more of a find. Rooms are effortlessly elegant, decked out in restrained tones of fawn and cream; most have Buttermere views, and there's fresh-baked bread and Woodall's bacon on the breakfast table. The house even has artistic cachet – it featured in a 1798 landscape by JMW Turner.

Bridge Hotel (☎ 017687-70252; www.bridge-hotel.com; Buttermere; r incl dinner £158-210; ℗) For fancier accommodation, head over to Buttermere's second splendid inn, built beside the village's humpbacked bridge. Behind the whitewashed frontage you'll discover classy rooms, all with frilly fabrics and comfy armchairs (but no tellies due to the dodgy signal); downstairs, there's a beamed bar and a table d'hôte restaurant serving braised venison, slow-roasted lamb and the valley's best Sunday lunch.

Fish Hotel (☎ 017687-70253; www.fish-hotel.co.uk; d with 2-night minimum £170; ℗) Buttermere's most famous pub is known for its connections with the Maid of Buttermere (opposite), but it's worth a look for its grub and ales, too. There's not too much decorative dazzle in the rooms, but the restaurant boasts plates of Crummock trout and Cumbrian tatie pot (mains £8 to £16), washed down with local brews.

Ullswater

Second only in stature and stateliness to Windermere, the elegant lake of Ullswater cuts a regal 8-mile sweep through the eastern fells, stretching between the small villages of Pooley Bridge in the north and Glenridding and Patterdale in the south. Gouged out by a long-extinct glacier, it's arguably one of the most dramatic of all the Lakeland valleys, with each shore flanked by lofty mountains and serrated summits, topped off at its southern end by the unmistakeable razor ridges leading up to Helvellyn, England's third-highest mountain.

Storybook steamers have been puttering their way across the waters since 1859, and the lake's shorelines are lined with ancient stands of birch, oak and hazel. Overlooking the lake are the woodland parks of Gowbarrow and Glencoyne, whose annual daffodil displays were canonised by Wordsworth in one of his best-loved poems. But Ullswater is a long way from a well-kept secret these days, and it can feel frustratingly logjammed in summer; you can usually find more solitude in the little-visited valleys on the lake's eastern side, or by venturing away from the lakeshore altogether to explore the rolling parkland of the Lowther estate and the wild valley of Haweswater out to the southeast. And if it's wide-angle panoramas you're seeking, there aren't many to match the view from the sky-top summit of Kirkstone Pass, the highest road pass in the national park.

HIGHLIGHTS

- Tame your nerves on the tightrope walk along Striding Edge to **Helvellyn** (opposite)
- Hop aboard the historic **steamers** (p167) on Ullswater
- Wander among Wordsworthian daffodils around **Gowbarrow Park** (p170)
- Visit Cumbria's most beautiful mountain chapel, **St Martin's** (p174) in Martindale
- Take a wildlife safari around the estate of **Lowther Park** (p175)
- Scan the skies around **Haweswater** (p176) for England's last golden eagle

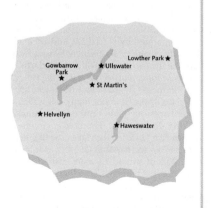

- Area of largest lake (Ullswater): 3.41 sq miles
- Ullswater 'Steamers' passengers in 2007: 187,469
- Number of daffodil varieties in Britain: 27,000 to 35,000

ITINERARY 1
HELVELLYN HIKE
8 miles/6 to 7 hours/Patterdale to Glenridding

The classic Helvellyn route is the ridge scramble along **Striding Edge**, a strenuous challenge even for experienced walkers, with dizzying drops and some all-fours scrambling – don't try it if you're even slightly wary of heights, steer clear in wintry conditions and come suitably prepared.

There are several possible routes, but one of the most rewarding starts along the gorgeous Grisedale Valley. Head west from Patterdale and, after about half a mile, cross **Grisedale Beck** via a humpback bridge before ascending the flank of **Birkhouse Moor**. After a long, steep climb you'll reach the **Hole-in-the-Wall** landmark, a good place to take a breather, with grand views up to the Helvellyn summit, the glacial Red Tarn and the dramatic spine of Striding Edge.

Head southwest beneath **Bleaberry Crag** and over the rocky mound of **High Spying How** before venturing onto the ridge itself. Several trails wind their way along the edge, offering various degrees of difficulty; whichever you choose, take it carefully. At the end of the ridge it's a scramble over the rock tower known as the **Chimney** (or along the easier right-hand trail) and up another sharp, rocky section to the summit (3116ft), where you'll be rewarded with fabulous views southeast to **St Sunday Crag**, northeast to the pointy peak of **Catstycam** (2917ft), west to Thirlmere and east to Ullswater.

Three memorials can be found around the summit: the first to Robert Dixon, who slipped off the peak while following a foxhounds' trail, and a second to the headstrong climber Charles Gough who, in 1805, became the first recorded person to fall off the mountain. A third memorial marks the point where two daring pilots, John Leeming and Bert Hinkler, landed their plane on 22 December 1926. Some people will do anything to avoid a walk!

After the dizzying challenge of Striding Edge, the descent via **Swirral Edge** is a doddle, with a clear trail winding down between Catstycam and **Red Tarn**. You can now either retrace your steps back to Patterdale or take the alternative route along **Red Tarn Beck**, passing Greenside Mine before descending to Glenridding.

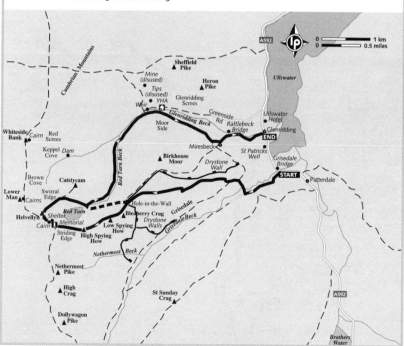

ITINERARY 2
ULLSWATER DRIVE
24 miles/5 to 6 hours/Penrith to Ambleside

This scenic spin takes in all the best bits of the Ullswater valley, with a trip across the lake thrown in for good measure. Kick the day off in **Penrith** (p204), with an early morning detour to either the **Rheged Discovery Centre** (p208) or the stately home of **Dalemain** (opposite). Then it's west along the A592, recently voted as one of Britain's top 10 drives; the road swings and swerves all the way along the lake shore of Ullswater, offering sweeping views over the lake and the cloud-covered fells to the east. Stop off at **Gowbarrow Park** (p170) and stretch your legs with a woodland stroll up to **Aira Force** and **High Force**, followed by a ploughman's and a pint at the homely **Royal** (p171) in Dockray.

After lunch, drive on into **Glenridding** (p171) and park in the village car park before catching a leisurely afternoon cruise across the lake with **Ullswater 'Steamers'** (opposite). If you fancy a walk, you could hop off the launch for a wander back to the village from the pier at **Howtown** (p174); alternatively, stay on the boat and save yourself for afternoon tea at **Fellbites Cafe** (p173) or **Greystones Coffee House** (p173).

The most spectacular stretch of driving is saved for last; from Glenridding the road rolls past Patterdale (p171) through the southern side of the Glenridding valley and up past **Brothers Water** and **Hayeswater** before finally topping out at the **Kirkstone Pass** (p174), the highest point in the Lake District accessible by automobiles. There's a handy car park near the summit of the pass from where you'll have a sweeping view over Brothers Water and the surrounding fells.

Once you've taken your snaps and admired the views, hop back in the motor for the downhill dodgem ride to **Troutbeck** (p75). History buffs will want to make a stopoff at the former yeoman's farmhouse of **Townend** (p75), while horticultural types will prefer the landscaped gardens of **Holehird** (p75). The road trip ends in the busy market town of **Ambleside** (p76), where you'll find a hearty supper at **Zeffirelli's** (p82) or **Tarantella** (p82).

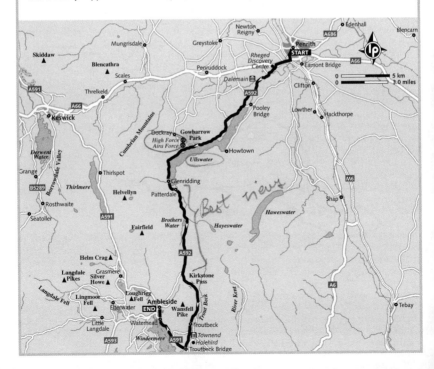

ULLSWATER & AROUND

Wordsworth and Wainwright both adored it, and it has been compared to countless other lakes around the globe, but England's second-largest water has an imperial grandeur all of its own. Ullswater owes its distinctive zigzag shape to the intractable toughness of the surrounding fells; long ago, the glacier that carved out the lake bed was forced off course by the varying densities of granite, Skiddaw slate and limestone in the nearby mountains, creating the lake's three distinct dog-leg sections. The elegant steamers that have been plying its waters for the last century and a half are some of the oldest and loveliest in the Lakes, and if you've been saving yourself for the picture-perfect cruise, this is probably where you'll find it.

DALEMAIN

Driving southwest along the main A592 road from Penrith, a dense cover of overhanging trees and hedgerows thins out suddenly to reveal the striking, salmon-pink facade of Dalemain (☎ 017684-86450; www.dalemain.com; adult/under 16yr £7.50/free, gardens only £3; ☉ 11.15am-4pm mid-Mar–mid-Oct), standing proud amid sheep-filled fields a mile from the northerly tip of Ullswater.

With a name deriving from the Old Norse for 'manor in the valley', this elegant country estate traces its roots back to the reign of Henry II; the present-day Georgian facade was constructed during the mid-18th century, but behind its orderly frontage are the remnants of a 12th-century pele tower and an Elizabethan manor.

Inside it's the picture of a quintessential English country house – half *Gosford Park* set, half three-dimensional *Cluedo* board, with a bewildering maze of passages, spiralling staircases and interconnecting rooms to explore. Since 1679 the house has been in the hands of the Hasell family, and it still feels very much like a family home; photos and heirlooms are dotted around among the assortment of antique pots, burnished furniture and sombre oil portraits.

Guided tours run during the morning, and after lunch you can wander around at will. Highlights include the splendid Georgian 'Chinese Room' with its hand-finished oriental wallpaper, and the Tudor 'Fretwork Room', notable for its oak panelling and plastered ceiling; antiques fans will spot fine collections of Chippendale furniture, vintage toys and countless pieces of priceless porcelain. Meanwhile the servants' quarters offer a fascinating insight into the *Upstairs, Downstairs* life of the house: the huge kitchen and cramped housekeeper's quarters provide a timely reminder of the blood, sweat and toil that went into maintaining the Georgian gentry's lavish lifestyles.

Outside, the grounds feature a Tudor knot garden and a wonderful rose walk, as well as the 16th-century Great Barn (one of the oldest in England), which houses small museums on agriculture and the hardy fell pony. In the base of the 12th-century Norman pele tower is another museum dedicated to the Westmorland and Cumberland Yeomanry regiment, founded in 1819 and disbanded shortly after WWI.

The house hosts lots of festivals and events throughout the year, including country shows, tractor meets, classic car displays and the wonderfully British **Marmalade Festival** (www.marmaladefestival.com), where local cooks battle to bottle the best citrus, chunky, Seville orange and organic marmalades.

POOLEY BRIDGE

Nestled at the head of the lake alongside the babbling River Eamont, the tiny hamlet of Pooley Bridge is little more than a collection of country pubs, cottages and teashops, but in days gone by this was the main market centre for northern Ullswater. Spread along a pebbled shoreline and surrounded by woods and fields, it's still a pleasant base for exploring the lake, although the steady stream of tourist traffic robs the village of much of its charm in the busy summer season.

The **Ullswater 'Steamers'** (☎ 017684-82229; www.ullswater-steamers.co.uk; ♿) putter out from the Pooley Bridge jetty for the southern reaches of the lake, stopping at Howtown and Glenridding before looping back to Pooley Bridge. The company's oldest vessels have been in action on Ullswater for over a century: *Lady of the Lake* was launched in 1877, followed by *Raven* in 1889. These two grand old ladies have been joined by a couple of younger fillies: the *Lady Dorothy* (transported from Guernsey in 2001) and the *Totnes Castle* (launched in 2007, and rechristened the *Lady Wakefield*).

ULLSWATER

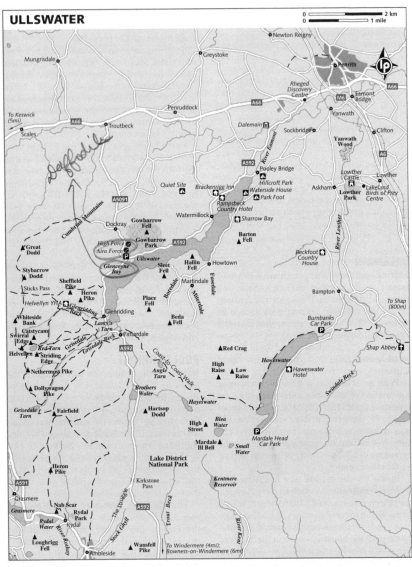

Up to 12 daily ferries run in summer, dropping to three in winter. Returns from Pooley Bridge are £4.80/2.40 per adult/child to Howtown, or £11.30/5.65 to Glenridding and back. A special walker's ticket covers travel between any three stages and costs £9.90/4.95. Bikes and dogs are allowed on board depending on space, and wheelchair access is usually possible (although the height of the lake sometimes causes problems, so it's worth ringing ahead).

There's no tourist office in the village, although there's a small **information point** (☎ 017684-82229; 9am-5pm Easter-Oct) next door to the Crown Inn.

Sleeping

CAMPING

Hillcroft Park (☎ 017684-86363; Roe Head Lane; sites £11-20; ⊙ Mar-Oct) This friendly campsite is a stroll from the village so it gets crammed in summer – if you prefer not to rub guy ropes with your neighbour you're better off looking elsewhere. The lake views are grand and the village pubs are on your doorstep, but the two amenities blocks are looking tired.

Waterside House (☎ 017684-86332; www.waterside farm-campsite.co.uk; sites per 2 adults, tent & car £12-18, motor homes £12-18; ⊙ Mar-Oct) Plump for this lovely lakeside site if you don't mind jostling for position with a Swaledale or two. Electric hook-ups are available for caravans, specific fields are geared to general or family campers, and the facilities are bang up to date. Canadian canoes, row boats and 'sea cycles' are available for hire if you feel like getting out on the water.

Park Foot (☎ 017684-86309; www.parkfootullswater .co.uk; Howtown Rd; sites incl 2 adults, tent & car £12-24, caravans £16-31; ⊙ Mar-early Nov) Further south on the Howtown road, this site is the best for family facilities, including tennis courts, bike hire, pony trekking, two playgrounds and a kids' activity club.

MIDRANGE

Ullswater View (☎ 017684-86286; www.theullswater view.co.uk; Watermillock; d £68-100; P ⊙) The name's a giveaway – all the rooms at this modernised stone house in Watermillock have a lake outlook, and a recent refurb has spruced up the decor: beige-tiled bathrooms, fancy sinks and flat-screen TVs lend character to the rather boxy layouts.

Pooley Bridge Inn (☎ 017684-86215; www.pooley bridgeinn.co.uk; d £75-100; P) Break out the lederhosen; this weird inn looks like it's upped sticks from the Alsatian Alps and set up shop in Pooley Bridge. Hanging baskets, cartwheels and balconies decorate the exterior, and inside you'll find dinky rooms heavy on the florals and oak beams. The stable restaurant (mains £8 to £16) is worth a look for baked trout and solid sausage and mash, served among beams, stone and parquet floor.

Brackenrigg Inn (☎ 017684-86206; www.brackenrigg inn.co.uk; Watermillock; d £79, incl dinner £119; P) Perched by the road 2 miles southwest of Pooley Bridge, this whitewashed hostelry has a reputation for grub and ales stretching back two centuries. Rooms are plainish in country cream, so it's worth insisting on a lake view (despite the A592 being in the way). The menu is strong on fish, meat and game and there's a choice of grassy terrace, cosy bar or dining room.

our pick **Rampsbeck Country Hotel** (☎ 017684-86442; www.rampsbeck.co.uk; Watermillock; s £95, d £70-125, ste £145; P) This terrific family-run retreat near the Brackenrigg Inn is surrounded by striped lawns and lush gardens, and boasts one of the best lakeside spots anywhere on Ullswater. Rooms are an sweetly endearing blend of old and new: wooden wardrobes, wallpapers, roll-top baths and braided drapes meet flashy fabrics and fancy Bose radios. For maximum character ask for Silver Crag, with half-tester bed and private balcony, or Ullswater, with four-poster and lake outlook. A three-/four-course dinner menu is available for £43/49.50.

SOMEWHERE SPECIAL

our pick **Quiet Site** (☎ 07768-727016; www.thequietsite.co.uk; sites £12-27, caravans £17-27, pods £30; P ⊙) Who said camping couldn't be chic? Huddled on the hillside halfway between Pooley Bridge and Gowbarrow Park, this isn't just one of Ullswater's best campsites, it's one of the top spots in the whole national park. As its name suggests, it's gloriously quiet: the grassy camping fields are spread out under shady trees with plunging views over Ullswater (sloping sites are cheaper), and the sparkling showers and atmospheric pub are housed in converted farm buildings, making a welcome change from pre-fab portable cabins. It's also scooped several awards for its ecofriendliness, which includes reed-bed sewage treatment, harvested waste water, on-site recycling and timber-framed 'eco-pods'. David Bellamy has given it his seal of approval, and who are we to argue with England's bewhiskered biologist?

The campsite is signed from the main A592 just after the Brackenrigg Inn, from where it's an uphill drive of about 1.5 miles.

ULLSWATER

TOP END

Sharrow Bay (☎ 017684-86301; www.sharrowbay.co.uk; d £185-420; ℗ 🛜) You might need a second mortgage to stay at this legendary Lakeland getaway, but for swag-draped splendour, there are few places to top it. Rooms are split between the main house, a farmhouse conversion and an Edwardian gatehouse; chaise longues, antique armchairs, ornate chandeliers and canopied beds come as standard, there's a Michelin-rated restaurant (dinner from £55), and of course a private jetty and boathouse. It's snooty and expensive, but if you're after that once-in-a-lifetime megasplurge, Sharrow Bay certainly shouldn't disappoint.

Eating

Sun Inn (☎ 017684-486205; mains £5-12) Pooley Bridge's best boozer is a Jennings establishment, so the beer is guaranteed to be good. Inside you'll find the usual wood-panelled and crackling-fire cosiness, with a *carte du jour* of chicken-and-ham pies and haddock lasagnes; there's a wooden fort outside to keep the nippers entertained.

Granny Dowbekin's Tearooms (☎ 017684-86453; Pooley Bridge; mains £5.95-7.95; ☉ 10am-5pm daily) This popular brook-side tearoom makes an ace option for afternoon tea. Top tips are the 'scramberland' all-day brekkie (Cumberland sausage and scrambled egg) and the trademark Ullswater pie (chicken, ham, apple, apricot and ginger), served with tangy Branston pickle.

Getting There & Away

The most useful bus to Pooley Bridge is the 108, which runs between Patterdale (25 minutes) and Glenridding (20 minutes) before stopping at Pooley Bridge and continuing to Penrith (20 minutes). There are two car parks in the village (one on either side of the humpbacked bridge), but you'll need to be there early to bag a summer spot.

GOWBARROW PARK & AIRA FORCE

Southwest of Pooley Bridge, the A592 ducks and dives along Ullswater's western shore, with occasional breaks in the trees affording glimpses of the lake and the broody fells beyond. After 5 miles you'll reach the small car park at Gowbarrow Park, which marks the start of the half-hour stroll to one of the most famous Lakeland waterfalls, Aira Force. The 230ft cascade starts high in the surrounding hills and makes for a furious sight after heavy rain, with its clashing waters tumbling down beneath a stone footbridge into a densely wooded ravine lined with spruce, fir, pine

THE ULLSWATER DAFFODILS

A short way south from Gowbarrow Park towards Ullswater is the little inlet of **Glencoyne Bay**, where during a springtime walk on 15 April 1802 Dorothy and William Wordsworth famously stumbled across the sprightly stand of daffodils that inspired one of WW's most famous poems (not to mention one of the most quoted verses in the literary canon):

I wandered lonely as a clouder vales and hills,
That floats on high o'
When all at once I saw a crowd,
A host, of golden daffodils;
Beside the lake, beneath the trees,
Fluttering and dancing in the breeze.

Interestingly, William didn't actually complete his poem until two years later in 1804, and many of its famous phrases seem to have been inspired as much by his sister's journal as by his own recollections. Dorothy's delicate observations are a clear demonstration of her own poetic sensibilities: in her diary she recalls how the daffodils 'rested their heads upon these stones as on a pillow for weariness and the rest tossed and reeled and danced and seemed as if they verily laughed with the wind that blew upon them from over the lake, they looked so gay ever glancing ever changing'.

Needless to say, springtime is the best time to visit if you want to see the blooms, but try to resist the urge to pick them unless you fancy a slap on the wrist from a passing NPA warden.

and cedar. Red squirrels are frequent visitors to the woods around the falls, so keep your eyes peeled.

If the inevitable crowds around the falls are a little too much, you can continue your walk along the wooded trail to **High Force** and **Dockray**, where the pleasant country pub, the **Royal** (☎ 017684-82356; Dockray; mains £6-14), makes an ideal place for a pint and a bacon butty before tackling the return walk.

Another trail leads through the woods along the lakeshore before rounding the viewpoint at Yew Crag and skirting the upper fell slope. Alternatively, it's a tough slog to the summit of **Gowbarrow Fell** (1578ft), but the views over Ullswater are famously grand, and you'll certainly leave most of the waterfall crowds well behind. The surrounding estate of Gowbarrow Park was founded by the Howard family (owners of nearby Greystoke Castle) as a hunting park and leisure garden, centred around the curious tetra-turreted building of Lyulph's Tower.

GLENRIDDING & PATTERDALE

Clustered around the lake's southern reaches, 3 miles south of Gowbarrow, are the side-by-side villages of Glenridding and Patterdale, backed by some of the most striking mountain scenery anywhere in the Lakeland. High in the western hills loom the spectres of Great Dodd, Stybarrow Dodd, Raise, Nethermost Pike and Dollywagon Pike, connected by the high point of Helvellyn and its classic twin ridge walks via Striding Edge and Swirral Edge. Thousands of plucky hikers descend on the villages every year to tackle the area's exhilarating trails and admire the splendid Lakeland scenery, but apart from the views there's not a huge amount to keep non-walkers entertained.

Information

Glenridding Cyber Cafe (www.glenriddingcybercafe .co.uk; per half hr £1; ⏰ 10am-11pm) Inside Kilner's Coffee House at the Glenridding Hotel.

Post Office (Glenridding; ⏰ 8.30am-5.30pm Mon, 8.30am-3.30pm Tue, 8.30am-noon Wed-Thu)

Ullswater Tourist Office (☎ 017684-82414; ullswater tic@lake-district.gov.uk; Beckside car park; ⏰ 9am-5.30pm Apr-Oct)

www.patterdale.org District information with links to local businesses.

www.ullswater.co.uk Local website with advice on accommodation, activities and walks.

Sights & Activities

Glenridding is by far the busier of the two villages, ranged along the banks of the jangling beck after which the village is named. Originally Glenridding was established as a mining settlement to tap the rich lead reserves at nearby Greenside Mine; power was provided by several waterwheels along the beck, and much later by a series of dams erected at tarns high up in the surrounding mountains, most notably at High Dam and Keppel Cove, which infamously burst its banks in 1927 causing widespread devastation in the valley below.

The last lead mines closed down in the mid-1960s and Glenridding has since turned its attention almost entirely to the tourism trade, with a smattering of tearooms, outdoors shops, B&Bs and a brace of village stores scattered around its part-cobbled street. Down by the lake shore you'll find the southerly pier for the Ullswater 'Steamers' (p167), which putter north across the lake to Howtown (adult/child £8.40/4.20) and Pooley Bridge (£11.90/5.65).

A mile further south from Glenridding, Patterdale is little more than a conglomeration of cottages and a large slate-fronted hotel strung along the lakeshore. The tiny church of **St Patrick's**, at the northern end of the village, is worth a look for some tapestries by the seamstress Ann Macbeth, who lived here between 1921 and 1943 and belonged to the influential 'Glasgow School' (which also counted Charles Rennie Mackintosh among its members).

WALKING

For the vast majority of visitors, the villages are simply convenient staging posts for exploring the surrounding fells. Obviously the main target is Helvellyn (p165) and thousands of visitors clamber up to the summit every year. It was a favourite walk of Wainwright's, and seems also to have exercised a peculiarly powerful hold over Wordsworth: the mountain crops up frequently in his work, and he continued to climb it well into his 70s. One of the most famous portraits of the poet, completed by the painter Benjamin Haydon in 1842, depicts Wordsworth deep in thought with Helvellyn as a suitably Romantic backdrop.

Even if you don't feel up to the main Helvellyn event, there are plenty of other hikes to tackle, including the easy half-hour amble to **Lanty's Tarn**, which starts just south of Glenridding, and the more challenging 3.5-mile valley hike up to **Grisedale Tarn** from Patterdale. Local legend maintains that Grisedale Tarn is the final resting place of the Cumbrian crown, which was supposedly brought here after King Dunmail was defeated in 945. From here there's an alternative route to the Helvellyn summit via Dollywagon Pike and Nethermost Pike.

Another good option from Glenridding village is to follow the trail up Glenridding Beck for half a mile to Rattlebeck Bridge, or for a further mile to the remains of the **Greenside Mine** and the former mine-workers' cottages now occupied by the Helvellyn YHA (right); you'll be rewarded with a grand view of the Helvellyn Range without having to summon the courage to face them head on. For a longer walk, you could ascend to **Sticks Pass** and **Stybarrow Dodd** – offering seriously stupendous views – with a possible return via Sheffield Pike, Heron Pike and Glenridding Dodd.

For a longer-distance route, many walkers opt for the hike to **Hallin Fell**, the standalone hummock of land that looms above Howtown on the lake's eastern shore, offering a panorama of peaks including High Raise, Beda Fell and Place Fell. You could catch the launch back to Patterdale or opt for a return route via the tops of Steel Fell and Place Fell; if you walk the whole way, count on covering a distance of around 6 to 8 miles.

Alternative fell-walkers' targets include the old Roman road over the top of **High Street**, which, at 2717ft, is one of the highest peaks east of Ullswater, or the circuit of Hartsop-above-How, Hart Crag and Fairfield, with a stunning descent via Deepdale Hause and St Sunday Crag.

SAILING

The **Glenridding Sailing Centre** (☎ 017684-82541; www.glenriddingsailingcentre.co.uk; The Spit, Glenridding) hires out canoes (£15/35/60 for one hour/three hours/full day) and kayaks (£8/20/40 for one hour/three hours/full day), as well as boats, dinghies and single-handers (£70 to £100 per day). Sailing courses are available for landlubbers looking to earn their watery stripes.

Row boats and outboard-powered vessels can be hired by the hour, half day and day from **St Patrick's Boat Landings** (☎ 017684-82393; Glenridding) and **Ullswater Marine** (☎ 017684-86415; Watermillock). Remember there's a 10mph speed limit on the lake.

Sleeping

CAMPING

Side Farm Campsite (☎ 017684-82337; andrea@sidefarm .fsnet.co.uk; Patterdale; 2 adults & car £11; ⏴ Easter-Oct) Patterdale's camp ground is more basic, with 60-odd pitches spread out over a spacious farmer's field overlooking Ullswater. Big groups and fires aren't allowed, so things are pretty tranquil, except during the summer rush when it's crammed. Facilities include basic shower blocks, a laundry and a small sticky-bun teashop.

Gillside Farm Campsite (☎ 017684-82346; www .gillsidecaravanandcampingsite.co.uk; Glenridding; 2 adults, tent & car £14; ⏴ Mar–mid-Nov; P) Glenridding's village campsite makes a lovely spot to pitch, peacefully situated on a working farm run by the friendly Lightfoots (who'll supply fresh milk and eggs for breakfast). Fell tops glower in all directions and there's a camping barn in case the weather takes a turn for the worse.

BUDGET

Helvellyn YHA (☎ 0845 371 9742; helvellyn@yha.org .uk; Greenside; dm £12.95; ⏴ reception 7.30am-10am & 5-10.30pm Easter-Oct) It's not as remote as Black Sail (p140), but for that high-altitude rush Helvellyn's hostel is still a treat. Converted from former miners' dwellings, it's perched 900ft above Glenridding along the rough track to Helvellyn, so it's a hiker's fave; meals and guided walks are laid on by the hostel staff, and there's plenty of dorm space crammed in among its sturdy stone walls.

Patterdale YHA (☎ 0845 371 9337; patterdale@yha .org.uk; dm £12.95; ⏴ reception 7.30am-10am & 5-10.30pm Easter-Oct) Purpose-built hostel by the Patterdale shoreline, decked out in funky colours and kitsch artwork to match its retro mid-1970s architecture. It's packed with quirks, from the wood-panelled, wall-mounted bunk beds to the groovy A-framed cafe-bar, and makes a nice change from the slightly stuffy surroundings of some Lakeland hostels. Only a few doubles, though, so book early if you prefer your privacy.

MIDRANGE

Grisedale Lodge (☎ 017684-82155; www.grisedalelodge .co.uk; s £40, d £75; P) Spot woodpeckers and blue tits from your window at this lawn-fringed B&B in Grisedale, between Glenridding and Patterdale. Both doubles (one with a private bathroom, the other en suite) are

TV-free, so late-night noise isn't a problem, but if you get tube withdrawal symptoms there's a guest TV lounge with Freeview and hiking books.

Mosscrag (☎ 017684-82500; www.mosscrag.co.uk; s £42.50-47.50, d £64-80; P) On the main Glenridding lane, this old-school guest house overlooks Glenridding Beck and offers six pine-and-cream rooms straight out of the Brit B&B textbook – plastic tea trays, floral curtains and the kind of crazy carpets that went out of fashion with bell-bottom flares.

Old Water View (☎ 017684-82175; www.oldwaterview .co.uk; Patterdale; s £45, d £70; P) Six spick-and-span rooms in Patterdale all with individual decorative tics. 'Little Gem' has a barn-door overlooking a babbling brook, split-level 'Bothy' has a mum-and-dad's double with attic singles for the kids, and 'Place Fell' is jammed under the rafters (look out for Wainwright's autograph on the wall – this was apparently the great man's favourite room).

Cherry Holme (☎ 017684-82512; www.cherryholme .co.uk; Glenridding; s £60, d £100-120; P ☎) This spacious house on the eastern edge of Glenridding is a cut above its competitors, with lashings of blond pine, LCD TVs and a Nordic-style steam room, although the rooms are pricey considering their plainness.

Glenridding Hotel (☎ 01768-482228; www.bw -glenriddinghotel.co.uk; d £84-125; P ☎ ☎) Glenridding's big lakeside hotel has been hoovered up by Best Western, so the rooms have about as much character as a cardboard box – but if you like your facilities (gym, sauna, swimming pool) and don't mind corporate colours, you'll be happy enough (watch out for those added extras, though). The Ratcher's Restaurant (mains £11.95 to £16.95) is Glenridding's main eatery, or there's more relaxed food at the Ratcher's Tavern next door.

TOP END

Inn on the Lake (☎ 017684-82444; www.innonthe lakeullswater.co.uk; Glenridding; s £81, d £128-220; P ☎) The traditional hotel choice, with plenty of facilities, but light on charm. The lakeside aspect is fantastic, and as long as you can look past the stuffy, generic decor, you'll have a choice of mountainous or watery views and lots of spoils including jacuzzi baths, croquet lawn and a private shoreline. The restaurant is smart-casual, but the lovely beamed Ramblers Bar is more laid-back.

Eating

Greystones Coffee House (☎ 017684-82392; www .greystonesgallery.co.uk; Glenridding; lunches & cakes £3-10; ☉ 9am-5pm) Colourful cafe and gallery serving cappuccinos, wraps and cakes among exhibitions of local artwork and photography.

Traveller's Rest (☎ 017684-82298; Glenridding; mains £5.50-15) Typically friendly Cumbrian pub with fire-lit lounges, a fell-view patio and a hearty bar menu. Hungry hikers come from miles around for the Traveller's Mixed Grill (£14.70) of rump steak, lamb chop, gammon, black pudding and Cumberland sausage, crowned with a fried egg. The pub is a 500m walk uphill from the A592.

Fellbites (☎ 017684-82664; Glenridding; lunch £6-12, evening menu 2-/3-courses £17.50/21.30; ☉ lunch daily, dinner Thu-Sat) Hikers and sightseers congregate in this converted stone barn beside the beck, tucking into all-day breakfasts, spuds and chunky sandwiches, or more satisfying plates of trout, chicken, duck and lamb shank by night. There's a daily roast, too.

Shopping

The village's only shops are both beside the main road in Glenridding: for general supplies try **Glenridding Mini Market** (☎ 01768-482322) or **Sharman's of Glenridding** (☎ 017684-82221; ☉ 8am -6pm, later in summer), which has the village's only cash machine and also hires hiking boots just in case you've left yours at home.

For outdoor gear, head for **Catstycam Outdoor Shop** (☎ 017684-82351; Glenridding; ☉ 9am-5.30pm Mon-Sat, 10am-4pm Sun), which has a second outlet in Pooley Bridge.

ENGLAND'S HARDIEST HIKERS

While you're tackling the challenges of Helvellyn, spare a thought for the steel-legged Helvellyn Weatherline Assessors, who are employed by the national park to climb the mountain every day between December and March to assess the risk of possible avalanches and routine weather conditions such as wind chill, snow depth and temperature. The information is recorded on the **Lake District Weatherline** (☎ 0870 055 0575; www.lake-district.gov.uk /weatherline) a vital weather service relied upon by hundreds of thousands of hill walkers every year.

Getting There & Around

Bus 108 runs from Penrith to Patterdale via Pooley Bridge and Glenridding (six Monday to Friday, four on Sunday). The 517 (Kirkstone Rambler; three daily July and August, otherwise weekends only) travels over the Kirkstone Pass from Bowness and Troutbeck, stopping at Glenridding and Patterdale.

The **Ullswater Bus and Boat** ticket (adult/child £13.60/6.85) combines a day's travel on the 108 with a return trip on an Ullswater 'Steamer'.

HOWTOWN & MARTINDALE

The narrow, twisty road winding along the lake's eastern edge to the miniscule hamlet of Howtown is best avoided if you're a bad reverser – it's single-track pretty much the whole way from Pooley Bridge, and passing places are few and far between. A much better way to arrive is via the Ullswater 'Steamers' (p167), which call in at the village jetty en route from Glenridding and Pooley Bridge. There's precious little to see in the village itself: the main reason for visiting is an expedition into the nearby peaks, either the ascent of **Hallin Fell** followed by the lakeshore walk back to Patterdale, or the more challenging charge up Fusedale, High Raise and Angle Tarn, taking in the old Roman road of **High Street** en route.

Apart from the fells, the 2-mile toil up to the church of **St Martin's** is well worth the effort. Sitting high in the hilltops above the Martindale valley, this is one of the most beautiful of all the Lake District's mountain chapels – sheltered under the boughs of a 1000-year-old yew, with a flagstoned interior housing a 17th-century pulpit and a 500-year-old church bell.

The only place to stay is the bewitchingly backward **Howtown Hotel** (☎ 017684-86514; Howtown; d from £60), which steadfastly refuses to kowtow to the expectations of contemporary travellers. There are no phones, no TVs and precious few mod-cons, and its interior design seems to have stalled around the early 1900s (think stuffed deer's heads rather than designer furnishings), but it still manages to be irresistible. Rooms with views of fells and fields, friendly service and simple country food make this an ideal refuge from the stresses of 21st-century existence. The picnics are superb, too.

KIRKSTONE PASS

South of Ullswater the main A592 swings and careens along the valley floor before shooting up past the modest splashes of Brothers Water and Hayeswater en route to Kirkstone Pass – at 1489ft the highest mountain pass in Cumbria open to road traffic.

It's one of the most scenic stretches of tarmac anywhere in the national park, but it's not always easy going: the upper section of the road, as you pass the whitewashed **Kirkstone Pass Inn** (☎ 015394-33888; www.kirkstonepassinn.com; mains £5-15) and begin the long, snaking descent down the Rothay Valley to Ambleside, is rather ominously known as the 'Struggle'. Every winter unsuspecting drivers are caught out by surprise patches of black ice and snow, only to find themselves coming to an abrupt stop against an inconveniently positioned drystone wall. Historically the surrounding hillsides were important slate-mining areas, and the industry is still in full swing around the Kirkstone Quarry – you can see examples of local stone craft in the Kirkstone Slate Gallery (p96) in Skelwith Bridge.

The 517 Kirkstone Rambler travels up and over the pass from Glenridding, stopping outside the inn before heading to Troutbeck, Windermere and Bowness. There are three daily buses in July and August, otherwise the service runs only on weekends.

LOWTHER TO HAWESWATER

Eastwards from the deep valleys and interlocking hills around Ullswater, the countryside opens out onto the broad green pastures of the Lowther Park estate, the family seat of the aristocratic Lowther family, who still own huge swathes of land across the Lake District. To the south, a narrow road runs through the pocket-sized village of Bampton to one of the national park's least developed valleys, Haweswater, while to the southeast you'll find one of the Lake District's most atmospheric ecclesiastical landmarks, the tumbledown ruins of Shap Abbey.

The only public transport is via the 111 bus, which runs two or three times daily between Penrith, Yanwath, Askham, Bampton and Burnbanks (near Haweswater).

WICKED JIMMY

It's difficult to imagine the spectacular power once wielded by the Lowthers, the aristocratic dynasty that has been lording it over this part of England for the last 800 years. There's been a Lowther in Cumbria since at least the 13th century, and they've been an almost permanent fixture in English upper-crust society ever since, serving as peers, MPs, earls, barons, sheriffs, courtiers, generals, parliamentary advisers and feudal landowners.

Perhaps the most notorious family member is **Sir James Lowther** (1736–1802), later the 1st Earl of Lonsdale, who became one of the richest men in 18th-century England thanks to his inheritance of three vast fortunes (including the Lowther estate, the entire town of Whitehaven and a cash sum equivalent to a quarter of total British exports at the time).

Despite his unimaginably huge fortune, he was notoriously unpopular, with a reputation for meanness, arrogance, cruelty and licentiousness (explaining his decidedly unflattering nicknames of Wicked Jimmy, the Bad Earl, the Gloomy Earl and Jimmy Grasp-All). Lowther was married twice and had a string of local mistresses; in his scurrilous memoir, *Reminiscences of the Lake Poets*, Thomas de Quincey relates the rather dubious legend that the earl kept one of his young conquests embalmed in a glass-topped coffin at Lowther Castle. Necrophiliac tendencies aside, the earl was certainly tight-fisted: William Wordsworth's father, John, served as his steward and estate manager for over 20 years, but was still owed more than £4000 by the time Sir James popped his clogs in 1802. The debt was eventually settled by the earl's heir, William Lowther, and paid to the surviving Wordsworth children; legend has it that when the Bad Earl was buried in 1802, the ground shook so violently the vicar almost fell into the grave.

LOWTHER PARK

Askham village marks the westernmost extent of **Lowther Park** (☎ 01931-712378; www.lowther.co.uk), a huge country estate encompassing great tracts of woodland, forest, hunting park and pasture, an organic farm and a red squirrel reserve at Whinfell Forest. Guided **wildlife safaris** conducted by the estate's gamekeepers can be arranged by phoning the Lowther Park offices. Depending on the season you might spy anything from rutting roe deer to kestrels, badgers, otters, buzzards, peregrine falcons and, if you're really lucky, a red squirrel or two. For a further wildlife fix, the **Lakeland Birds of Prey Centre** (☎ 01931-712746; Lowther Castle; adult/child £6/3; ☼ 11am-5pm Apr-Oct) provides daily demonstrations by its population of hawks, falcons, eagles and owls.

The estate's most spectacular feature is undoubtedly the crenellated ruin of **Lowther Castle**. Covered in turrets, battlements and corner towers, the house was built by the Victorian architect Robert Smirke, who also designed the British Museum and the Covent Garden Theatre in London, but its upkeep proved too costly even for the prodigiously prosperous Lowthers. The house fell into disrepair around the turn of the century, although long-held plans to renovate the castle finally seem to be coming to fruition thanks to a £9 million development plan from the Northwest Regional Development Agency. At the time of writing there's still no fixed date for the reopening – check up on the latest progress at www.transforminlowther.co.uk. In the meantime the castle is occasionally open to the public, and its grounds play host to a variety of events including the historic **Lowther Horse Driving Trials and Country Fair** (p23).

Campers and caravanners can stay at the **Lowther Holiday Park** (☎ 01768-863631; www.lowther-holidaypark.co.uk; Eamont Bridge; sites incl tent or caravan, car & up to 6 people £22.50-30; ☼ mid-Mar–Nov), which also rents out holiday cottages.

ourpick George and Dragon (☎ 01768-865381; www.georgeanddragonclifton.co.uk) in the village of Clifton is gorgeously refurbished and sources its produce straight from the estate's organic farm. Reclaimed benches, flagstoned hearths and a big fire blazing in the grate make this an irresistible spot for Sunday lunch (from £8.95); period prints and sepia photos explore the Lowthers' long history, while the hand-written blackboards are jam-packed with lamb shank, fillet steak and roasted chicken. Plans are afoot to add upstairs rooms.

HAWESWATER

There are few places in Cumbria that feel as wild and empty as the valley of Haweswater, a long grey slash of water ringed by orange-brown fells and lonely hilltops. South of

---

DETOUR – SHAP ABBEY

Standing in a lonely spot next to the River Lowther, about half a mile west of its namesake village, Shap Abbey was the last great abbey to be founded in England, and the last to be dissolved by Henry VIII's dissolution. It was established in 1199 by a group of Premonsterian canons, and reached the height of its powers during the early 16th century, when the striking bell tower was added to the abbey's west front. This tumbledown tower is now practically all that remains of this once-splendid abbey; the rest of the stone was carted off to build the walls of Shap Market Hall and nearby Lowther Castle.

Askham, a minor road runs through the village of Bampton all the way to the car park at Burnbanks at the lake's northern end, before tracking along the eastern shore and coming to a dead stop near the lake's southerly tip (where there's a second official car park at Mardale Head).

Seen on a brooding winter's day, topped by overhanging clouds and ribbons of mist, the lake makes for one of the most unforgettable sights in the national park, but it's actually not a natural body of water; Haweswater was dammed in the early 1930s to create the Lake District's second reservoir, drowning the little farming community of Mardale in the process; the village later inspired Sarah Hall's moving novel, *Haweswater,* as well as the name of the satirical newspaper the *Mardale Times* (www.mardaletimes.com). Film buffs might also recognise the lake from its appearance in the cult British flick *Withnail & I.* The construction of the dam raised the water level by 95ft, doubling the length of the lake to create the new 4-mile reservoir. Although most of the village was demolished prior to the flooding of the valley, during especially dry periods the old stone bridge and drystone

walls sometimes make an eerie reappearance above the waterline.

Haweswater is also home to one of the RSPB's largest **bird reserves** (☎ 01931-713376; haweswater@rspb.org.uk) with a fluctuating population of buzzards, peregrine falcons, ring ouzels and dippers. The star attraction of the lake, however, is England's last remaining golden eagle, which can often be seen soaring above the water during the summer months. There's a special **viewpoint and bird hide** in the Riggindale Valley, about 1.5 miles walk from the Mardale Head car park. It's open year round, but RSPB wardens man the hide on weekends from April to October, and can hopefully help you spot Haweswater's regal eagle.

Apart from birdwatchers, often the only other visitors to the valley are hill walkers setting out on the classic circuit up the Riggindale Valley via High Street (2717ft), Mardale Ill Bell (2493ft) and Harter Fell (2552ft).

Sleeping & Eating

Beckfoot Country House (☎ 01931-713241; www .beckfoot.co.uk; near Helton; s £30-45, d £80-90; ⦿ Mar-Dec; Ⓟ) Halfway between Askham and Bampton, this remote country manor is surrounded by peaceful paddocks, some of which are grazed by the owner's Shetland ponies. It's a wonderfully backward kind of place, filled with ticking clocks, chaise longues and country knick-knacks, and the rooms are mostly huge.

our pick Haweswater Hotel (☎ 01931-713235; www.haweswaterhotel.com; s £50-80, d £80-100; Ⓟ) Ditch the mobile, unplug the laptop, and revel in the splendid isolation of this remote, oh-so-English hotel, built to replace Mardale's drowned Bull Inn in the late 1930s and still the only place to stay in the valley. Clad in ivy, teeming with antiques and offering views of Haweswater from every room, it's a backcountry retreat par excellence – old fashioned, yes, but you couldn't ask for a snugger spot. A two- or three-course dinner is available for £24.95/29.95.

Cumbrian Coast

Most visitors to the Lake District never stray beyond the boundaries of the national park, but they're missing out on one of the county's forgotten gems – its bleakly beautiful coastline, a gentle panorama of sandy bays, grassy headlands and bottle-green pastures stretching from the sands of Morecambe Bay to the shores of the Solway Coast.

Historically, Cumbria's coastal ports provided an outlet for its mineral mines and slate quarries, and this legacy of industrial activity lingers on in many corners of the coast, especially the old port of Whitehaven, the red-brick city of Barrow-in-Furness and the nuclear reprocessing plant at Sellafield. But outside the scattered pockets of industry, the coast is just as gloriously green as the rest of Cumbria – landscaped grounds and tidal salt marshes surround the stately home of Holker Hall, while orderly promenades line the seafront of Grange-over-Sands, and Cartmel conceals one of Cumbria's most beautiful medieval priories.

Comedy fans make the pilgrimage to the little market town of Ulverston, famous as the birthplace of the bumbling British comedian Stan Laurel, while out to the west, twitchers seek gulls and kittiwakes around the bird reserves of St Bees and the Solway peninsula. Halfway between Barrow-in-Furness and Whitehaven is the Roman settlement of Ravenglass, which marks the westernmost boundary of the Lake District; we've covered it in our Western Lakes chapter on p130.

HIGHLIGHTS

- Indulge in Cumbria's tastiest afternoon tea at **Hazelmere Cafe** (p181) in Grange-over-Sands

- Pay comedy homage at the charmingly chaotic **Laurel and Hardy Museum** (p185) in Ulverston

- Play lord of the manor around the grounds of **Holker Hall** (p183)

- Sample the stellar food at Simon Rogan's restaurants in **Cartmel** (p183)

- Delve into the salty seafaring heritage of **Whitehaven** (p189)

- Join the twitchers in the grassy dunes of **Hodbarrow Nature Reserve** (p188) and **St Bees** (p191)

- Number of visitors to the Dock Museum in 2007: 70,563
- Highest point (Black Combe): 1969ft
- Number of breeding seabirds in Morecambe Bay: 20,000

ITINERARY 1
BLACK COMBE CLIMB   8 miles/4 hours/Whicham

Despite its modest height, this often-overlooked fell is one of Cumbria's best-kept secrets, looming dramatically over the county's western coastline and offering panoramic views all the way from Solway down to the Duddon Sands and Morecambe Bay. Catch the Combe on the right day and you might even glimpse the distant crests of Snowdonia a couple of hundred miles to the south.

This moderate hike starts from the fell's southern side, near the little village of **Whicham**. Follow the public bridleway behind the village church as it climbs up fairly steeply alongside **Moorgill Beck**. As you walk remember to look out over the Irish Sea; you might well be able to spot the silhouette of the Isle of Man far out on the western horizon, as well as the dark hump of Walney Island squatting just off the Furness Peninsula to the south. The trail briefly levels out around **Townend Knotts** before beginning another leg-sapping ascent up the fell-side to the **summit** (1969ft), which you should reach after another hour or so of walking. The top is marked by a trig point and a drystone wind shelter, as well as a small tarn just to the south.

Unlike most of the other Lakeland fells, Black Combe stands almost in isolation, so there's practically nothing to obstruct the 360-degree coastal views to the south and west, and to the distant mountains that stack up impressively inland. The only drawback to such a gloriously isolated spot is the inevitable breeze that often blows in from the sea – it can be pretty windy up top, so a warm coat and an extra fleece might well come in handy!

The descent route tracks northeast past the crag of **Blackcombe Screes** before meandering northwest through disused quarries and sheepfolds. The views as you descend the grassy slope are really grand, so there's no need to rush. The path then swings south over **Hall Foss** and **Holegill Beck**, skirting beneath the craggy slate of the fell's western side, then meanders along the mountain's southern reaches before joining up with the main path back to Whicham.

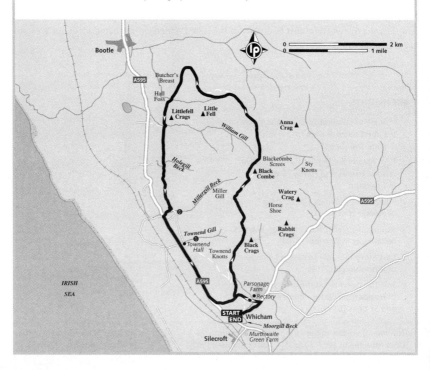

ITINERARY 2
ULVERSTON CYCLE
15 miles/4 to 5 hours/Ulverston

This moderate cycle provides a taster of the long-distance **Walney to Wear Cycle Route** (www
.cyclingw2w.info) between Ulverston and Low Wood before veering up into the peaceful Rusland
Valley. It's fairly well signposted most of the way, and although there are a few tough hills to contend with, it travels through peaceful countryside and is well within most bikers' capabilities. The
route has quite a few twists and turns, so a good-quality Ordnance Survey map is essential.

Start out in Ulverston at **Gill Cycles**, and turn right along Stanley St, following signs for 'Bike
Route 20' past the hospital, along Garden Tce and onto the B5281 out of town. Climb uphill
past the houses and at the next junction bear right, continuing to follow the bike route signs
en route to the hamlet of **Penny Bridge**.

Once you reach the village, look out for the right-hand turn near the start of the houses, which
passes the **Ship Inn** (an ideal sustenance stop) before crossing onto a stone track that heads
under the main A590. A footbridge crosses over the **Greenodd Sands** estuary before joining up
with a section of trail along the banks of the **River Leven** all the way to the B5278; turn left into
Haverthwaite, the starting point for the Lakeside and Haverthwaite Railway (p71).

From here the route has two possible options: if you're feeling fit, you could make a long loop
along either side of the secluded **Rusland Valley**, passing the **Rusland Moss National Nature
Reserve** on the way. For a shorter route, once you've crossed over the A590, turn left and cycle
on to the village of **Booth**; look out for a right-hand turn near the **White Hart** pub (signposted
to Greenodd & Ulverston). The next section is slightly tricky: ignore the two roads on your right,
turn right at the next T-junction, then left just before **Tottlebank Farm**. You'll pass through some
stretches of woodland before crossing over the A5092 back into Penny Bridge, where you rejoin
the Walney to Wear route back to Ulverston.

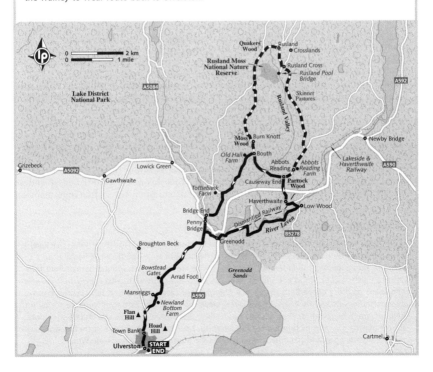

CUMBRIAN COAST

GETTING AROUND

The Furness Railway and Cumbrian Coast lines follow a long 120-mile loop from Lancaster to Carlisle, stopping at Grange-over-Sands, Ulverston, Barrow-in-Furness, Millom, Ravenglass, Whitehaven and Workington. Direct trains run every couple of hours, with extra connecting services north and east from Barrow; services are limited on Sunday.

The Cumbrian Coast Day Ranger (adult/child/railcard holder £15/7.50/9.90) buys a day's travel on the Cumbrian Coast line; see individual town headings for other fares.

SOUTH COAST

GRANGE-OVER-SANDS

pop 4098

Overlooking the sandy expanse of Morecambe Bay, the quiet seaside town of Grange-over-Sands was founded as a granary store for the monks of Cartmel Priory nearby, but was changed beyond recognition by the massive boom in Victorian and Edwardian tourism following the arrival of the railway in the mid-19th century. Hundreds of grand holiday villas and oversized hotels sprang up around the town's hilly streets to cater for the influx of day trippers and train travellers who arrived en masse to stroll the seafront and suck up the bracing seaside breeze (thought to be a palliative for everything from asthma to arthritis).

Grange's gentrified heyday has long since faded, and these days it's mainly frequented by retirees whiling away their twilight years. Once you've had a stroll along the elegant promenade, wandered the ornamental gardens and bimbled around the town's shops, there's not a great deal to keep you entertained, but the town makes a handy base for exploring the rest of the southern coast.

If you're feeling energetic, the half-an-hour stroll up **Hampsfell** offers great views across the bay and (if the weather plays ball) inland to Coniston, Helvellyn and the Langdale Pikes. The best vantage point is the **Hampsfell Hospice**, a little building constructed in 1846 by the vicar of Cartmel as a traveller's shelter.

Back in Grange, the **tourist office** (☎ 015395-34026; grangetic@southlakeland.gov.uk; Victoria Hall, Main St; ⏰ 10am-5pm Easter-Oct) can fill you in on local happenings.

Sleeping

Lymehurst Hotel (☎ 015395-33076; www.lymehurst .co.uk; Kents Bank Rd; s £35-38, d £76-90; **P**) By far Grange's best guest house, with a hint of stately style left from the town's Edwardian heyday. Light, contemporary rooms ditch the clutter for simple pine, creamy walls and ice-white linen, and there's a shiny brass bed in the premier room. The restaurant is worth investigating, too – chef-owner Kevin Wyper dabbles with fusion flavours (dinner 2-/3-course menu £20.50/26.50), and also takes charge of the top-notch brekkie.

Hampsfell House (☎ 015393-32567; www.hampsfell house.co.uk; s £40, d £50-80; **P**) China blues and soothing mauves predominate at this long-standing B&B on Hampsfell Rd, which offers nine thoroughly modern rooms overlooking shrub-filled gardens.

Thornfield House (☎ 015395-32512; www.grange guesthouse.com; Kents Bank Rd; d £58-70; **P**) Nothing groundbreaking, but if you're happy with lemon yellows and peachy pastels, plus a decent fry-up for breakfast, then you'll be comfy enough. On-site parking is a bonus.

Graythwaite Manor (☎ 015395-32001; www .graythwaitemanor.co.uk; Fernhill Rd; s £69.50, d £126-139; **P**) Splash out on countrified splendour at this chimney-covered Grange mansion.

SOMETHING SPECIAL

ourpick **No 43** (☎ 01524-762761; www.no43.org.uk; The Promenade, Arnside; r £110-140; **P**) Holy mackerel – or should that be holy cockle? This seductive little number isn't exactly what you'd expect to stumble across among the faded old town houses of Arnside. It's a boutique barnstormer from start to finish: wicker, wood and gilded wallpapers rub shoulders with crisp sheets, fluffy towels and soaps courtesy of the Bath House in Sedbergh. Tones are achingly tasteful – ochres, creams, cappuccinos – and rooms 2 and 7 have lovely views over the Kent Estuary. If you're a sucker for luxuries, you'll be spoilt for choice: some rooms have Bose sound systems and Belfast-style sinks, others plasma TVs and picture flame fires. Even the breakfast has boutique cachet: Saddleback bacon, organic eggs and handmade breads from the Munx bakery in Staveley. Wow.

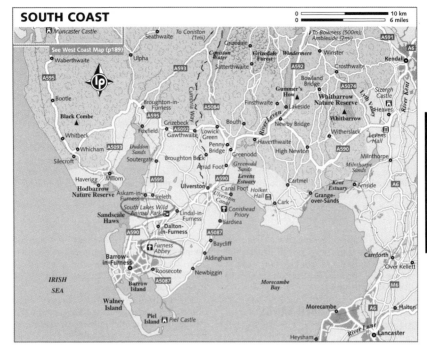

CUMBRIAN COAST

It's been seemingly pickled in aspic since the mid-1930s – a Union-jacked flagpole stands outside, leather armchairs and ticking grandfather clocks fill the creaky corridors, and there's a wood-panelled lounge straight out of a Hercule Poirot novel. Rooms are spacious and stuffy; latticed windows afford views of trimmed lawns.

Netherwood Hotel (☎ 015395-32552; www.nether wood-hotel.co.uk; Lindale Rd; d £150; P 🖳 🐕) Another ridiculously over-the-top pile on Grange's outskirts, built for the Fallowfield family, and still resplendent with gables, gardens and grand rooms. It's more corporate these days, but there's still plenty of corniced character, and the facilities (sauna, gym and swimming pool) keep its corporate clientele happy.

Eating
our pick **Hazelmere Cafe** (☎ 015395-32972; 1-2 Yewbarrow Tce; sandwiches £4-6, mains £6-10; 🕙 10am-5pm summer, 10am-4.30pm winter) Is this the finest afternoon tea in Cumbria? Well, according to the Tea Guild it is – and with a choice of over 30 different brews, it's not really surprising.

Pine tables, sandwich towers and china teapots conjure an olde-worlde air, and the menu is stuffed with English classics – Morecambe Bay shrimps, rabbit pie, venison sausage and crumbly cheese toasties, plus a bounty of buns, Bakewell tarts, macaroons, jam sponges and walnut gateaus. Takeaway treats are available at the bakery next door.

Higginsons (☎ 015395-34367; Keswick House, Main St) Head to this renowned butcher for the finest pies, pasties, sausages and meats for miles around.

Getting There & Away
Both the train station and bus stop in Grange-over-Sands are downhill from the tourist office.

Grange is on the Furness Railway line, with frequent connections north to the towns of the Cumbrian Coast en route to Carlisle (£24.50, one hour), south to Lancaster (£4.40, 30 minutes) and west to Cark-in-Cartmel (£2.20, 10 minutes), a small train station about 2 miles southwest of the village of Cartmel.

Bus 532 travels eight to 10 times daily from Monday to Saturday between Grange, Kents

CUMBRIAN COAST

MORECAMBE BAY CROSSING

Before the coming of the railway, the sandy expanse of Morecambe Bay provided the only reliable route into the Lake District from the south of England. The traditional crossing is made from Arnside on the eastern side of the bay over to Kents Bank, near Grange-over-Sands. It has, however, always been a risky journey. Over 115 sq miles of tidal sand and mud flats (the largest such area in Britain) are revealed at low tide, but the bay is notorious for its treacherous quicksands and fast-rising tide (said to move at the speed of a galloping horse). Even experienced fishermen have lost carts, ponies and tractors in the capricious sands, and there have been numerous strandings, most recently in 2004, when at least 21 Chinese cockle pickers were tragically caught by the tide and drowned (an incident that inspired Nick Broomfield's 2006 film, *Ghosts*).

It's possible to walk across the flats at low tide, but only in the company of the official **Queen's Guide**, a role established in 1536. Cedric Robinson, a local fisherman, is the 25th official Queen's Guide, and leads walks across the sands throughout the year. You'll need to register a fortnight in advance – ask at the Grange tourist office for details of the next crossing. The 8-mile trudge takes around 3½ hours.

Find out more about this unique waterway at www.morecambebay.org.uk.

Bank, Allithwaite, Flookburgh and Cartmel, and also stops at the nearby Cark-in-Cartmel train station. Bus X35 from Kendal stops at Grange (30 minutes, hourly) on its way to Ulverston (one hour).

AROUND GRANGE-OVER-SANDS

Cartmel
pop 1798

Green fields and flowery hedgerows fan out across the countryside around the cobbled village of Cartmel. Arranged around a quaint market square, this charming hamlet has three claims to fame – its 12th-century priory, its pocket-sized racecourse and its world-famous sticky toffee pudding, still prepared to its original recipe at the **Cartmel Village Shop** (☎ 015395-36201; www.stickytoffeepudding.co.uk; The Square; ⊙ 9am-5pm Mon-Sat, 10am-4.30pm Sun).

The market square dates back to medieval times, and although its original market cross has long gone, the old granite fish slabs where the daily catch would once have been displayed and a vintage water pump are still in situ. Whitewashed inns and higgledy-piggledy houses line the sides of the square, while a winding lane leads through the medieval gatehouse to **Cartmel Priory** (☎ 015395-36261; www.cartmelpriory.org.uk; ⊙ 9am-5.30pm May-Oct, 9am-3.30pm Nov-Apr), one of the few priories to have survived the ravages of the Dissolution practically unscathed. Inside the priory is wonderfully plain and unadorned; light filters in through the stained-glass **east window**, lighting up the wooden pews and ancient tombs set into the flagstoned floor. Note the skulls and

hourglasses carved into many tombstones, memento mori to pious parishioners. Outside look up for the priory's most unusual feature: its square belfry tower, set diagonally across the original lantern tower.

The smattering of smart toy shops, vintage booksellers and posh restaurants around the village hint at Cartmel's other well-heeled attraction – its historic **racecourse** (☎ 015395-36340; www.cartmel-racecourse.co.uk). Racing officially dates back in Cartmel to 1856, but mule races were being practised here by the local monks as far back as the 15th century. Needless to say, these days it's strictly a thoroughbred affair, and on race days the village streets are awash with upper-crust punters decked out in wax jackets and wellies. Race fixtures are mainly held between May and August; accommodation in Cartmel is like gold dust on race days.

SLEEPING & EATING

Prior's Yeat (☎ 015395-35178; www.priorsyeat.co.uk; Aynsome Rd; s/d £32/64; **P**) Apart from the pubs, the village is short on decent B&Bs. This red-brick Edwardian house is the best option, with a trio of rooms (a twin in duck-egg blue, and a brace of doubles in flowery wallpaper and pine). There's bike storage, and the owners will happily pack you a picnic lunch.

Hill Farm Cartmel (☎ 015395-36477; www.hillfarmbb.co.uk; s £40-45, d £80-100; **P**) Farmhouse digs surrounded by gardens, duck ponds and Constable countryside half a mile from Cartmel's market square. The house dates from the 1530s, so the rooms are small but ooze rough-stoned, low-ceilinged charm.

Cavendish Arms (☎ 015395-36240; www.thecavendish arms.co.uk; mains £7.50-16.95) Behind the medieval gateway, covered with hanging baskets, this is the pick of the town inns – not a full-blown gastropub, but getting there. Sophisticated dishes – guinea fowl supreme, venison steak in Cumberland sauce – are served amid heavy beams, sturdy furniture and a log fire. Rooms are pub-plain, but cosy (double £60).

King's Arms (☎ 015393-36259; www.kingsarmscartmel .co.uk; mains £8-14) Tucked at the edge of the market square, this smart country boozer is a good bet for pub grub, plus Barngates and Hawkshead ales on draught. Racing memorabilia enlivens the interior; the best rooms overlook the rear garden (double £60 to £80).

ourpick Rogan and Company (☎ 015395-35917; mains £13.50-18.50; ✆ lunch & dinner) Simon Rogan's second Cartmel outpost provides the culinary cachet without the sky-high price of L'Enclume (see below). For our money, it's a much more satisfying experience. The decor is fittingly chic, combining the 16th-century shell of the original building with the requisite razor-sharp lines, white walls and tastefully chosen tones, but unlike at L'Enclume, you might actually leave with a full tummy. Generous hunks of *croustillant* of duck or herby halibut with anchovy fritters keep the cooking cutting edge without costing the earth.

L'Enclume (☎ 015395-36362; www.lenclume.co .uk; Cavendish St; lunch 2/3 courses £18/25, dinner menu £50/70/90; ✆ lunch weekends, dinner daily) Gird your gastronomic loins – this Michelin-starred establishment is renowned for its boundary-pushing cooking, concocted by head-chef Simon Rogan, although you may need an interpreter to make heads or tails of the menu (unless you're already au fait with egg drop hot and sour soup or eel-veal ragout). It's stuffy, but if you're a sucker for the most nouveau of nouveau cuisine you'll be wowed. Chichi rooms (ranging from £98 to £188) are rather disappointing, considering the price tag.

ourpick Howbarrow Organic Farm (☎ 015395-36330; www.howbarroworganic.co.uk; ✆ farm shop 10am-5pm Wed-Sat; Ⓟ) Gone gaga for the good life? Then don't leave Cartmel without visiting this 100% organic farm, renowned for its seasonal fruit and veg boxes, all grown with loving pesticide-free care on the surrounding fields. The farm shop overflows with locally sourced goodness – jams, beers, cheeses, meats and chutneys – and there are two simple rooms (£57.50) that share a bathroom, if you fancy overnighting.

GETTING THERE & AWAY

Bus 530/532 travels from Cartmel to Grange (40 minutes) eight to 10 times daily from Monday to Saturday, stopping en route near Cark-in-Cartmel station, about 2 miles southwest of the village. From here there are regular connections every couple of hours east to Grange (£2.20, 10 minutes) and west to Ulverston (£2.40, 10 minutes).

Holker Hall & Lakeland Motor Museum

Few of Cumbria's stately homes can top the red-brick splendour of **Holker Hall** (☎ 015395-58328; www.holker-hall.co.uk; adult/child house & grounds £9.25/5, grounds only £5.95/3, incl motor museum £11.50/6.50; ✆ house 11am-4pm Sun-Fri mid-Mar–Nov, gardens 10.30am-5pm Sun-Fri mid-Mar–Nov, closes at 4pm in shoulder months), owned by just three Cumbrian families (the Prestons, Lowthers and Cavendishes) over the last 500 years.

Though parts of Holker Hall date from the 16th century, the west wing was entirely rebuilt following a devastating fire in 1871. This is the only section open to the public (the present-day Cavendishes still live in the other bits), and it's an architectural wonder, topped with mullioned windows, gables and copper-topped turrets, and filled with wood-panelled rooms, historic portraits and a ridiculously grand staircase leading to the upper floors.

Among the highlights are the Drawing Room, packed with Chippendale furniture and historic oil paintings, and the Library, containing an antique microscope belonging to Henry Cavendish (discoverer of nitric acid) and over 3500 antique books (some of which are fakes, designed to conceal light switches when the house was converted to electric power in 1911). But the showstopper is the Long Gallery, notable for its plasterwork ceiling and glorious English furniture – look out for the 19th-century sphinx-legged table and a wonderful walnut cabinet inlaid with ivory and rosewood.

For many visitors, however, Holker's stunning landscaped grounds are the highlight. Encompassing 10 hectares, the estate includes rose gardens, rhododendron arbours, woodland, ornamental fountains, stately terraces and rare trees, including one enormous 72ft lime, thought to be the largest in England. The highly prized cuts of the estate's deer, shorthorn cattle and salt marsh sheep are sold at the **Holker Food Hall** (☎ 015395-59084; www.holkerfoodhall .co.uk; ✆ 10.30am-5.30pm, 10am-4pm winter).

CUMBRIAN COAST

CUMBRIAN COAST

SOMETHING FOR THE WEEKEND

For this quick coastal getaway, start things off in style with a night at **No 43** (p180) in Arnside. Then it's a leisurely spin round the bay for lunch at the **Hazelmere Cafe** (p181) followed by an afternoon exploring the antiques and natural attractions of **Holker Hall** (p183). Backtrack to Cartmel for a look around the **priory** (p182), a visit to the **Cartmel Village Shop** (p182) and a slap-up feed at **Rogan and Company** (p183), or **L'Enclume** (p183) if you're feeling flush.

Overnight at **Hill Farm Cartmel** (p182) and spend Sunday exploring the west coast; detour via **Furness Abbey** (p187), take a romantic walk around **Millom** (p188) and have lunch at **Zest Harbourside** (p191). Stroll around **Whitehaven** (p189) before driving up the **Solway Coast** (p192) and indulging yourself at the **Willowbeck Lodge** (p200) just outside Carlisle.

The Courtyard Cafe at Holker Hall has a blackboard of lunchtime specials from around £6, with jacket spuds and sandwiches featuring alongside more generous ploughman's lunches, mackerel fillets and partridge pies.

If you've got an hour or two it's worth visiting the **Lakeland Motor Museum** (☎ 015395-58509; adult/6-15yr £7/4.50; 🕙 10.30am-4.45pm Feb-Nov) inside the former estate stables. The collection of classic machines includes Austins, Jaguars and Cadillacs, antique Norton motorbikes and even a royal-blue Bentley belonging to Donald Campbell (see p114). A separate section explores the Campbell legend and houses a replica of his jet-powered vessel, the *Bluebird*. There's even a replica of a pre-war petrol station from the 1930s, complete with vintage signs and petrol pumps.

ULVERSTON
pop 11670

The workaday market town of Ulverston isn't the comeliest of Cumbrian towns, and with a long industrial history it's hardly surprising it feels a little dowdy in spots. Cobbled streets radiate out from the main square, which has been the focus of local attention ever since the town received its market charter during the 13th century. Ulverston is handily plonked within reach of the southern Lakes and the west coast; walkers and cyclists tackling the long-distance Cumbria Way (p186) kick off their expeditions in the town, while comedy fans make a beeline for the town's shrine to Laurel and Hardy.

Information
Library (☎ 01229-894151; Kings Rd; internet per half hr/hr £1/2; 🕙 9am-6pm Mon & Thu, 9am-5pm Tue & Fri, 9am-1pm Wed, 9.30am-1pm Sat)
Post Office (County Sq; 🕙 9am-5.30pm Mon-Fri, 9am-12.30pm Sat)

Tourist Office (☎ 01229-587120; ulverston.tourism@southlakeland.gov.uk; County Sq; 🕙 9am-5pm Mon-Sat, 10am-4pm winter) Inside the Coronation Hall.
www.ulverston.net Town website.

Sights
ULVERSTON CANAL
Ulverston grew up as a centre for leather, copper and iron ore, and in 1796 England's deepest, widest canal was extended from the coast to facilitate access to deep-water shipping. Unfortunately the arrival of the Furness Railway in the mid-1840s scuppered the canal's long-term profitability, and it was closed down for good in the early 20th century. It is now owned by the pharmaceutical company GlaxoSmithKline, which has a large factory beside the canal. The canal towpath starts near **Canal Head**, a 10-minute walk from the town centre, and offers a lovely 2-mile walk to the shores of Morecambe Bay with its resident population of cormorants, coots, ducks and herons.

HOAD MONUMENT
The town's most prominent monument is the pointy-fingered **tower** on Hoad Hill, built to commemorate the explorer, author and Secretary to the Admiralty Sir John Barrow (1764–1848), who helped map much of the Arctic and participated in the search for the northwest passage. The views are wonderful, stretching north towards Langdale, Coniston and Helvellyn and south to Morecambe Bay; the monument is open (indicated by a flying flag) most Sunday afternoons in summer and on Bank Holidays, but you can visit the hill at any time of year. Walk up Soutergate and Chittery Lane to find the path up the monument, or follow the alternative trail from Hoad Lane off Newland Rd.

LAUREL & HARDY MUSEUM

Ulverston's other attraction is the **Laurel and Hardy Museum** (☎ 01229-582292; www.laurel -and-hardy.co.uk; 4c Upper Brook St; adult/child £3/2; ☻ 10am-4.30pm Feb-Dec), founded by the avid Laurel and Hardy collector Bill Cubin in 1983. Stan Laurel, the spindlier half of the duo, was born in Ulverston in 1890, and the museum is carpeted from floor to ceiling with movie memorabilia: newspaper clips, cuttings, posters, figurines and even a few film props. Best of all there's a tiny little cinema where you can catch screenings of the duo's classic flicks.

The museum's founder died back in 1997 and it's now run by his family; at the time of writing, long-held plans to move into more spacious (but altogether less characterful) premises were nearly set to go ahead – check the website for news.

LANTERNHOUSE

For contemporary artwork, the **Lanternhouse** (☎ 01229-581127; www.lanternhouse.org; The Ellers; admission varies) is occupied by a community of funky cultural types known as Lanternhouse International, with regular exhibitions of everything from digital video to conceptual sculpture. The building is almost as quirky as the artwork – part converted school, part reclaimed barn, part modern concrete tower, topped off by a cast-iron pinnacle. The gallery -cum-exhibition space is off the Tank Sq roundabout at the end of Market St.

CUMBRIAN COAST

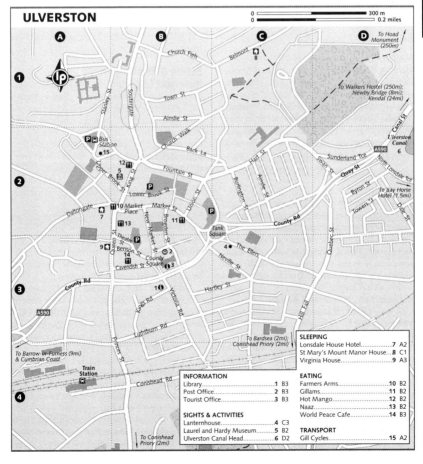

ULVERSTON

0   300 m
0   0.2 miles

THE CUMBRIA WAY(S)

Ulverston marks the southerly start of the long-distance **Cumbria Way** (www.thecumbria way.info), which winds up through the Lake District via Coniston, Langdale, Keswick, Caldbeck and Carlisle, covering a total distance of around 70 miles (depending on your exact route). The trail was devised by the Rambler's Association and completed in the mid-1970s, but it wasn't completely waymarked until 2007.

A sister route for cyclists, the **Cumbria Way Cycle Route** (www.cumbriawaycycleroute .co.uk) covers a broadly similar route. The sustainable transport organisation **Sustrans** publishes a detailed booklet (go to www .sustransshop.co.uk and search for 'Cumbria Way'), which includes accommodation tips along the way.

MARKETS

Ulverston's lively market, centred on Market Pl, fills the town's streets every Thursday, with a smaller market on Saturday and a local **food fair** every third Saturday of the month. There are also special summer markets every Saturday in June, July and August, and a Christmas Festival the last weekend in November when everyone parades round town in Dickensian garb. Gawd bless ya.

Sleeping

Walkers Hostel (☎ 01229-585588; www.walkershostel .co.uk; 1 Oubas Hill; dm £16.50; ✷ reception 4-6pm & 9-10.30pm) The town's indie hostel has been a Cumbria Way base for donkey's years, and the owners still run it along the same laid-back, eco-conscious lines. Dorms are cramped, but there's a tidy kitchen and a lounge stocked with walking books. The hostel is 10 minutes' walk on the A590 towards Kendal.

St Mary's Mount Manor House (☎ 01229-849005; www.stmarysmount.co.uk; Belmont; s £35, d £45-75; **P**) By far the town's nicest B&B, perched on the hill with spick-and-span rooms furnished with brass beds, half-testers and original fireplaces. It's cluttered, but some rooms have bubbly baths and there's a choice of garden or Morecambe Bay views.

Virginia House (☎ 01229-584844; virginia@ulverston hotels.wanadoo.co.uk; 24 Queen St; s £35-50, d £55-60) Bang in the middle of town, this creaky Victorian town house is rooted in another era –

expect period knick-knacks, pastel pictures and old-style decor – but you couldn't ask for a handier location.

Lonsdale House Hotel (☎ 01229-581260; www .lonsdalehousehotel.co.uk; 11 Daltongate; r £85-120; **P** ✷) The only real hotel in Ulverston's centre, this is a smart Georgian building with 20 rooms finished in tartans, magnolias and rosy drapes. Top rooms have four-poster beds and jacuzzis, and the quietest ones overlook the lovely Gothic-walled garden.

Bay Horse Hotel (☎ 01229-583972; www.thebayhorse hotel.co.uk; Canal Foot; d £85-120; **P** ✷) If you don't mind staying out of town, the best rooms are at the Bay Horse, perched on the pebbly sands of the Levens Estuary (ask to borrow some binoculars if you're a bird spotter). The style is a little behind the times, but the restaurant is well known for its upmarket nosh: venison, ostrich and salt marsh lamb shank (mains £21.50 to £25). Follow the signs to Canal Foot from the A590.

Eating & Drinking

World Peace Cafe (☎ 01229-587793; www.worldpeace cafe.org; 5 Cavendish St; mains £3-6; ✷ 10am-4.30pm Tue-Sat) Realign your chakras over cappuccino and cake at this holistic cafe, an offshoot of the Manjushri Buddhist Centre. Ingredients are organic and fair trade, the decor is simple, light and soothing, and there's a meditation centre on the 1st floor for the super-stressed.

Gillams (☎ 01229-587564; 64 Market St; lunch £3-8; ✷ Mon-Sat) The vintage bike propped up outside hints at the age of this place, which has been serving tea to Ulverstonian punters since the 1890s. It's run along veggie-organic principles these days (even vegans have a decent choice): count on pies, sandwiches, toasties and scones served by waistcoated waitresses in slate-floored surrounds. Lovely.

Hot Mango (☎ 01229-584866; 27 King St; lunch £5-8; ✷ 9am-4pm Tue-Sat) Spicy cafe-brasserie dishing up posh ploughman's, big and little brekkies and a fish-finger sandwich with gherkins and mayo. Tiled floors, pine furniture, cool vibe.

Farmers Arms (☎ 01229-584469; 3 Market Pl; mains £6-14) Lively pub on the market square, with a well-deserved foodie reputation. Forget pub pies – here it's all halibut steak, sticky-cherry duck, steaming mussels and sea-fresh langoustines. Beer's not bad, either.

Naaz (☎ 01229-588947; 15-17 Queen St; mains £10.80-12.50; ✷ dinner) Miles better than your curry house standar', this Indian restaurant offers more adventurous flavours than the usual bhunas and birianis – try chicken Hyderabadi (cooked in a cashew nut paste) or Rajasthani gosht (lamb and tamarind stew).

Getting There & Away

Ulverston has regular train connections to Whitehaven (£10.10, 1½ hours) and Carlisle (£14.50, two to 2¼ hours), and in the opposite direction to Grange (£4, 15 minutes), Arnside (£4.70, 20 minutes) and Lancaster (£6.90, 40 minutes). The station is five minutes' walk south of the centre.

The hourly X35 travels from Ulverston via Haverthwaite (where you can connect with the Lakeside and Haverthwaite Steam Railway, see p71), Newby Bridge, Grange-over-Sands and Kendal from Monday to Saturday (three times on Sunday).

AROUND ULVERSTON
Conishead Priory

Two miles south of Ulverston along the A5087, **Conishead Priory** (☎ 01229-584029; www .nkt-kmc-manjushri.org; admission free; ☻ 2-5pm weekdays, noon-5pm weekends & Bank Holidays Easter-Oct, 2-4pm Nov-Easter) started life as an Augustinian priory in the 12th century, and has since served as stately home, military hospital, miners' retreat and spa hotel, but its current guise is the most curious. Since the mid-1970s the building's distinctive 100ft Victorian Gothic towers have been owned by the Manjushri Buddhist organisation, and it's now home to a spiritual retreat and Europe's only Kadampa Buddhist Temple.

Entry to the grounds is free, and if you want to see inside the house, there are guided weekend tours (£2.50) at 2.15pm and 3.30pm (notable features include a vaulted Great Hall, and an impressive Oak Room containing

17th-century wood panelling). Alternatively meditation retreats are available for those interested in delving a little deeper.

A little further south is the coastal harbour of **Bardsea**, a nice place for a paddle and a picnic when the sun is shining.

Furness Abbey

The Cistercian monks of **Furness Abbey** (EH; ☎ 01229-823420; adult/child £3.50/1.80; ☻ 10am-5pm Mar-Sep, 10am-4pm Sat & Sun Oct-Mar) were once among the richest and most powerful in northern England, controlling a huge swathe of land stretching from present-day Lancashire to the Central Lakes, and laying down the blueprint for many traditional Cumbrian industries including sheep farming, iron smelting, quarrying and, of course, beer brewing. But their dominion was brought to an ignominious end during the Dissolution, and these days the rosy-red ruins offer only the barest hint of the abbey's former grandeur.

An informative audio guide provides an overview of the abbey's history. While the roof and most of the walls have long since crumbled into nothingness, you can still discern the abbey's essential footprint: various arches, windows and the north and south transept walls are still standing, along with the shell of the bell tower and the remnants of the underground drainage system. A rather fanciful legend maintains that a subterranean tunnel leads beneath the abbey all the way to Piel Castle, enabling the monks to escape during times of trouble. Before you leave, the small museum is worth a look for two rare knights' effigies and a collection of other stone carvings.

The abbey is 8.5 miles from Ulverston. Several buses, including the hourly X35, stop nearby.

CUMBRIAN COAST

DETOUR – THE DOCK MUSEUM

The busy port city of **Barrow-in-Furness**, sprawling along the coastline to the southwest of Ulverston, isn't the prettiest city in England, but it's worth visiting for the **Dock Museum** (☎ 01229-876400; www.dockmuseum.org.uk; admission free; ☻ 10am-5pm Tue-Fri, 11am-5pm Sat & Sun Easter-Oct, 10.30am-4pm Wed-Fri, 11am-4.30pm Sat & Sun Oct-Easter), which charts the story of how this modest fishing harbour was transformed into one of the thumping powerhouses of the Industrial Revolution. In its heyday, Barrow was the world's leading iron and steel city, as well as a massive centre for shipbuilding and manufacture (BAE Systems still has a major shipbuilding presence in Barrow). The museum's striking pyramid-shaped building stands above the city's old Victorian dry dock, and houses exhibitions exploring the city's shipbuilding heritage from the days of early steam liners to modern state-of-the-art submarines.

CUMBRIAN COAST

THE KING OF PIEL

The small lump of rock known as **Piel Island** sits in the mouth of the channel between the Cumbrian mainland and the long sandy strip of Barrow Island. The island's only buildings are the ruins of **Piel Castle** (EH; admission free; ☉ daily), a defensive outpost built in the 14th century by the monks of Furness Abbey, and the **Ship Inn**, whose landlord is traditionally crowned the 'King of Piel' – a custom that supposedly dates back to 1487, when the short-lived pretender to the English crown Lambert Simnel landed on the island and declared himself monarch.

At the time of writing the pub was undergoing restoration, but you can visit the island and castle in summer by ferry. For more details contact the skippers **Steve Chattaway** (☎ 07516-453784; pielisland@tiscali.co.uk) or **Alan Cleasby** (☎ 07798-794550), or the local guiding company **Murphy's Miles** (☎ 01229-473746; murphysmiles@hotmail.co.uk), which leads guided walks across the sands during low tide.

South Lakes Wild Animal Park

Budding Doctor Doolittles will adore this fantastic **animal park** (☎ 01229-466086; www.wild animalpark.co.uk; Broughton Rd; adult/child £7/4; ☉ 10am-5pm Easter-Nov, 10am-4.30pm Nov-Easter) just outside Dalton-in-Furness. Beasties and birdies of every shape, size and configuration roam the themed enclosure spaces: spectacled bears, Colombian spider monkeys and capybaras populate South America; wallabies, kangaroos, emus and ibis roam Down Under; lemurs indulge in tree-swinging antics in Madagascar; and Sumatran and Amur tigers stalk the Asian enclosure. As always though it's Africa that steals the show, with its marvellous menagerie of giraffes, hippos, meerkats, mandrills, baboons and golden-coated lions. For a truly unforgettable experience, £100 buys the chance to be a keeper for a day and really get up close and personal with the animals.

The park is half a mile east of Dalton-in-Furness, off the A590 from Ulverston. Follow the brown elephant signs.

Millom, Haverigg & Bootle

Nestling beneath the looming dome of Black Combe (1969ft) to the west of Duddon Sands, the quiet coast between Millom and Bootle makes an attractive detour, dotted with sandy pockets, grass-backed dunes and little harbours.

The stout port of Millom is best known for its RAF base (now an aviation museum) and its long association with the prodigiously whiskered poet Norman Nicholson, who lived here for over 70 years between 1914 and his death in 1987. Nicholson was known for his simple, direct poetic style and his enduring fascination with Cumbrian life – much of his work deals with local heavy industries,

and his poetry echoes with the rhythms and dialects of local people. More than 20 years after his death, he remains one of the county's best-loved wordsmiths; a vivid stained-glass window in St George's Church in Millom commemorates his life and work.

If Nicholson's poems have piqued your interest, the adorable **Millom Folk Museum** (☎ 01229-772555; www.millomfolkmuseum.com; Old Station Bldg, Station Rd; adult/child £5/3; ☉ 10.30am-4.30pm Tue-Sat) commemorates everything from the local industries of swill making and smithing to the gritty realities of life for the local iron miners. Replica shop fronts create the air of a period shopping arcade, and there's a small display on Nicholson's work.

Birdwatchers and nature buffs should head for the nearby **Hodbarrow Nature Reserve** (☎ 01229-778011), an RSPB site reclaimed from an old iron-ore works. The reserve is now home to a population of widgeons, goldeneye ducks and pintails, while grebes, coots, swans, geese and teal are frequent visitors to the enclosed lagoon. If you're really lucky you might spot a natterjack toad, one of England's most endangered amphibians.

Further along the coast are the small sandy beaches at Haverigg and **Silecroft**. For a fun way to explore the sands, the **Murthwaite Green Trekking Centre** (☎ 01229-770876; www.murthwaite green.co.uk; Silecroft) offers pony treks and horse rides; prices range from £20 for an hour's ride up to £60 for a half day, but they're very popular, so you'll need to book.

SLEEPING

Cambridge House Hotel (☎ 01229-774982; www .cambridge-house-hotel.co.uk; 1 Cambridge St, Millom; s £35, d £60) This sombre B&B looks a bit unpromising from the outside, but it's decent enough as long as you're content with flouncy spreads, old carpets and pre-fab pine. It's old school, but cute in a museum-piece sort of way.

Bankfield House (☎ 01229-772276; www.bankfield house.com; Millom; s £45-60, d £70-90; P) This grey-fronted Millom guest house is a great base; once a farm dwelling it has been converted to provide five pleasant rooms stocked with thick throws and puffy cushions (plus a spa bath and four-poster in the priciest one). Two hectares of grounds keep the views tranquil.

EATING
Millstones (☎ 01229-718775; Bootle; mains £3-10; ⏰ 10am-5.30pm Tue-Sat) Stonking deli-cafe-bakery filled with the fresh-baked aroma of crusty organic bread, hot pies and lemon drizzle cakes. There's an excellent food shop selling Cumbrian produce, cheeses and charcuterie, and a crafts store where you can pick up woolly jumpers and hand-tooled woodcrafts.

ourpick Woodall's of Waberthwaite (☎ 01229-717237; www.richardwoodall.com; Waberthwaite) Her Majesty the Queen gets her breakfast bangers and bacons from this award-winning butcher, so you can't quibble with the provenance – and it's been in business for eight generations, so they should know how to stuff a sausage by now. The dry-cured bacons and smoked hams are especially scrumptious.

GETTING THERE & AWAY
Cumbria Coast trains stop every two hours at Millom from Ulverston (£6.90, 45 to 60 minutes) and Barrow-in-Furness (£4.20, 25 minutes), before travelling north via Ravenglass (£2.60, 15 minutes) and Whitehaven (£7.90, 45 minutes).

WEST COAST

WHITEHAVEN
pop 23,795
Historically Cumbria's coastal ports provided a vital outlet for the county's heavy industries, and during the Industrial Revolution its harbours teemed with tall ships and trading vessels bound for the far-flung corners of the British Empire. Thanks to this ocean-going trade, the port of Whitehaven mushroomed into the third-largest in England, with a fortune founded on the lucrative trade in coal, iron and spices (as well as less salubrious cargoes of illicit liquor and slaves). Whitehaven's transatlantic trade has long since sailed into

the sunset, and these days you're more likely to see swanky yachts rather than spice freighters moored up along its harbour, but there's still a faint trace of Georgian grandeur hanging around its briny old streets.

Information
Branches of Natwest, Lloyds and HSBC can be found on Lowther St.
Library (☎ 01946-852900; Lowther St; internet per half hr/hr £1/2; ⏰ 9.30am-7pm Mon, Tue & Thu, 9.30am-4pm Wed & Sat, noon-4pm Sun)
Michael Moon's Bookshop (☎ 01946-599010; 19 Lowther St; ⏰ 9.30am-5pm Mon-Sat) Endearingly eccentric antiquarian and second-hand bookshop, perfect for extended browsing. Sometimes closed on Wednesday in winter.

CUMBRIAN COAST

CUMBRIAN COAST

Police Station (Scotch St; ⊙ 8am-midnight)
Post Office (10 Market Pl; ⊙ 9am-5.30pm Mon-Fri, 9am-noon Sat)
Tourist Office (☎ 01946-598914; tic@copelandbc.gov.uk; Market Pl; ⊙ 9.30am-4.30pm) In the Market Hall near the town centre.

Sights
THE TOWN
Whitehaven's regimented grid of streets is a stark contrast to the higgledy-piggledy, haphazard town planning characteristic of most English ports, and the town was in fact one of the first in England to be laid out according to a predetermined architectural plan. Inspired by Christopher Wren's plans for the rebuilding of London following the Great Fire of 1666, the local landowner Sir John Lowther oversaw a huge 17th-century building boom in Whitehaven: at the time of his birth, in 1642, around 200 people lived in and around Whitehaven, but when he died 64 years later in 1706, the population had grown almost tenfold.

The town reached its peak in the mid-1700s, by which time the port had become the third-busiest harbour in England (topped only by London and Bristol), but during the 18th and 19th centuries the rise of the railway and increased competition from other British ports led to a long decline in the town's fortunes. During the 18th and 19th centuries slums sprang up around the Georgian streets and Whitehaven was largely abandoned by

---

JOHN PAUL JONES

One of the most notorious incidents in Whitehaven's history occurred during the American War of Independence, when the town was attacked by the American naval commander John Paul Jones (actually a Scot, born in Arbigland in 1747). Jones convinced his reluctant crew to mount a daring night raid on Whitehaven, hoping to strike a fearsome blow against one of Britain's key ports. Unfortunately strong winds and tides, coupled with a shortage of ammunition, a semi-mutinous crew and the troublesome distractions of Whitehaven's taverns and brothels, meant the raid was a total flop; of the 200-odd ships stationed in Whitehaven's harbour, Jones sank just a single lowly coal barge.

---

local industrialists. Many native Cumbrians emigrated to the New World in search of a better life, including the local girl Mildred Warner, who married a Virginian merchant and became grandmother of the first president of the United States, George Washington.

As a result, Whitehaven's fine 17th-century architecture remained practically untouched by Victorian redevelopers, and the town is one of the best examples of Georgian planning anywhere in England (locals often like to claim Whitehaven provided the architectural inspiration for the ultra-ordered streets of New York). A long restoration program has polished up many of the merchants' mansions and sea captains' houses, and a set of five booklets (some written in period parlance) outline guided walks around the town's landmarks – ask for the *Quest Trail* leaflets (£1.95 to £3.95) at the tourist office.

THE BEACON
The tall tower at the end of the harbour is the **Beacon** (☎ 01946-592302; www.thebeacon-whitehaven.co.uk; West Strand; adult/under 16yr £5/free; ⊙ 10am-4.30pm Tue-Sun), which explores the town's distinguished history of transatlantic trade, shipbuilding and salt making, and its not-so-distinguished history of smuggling and slave trading. Fresh from a £2.2 million refurbishment, the building is split over four floors, each devoted to a different theme: Work and Play on the 2nd, Tides and Trades on the 3rd and the Viewing Gallery and Weather Zone on the top floor, where you can view the town through a high-powered telescope and try your hand at presenting a TV weather forecast.

THE RUM STORY
The fun (if irresistibly tacky) waxworks at the **Rum Story** (☎ 01946-592933; www.rumstory.co.uk; Lowther St; adult/child £5.45/3.45; ⊙ 10am-4.30pm) delve into Whitehaven's long associations with 'the dark spirit'. Sometimes legally imported, sometimes covertly smuggled, this sweet firewater underpinned the town's success during the 18th century, and probably provided much-needed solace during the darker days that followed. Among the various exhibits you can stop off at an 18th-century sugar workshop, delve into a debauched 'punch tavern' and ponder a weird exhibit showing Lord Nelson's body being pickled in rum following the Battle of Trafalgar.

ST NICHOLAS' CHURCH
This red-brick **chapel** on Lowther St has been the centre of Whitehaven worship for over three centuries. Originally built during the 17th century, and redeveloped in showy Victorian style in 1883, the church was savaged by fire in 1971; only the original clock tower remains, with the former nave now taken up by an ornamental garden. Look out for memorials commemorating workers killed in the local coal pits – over 1200 people had lost their lives by the time the mines finally fell silent in the early 20th century.

Sleeping
Glenfield (☎ 01946-691911; www.glenfield-whitehaven .co.uk; s £35, d £55-65; **P**) Traditional brick guest house in the heart of Whitehaven's conservation district, offering six rooms decked out in shipshape Victorian fashion: Corkickle is the roomiest, with original fireplace and sofa chairs, while Fleswick and Nannycatch are finished in peachy stripes, and apple-green Ingwell is tailored for single travellers.

Georgian House Hotel (☎ 01946-696611; 9-11 Church St; www.thegeorgianhousehotel.net; s £79, d £89-99; **P** 🛜) For hotel digs, try this former sea captain's residence in the town centre. Period Georgian trappings blend with up-to-date comfort: turned-wood bed frames, flashy wallpapers and thick carpets keep things cosy, although rooms err towards the corporate.

our pick **Moresby Hall** (☎ 01946-696317; www .moresbyhall.co.uk; Moresby; s £80-100, d £100-140; **P**) Itching for Grade-I–listed grandeur? Then head out of Whitehaven to this converted manor, with its overflow of antiques, lofty ceilings, ordered lawns, and surreally symmetrical frontage erected in 1620. Rooms are luxuriously appointed offering hydro-massage showers and Gilchrist and Soames bath stuffs, plus grand four-posters in De Asby and Copeland, and crimson-and-cream fabrics and Vetriano prints in Pekerige. Old fashioned, yes, but an aristocratic spoil.

Eating
Zest Harbourside (☎ 01946-66981; 8 West Strand; mains £6-12; ☽ breakfast, lunch & dinner) On the Whitehaven harbour this sister restaurant to Zest (see right) has a more chilled approach – wraps, paninis and 'blinding butties' are the mainstays, alongside fish stews, crab cakes and spicy meatballs. Chrome fittings and globe lanterns keep the feel funky.

Above Restaurant (☎ 01946-696611; 8-11 Church St; mains £8.50-15.95; ☽ dinner Tue-Sat, lunch Sun) The in-house bistro at the Georgian House is a cut above your average hotel diner, but the food is solid rather than stellar: think Cajun chicken, T-bone steak and Cumbrian Lass (chicken stuffed with cheese, Parma ham and sausage meat).

Zest (☎ 01946-692848; Low Rd; mains £12-17; ☽ dinner Wed-Sat) Zesty by name, zesty by nature, this spanking brasserie just outside town offers some of the best modern Brit cooking in western Cumbria. Top-quality local ingredients and a hint of fusion flavours have attracted a string of well-heeled diners – Tony Blair, Abi Titmuss and the local Cumbrian wordsmith Hunter Davies have all dropped by to have a gander at the grub. The restaurant is about half a mile along the B5345 towards St Bees.

Entertainment
Rosehill Theatre (☎ 01946-692422; www.rosehill.co.uk; Moresby, Whitehaven; ☽ box office 10am-5pm Mon-Fri & 1 hr before performances) Quirky little theatre and arts venue on Whitehaven's outskirts, showcasing recent and classic films, touring productions and the occasional live gig.

Getting There & Away
Whitehaven is on the Cumbrian Coast Line; trains travel every two hours north along the Solway Coast ports to Carlisle (£8.50, one hour 10 minutes), and south to Ravenglass (£3.80, 30 minutes) and beyond.

Bus 6 travels to Egremont, Gosforth, Seascale, Ravenglass and Muncaster Castle five times daily Monday to Saturday; on Sunday, the X6 service continues on to Millom and Barrow-in-Furness. For St Bees, catch the 20 (six daily Monday to Saturday, four on Sunday).

AROUND WHITEHAVEN
To the south of Whitehaven twitchers gather around the rust-coloured headland of **St Bees** (☎ 01697-351330; stbees.head@rspb.org.uk) to see the large colonies of guillemots, herring gulls, fulmars and kittiwakes nesting around the RSPB reserve, while walkers set out on Alfred Wainwright's classic long-haul Coast-to-Coast walk (p102).

Few visitors travel north of Whitehaven to explore the stretch of coastline curving around the county's northwestern peninsula, and that's a shame – while it's not the most

---

AN ATOMIC TALE

Few places stir up such a maelstrom of controversy as the billowing chimneys and sprawling reactor halls of **Sellafield Nuclear Plant**, halfway between St Bees and Ravenglass. Originally built as an ammunitions dump and TNT factory, after WWII the nearby site of Windscale was chosen as the site for Britain's first plutonium-manufacturing reactors (needed to supply the country's burgeoning nuclear arsenal). In 1956 they were joined by four Magnox reactors at Calder Hall, creating the world's first commercial nuclear power station.

In a country still reeling from postwar rationing, huge unemployment and a shattered national infrastructure, the opening of Windscale seemed to sum up the nation's hopes for a newer, brighter, shinier future. But the dream soon turned sour: in 1957 a fire tore through the Windscale reactor hall forcing its emergency closure, and though the initial fallout was hushed up, it soon emerged that Windscale was also to be the site of the world's first large-scale nuclear disaster. Huge amounts of radioactive material contaminated local land, milk production and animal crops, and eventually drifted as far afield as Wales, Scotland and the Irish west coast.

It was the first of a long line of controversies. The Windscale site, subsequently renamed Sellafield in 1981 and now the UK's largest nuclear-reprocessing facility, has been dogged by non-stop claims of environmental damage and radioactive pollution over the last 50 years – not least by the Irish government, who have long campaigned for an embargo on the release of reactor water into the Irish Sea. And even with a new generation of British nuclear power stations on the horizon, Sellafield's own future is still very much in the balance. The site has been scheduled for gradual decommissioning over the next decade, but its total closure would represent a huge blow to local employment; many local people have lobbied hard for a new power station to be built on the Sellafield site, while rival environmentalists have lobbied equally strongly for its permanent closure.

If you want to find out more, drop into the **Sellafield Visitor Centre** (☎ 019467-28333; ⓧ 10am-4pm Mon-Fri), which has an exhibition exploring the site's controversial history and its equally thorny future.

---

conventionally beautiful patch of shoreline in Britain, it's worth an afternoon's exploration, with an intriguing history of smuggling and rum running, and several quiet coastal villages that feel light years away from the hustle and rush of the busier Lakeland towns.

Further north are the old harbours of Workington and nearby **Maryport**, where you'll find the **Lake District Coast Aquarium** (☎ 01900-817760; www.lakedistrict-coastaquarium.co.uk; South Quay, Maryport; adult/child £5.75/3.75; ⓧ 10am-5pm) and its deep-sea denizens, including cuttlefish, conger eels, rays, starfish and a population of playful sea horses.

North of Maryport a long, flat expanse of windblown dunes stretches past the straggling seafront village of Allonby and neat and tidy **Silloth**, marking the start of the **Solway Coast** (☎ 01697-333055; www.solwaycoastaonb.org.uk). This protected nature reserve extends along the coast to Rockcliffe Marsh near Carlisle, and

is important for its coastal salt marshes and populations of migratory seabirds. Strong offshore winds also attract the county's kite-surfers and kite buggiers, and there's nowhere better in Cumbria to catch a sunset.

For general information, drop into the **Solway Coast Discovery Centre** (☎ 016973-31944; sillothtic@allerdale.gov.uk; Silloth; ⓧ 10am-4pm Mon-Thu, 10am-1pm & 2-4pm Fri) in Silloth, which has a small exhibition (adult/child £2.50/1.50) detailing the area's natural habitats.

Getting There & Away

Several towns on the Solway Coast are served by the Cumbrian Coast railway from Whitehaven, with stations at St Bees, Workington and Maryport, and others inland at Aspatria and Wigton before journey's end in Carlisle. The 60 bus runs between Maryport, Allonby and Silloth 11 times daily from Monday to Saturday.

Inland Cumbria

Jammed hard against the Scottish frontier, trammelled westwards by the Lakeland fells and eastwards by the barren sweep of the Pennines, inland Cumbria has long served as a historical crossroads. Generations of Picts, Celts, Romans and Reivers have all battled each other for supremacy over this strategic patch of land down the centuries, and 2000 years of conflict have left a permanent smudge on the landscape.

Fortified pele towers, crumbling abbeys and ruined castles litter the hilltops around the old market towns of Penrith, Appleby and Kendal, while the red-brick battlements of Carlisle Castle have stood watch over England's northern border for seven centuries. The most obvious reminder of the area's tempestuous past, however, is provided by the Vallum Aelium, otherwise known as Hadrian's Wall, which still forms a forbidding barrier almost two millennia after the first stone was laid; you can still visit the foundations of one of Britain's best-preserved Roman garrison forts at Birdoswald, near Gilsland. And if you're a railway aficionado, there's no finer train trip in England than the landmark Settle-Carlisle Railway, which clatters for 72 stunning miles across the rugged Yorkshire Dales en route to Cumbria's history-packed capital.

HIGHLIGHTS

- Check out some medieval graffiti at **Carlisle Castle** (p197)
- Revel in England's most scenic railway journey on the **Settle-Carlisle Line** (p201)
- Stock up with local goodies from **Low Sizergh Barn** (p214), Penrith's **JJ Graham** (p207) and the **Village Bakery** (p209) in Melmerby
- Imagine yourself in the shoes (or sandals) of a Roman legionary at **Birdoswald Roman Fort** (p203)
- Marvel at the over-the-top topiary of **Levens Hall** (p214)
- Ponder one of England's largest – and strangest – stone circles at **Long Meg and Her Daughters** (p206)

★ Carlisle
★ Birdoswald Roman Fort
★ Settle-Carlisle Line
★ Melmerby
★ Long Meg & Her Daughters
★ Penrith
★ Low Sizergh Barn
★ Levens Hall

▪ Number of visitors to Rheged in 2007: 467,452	▪ Number of viaducts on the Settle-Carlisle Railway: 22	▪ Date of Kendal mintcake invention: 1869

ITINERARY 1
PENRITH CYCLE   16 miles/3 to 4 hours/Penrith

This moderate spin travels through the green countryside south of Penrith. It's a quiet ride that follows mostly minor roads (apart from one short section along the A6), so traffic shouldn't be a major headache. There are a few hilly sections to contend with however, so take things easy.

Start the day in **Penrith** (p204) with an indulgent brunch at **No 15** (p207). Head back to the bus station on Sandgate, turn right onto Benson Row and Folly Lane, then follow the blue 71 signs out of town. Pass under the busy A66 to reach the River Eamont and the tumbledown remains of **Brougham Castle** (p205), a medieval keep built on the foundations of a much earlier Roman fort.

Beyond the castle, turn right at the crossroads and head on past **Brougham Hall** (p206) and the stone circle known as **King Arthur's Round Table** (p206). Turn left past **Mayburgh Henge** (p206) and spin on to Yanwath, where the **Gate Inn** (p207) makes a fantastic spot to stop for lunch (our tip is the venison burger).

From Yanwath follow the road south, travelling through the green fringes of Lowther Estate all the way to the pleasant village of **Askham**. Turn left past **Askham Hall**, cross the River Lowther and admire the views over **Lowther Castle** (p175). You could also break the journey with a visit to the nearby **Lakeland Birds of Prey Centre** (p175), famous for its collection of hawks, eagles and owls.

The next section of the route joins up briefly with the A6. Turn left onto the main road and take care, as it can be busy. Continue north along the A6 and look out for the right-hand turn just after you pass under the M6. Follow this minor road as it passes the railway track and continue east to the next junction. Nearby is the intriguing **Wetheriggs Pottery** (☎ 01768-892733; www .wetheriggs-pottery.co.uk), where local artisans conjure up all kinds of earthenware.

Take the next right-hand turn, following Moor Lane (you should see a blue sign for the NCN71). From here it's an easy ride back to Brougham Castle and journey's end at Penrith.

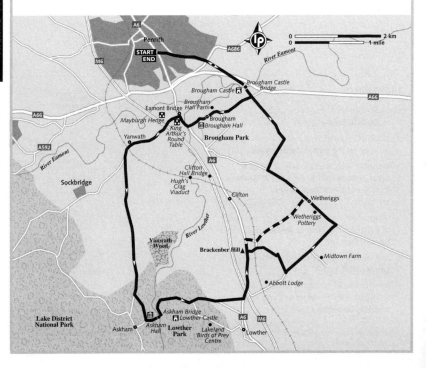

ITINERARY 2
ROAD TO THE PENNINES   20 miles/1 to 2 hours/Penrith to Alston

Get ready for grandstand views – the Automobile Association (AA) has dubbed the fabulous road trip from Penrith to Alston along the A686 one of Britain's top 10 drives, and with good reason. The road cuts from the lush greenery of the Eden Valley into the barren and beautiful heights of the Northern Pennines, passing through a string of picturesque villages en route and offering truly grand views over some of northern England's most impressive countryside.

Pick up some supplies for the day from the endearingly old-fashioned food emporium **JJ Graham** (p207), right in the heart of Penrith town. Head east from town along the A686 to **Langwathby**, and make an optional detour to the huge stone circle of **Long Meg and Her Daughters** (p206) near the village of **Little Salkeld** (despite the signs en route, the circle actually has nothing to do whatsoever with the druids).

Backtrack to the main road and swing through **Melmerby**, perhaps making a lunch stop at the **Village Bakery** (p209), famous for its home-baked breads and cakes. Once you've fuelled up it's time to tackle the main event: the long, looping climb all the way to **Hartside Summit** (1904ft), without doubt one of the most spectacularly sited road passes anywhere in England. The switch-backing road makes for lively driving, and the views open up as you climb sharply up the side of the ridge. At the top of the pass you'll be able to take a break at a car park and small roadside **cafe**. The panorama from here is quite staggering, stretching across the valley all the way to the distant Lakeland fells – see if you can spot the tops of Helvellyn, Great Gable and Skiddaw way, way out to the west.

Keep following the A686 as it trundles along a narrow ridge road, passing through the bracken-covered fields, plunging dales and austere countryside so characteristic of the Pennines. Eventually you'll wind up in England's highest market town at **Alston** (p209), where you can continue the adventure aboard the trains of the **South Tynedale Railway** (p209).

INLAND CUMBRIA

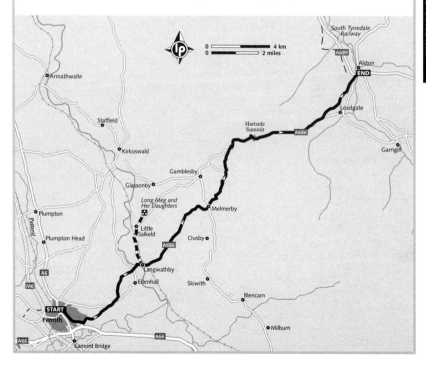

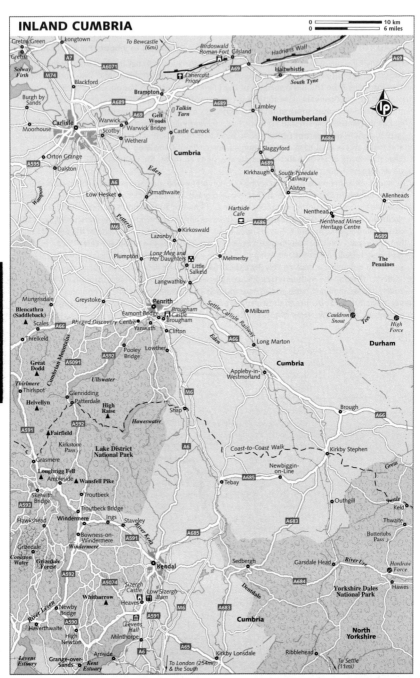

INLAND CUMBRIA

0 ———— 10 km
0 ———— 6 miles

CARLISLE

pop 69,527

Precariously perched on the stormy border between England and Scotland, the red-brick city of Carlisle has been in the thick of the action for 2000 years. Overlooking the bleak frontier once known ominously as the 'Debatable Lands', it's witnessed more sieges, sackings and pillagings than practically any other city in England, and the remnants of its martial past can still be seen dotted around the city's streets, including the original medieval gatehouses and forbidding rust-red castle.

Much later the city became a thumping powerhouse of the Industrial Revolution, as well as an important terminus for seven Victorian railway companies, but these days most of the heavy industry has moved on, and Carlisle has reinvented itself as a lively centre for shoppers, students and rowdy weekend revellers. The old girl has been battered a bit over the centuries, and she might not have the star quality of some of the north's other revitalised cities, but she's still got a big-city buzz.

HISTORY

A Celtic camp or *caer* provided an early military station for the Romans, who founded a key stronghold known as Luguvalium, which became the northwest's main administrative centre following the construction of Hadrian's Wall. After centuries of intermittent conflict between Picts, Saxons and Viking raiders, the Normans seized Carlisle from the Scots in 1092. Later, throughout the Middle Ages, the English developed Carlisle as a military stronghold, enlarging the walls, citadels and the great gates, and the city became an important strategic base for Royalist forces during the Civil War. Peace came to Carlisle with the Restoration, and the city developed as an industrial centre for cotton and textiles after the arrival of the railway in the mid-19th century.

ORIENTATION

From the M6, the main routes into town are London Rd and Warwick Rd. The train station is south of the city centre, a 10-minute walk from Town Hall Sq (also known as Greenmarket) and the tourist office. The bus station is on Lonsdale St, about 250m east of the square. Most of the town's B&Bs are dotted along Victoria Pl and Warwick Rd.

INFORMATION

@CyberCafe (☎ 01228-512308; www.atcybercafe .co.uk; 8-10 Devonshire St; per hr £3; ☻ 10am-10pm Mon-Sat, 1-10pm Sun)

Banks Natwest (English St), Lloyds (Lowther St), HSBC (Bank St), Barclays (Bank St)

Cumberland Infirmary (☎ 01228-523444; Newtown Rd) Half a mile west of the city centre.

Laundrette (☎ 01228-818241; Beaconsfield St)

Police Station (☎ 0845 33 00 247; English St; ☻ 8am-midnight)

Post Office (20-34 Warwick Rd; ☻ 9am-5.30pm Mon-Fri, 9am-12.30pm Sat)

Tourist Office (☎ 01228-625600; www.historic-carlisle .org.uk; Greenmarket; internet per 15 min £1; ☻ 9.30am-5pm Mon-Sat, 10.30am-4pm Sun Jul-Aug, 9.30am-5pm Mon-Sat Mar-Jun & Sep-Oct, 10am-4pm Mon-Sat Nov-Feb)

Waterstones (☎ 01228-542300; 66-68 Scotch St; ☻ 9am-5.30pm Mon-Sat, 10am-4pm Sun) Large chain bookshop stocking new titles and local books.

SIGHTS

Carlisle Castle

Carlisle was founded as a military city, and the brooding, rust-red **Carlisle Castle** (☎ 01228-591922; adult/child £4.50/2.30; ☻ 9.30am-5pm Apr-Sep, 10am-4pm Oct-Mar) provides a timely reminder of the conflicts that have shaped the city's history. The castle began as a Celtic and Roman stronghold; a Norman 'motte and bailey' fort was constructed in 1092 by King William II, and reinforced in stone by Henry I. Later additions were made by Henry II, Edward I and Henry VIII, who tacked on the 'cannon-proof' circular towers.

Thanks to its position in the frontline of England's defences, Carlisle Castle has witnessed a host of sieges. In 1315 the English-held castle was encircled by Robert the Bruce after his victory at Bannockburn, but eventually sat out the siege under their determined commander, Andrew de Harcla. Another notorious eight-month siege occurred during the Civil War in 1644, when the 700-strong Royalist garrison were starved into submission by the Parliamentarian General Lesley; the defenders survived by eating rats, mice and the castle dogs before finally surrendering in 1645 (a fascinating day-by-day account was kept by the 18-year-old Isaac Tullie, after whom the city's Tullie House Museum is named). The Jacobite siege of 1745 was less protracted: Bonnie Prince Charlie's army besieged Carlisle for just six days before the defenders caved in.

Mary Queen of Scots was imprisoned here in 1568, and you can visit the remains of the tower where she was held; look out too for medieval graffiti in the castle gaol, and the famous 'licking stones', which Jacobite prisoners supposedly lapped for moisture to keep themselves alive. Meanwhile you can indulge those secret *Braveheart* fantasies up on the castle's crenellated battlements.

Admission includes entry to the Kings Own Royal Border Regiment Museum, which explores the history of Cumbria's Infantry Regiment. There are guided tours of the castle from April to September.

Carlisle Cathedral

Carlisle's sandstone **cathedral** (☎ 01228-548151; www.carlislecathedral.org.uk; donation £2; ☺ 7.30am-6.15pm Mon-Sat, 7.30am-5pm Sun) – the only cathedral in Cumbria – began life as an Augustinian priory church in 1122, before being elevated to cathedral status 11 years later, when its first abbot, Athelwold, became the first Bishop of Carlisle. The building's notable features are the 15th-century carved choir stalls, the dramatic barrel-vaulted roof and the delicate column capitals, depicting labours associated with each month, but there's no chance of missing the centrepiece: at over 50ft high, the dramatic 14th-century **East Window** is one of England's largest and most spectacular Gothic windows. During the 1644–45 siege of Carlisle, two-thirds of the nave was torn down by Parliamentarian troops to reinforce their defences, and serious restoration wasn't completed until the mid-19th century.

Other priory buildings dotted around the cathedral include the 16th-century **Fratry** and the **Prior's Tower**.

Tullie House Museum

Carlisle's excellent **museum** (☎ 01228-534781; www.tulliehouse.co.uk; Castle St; adult/under 18yr £5.20/free; ☺ 10am-5pm Mon-Sat & 11am-5pm Sun Jul-Aug, 10am-5pm Mon-Sat, noon-5pm Sun Apr-Jun & Sep-Oct, 10-4pm Mon-Sat, noon-4pm Sun Nov-Mar) explores the foundation of the city, life under Roman rule and the development of modern Carlisle.

The upstairs **Border Galleries** set the archaeological context with displays on the city's Iron Age, Celtic and Roman history. There's a life-size replica of a section of Hadrian's Wall, and artefacts including Viking burial items, a huge Iron Age cooking cauldron, Roman hairpins, gaming dice, sandals and some excruciating-looking surgical instruments. There's also a collection of Roman tablets unearthed along Hadrian's Wall, including a famous one depicting a Roman cavalryman trampling over the bodies of vanquished native Britons, as well as galleries dedicated to Lakeland geology, the Border Reivers and the Jacobite siege of Carlisle Castle. On your way out, look out for the Muckle Toon Bell, which was rung to warn of impending raids and features a hefty crack in one side sustained during a town hall fire in the 1880s.

On the ground floor is the **Carlisle Life Gallery**, which explores the city's social history through photos, films and local people's stories. Nearby **Old Tullie House** concentrates on fine arts, sculpture and porcelain housed in a wonderful 17th-century Jacobean house, and the basement **Millennium Gallery** is a rather odd mishmash of mineral displays, geology, architecture and a glass-bricked 'whispering wall'.

Once you've done the tour, a subway leads underneath the A595 to Carlisle Castle.

Guildhall Museum

This tiny **museum** (☎ 01228-532781; Greenmarket; admission free; ☺ noon-4.30pm Tue-Sun Apr-Oct) is housed in a wonky 15th-century town house built for Carlisle's trade guilds. Among the modest exhibits are a ceremonial mace, the city's medieval stocks and a section of exposed wall showing the building's wattle-and-daub construction.

TOURS

Open Book Visitor Guiding (☎ 01228-670578; www.greatguidedtours.co.uk) offers tours of Carlisle from April to September, including visits to Carlisle Castle and Hadrian's Wall.

SLEEPING

Carlisle's accommodation is a bit underwhelming – the choice boils down to big, faceless chain hotels in the centre (Travelodge, Ibis and Premier Inn all have a presence) or small B&Bs scattered around the outskirts.

Budget

Carlisle YHA (☎ 0870 770 5752; deec@impacthousing.org.uk; Bridge Lane; dm £21; ☺ Jul-Sep) Lodgings at the old Theakston Brewery now provide student digs for Carlisle University; rooms are available during the summer hols.

Midrange

Cornerways (☎ 01228-521733; www.cornerwaysguest house.co.uk; 107 Warwick Rd; s £30-35, d £55-65; **P** 🛜) One of the cheapest B&Bs, on the corner of Warwick Rd in the city's conservation district. It's basic – functional rooms, shared bathrooms, musty carpets – but period Victorian touches cheer things up.

Langleigh Guest House (☎ 01228-530440; www .langleighhouse.co.uk; 6 Howard Pl; s/d £35/70; **P**) You'll be bowled over by exuberant hounds as you cross the threshold of this sweet, rather chaotic guest house. The house is a rambling Victorian affair, with a muddle of rooms stuffed with gilded mirrors, marble fireplaces and porcelain pots; they're cosy, if cluttered.

Derwentlea (☎ 01228-409706; www.derwentlea .co.uk; 14 Howard Pl; s/d £35/70; **P**) Red leather armchairs and ticking mantle clocks set the period vibe at this traditional brick B&B. Soft beds, wall mirrors and dressing tables distinguish the prissy rooms; there's bike storage and a ground-floor room for mobility-restricted guests.

Angus Hotel (☎ 01228-523546; www.angus-hotel .co.uk; 14-16 Scotland Rd; s/d/f £52/70/81; **P** 🛜) Ignore the hotel billing – this is a B&B trading above its station. Eleven rooms, some with puce-and-purple walls and cast-iron beds, others with straightforward shades and MDF furniture. The downstairs restaurant, Almonds Bistro (mains £8 to £15), isn't a bad bet for supper.

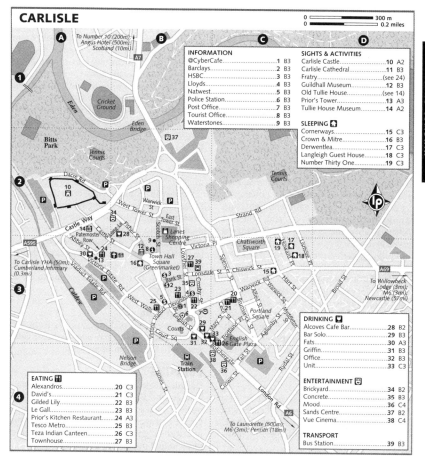

CARLISLE

0 ———— 300 m
0 ———— 0.2 miles

INLAND CUMBRIA

INFORMATION	
@CyberCafe	1 B3
Barclays	2 B3
HSBC	3 B3
Lloyds	4 B3
Natwest	5 B3
Police Station	6 B3
Post Office	7 B3
Tourist Office	8 B3
Waterstones	9 B3

SIGHTS & ACTIVITIES	
Carlisle Castle	10 A2
Carlisle Cathedral	11 B3
Fratry	(see 24)
Guildhall Museum	12 B3
Old Tullie House	(see 14)
Prior's Tower	13 A3
Tullie House Museum	14 A2

SLEEPING	
Cornerways	15 C3
Crown & Mitre	16 B3
Derwentlea	17 C3
Langleigh Guest House	18 C3
Number Thirty One	19 C3

EATING	
Alexandros	20 C3
David's	21 C3
Gilded Lily	22 B3
Le Gall	23 B3
Prior's Kitchen Restaurant	24 A3
Tesco Metro	25 B3
Teza Indian Canteen	26 C3
Townhouse	27 B3

DRINKING	
Alcoves Cafe Bar	28 B2
Bar Solo	29 B3
Fats	30 A3
Griffin	31 B3
Office	32 B3
Unit	33 C3

ENTERTAINMENT	
Brickyard	34 B2
Concrete	35 B3
Mood	36 C4
Sands Centre	37 B2
Vue Cinema	38 C4

TRANSPORT	
Bus Station	39 B3

Number Thirty One (☎ 01228-597080; www
.number31.co.uk; 31 Howard Pl; s/d from £60/95; P 💻)
Carlisle's top city-centre B&B, with a dash
of flashy flair other places can only envy. All
three rooms have their own design touch:
Oriental overtones and a dragon-print head-
board in the Green Room, Edwardian knick-
knacks and an antique fireplace in the Blue
Room, and flowery fabrics and an overhead
bed canopy in the Yellow Room.

Crown & Mitre (☎ 01228-525491; www.peel
hotels.co.uk/hotels; s £90-95, d £105-120; P 🛜)
Splendiferous chimney-topped pile overlooking the main square, built from crimson brick in fine Edwardian style. Grand
hallways and a wonderful old staircase lead
off from the posh lobby, but the rooms are
depressingly corporate – more Travelodge
than turn-of-the-century.

our pick Willowbeck Lodge (☎ 01228-513607; www
.willowbeck-lodge.com; Lambley Bank, Scotby; d £100-120;
P 🛜) The architects have gone doolally at
this palatial B&B, 3 miles east of the city. It's
a marvel, boasting six rooms in creams and
taupes, with luxury spoils including corner
tubs, broadband internet and LCD TVs. The
centrepiece is the 22ft-high gabled lounge
overlooking a private pond frequented by
wild birds – rather fabulous, really.

EATING
Cafes & Quick Eats

Townhouse (☎ 01228-590955; 34 Lowther St; lunch
£3.95-5.15; 🕙 9am-5pm Mon-Sat) Funky Lowther St
hangout, chock-a-block with fairy lights and
handwritten chalkboards offering gourmet
coffees, paninis and jacket spuds. Porridge is
served two ways: take it like a northerner with
cold milk, or with cream and fruit if you're a
southern softie.

Prior's Kitchen Restaurant (☎ 01228-543251;
lunches £4-6; 🕙 9.45am-3pm or 4pm Mon-Sat) Hidden
away in the vaulted cellar of the former fratry, this basement tearoom is an old fave for
city-centre shoppers and ladies who lunch.
Crumbly cakes and a light-and-easy menu
of quiches, sarnies and pies keep the clientele
well fed.

Restaurants

Alexandros (☎ 01228-592227; 68 Warwick Rd; meze
£3-6, mains £10-16; 🕙 dinner Mon-Sat) Cheery (and
cheesy) Greek grub just outside the centre,
with the usual selection of meze, kebabs
and calamari.

Le Gall (☎ 01228-818388; 7 Devonshire St; mains
£5.95-11.95; 🕙 lunch & dinner) Despite the name,
this bistro is more fusion than French, with
a choice of fajitas, burgers, salads and stir-
fries. The atmosphere is modern and muted,
with lots of stripped wood and blond pine,
and it's a pleasant escape from the buzz of
nearby Botchergate.

Gilded Lily (☎ 01228-593600; 8 Lowther St; mains
£6.75-16.95; 🕙 lunch & dinner) Lodged in a converted
bank, with a soaring lantern skylight still in
situ, the Lily is as popular for cocktails as for
its gastropub-style cuisine – duck breast on
potato rōsti, or haddock on buttered spinach.
It's finished with bespoke wallpapers, chrome
and a smattering of olde-worlde style.

our pick Teza Indian Canteen (☎ 01228-525111; 4a
English Gate Plaza; mains £7.95-13.95; 🕙 lunch & dinner Mon-
Sat) Wave goodbye to those tired vindaloos –
this 21st-century Indian stands out from
Carlisle's other curry houses like a Bollywood
superstar. It shimmers with chrome, plate glass
and minimalist furniture, and champions a
new breed of Indian cuisine – Keralan fish
curry, tiger prawns with coriander and cloves,
and slow-cooked lamb in pickled ginger.

David's (☎ 01228-523578; 62 Warwick Rd; lunch £8-12,
dinner £13.95-20.50; 🕙 lunch & dinner Tue-Sat) High-
falutin' fare – venison, guinea fowl, duck –
served in town-house surroundings. Cutlery
gleams, candles flicker and the napkins are
sharp enough to slice your finger on, but it
might feel too toffee-nosed for some.

Number 10 (☎ 01228-524183; 10 Eden Mount; mains
£13-21; 🕙 dinner Tue-Sat) The city's best modern
British–orientated address, with an admirable
dedication to Cumbrian produce (shrimps
and cockles from Morecambe Bay, lamb and
beef straight from the fell farms and cheese
from local dairies). The dining room is light
and unfussy, and the quality is consistent, so
it gets busy – book ahead.

Self-Catering

Self-caterers can pick up supplies from the
Tesco Metro (☎ 0845 677 9135; Victoria Viaduct; 🕙 8am-
8pm Mon-Fri, 8am-7pm Sat, 10am-4pm Sun).

DRINKING

Carlisle's nightlife centres on the wall-to-wall
bars around Botchergate, but it gets notoriously troublesome at chucking-out time; if
you've ever wondered what the phenomenon
of British binge drinking is all about, this is the
place to find out. Mind how you go.

SETTLE-CARLISLE RAILWAY

There's nothing quite like rattling along the rails watching the English landscape rush by, and if you're a passionate steam junky, Cumbria will seem like choo-choo heaven. Several railways chug their way around the county, but the most historic is the **Settle-Carlisle Railway** (www.settle-carlisle.co.uk), which cuts across the Yorkshire Dales and the Eden Valley from Leeds to Carlisle, with stops at Settle, Kirkby Stephen and Appleby.

It's one of England's most stunning train journeys, traversing moor, heath, pasture and valley, not to mention 14 tunnels and the 24-arched Ribblehead viaduct, one of the great triumphs of Victorian engineering. The line required the blood, sweat and graft of 6000 'navvies' to complete at a cost of £3.5 million (twice the original estimate), and work was halted several times due to freezing weather conditions, floods, blizzards and even a smallpox outbreak. The railway was finally opened for business in 1876, and over a century later in 1998, a memorial stone was laid in the churchyard of St Mary's in Mallerstang to commemorate the scores of workers who lost their lives during its construction.

Sample fares are Leeds to Carlisle single/return £23.10/27.80, Settle to Carlisle £16.80/20 and Appleby to Carlisle £8.10/8.60. There are also Settle-Carlisle Day Ranger tickets for £25/12.50 per adult/child, or Settle-Carlisle Rover Tickets allowing four days travel in eight for £44/22. The line is also covered by regional Day Rover and Ranger tickets – see p228 for details.

Fats (☎ 01228-511774; 48 Abbey St; 11am-11pm) Slate, steel and an open fireplace attract a classy clientele to Fats. World beers behind the bar, with open-mic nights, scratch sessions and hot-tip DJs to pull in the punters.

Alcoves Cafe Bar (☎ 01228-536945; 18 Fisher St; 6pm-late Tue-Sat) The latest venture from the Cafe Sol crew, tucked along a narrow alley near the cathedral. There's a different musical vibe every night, and the feel is a good deal more chilled than the Botchergate hullabaloo.

Bar Solo (☎ 01228-631600; 1 Botchergate) Late-night tapas, Hispanic-themed cocktails, and Sol beers at a tiny corner bar on the edge of Botchergate.

Griffin (☎ 01228-598941; Court Sq) Traditional Brit boozer in a former bank with Jennings ales on tap. It's less rowdy than most of the Botchergate pubs, but you'll still have to brave the bouncers on weekends.

Unit (☎ 01228-514823; Botchergate; 24hr) Plasma screens, DJ decks and plenty of neon and chrome (not to mention a round-the-clock licence) make the Unit one of Carlisle's favourite after-hours drinking dens.

Office (☎ 01228-404303; Botchergate) Expansive, industrial-style bar with DJs spinning breakbeat, chunky house and hip hop.

ENTERTAINMENT

There are plenty of chart-pop and chunky house clubs in and around Botchergate, including super-cheesy **Mood** (☎ 01228-520383; 70 Botchergate), but the musos generally check out the line-up at **Concrete** (14 Lowther St; admission from £6).

The **Sands Centre** (☎ 01228-625222; www.thesandscentre.co.uk) is the city's main entertainment and music venue, hosting everything from touring bands to trade shows in a purpose-built building just outside the centre; it's about a 10-minute walk from town. Another option is the **Brickyard** (☎ 01228-512220; www.thebrickyardonline.com; 14 Fisher St), Carlisle's oldest gig venue, which concentrates on indie, rock and metal, and often attracts a breaking NME name or two. It's housed in the former Memorial Hall near the castle. For the latest mainstream flicks check out the huge seven-screen chain **Vue Cinema** (☎ 08712 240 240; 50 Botchergate).

GETTING THERE & AWAY
Bus

Carlisle is Cumbria's main transport hub. National Express coaches travel from the bus station on Lonsdale St to London (£33.50, 7½ hours, three direct daily, with extra buses via Birmingham), Glasgow (£17.70, 2¾ hours, nine daily) and Manchester (£24.50, three hours, five daily).

The most useful services to the Lakes are the 600 to Cockermouth (nine Monday to Saturday), which connects through to Whitehaven (30 minutes, eight Monday to Saturday), and the 554 to Keswick (70 minutes, three daily), connecting with the 555/556 Lakeslink to Windermere and Ambleside.

The 104 operates to Penrith (40 minutes, hourly Monday to Saturday, nine on Sunday), and bus AD122 (the Hadrian's Wall bus; six daily late May to late September) connects Carlisle and Hexham.

Train

Carlisle is also the county's busiest rail link. It's on the main West Coast line from London Euston (advance £39.50 to £49, off-peak £86.10, anytime £123.50, 3¼ to 4¼ hours) to Glasgow (advance £6.50 to £14.50, off-peak £7.20, anytime £33.50, 1¼ to 1½ hours), with hourly connections in either direction. It's also the terminus for several regional railways.

Cumbrian Coast Line Tracks the coastline in a long loop from Carlisle to Lancaster (£23.20, 3½ to five hours depending on connections), with stops including Whitehaven, Ravenglass, Barrow-in-Furness, Cartmel and Grange-over-Sands provided in partnership with the Furness Line.

Settle-Carlisle Railway See boxed text, p201.

Tyne Valley Line (www.tynevalleyrail.org.uk) Sometimes referred to as the Hadrian's Wall line, this follows the rough course of the wall from Carlisle to Newcastle-upon-Tyne (£12.10, 1½ hours), with stops at Hexham, Alston, Haltwhistle and Brampton.

For details of Day Ranger and Rail Rover tickets covering travel on these lines, see the Transport chapter on p233.

GETTING AROUND

For taxis in Carlisle, try the following:
Citadel Station Taxis (☎ 01228-523971)
County Cabs (☎ 01228-596789)
Radio Taxis (☎ 01228-527575)

AROUND CARLISLE

While most people make a headlong dash out of Carlisle for the M6, the open countryside around the city is worth taking a couple of days to explore. This is one of the most history-heavy corners of Cumbria: to the east, you can make the pilgrimage to the great ecclesiastical seat of Lanercost Priory, before exploring the remains of Hadrian's Wall around Brampton and the crumbling garrison fort at Birdoswald. If you've got time, there's also a famous Anglo-Saxon cross at Bewcastle.

BRAMPTON & AROUND

The stout sandstone market town of Brampton lies 7 miles northeast of Carlisle and 2 miles west from the remains of Hadrian's Wall. Founded around the 7th century and later an important terminus on the Tyne Valley Railway, the town now makes an ideal exploration base, with a smattering of boutiquey B&Bs dotted around the countryside, and a more relaxed feel than the hustle and rush of nearby Carlisle.

Sights
BRAMPTON TOWN

Notable for its winding exterior staircase, arched windows and weather-vane turret, Brampton's octagonal **Moot Hall** was built in 1817 and is now occupied by the **Brampton Tourist Office** (☎ 016977-3433; tourism@carlisle.gov.uk; 🕒 10am-5pm Mon-Sat Easter-Sep, 10am-4pm Oct-Easter).

The town's other landmark is **St Martin's Church** (www.stmartinsbrampton.org.uk; 🕒 9.30am-4.30pm), designed by the architect Philip Webb, a key figure in the Pre-Raphaelite movement and a partner in the influential interior design company run by the artist Edward Burne-Jones, the poet-painter Dante Gabriel Rossetti and the celebrated English designer William Morris (whose workshop fabricated the church's gorgeous stained-glass windows).

Two miles south of town is the 26-hectare boating lake of **Talkin Tarn**, scooped out by an ancient glacier and now surrounded by walking trails and 48 hectares of quiet woodland. The nearby **Gelt Woods RSPB Reserve** is a popular haven for twitchers and bird spotters.

LANERCOST PRIORY

About 3 miles northeast of the town centre is the rosy ruin of **Lanercost Priory** (EH; ☎ 01697-73030; adult/child £3/1.50; 🕒 10am-5pm daily mid-Mar–Sep, 10am-4pm Thu-Mon Oct, 9am-4pm Sat & Sun Nov-Dec), situated at the old crossing over the River Irthing. Second only in stature to the abbey in Furness (p187), Lanercost was founded by Augustinian monks in the mid-12th century, but had a chequered history; marauding Scottish raiders sacked the building at least four times during its history, and it suffered the same sorry fate as Cumbria's other priories during Henry VIII's Dissolution. Fortunately Lanercost was saved from total collapse by the Victorian architect Anthony Salvin, who restored part of the building and converted it for use as a parish church in the mid-19th century.

BIRDOSWALD ROMAN FORT

Just east of Lanercost Priory, the remains of one of England's great ancient monuments wind across the flat fields. **Hadrian's Wall** once stretched for just over 70 miles between Wallsend and Bowness-on-Solway, and was manned by several thousand legionaries operating from garrison forts positioned along the wall's length. Though most have long since been plundered for building supplies, you can still visit one at **Birdoswald Roman Fort** (☎ 01697-747602; adult/child £4.50/2.30; ☺ 10am-5.30pm mid-Mar–Sep, 10am-4pm Oct-Mar). Built to replace an earlier timber-and-turf fort, Birdoswald would have been the operating base for around 1000 Roman soldiers; excavations have revealed three of the four gateways, as well as granary stores, workshops, exterior walls and a military drill hall. A visitor centre explores the fort's history and the background behind the wall's construction.

Sleeping & Eating

Tantallon House (☎ 016977-47111; www.hadrians-wall -bed-and-breakfast.co.uk; Gilsland; s £40, d £70-80; P ☎) Terrific gabled B&B in Gilsland, a stone's throw from Birdoswald. The two rooms are huge and airy, with Victorian hearths and sash windows overlooking shrub-filled gardens; don't forget to visit the little aviary and say hello to Hoot the Owl.

our pick **Willowford** (☎ 016977-47962; www.willow ford.co.uk; Gilsland; s £50, d £75-120; P) Hadrian's Wall steamrollers right through the grounds of this eco-conscious farm just outside Gilsland. There's a choice of rooms in the main house or a beautifully converted milking parlour; all boast the same combo of elegant design (exposed stone, stripped wood, slate) and environmental friendliness (fleece insulation, waste-wood heating, double-glazing). You'll

spot Swaledale ewes and free-range chickens from your window.

Weary (☎ 01228-670230; www.theweary.com; Castle Carrock; d £110-150; P ☎) Don't be fooled by the old inn exterior – inside this flashy bolthole is all monsoon showers, twisted willow, Egyptian cotton and Bang and Olufsen phones. The restaurant (mains £11.95 to £24.95) is more Soho hangout than country pub – light streams from an overhead skylight and the menu is a textbook of modern Brit cuisine (goose breast, swordfish steak, venison with beetroot).

Crosby Lodge (☎ 01228-573618; www.crosbylodge .co.uk; Crosby on Eden; lunch menu £28, dinner menu £38; P) Ostentatious country house straight out of a Jane Austen novel: lofty Georgian windows overlook tended parkland, and the interior is an antique shop of burnished dressers and sleigh beds (double £160). You'll be drenched with spoils – Molton Brown goodies in the bathrooms, chaise longues in the drawing room and beef entrecôte on the supper table. Golly.

Getting There & Away

A number of buses run from Carlisle bus station, including the 685 to Brampton (20 minutes, hourly Monday to Saturday, four on Sunday), Gilsland (40 minutes) and Newcastle (two hours 20 minutes), and the less frequent 95 to Brampton (20 minutes, four to six Monday to Saturday).

There's also the special AD122/185 bus (aka the Hadrian's Wall Bus) that runs from Carlisle Courts via Brampton (20 minutes, seven daily mid-March to November), Lanercost Priory (35 minutes), Birdoswald Fort (45 minutes) and Gilsland (50 minutes).

There are around six daily trains from Carlisle to Brampton (£3.80, 15 minutes) and Haltwhistle (£6, 30 minutes).

INLAND CUMBRIA

DETOUR – BEWCASTLE CROSS

If you've already paid a visit to the Gosforth Cross (p136), it's worth making the comparison with the Bewcastle Cross, which stands in the village churchyard of Bewcastle, 14 miles north of Brampton. This 14ft stone pillar dates from the 7th to 8th centuries and is one of the oldest known Anglo-Saxon crosses in England. Its four faces are covered with runic inscriptions, vines, animals, figures and Christian symbols.

Though the cross is badly weathered and the upper section has broken away, archaeologists believe it was erected for King Alcfrith, who made a failed bid for the Northumbrian crown in the mid-7th century. A similar Anglo-Saxon stone, known as the Ruthwell Cross, can be seen in Annan just across the Scottish border; it was carved around the same time, possibly by the same Northumbrian stonemasons.

PENRITH & THE EDEN VALLEY

pop 14,882

There's a flavour of bygone days hanging around the crimson-bricked streets of Penrith, one of eastern Cumbria's most atmospheric market towns and, until 1070, its regional capital. Vintage shop fronts, traditional greengrocers and wonky-roofed pubs line its cobbled alleys and busy shopping arcades, and the focus of daily life still revolves around the medieval market square. While it might not have the chocolate-box appeal of some other Lakeland towns, Penrith makes a lively and convenient gateway for exploring the eastern Lakes and the nearby Eden Valley.

HISTORY

Celtic tribes and Roman garrisons recognised the strategic importance of Penrith, and founded forts on the site of the present-day town; Penrith's name derives from the Celtic words *penn* and *rid* meaning either 'hill ford', 'main ford' or 'red hill'.

During the 9th and 10th centuries the town was allied with the Scots as part of Strathclyde, and served as the capital of a semi-autonomous kingdom until 1070. It was later annexed by the English in 1295, leading to a century of conflict with the Border Reivers, who sacked the town three times, prompting the construction of a defensive pele tower (later reinforced as Penrith Castle) and a warning beacon at the top of Beacon Hill.

Penrith was granted its market charter in the 13th century, and grew into an important trading centre, with markets centring on Corn Market, Dockray, Sandgate, Burrowgate, Castle Mart and Market Pl. Following the arrival of the railway in the mid-19th century, Penrith became a bustling industrial base, especially for tanners, weavers, tailors, coopers and saddle makers; in 1907 the town boasted 57 inns (each associated with a particular trade or guild) for a population of just over 9000 people.

ORIENTATION

Penrith's train station is at the top of the hill to the southwest of town, about a 10-minute walk from the centre via Brunswick Rd or Castlegate. The bus station is next to the large car park off Sandgate. The main shopping streets are Middlegate and Devonshire St, which lead southeast through the town centre towards the central market square. Ullswater Rd leads southwest from the centre past the train station before linking with the A66 and the M6 motorway.

INFORMATION

Branches of Lloyd's, HSBC and Barclays are located on Market Sq.

Penrith Library (☎ 01768-242100; St Andrew's Churchyard; internet per half hr/hr £1/2; ☺ 10am-7pm Mon & Tue, 10am-1pm Wed, 10am-5pm Thu & Fri, 10am-4pm Sat & Sun)

Police Station (Hunter Lane; ☺ 8am-midnight)

Post Office (Crown Sq; ☺ 9am-5.30pm Mon-Sat, 9am-12.30pm Sat)

Tourist Office (☎ 01768-867466; pen.tic@eden.gov.uk; Middlegate; ☺ 9.30am-5pm Mon-Sat, 1-4.45pm Sun)

SIGHTS

Penrith Castle

Opposite the station are the ruins of the 14th-century **Penrith Castle** (☺ 7.30am-9pm Easter-Oct, 7.30am-4.30pm Oct-Easter), built by William Strickland (later Bishop of Carlisle and Archbishop of Canterbury). The castle was substantially reinforced by Richard, Duke of Gloucester (later Richard III), to resist Scottish raids, which had previously razed the town three times in 1314, 1345 and 1382. Richard embellished the castle with a new banqueting hall and residential quarters before becoming King of England in 1483 following Edward IV's death; he was killed just two years later at the Battle of Bosworth Field and the castle fell into disrepair.

Penrith Museum

Penrith's tourist office houses a quirky **town museum** (admission free; ☺ 9.30am-5pm Mon-Sat, 1-4.45pm Sun) displaying local historical objects. Look out for antique clocks from the town's heyday as a clock-making centre, ceremonial keys, and a wrestling belt belonging to William Jameson, a former champion Cumbrian wrestler (memorably described as 'a polar bear on its hind legs in a grey flannel shirt').

There's also a display on Percy Topliss, the notorious army fraudster, impostor and con man sometimes known as 'the Monocled Mutineer'. Following a career of forgery, impersonation, black marketeering and general skulduggery, Topliss murdered a taxi driver and wounded two policemen and went on the

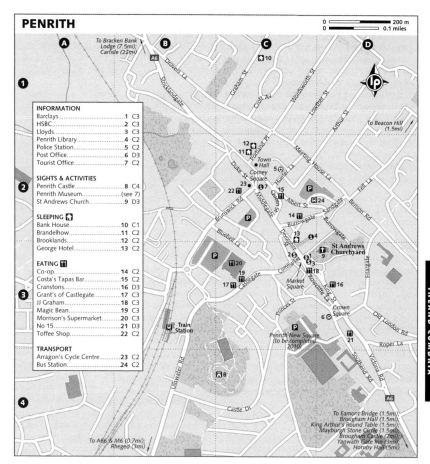

PENRITH

INFORMATION
Barclays	1 C3
HSBC	2 C3
Lloyds	3 C3
Penrith Library	4 C2
Police Station	5 C2
Post Office	6 D3
Tourist Office	7 C2

SIGHTS & ACTIVITIES
Penrith Castle	8 C4
Penrith Museum	(see 7)
St Andrews Church	9 D3

SLEEPING
Bank House	10 C1
Brandelhow	11 C2
Brooklands	12 C2
George Hotel	13 C2

EATING
Co-op	14 C2
Costa's Tapas Bar	15 C2
Cranstons	16 D3
Grant's of Castlegate	17 C3
JJ Graham	18 C3
Magic Bean	19 C3
Morrison's Supermarket	20 C3
No 15	21 D3
Toffee Shop	22 C2

TRANSPORT
| Arragon's Cycle Centre | 23 C2 |
| Bus Station | 24 C2 |

INLAND CUMBRIA

run; he was eventually killed during a gunfight with local bobbies near Penrith, and was buried in an unmarked grave in Beacon Edge Cemetery. You can see the monocle he often used as part of his disguise in the museum's display cabinet.

St Andrew's Church
Built from the distinctive local red sandstone, St Andrew's Church was constructed during the 18th century on the site of an earlier chapel, parts of which survive in the 14th-century church tower. In the churchyard are the weathered remains of two Celtic crosses and four 10th-century tombstones, known as the **Giant's Grave**; local legend maintains they mark the burial site of Owen Caesarius, the

rightful king of Cumbria. Nearby is the **Giant's Thumb**, another badly weathered Norse cross believed to date from the 10th century.

Brougham Castle & Around
Straddling the banks of the River Eamont, on the foundations of the old Roman fort of Brocavum, **Brougham Castle** (pronounced 'broom', EH; ☎ 01768-862488; adult/child £3/1.50; ☼ 10am-5pm mid-Mar–Sep; ⌖) was begun in the early 13th century by the local notable, Robert de Vieuxpoint, and reinforced by the Clifford family as a defensive stronghold against Scottish raids. You can clamber up to the top of Vieuxpoint's striking central keep for fabulous views over the Eden countryside, and there are Roman tombstones on display in the castle grounds.

INLAND CUMBRIA

DETOUR – LONG MEG & HER DAUGHTERS

The third-largest prehistoric stone circle in England, **Long Meg and Her Daughters**, stands in the centre of a rolling field near the village of Little Salkeld, 6 miles northeast of Penrith. It's thought that the circle would have originally contained up to 77 uprights; today only around 27 are still standing in their original places, while many more have toppled over or been shifted over the course of the centuries.

Local legend maintains that the circle was once a coven of witches, zapped into stone by a local wizard. The circle is also said to be uncountable (if anyone manages twice the spell will be lifted) and a terrible fate awaits anyone who disturbs the stones. Just outside the circle stands Long Meg herself, a 12ft red sandstone pillar decorated with faint spiral traces; another local legend says that the stone would run with blood if it were ever damaged.

The circle is situated along a minor road three-quarters of a mile north of Little Salkeld, just off the A686. Follow the signs to the 'Druid's Circle'.

On your way back to town, it's worth detouring via the 14th-century mansion of **Brougham Hall**, which houses a craft centre, chocolate shop, tearoom and smokehouse, before strolling around the Stone-Age earthwork known as **King Arthur's Round Table**. The standing stones that marked the spot have long since disappeared, although you can still make out the monument's central plateau and encircling ditch; the site was clearly connected with a second, much larger henge at **Mayburgh** a few hundred metres to the west.

SLEEPING

Penrith's best B&Bs are side by side along Portland Pl, although there's a second cluster of more downmarket places along Victoria Rd.

Brandelhow (☎ 01768-864470; www.brandel howguesthouse.co.uk; 1 Portland Pl; s £32.50, d/tw £65) Spick-and-span rooms jazzed up by thoughtful extras such as mini-fridges, bathrobes, bickies, and complimentary slabs of Bootle gingerbread or Lanie's Expedition flapjacks on arrival. The bedrooms concentrate on country pine, cream and golds: Willow has a garden view, Woodland has a cast-iron bed frame, while the Meadow Suite has a lovely bay window and bags of space.

Brooklands (☎ 01768-863395; www.brooklandsguest house.com; 2 Portland Pl; s £30-35, d £65-75) Next door to Brandelhow, this guest house is a notch up the comfort ladder. Some rooms feature rich purples and pine four-posters, while others go for soothing magnolias and flower prints. For the full swank-factor you'll want the fluffy-pillowed suite, with brass bedstead and wall-mounted TV.

Bank House (☎ 01768-868714; www.bankhousepenrith .co.uk; Graham St; s £38, d £68-76; 🛜) Unpretentious Cumbrian guest house that does all the basics right (including a kingly breakfast of fresh-baked granary loaf and coiled Cumberland sausage). The rosy-pink twin room might be too lacy for some, but the other doubles are more neutral, with DVD players and wooden beds.

Hornby Hall (☎ 01768-891114; www.hornbyhall.co.uk; Brougham; d £50-84; **P**) Another off-beat retreat, housed in a Grade-II–listed manor house 3 miles southeast of Penrith in Brougham. The five musty rooms overlook manicured grounds; two are reached via a Hogwarts-esque spiral staircase, and breakfast is served in the 16th-century dining hall with its original stone hearth and Victorian range.

Bracken Bank Lodge (☎ 01768-898241; www .brackenbank.co.uk; Lazonby; d £70-140; **P** 🛱) Secretly harbouring *Brideshead Revisited* daydreams? Then head for this august country house in the village of Lazonby, languishing in grounds filled with red deer, pheasants and tinkling fountains. It's an upper-class treat with sporting prints and hunting trophies in the dining room, bedrooms furnished with roll-top baths, tartans and four-poster beds, and breakfasts cooked up on the antique aga. There's even a snooker hall and gun room.

George Hotel (☎ 01768-862696; www.lakedistrict hotels.net/georgehotel; Devonshire St; s £79-103, d £106-172; **P**) The town's solid old hotel looks rather venerable, but inside (most) rooms have been given a facelift: cool tones of duck-egg blue, taupe and gold combine with LCD TVs, throw cushions and shiny bathrooms. Cheaper rooms are showing their age, and the vibe in the restaurant is classic: expect old armchairs, heavy drapes and portions of Lancashire hotpot and Hawkshead trout (mains £9.50 to £16.50).

EATING

Costa's Tapas Bar (☎ 01768-895550; 9 Queen St; tapas £4.50-10; ☺ dinner Tue-Sun) Hispanic mementoes cover every inch of wall space at this tapas joint. While the atmosphere's a tad cheesy, the food's authentically Spanish: 40 tapas choices are backed up by paella just like mama used to make.

No 15 (☎ 01768-867453; 15 Victoria Rd; lunches £6-10; ☺ daily) Coffee connoisseurs and arty types congregate in Penrith's sleek and groovy cafe-gallery. Blackboard specials of wraps, salads and home-baked pies are chalked up behind the bar, and there are displays of photography and art in the gallery annexe.

Magic Bean (☎ 01768-867474; Poet's Walk; mains £6-14; ☺ lunch & dinner Mon-Sat) This mews restaurant has a split personality: light lunches and afternoon teas are served during daylight hours, but by night spicier Indian-influenced flavours take over. Try unusual dishes such as *niligiri machli* (cod curry with chilli and coriander) and chicken *chettinad* (cooked with black pepper and mace).

Grants of Castlegate (☎ 01768-895444; Castlegate; mains £8-15; ☺ lunch & dinner Wed-Sun) Shiny split-level bistro on Castlegate, plundering global flavours for its catch-all menu – expect everything from stir-fries and chicken breast to risotto and ravioli. It's bright and modern, and popular with Penrith's wine-bar crowd.

ourpick **Yanwath Gate Inn** (☎ 01768-862886; www.yanwathgate.com; Yanwath; mains £13.95-18.95) Two miles southwest of Penrith, the Yanwath always features at the top of the Cumbrian foodie critics' list. It's one of the county's original gastropubs, known for its inventive takes on traditional dishes: salt marsh lamb and crispy pork belly sit alongside venison burgers, smoked eel salads and a fantastic Gate Inn Platter. The setting has bags of A-framed, wood-panelled character, and there are local cheeses and beers to round things off with a gastronomic bang.

Self-Catering

ourpick **JJ Graham** (☎ 01768-862281; www.jjgraham .co.uk; 6-7 Market Sq) For chocolates, pies, puddings and cold cuts, nowhere beats this historic grocer's shop, in business since 1793. Wicker baskets are filled with warm crusty bread, glass chiller cabinets are crammed with tempting treats, and assorted cakes and biscuits are stacked up on the counter tops.

For more sweet treats head to the **Toffee Shop** (☎ 01768-862008; www.thetoffeeshop.co.uk), which has been serving up tooth-cracking toffees and tasty fudges for nearly 100 years. Savoury items, including award-winning Cumberland sausages, hams and bacons are sold at **Cranstons** (☎ 01768-868680; Ullswater Rd), established in 1914, or for more basic supplies, head for the town centre **Co-op** (Burrowgate; ☺ 8am-8pm Mon-Fri, 8am-6pm Sat), or **Morrison's Supermarket** (Brunswick Rd; ☎ 8am-8pm Mon-Wed & Sat, 8am-9pm Thu-Fri, 10am-4pm Sun) near the station.

Penrith's **farmers market** fills Market Sq on the third Tuesday of every month from 9.30am to 2pm.

GETTING THERE & AROUND
Bike Hire

Bikes can be hired from **Arragon's Cycle Centre** (☎ 01768-890344; www.arragons.com; Brunswick Rd; ☺ 9am-5.30pm Mon-Sat) or **Cycle Active** (☎ 01768-840400; www.cycleactive.co.uk) at nearby Brougham Hall.

INLAND CUMBRIA

SOMETHING FOR THE WEEKEND

Begin the weekend break with a night of pampering at **Willowbeck Lodge** (p200). On Saturday morning take a few hours to explore Cumbria's capital city, factoring in visits to **Carlisle Castle** (p197) and the excellent **Tullie House Museum** (p198). Have a light lunch – **Teza Indian Canteen** (p200) and the **Gilded Lily** (p200) are both great options – and then head out of the city for an afternoon exploring **Brampton** (p202), **Lanercost Priory** (p202) and the thought-provoking ruins of **Birdoswald Roman Fort** (p203). Check into the supremely swish **Weary** (p203) or the lavishly appointed **Crosby Lodge** (p203) and indulge in a luxurious supper and sleep.

On Sunday head south to **Alston** (p209) and follow our **driving itinerary** (p195) in reverse all the way to **Penrith** (p204). Have Sunday lunch at **Yanwath Gate Inn** (above), and spend the rest of the day exploring the town and surrounding countryside, perhaps adding in a detour to **Haweswater** (p175) or **Lowther Park** (p175). Round things off with a memorable night at **Bracken Bank Lodge** (opposite) or the slightly stuffy **George Hotel** (opposite), or settle into comfortable B&B digs at **Brandelhow** (opposite) or **Brooklands** (opposite).

Bus

The bus station is northeast of the centre, off Sandgate. Bus 104 runs between Penrith and Carlisle (45 minutes, hourly Monday to Saturday, nine on Sunday). Bus X4/X5 (13 Monday to Saturday, six on Sunday) travels via Rheged, Keswick and Cockermouth en route to the Cumbrian Coast.

Train

Penrith is on the main West Coast line, with hourly connections through to Carlisle (£6.70, 20 minutes), Kendal (£11.20, 30 minutes), Lancaster (£12.50, 35 to 50 minutes) and the south. For connections to Windermere, change at Kendal.

AROUND PENRITH

RHEGED

Cunningly disguised as a Lakeland hill 2 miles west of Penrith, **Rheged** (☎ 01768-686000; www.rheged.com; 🕑 10am-6pm) houses a large-screen Imax cinema and an exhibition on the history and geology of Cumbria, as well as a retail hall selling Cumbrian goods, from handmade paper to chocolate and chutneys.

The cinema offers a regularly changing line-up of around six films, shown on a loop throughout the day. A new flick starts hourly; one film costs £4.95/3 per adult/child, with each extra film costing £3/2.

The frequent X4/X5 bus between Penrith and Workington stops at the centre.

APPLEBY-IN-WESTMORLAND

Tucked in an ox-bow curve of the River Eden, the sweet market town of Appleby was once the second most important in the Eden Valley, and until the formation of the new district of Cumbria in 1974 served as Westmorland's county town. It's a sleepy, charming slice of old England, with traditional butchers, villagey shops and tearooms dotted along its central street, Boroughgate, which slices through town to the sandstone facade of **St Lawrence's Church** and the **Cloisters**, a pleasant covered arcade built by Robert Smirke (who also designed Lowther Castle).

The town's most famous resident was the redoubtable Lady Anne Clifford, a local aristocrat and part-time philanthropist who devoted much of her life to restoring neglected estates, churches and castles. One of her pet projects was the Norman keep of **Appleby Castle** (closed to the public), which stands at Boroughgate's southern end and served for several centuries as the family seat of the Clifford family.

Appleby's other claim to fame is its historic **horse fair**, which has been in business since 1685 and still attracts a technicolour pageant of painted gypsy wagons to the town's streets every June. The four-day fair centres on Fair Hill (previously known by the more macabre name of Gallows Hill); a local tradition involves riders wading into the River Eden on horseback to wash their steeds.

For more details drop into the **Appleby Tourist Office** (☎ 017683-51177; tic@applebytown.org.uk; 🕑 9.30am-5pm Mon-Sat, 11am-3pm Sun Apr-Oct, 10am-1pm Mon-Thu, 10am-3pm Fri, 10am-2pm Sat Nov-Mar) at the top of Boroughgate.

Sleeping & Eating

Bank End House (☎ 017683-52050; www.bankendhouse.co.uk; Appleby; s/d £45/70; P) Smartly built from local brick, this fine three-room B&B east of the Appleby centre ditches the usual chintz for whites, ochres and slate-greys. There's a funky brass-knobbed bed in the Barn Room, the Field Room has a continental sofa and oak bed frame, and the twin Copse Room has woodland views.

Marton House (☎ 017683-61502; www.martonhousecumbria.co.uk; Long Marton; s/d £50/75; P) Just a few rooms at this russet-coloured manor house in the village of Long Marton, but they're beauties: huge, relaxing and rural-cosy, with period interests ranging from original hearths to vintage baths. The house is grandly ringed by gardens, and breakfast is served in an orangery on summer mornings.

Tufton Arms (☎ 017683-51593; www.tuftonarmshotel.co.uk; Market Sq, Appleby; s £68-83, d £112-207; P) First a 16th-century coaching inn, then a Victorian house, now a spiffing town hotel with a *soupçon* of 21st-century flamboyance. All the rooms are different: plaster engravings and chandeliers meet muted paints and bespoke wallpapers in some, while others are the picture of restrained *Homes & Gardens* sophistication. It's dead in the centre of Appleby, and the classy bistro (mains £10.95 to £21.95) turns out the town's best food.

Getting There & Away

Appleby sits on the Settle-Carlisle Railway line, with connections west to Carlisle (single £7.60, return £8.10, 45 minutes, seven daily Monday to Saturday, five on Sunday) and southeast to Leeds (single £15.30, return £21). The most useful bus is the 563 from Penrith (30 minutes, nine Monday to Saturday, two on Sunday).

ALSTON

pop 2227

Surrounded by the bleak hilltops of the Pennines, isolated Alston's main claim to fame is its elevation: at 305m above sea level, it is the highest market town in England (although it can no longer boast a market). It is also famous among steam enthusiasts thanks to the diminutive **South Tynedale Railway** (☎ 01434-381696, talking timetable 01434-382828; www .strps.org.uk; adult/3-15yr return £5.50/2.50; ☙ Apr-Oct), which puffs and clatters through the hilly country between Alston and Kirkhaugh, along a route that originally operated from 1852 to 1976. The return trip aboard a steam or diesel locomotive takes an hour, with around five daily trains in midsummer.

Opposite the station is the **Hub Heritage Museum** (☎ 01434-382272; admission by donation; ☙ 11am-4pm on railway days), which houses a display of antique cars, old farming implements, period posters and sepia photos in a vintage railway goods shed.

Alston's library and **tourist office** (☎ 01434-382244; alston.tic@eden.gov.uk; Town Hall, Front St; ☙ 10am-5pm Mon-Thu & Sat, 10am-7pm Fri, 10am-4pm Sun) are in the Town Hall, at the foot of Alston's steep cobbled main street.

Sleeping & Eating

Alston YHA (☎ 0870 770 5668; The Firs; dm £11.95; ☙ Easter-Oct) Basic hostel with three dorms overlooking the South Tyne Valley. It's popular with walkers and cyclists on the Sea to Sea Cycle Route (C2C), so book ahead.

Lowbyer Manor (☎ 01434-381230; www.lowbyer.com; Alston; s £33, d £66-90) Handmade quilts (woven by the owner's relatives) and an endearing mix-and-match decor make this manor house Alston's cosiest B&B. The nine rooms range from a titchy single to a king-size four-poster suite overlooking Alston Moor. It's handy for the steam train – the station's only a stroll away.

Yew Tree Chapel (☎ 01434-382525; Slaggyford; s £39, d £68; ℗) Funky B&B in a converted church, overflowing with wit and style – the original organ and stained-glass windows form the lounge's centrepiece. The decor is boho-chic – with colourful furnishings and bric-a-brac, plus fresh bread, cinnamon toast and gourmet muesli for brekkie. It's in Slaggyford, 3 miles north of Alston.

Lovelady Shield (☎ 0871 288 1345; www.lovelady .co.uk; Nenthead Rd, Alston; d £100-170; ℗) The country hideaway par excellence, overflowing with swag-draped beds, flouncy curtains and posh wallpapers in white and gold. All rooms have sofa suites, widescreen TVs and wonderful views across the grounds, but it might be too stuffy for some.

Getting There & Away

Bus 888 travels twice daily to Newcastle (£8, 80 minutes), and once to Penrith (£6, 1¼ hours) and Keswick (£7, 1¾ hours). Bus 680 runs from Nenthead to Carlisle via Alston (four Monday to Saturday).

INLAND CUMBRIA

SOMETHING SPECIAL

Pastry-lovers and bun-buffs will want to make a beeline for two fabulous bakeries situated in the Eden countryside. The all-organic **Village Bakery** (☎ 01768-898437; www.village-bakery.com) in Melmerby is renowned for its sourdoughs, Russian ryes, French country loaves and granary breads, not to mention an irresistible selection of lemon drizzle cakes and dark chocolate tortes (made with fair-trade ingredients, of course).

Meanwhile the **Watermill** (☎ 01768-881523; www.organicmill.co.uk) in Little Salkeld is one of the last remaining mills in England powered in the time-honoured fashion using two overshot waterwheels. You can see the wheels in action on a **mill tour** (☙ 2pm & 3.30pm Mon, Tue, Thu, Fri & Sun Mar-Oct), before picking up organic breads, cakes and goodies at the tearoom. And if you really want to find out how the magic happens, special **courses** (1 day £65, 2 day £120) in bread making, milling and baking are offered every month.

DETOUR – NENTHEAD MINES

Over 40 miles of subterranean tunnels wind their way through the **Nenthead Mines** (☎ 01434-382037; www.npht.com; adult/child £4/free, with mine tour £7/3), sunk between the 17th and 19th centuries to extract the rich deposits of lead, zinc and other minerals buried beneath the Pennines rock. A one-hour guided tour takes in some of the gloomy mine workings; you'll need something warm to wear and sturdy shoes, as it's just 10°C underground. The tour visits several deep shafts and explains some of its powerhouse machinery; elsewhere you can visit the remains of an old smelt works and waterwheel complex, or try your hand at a spot of metal panning.

KENDAL

pop 28,398

Locally known as the 'Auld Grey Town' thanks to the sombre limestone and grey slate used in its buildings, Kendal occupies a hallowed place in the hearts of many hill walkers thanks to its sweet and powerfully pepperminty treat, Kendal mintcake. This calorific energy bar was concocted by accident by a local confectioner in the mid-19th century, and it's been a staple item in British rucksacks ever since (even making it to the top of Everest during Edmund Hillary and Tensing Norgay's landmark ascent in 1953). But Kendal is more than just its mintcake: it's also the ideal gateway to the southern Lakes, with some intriguing galleries and an excellent arts centre to explore, and the national park's eastern border just 10 miles to the west.

HISTORY

Brigantes and Romans both established themselves around Kendal, but the town only really took off once it received its market charter in 1189. Houses and shops were established along the central streets of Stricklandgate and Highgate, forming the distinctive layout of regimented plots linked by 'yards' leading from the main thoroughfare. Kendal later developed as a centre for cloth and wool – 'Kendal green' is mentioned in Shakespeare's *Henry IV*, and the town's

motto is *Pannus Mini Panis*, meaning 'wool is my bread'. During the Industrial Revolution the town was an industrial hub for everything from shoe and carpet manufacture to snuff making.

INFORMATION

Branches of HSBC, Barclays, Lloyds and Natwest line Highgate and Stricklandgate.

Kendal Laundrette (☎ 01539-733754; Blackhall Rd; 8am-6pm Mon-Fri, 8am-5pm Sat & Sun)

Library (☎ 01539-773520; 75 Stricklandgate; internet per half hr/hr £1/2; 9.30am-7pm Mon & Wed, 9.30am-5pm Tue & Fri, 9.30am-noon Thu, 9.30am-3.30pm Sat, noon-4pm Sun) Wi-fi available.

Post Office (75 Stricklandgate; 9am-5.30pm Mon-Fri, 9am-12.30pm Sat)

Police Station (Busher Walk; 8am-midnight)

Tourist Office (☎ 01539-725758; kendaltic@south lakeland.gov.uk; Highgate; 10am-5pm Mon-Sat) Inside the town hall.

Waterstones (☎ 01539-741771; 7 Westmorland Shopping Centre; 9am-5.30pm Mon & Wed-Sat, 9.30am-5.30pm Tue, 10.30am-5pm Sun)

SIGHTS
Kendal Museum

Housed in a former wool warehouse, Kendal's town **museum** (☎ 01539-721374; www .kendalmuseum.org.uk; Station Rd; adult/child £2.80/free; 10.30am-5.30pm Mon-Sat Apr-Oct, 10.30am-4pm Mon-Sat Feb-Mar & Nov-Dec) was founded in 1796 by a local natural-history enthusiast, William Todhunter (making it one of England's oldest museums). It's a typically eclectic mix – wandering its echoey halls you'll glimpse everything from Roman coins to Egyptian scarabs alongside medieval coin hoards and model boats, while the Natural History Gallery is crammed with spooky stuffed animals including a flamingo bagged in 1860 and a polar bear that once belonged to the Earl of Lonsdale. Alfred Wainwright, of *Pictorial Guide* fame, was honorary curator from 1945 to 1974; his former office has been reconstructed inside the museum, with many original Wainwright drawings and a collection of his possessions (including his rucksack, spectacles and well-chewed pipe).

Abbot Hall Art Gallery

This **gallery** (☎ 01539-722464; www.abbothall.org.uk; adult/under 18yr £6/free; 10.30am-5pm Mon-Sat Apr-Oct, 10.30am-4pm Mon-Sat Nov-Mar), housed in a lovely Georgian villa, displays one of the northwest's best collections of 18th- and 19th-century art, especially strong on portraiture and Lakeland landscapes. Look out in the beautifully restored rooms for works by Constable, Varley and Turner, as well as portraits by John Ruskin and local boy George Romney, born in Dalton-in-Furness in 1734, and a key figure in the 'Kendal School'.

Museum of Lakeland Life

Opposite Abbot Hall is the **Museum of Lakeland Life** (☎ 01539-722464; www.lakelandmuseum.org.uk; adult/child £4.50/3.20; ☼ 10.30am-5pm Mon-Sat Apr-Oct, 10.30am-4pm Mon-Sat Nov-Mar), which recreates various scenes from Lakeland activity during the 18th and 19th centuries, including spinning, mining, weaving and bobbin making. There's

also a reconstruction of the study of Arthur Ransome, author of *Swallows and Amazons*.

Kendal Castle

On the eastern bank of the River Kent stand the ruins of **Kendal Castle** (admission free), first constructed during the 13th century and later occupied by several baronial dynasties, including the Parr family (although local claims stating that Catherine Parr, sixth wife of Henry VIII, was born at the castle are probably more fiction than fact). Only a couple of solitary turrets of this once-powerful stronghold now remain, but the plateau offers fine views over town and countryside. From the town centre, follow Aynam Rd onto Parr St to get to the castle.

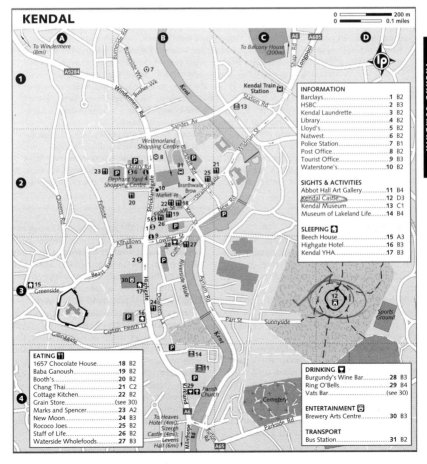

KENDAL

0 ———— 200 m
0 ———— 0.1 miles

INFORMATION
Barclays.................................**1** B2
HSBC.....................................**2** B3
Kendal Laundrette...................**3** B2
Library...................................**4** B2
Lloyd's...................................**5** B2
Natwest..................................**6** B2
Police Station.........................**7** B1
Post Office..............................**8** B2
Tourist Office..........................**9** B3
Waterstone's........................**10** B2

SIGHTS & ACTIVITIES
Abbot Hall Art Gallery...........**11** B4
Kendal Castle........................**12** D3
Kendal Museum.....................**13** C1
Museum of Lakeland Life........**14** B4

SLEEPING 🏠
Beech House.........................**15** A3
Highgate Hotel......................**16** B3
Kendal YHA...........................**17** B3

EATING 🍽
1657 Chocolate House............**18** B2
Baba Ganoush........................**19** B2
Booth's.................................**20** B2
Chang Thai.............................**21** C2
Cottage Kitchen.....................**22** B2
Grain Store.........................(see 30)
Marks and Spencer.................**23** A2
New Moon..............................**24** B3
Rococo Joes..........................**25** B2
Staff of Life...........................**26** B2
Waterside Wholefoods...........**27** B3

DRINKING 🍷
Burgundy's Wine Bar..............**28** B3
Ring O'Bells..........................**29** B4
Vats Bar............................(see 30)

ENTERTAINMENT 🎭
Brewery Arts Centre...............**30** B3

TRANSPORT
Bus Station...........................**31** B2

INLAND CUMBRIA

THE FELL-WALKERS' FRIEND

Anyone who's tackled the Lake District's hills will already be familiar with the towering figure of Lakeland hill walking, Alfred Wainwright (known to his followers just as AW). Born in Blackburn in 1907, Wainwright was an accountant by trade, but fell head over heels for the fells following a climb up Orrest Head (p64) in 1930. It was a chance encounter that inspired a lifelong passion.

Having arranged a move to the Kendal treasurer's office in 1941, Wainwright spent every available weekend ranging the region's hilltops. Initially for his own amusement he began documenting his walks through journals, maps and pen-and-ink drawings, but the more he walked, the more Wainwright became dissatisfied with existing guidebooks, which gave little indication of the geological quirks of each individual fell. So it was in 1952 that he embarked on his great project: having divided the area into seven sections according to the Ordnance Survey maps, he resolved to climb 214 Lakeland fells, recording each route in painstaking detail.

Factoring in the time taken up by his daytime job as Borough Treasurer, he reckoned it would take 13 years to complete averaging roughly one hand-written page per day. His routine was nearly always identical: he would rise early, travel to the Lakes by bus, climb all day, treat himself to a fish-and-chip supper, and then spend the following week writing up his notes and drawing illustrations from photographs he had taken while out on the hills.

When he first started Wainwright had fairly vague intentions of producing a book, but it soon became apparent that he was creating something unique: part walking guide, part illustrated artwork and part philosophical memoir. Helped by a local printer and his friend Henry Marshall (Kendal's chief librarian) Wainwright published his first volume, *The Eastern Fells* in 1955. It was an instant success and led to six subsequent books; the last volume, the *Western Fells,* was completed in 1966, exactly according to the schedule Wainwright had set himself. The original guides were followed by new books to the *Pennine Way* and the *Coast-to-Coast* (a long-distance route that he devised in 1973). Well over two million Wainwright books have now been sold since their original publication, but despite their success, the books were never a money-making scheme for Wainwright: he gave away most of his profits to local animal charities.

Wainwright died in 1991, and his ashes were scattered over the top of Haystacks, his favourite mountain. The guides have recently been updated by Wainwright's walking disciple, Chris Jesty, as requested in the great man's will, and the **Wainwright Society** (www.wainwright.org.uk) keeps an official record of the walkers who have climbed all 214 of AW's beloved summits. The BBC has even got in on the act with two series' worth of 'Wainwright Walks', fronted by Julia Bradbury.

SLEEPING

Kendal YHA (☎ 0845 371 9641; kendal@yha.org.uk; 118 Highgate; dm from £16.95; ⏰ reception 7.30am-10am & 1-11.30pm; 🖥) Housed in a mid-18th-century building next to the Brewery Arts Centre, this venerable hostel is a bit musty, but it's still the town's best budget base. Dorms are mostly four- to eight-bed, there's a spacious TV room and a pool room on the ground floor, but no kitchen.

Highgate Hotel (☎ 01539-724229; www.highgatehotel.co.uk; 128 Highgate; s/d/f £39/60/84; P) Built for Kendal's first doctor, this black-and-white town house could do with a spruce up, but it's pleasant enough, if far from plush. Large rooms have simple colour schemes, big chests of drawers and spongy beds, and you can plump for a view of street or car park.

Balcony House (☎ 01539-731402; www.balconyhouse.co.uk; 82 Shap Rd; s/d/f £40/60/75) Traditional B&B with a choice of doubles or twins, a spacious family room or a frilly four-poster suite. The decor's nothing special – stripy wallpaper, rosy prints – but luxuries include bathrobes, minifridges and DVD players in every room.

Heaves Hotel (☎ 01539-560396; www.heaveshotel.com; Heaves; s from £40, d £62-72; P) For truly regal digs head 4 miles south of Kendal along the A591 to this stately mansion, owned by the same well-to-do family for the last century. It's awash with extravagant Georgian features – stately staircases, corniced hallways, four-poster rooms – and cracking views of Austenesque parkland unfurl from every window. Go for the Gandy Room for something truly special.

Beech House (☎ 01539-720385; www.beechhouse
-kendal.co.uk; 40 Greenside; s £45-75, d £70-90; P 🛜)
Top B&B choice in Kendal by a country mile,
with a really inviting line-up of rooms: some
have velvet sofas and posh cushions, others
roll-top baths and his-and-hers sinks. The
overall feel is fresh and friendly; digital radios,
wi-fi and flat-screen TVs are standard.

EATING
Cafes
our pick **1657 Chocolate House** (☎ 01539-740702;
54 Branthwaite Brow; lunches £2-6) Chocaholics
can sink into cocoa-fuelled ecstasy at this
velvety-smooth cafe, where waitresses in
starched bonnets dish up 18 sorts of hot
chocolate including almondy Old Noll's
Potion, violet-infused Queen's Corsage or
bitter-choc Dungeon. Handmade chocs
and umpteen mintcake varieties are sold
in the cellar.

Cottage Kitchen (☎ 01539-722468; 24 Finkle St;
lunches £3-6; ☻ 9am-5pm Mon-Sat) Sheltering under
a cute blue awning, this longstanding Kendal
tearoom makes an ace place for morning
coffee or a country lunch; try three types
of scone (plain, fruit or cheese), authentic
cream teas (£3.50), or soup and a sandwich
for £5.

Waterside Wholefoods (☎ 01539-729743; Kent
View, Waterside; lunches £4-10; ☻ 8.30am-4.30pm Mon-
Sat) Chow down on chunky veggie chillis,
freshly made soups and wholemeal wraps at
this much-loved wholefood cafe. Needless to
say, ingredients are organic, locally sourced
and fair trade, and there are riverside tables
for when the sun peeps through the clouds.

Restaurants
Rococo Joes (☎ 01539-734655; 42 Stramongate; pizzas
£5.25-7.95; ☻ 10am-11pm Tue-Sat) Hand-spun dough
and unusual toppings including wild rocket,
goat's cheese, portobello mushrooms and
balsamic onion chutney make for the town's
top pizzas.

Grain Store (pizzas £6.50-7.95, mains £9.95-16.50;
☻ from 10am Mon-Sat) The Brewery Arts brasserie
is as buzzy and busy as ever. The gourmet
pizzas are still in evidence, plus hefty club
sandwiches and chargrilled wraps; things get
more sophisticated by night, with mains of
Barbary duck and Cloonacool Arctic char.

New Moon (☎ 01539-729254; 129 Highgate; mains
£9.50-14.95; ☻ lunch & dinner Tue-Sat) Kendal's flock

of fooderati come here for Med flavours mixed
with British ingredients. The decor is contemporary – clean lines and funky cutlery while
the menu ranges from lamb meatballs to a
huge 'Cumberland skillet'. The two-course
pre-theatre menu, served before 7pm, is great
value at £9.95.

Chang Thai (☎ 01539-720387; 54 Stramongate; mains
£9.95-15; ☻ dinner Tue-Sat) Thai food with a dash
of real class. Try *pla raad phrik* (crispy sea
bream) or *yum talay* (mussels, prawns and
squid), served up among rich burgundy wallpapers and dark-wood Buddhas.

Self-Catering
Kendal's **farmers market** is one of the county's best, and is held in Market Pl on the
final Friday of every month from 9.30am
to 3.30pm.

The town has two large supermarkets including an outpost of **Booth's** (☎ 01539-742370;
☻ 8am-7pm Mon-Sat, 10am-4pm Sun) in Wainwrights
Yard and a **Marks & Spencer** (☎ 01539-720665; Library
Rd) nearby.

Tucked away down a tiny backstreet, the
Staff of Life (☎ 01539-738606; www.artisanbreadmakers
.co.uk; Finkle St) bakes wonderful artisan breads,
while you can pick up olives, hummus and
deli treats at nearby **Baba Ganoush** (☎ 01539-
731072; 27 Finkle St).

DRINKING
Vats Bar (☎ 01539-725133; Highgate) Kendal's arty
set meet up to quaff cappuccinos and ales
around vintage beer vats at the Brewery Arts
Centre bar.

Burgundy's Wine Bar (☎ 01539-733803; 19 Lowther
St; ☻ 6.30pm-midnight Tue-Sat plus 11am-3.30pm Thu-
Sat, 7pm-midnight Sun) Despite the wine-bar tag,
this is one of the town's most down-to-
earth boozers, covered in old beer signs and
enough Scotch whiskies to keep you sozzled
till Christmas.

Ring O' Bells (☎ 01539-720326; Kirkland) The pick
of the town's pubs, where even the beer is
blessed – it's on consecrated ground next to
the parish church.

ENTERTAINMENT
Brewery Arts Centre (☎ 01539-725133; www.brewery
arts.co.uk; Highgate) Kendal's old brewery is now
an excellent arts complex, with two cinemas,
gallery space, a cafe, and a theatre hosting
dance, performance and live music.

GETTING THERE & AROUND
Bus
Kendal's handiest bus is the Lakeslink 555/556 (hourly Monday to Saturday, 10 on Sunday), which leaves Kendal en route to Windermere (30 minutes), Ambleside (40 minutes) and Grasmere (one hour), or Lancaster (one hour) in the opposite direction.

There are two daily buses from Kendal to Coniston (bus 505, one hour) via Windermere, Ambleside and Hawkshead, while the X35 travels south to Grange before returning via Haverthwaite Station, Ulverston and Barrow (hourly Monday to Saturday, four on Sunday).

Train
Kendal is on the Windermere (£3.50, 15 minutes, hourly) branch line from Oxenholme, which links up with the main West Coast line.

AROUND KENDAL

SIZERGH CASTLE
Three and a half miles south of Kendal along the A591, **Sizergh Castle** (☎ 015395-60070; adult/child £7.10/3.60, gardens only £4.70/2.40; ☺ gardens 11-5pm Sun-Thu mid-Mar–Nov, castle 1-5pm Sun-Thu mid-Mar–Nov) is renowned for its pele tower, built to protect the inhabitants from border raiders, and for the glowing Elizabethan-era wood panelling on display in the Inlaid Chamber, which was sold to London's Victoria & Albert Museum during hard times, and later returned after 100 years. The house is the feudal seat of the Strickland family, who have lived here for over seven centuries; look out for portraits of family notables as you wander around the house.

LOW SIZERGH BARN
For all-round Cumbrian deliciousness, the wonderful farm shop at **Low Sizergh Barn** (☎ 015395-60426; www.lowsizerghbarn.co.uk) stocks some of the Lakeland's finest home-grown produce – chutneys, honeys, jams and Cumbrian pudding, as well as milk, cheeses and other dairy goods from a 100% organic herd. The barn, which also boasts a craft gallery and a tearoom with views, is located on the A591 about half a mile south from Sizergh Castle.

LEVENS HALL
Two miles further southwest, just off the A6, is **Levens Hall** (☎ 015395-60321; www.levenshall.co.uk; house & gardens adult/child £10.50/4.50, gardens only £7/3.50; ☺ gardens 10am-5pm, house noon-5pm Sun-Thu Apr–mid-Oct), another fine Elizabethan manor built around a mid-13th-century pele tower. Jacobean furniture is on display throughout the house, and there are plenty of decorative quirks to pique your interest – items on display include Wellington's watch and Cromwell's suit of armour, while the stately dining room is (bizarrely) clad in burnished goat's leather. But the real draw is the stunning 17th-century topiary garden, a surreal riot of pyramids, swirls, curls, pompoms and peacocks straight out of *Alice in Wonderland*.

Once you've worked up an appetite, you can pop into the hall's lovely **Bellingham Buttery** (☺ 10am-5pm Sun-Thu) for a bottle or two of the house speciality, Morocco Ale, prepared to a secret recipe laid down in Elizabethan times.

The 555/556 (hourly Monday to Saturday) from Grasmere, Ambleside, Windermere and Kendal runs past the castle gates.

Directory

CONTENTS

This chapter provides general practical information for the whole of Cumbria and the Lake District. If you're looking for something more specific, consult the relevant area chapter or the Getting Started chapter (p18).

ACCOMMODATION

Whether it's historic country houses, boutique hotels, bargain-basement B&Bs or grandstand campsites, the Lake District has somewhere to stay to suit all tastes (and budgets). But while there's no shortage of accommodation, there's also no getting around the fact that this is far from the cheapest corner of England – especially if you pitch up in the high season in July and August, when space and prices are at a premium. Booking ahead, shifting your visit to the shoulder months, and opting for B&Bs and guest houses rather than pricey hotels can all help strip back the costs.

Where appropriate we've split our reviews into three categories – budget (under £50), midrange (£50 to £120) and top end (more than £120). We've generally quoted full prices for a double room in high season, so you might find some places will cut a deal in the quieter months. Broadly speaking the

standards of accommodation are high, although obviously you'll buy more creature comforts and designer flourishes the higher you move up the price ladder. There are a couple of accommodation-rating schemes that provide a rough (if generic) guide to standards – Visit Britain uses a one to five rosette rating, while the AA uses a one to five star rating. Both schemes tend to concentrate harder on facilities than on subjective impressions.

The **regional tourist board** (☎ 0845 450 1199; www.golakes.co.uk) is a useful place to start your search, and will arrange bookings for a £3 fee.

B&Bs and Guest Houses

The good old British B&B has taken its share of brickbats over the years – some deserved, some not so – and while the tired old clichés about chintzy wallpaper, Stalinesque landladies and saggy mattresses might still hold true for a few establishments, the average B&B has come on in leaps and bounds in recent years. With a little pre-trip research (and the help of this guidebook) you'll discover some seriously impressive places around the Lakes, including some that give the top-end hotels a run for their money.

The average B&B bed starts at around £30 to £40 for a single, or £60 to £80 for a double. Most B&Bs offer en suite or private bathrooms these days, but plumping for shared facilities can knock a few quid off the price tag. Even the most basic places offer clean (but not necessarily up-to-date) bedrooms and bathrooms, and a full fried breakfast (included in the room price), not to mention those essential items: twin-pack bickies, foil-wrapped teabags, UHT milk pots and, of course, a pocket-sized kettle. You'll nearly always have your own key to your room as well as the front door – thankfully the days of rigidly enforced B&B curfews (memorably recounted in Bill Bryson's *Notes from a Small Island*) are mostly a thing of the past.

It's worth remembering that many B&Bs don't accept credit or debit cards, and even if they do you might find a transaction charge added to your bill to cover the bank fees.

DIRECTORY

Camping

Whether you're a hiker keen to get a head start on the trail or a city type looking to rediscover the sights, sounds and smells of the countryside, for many people camping out is an essential part of the Lake District experience. There are some fantastic locations to choose from, ranging from spit-and-sawdust farm sites to facility-packed places loaded with the luxuries of a five-star resort. Some sites are geared towards caravans and motor homes, while others are tents only. At the simplest end of the spectrum, you'll be lucky to find much more than a field, a cold-water tap and a toilet block, but the fancier sites boast their own farm shops and even ecofriendly sleeping pods made from sustainably sourced timber. You can even stay in an authentic Mongolian yurt near Rydal Hall (p96) or a Sioux-style tipi near Newby Bridge (p72). For our top 10 favourites, see p21.

There are comprehensive listings at www .lakedistrictcamping.co.uk, and you can find out about the National Trust's three basic but spectacularly-sited campgrounds at www .nationaltrust.org.uk/campsites/lakedistrict. All the prices given in this book are for a tent and two adults unless otherwise stated. Generally you'll need to arrive before 10pm and leave by 11am the following morning, although policies vary at each campsite; not all places accept credit card payments, so check before you arrive.

Camping Barns

For campers who prefer something a little sturdier over their heads than a nylon flysheet, camping barns provide a bit more cover. The general rule is to imagine you're camping, but under a 'stone tent'; facilities generally include sleeping platforms, cold running water and a flush toilet, although some also offer cooking equipment, hot water, showers and a log fire, but you'll need your own sleeping bag and other camping gear. There are listings of over 15 barns at www.lakelandcam pingbarns.co.uk.

Hostels

In many ways the history of hostelling began right here in the Lake District – Thorney How, near Grasmere, was the first property purchased by the **YHA** (Youth Hostel Association; ☎ 0870 770 8868; www.yha.org.uk) back in 1931. The original ethos of the organisation was to provide friendly, affordable accommodation to enable more people to experience the pleasures of the English landscape, but things have moved on a long way since its foundation in the 1930s. Don't expect the drab, pre-fab buildings you may be used to elsewhere – the YHA has some truly stunning Lake District buildings, ranging from converted farmhouses and miners' cottages right through to a couple of converted mansions.

As always, facilities, rooms and standards of accommodation at each hostel are very different. Dorms are the norm, although a limited number of doubles and family rooms are available at many hostels; most have shared bathrooms and showers, as well as a TV lounge and usually a kitchen for guest use. Some also offer breakfast, usually included in the room price. Duvets, sheets and towels are provided at nearly all hostels. Prices range from around £9 to £15 per adult, or £6 to £10 per child depending on the hostel and season. Membership of the YHA offers a discount of up to £3 on the standard nightly fee and annual costs are £15.95 for adults, £9.95 for under-26s or £22.95 for two adults and their dependents. Unsurprisingly the Lake District YHAs are some of the busiest in the country and often get booked out during weekends and holidays, so plan ahead.

As well as the YHA hostels, there are independent hostels in Grasmere (p92), Windermere (p65) and Ulverston (p186). The **YMCA** (☎ 015395-31743; www.ymca.org.uk) also has its main outdoors centre at Lakeside on Windermere, although it tends to be booked out by activity holidays and school groups.

Hotels

There are lots of landmark country hotels scattered around the Lake District, ranging from historic hikers' hangouts such as the Old Dungeon Ghyll (p100) in Langdale to old-fashioned country pamper-pads such as Sharrow Bay (p170) and the Holbeck Ghyll (p68) in Windermere. The boundary between top-end B&Bs and hotels can sometimes be blurry, but in general you'll find hotels offer a higher standard of accommodation and service, as well as more comprehensive facilities such as gyms, in-house restaurants and swimming pools. Prices vary, but the cheapest hotels are likely to set you back between £100 and £120 per night, rocketing up to £250 or more at some of the fancier establishments.

It's worth figuring out what you're paying for to avoid disappointment – some of the newer Lake District hotels have opted for a strictly contemporary finish, while many of the older establishments have stuck doggedly to the frills-and-flounces Laura Ashley line.

Pubs & Inns

Coaching inns have been a feature of the Lakeland scenery for centuries (inns were often whitewashed to make them stand out to passing travellers). While a few flagship inns have gone down the upmarket gastropub route, most of the pubs in the Lake District are pretty traditional in feel, with plenty of slate flagstones, wood panelling and open fires, and with old-style rooms to match. Pubs generally charge similar room prices to B&Bs; count on £50 to £80 for a double.

Pubs are often the centre of the local social scene, especially in the smaller villages, and many have also established themselves as longstanding après-hike venues, so they're often a good place to hook up with fellow walkers and swap stories over a pint of ale or three.

Several have also established their own microbreweries – see p49 for some of our favourites.

Rental Cottages

Staying in B&Bs, especially if you're travelling *en famille*, can work out to be expensive, so many people plump instead for renting their own home away from home. There are hundreds and hundreds of rental properties in the Lakes – so many, in fact, that they've become a serious problem for many villages, where self-caterers often outnumber residents by a considerable margin in the summer months.

There's no doubt, however, that renting a cottage is one of the most cost-effective ways to visit the region, although facilities and standards vary widely and some properties can be plonked miles away from the nearest village, so it's worth thoroughly researching the surrounding area beforehand.

Coppermines & Lakes Cottages (☎ 015394-41765; www.coppermines.co.uk) The place to go if you're after a bolthole in the Coniston area.

Cumbrian Cottages (☎ 01228-599960; www.cumbrian -cottages.co.uk) More than 900 properties scattered across the county, including deluxe, pet-friendly and family-specific choices.

BOOK ACCOMMODATION ONLINE

For more accommodation reviews and recommendations by Lonely Planet authors, check out the online booking service at www.lonelyplanet.com. You'll find the true, insider low-down on the best places to stay. Reviews are thorough and independent. Best of all, you can book online.

Heart of the Lakes (☎ 015394-32321; www.heartof thelakes.co.uk) One of the best all-round selections in the Central Lakes, with a smaller section in Keswick and Ullswater.

Keswick Cottages (☎ 017687-78555; www.keswick cottages.co.uk) Unsurprisingly the specialist for Keswick, Braithwaite and the Newlands Valley.

Lakeland Cottage Company (☎ 015395-76065; www.lakelandcottages.co.uk) Plenty of properties in Windermere, Ambleside, Keswick, Ullswater, Borrowdale and the western Lakes.

Lakelovers (☎ 015394-88855; www.lakelovers.co.uk) Good-quality accommodation mainly based around the southern Lakes, with a mix of period and modern choices.

National Trust Cottages (☎ 0844 800 2070; www .nationaltrustcottages.co.uk) A limited selection of National Trust properties, most packed with period character.

Wheelwrights (☎ 015394-37635; www.wheelwrights .com) Loads of choice in and around Ambleside, Grasmere and the Langdale Valleys.

Windermere Lake Holidays (☎ 015394-43415; www.lakewindermere.net) Waterfront apartments and even a few houseboats available for rent.

ACTIVITIES

There's no shortage of ways to fill your days in the Lakes, especially if you're a lover of the great outdoors. Check out our special Outdoors colour section (p101) for advice on activities in the Lake District, or visit the excellent website at www.lakedistrictoutdoors.co.uk.

Activity Centres

Keen to get out in the countryside? Not sure what sport will suit? The following activity providers offer taster sessions of different outdoor pursuits.

Country Adventures (☎ 01254-690691; www.country -adventures.co.uk) Traditional outfit focussed on hill walking, scrambling and climbing.

Holmescales (☎ 01539-722147; www.holmescales .com; Old Hutton) Toys for big kids, including paintballing, quad biking, archery, shooting and amphibious 'Argo Cats'.

Kankku (☎ 015394-47414; www.kankku.co.uk; Windermere) Rattle out those loose fillings in an off-road 4WD adventure.

Outward Bound (☎ 0870 513 4227; www.outward bound-uk.org; Eskdale Green & Ullswater) The longstanding British favourite, especially among school and youth groups. Rafting, canoeing, abseiling – you name it, they do it. On-site accommodation is also available at both of the activity centres.

River Deep Mountain High (☎ 015395-31116; www .riverdeepmountainhigh.co.uk; Haverthwaite) Specialist in multi-activity holidays with weekend and weeklong breaks incorporating sailing, biking, kayaking, abseiling, and practically every other outdoor sport.

Rookin House (☎ 017684-83561; www.rookinhouse .co.uk; near Ullswater) Ever wanted to shoot a bow, steer a JCB, canter on a pony and drive an amphibious quad bike – all in the same weekend? Rookin House can help.

Summitreks (☎ 015394-41212; www.summitreks .co.uk; Coniston & Hawkshead) Long-established activity company offering everything from canoeing and ghyll scrambling to guided walks and orienteering.

Climbing

For advice on climbing in the Lakes, contact the **British Mountaineering Council** (☎ 0870 010 4878; www.thebmc.co.uk) or the **Fell & Rock Climbing Club** (www.frcc.co.uk), which publishes the definitive guidebook series covering Lakeland climbs. You might want to hone your skills on the climbing walls in Kendal and Keswick before you tackle the real thing; otherwise contact the following organisations for specific rock-climbing and mountaineering tuition:

Above the Line (☎ 019467-26229; www.wasdale.com; Wasdale Head)

Harold Edwards Mountaineering (☎ 019467-26229; www.haroldedwardsmountaineering.co.uk; Hutton Roof)

High Point (☎ 01931-713115; www.mountainguides .co.uk; Bampton)

Joint Adventures (☎ 015394-41526; www.jointadven tures.co.uk; Coniston)

Cycling

For something more adventurous than an easy day's spin around the Lakeland countryside, several travel companies offer special cycling packages specifically tailored around your routes and experience. Usually they'll provide self-guided route maps and sort out your accommodation en route; many also provide luggage transfers.

2 Wheel Treks (☎ 0845 612 6106; www.2wheeltreks .co.uk/cycling_lake_district.htm) National operator with a couple of Lake District–specific packages.

Country Lanes (☎ 015394-44544; www.country laneslakedistrict.co.uk; Windermere) Self-guided cycle tours lasting between three and seven days, offered by experienced Windermere-based company.

Cyclewise Training (☎ 017687-898775; www.cycle wisetraining.co.uk) Mountain bike tuition with the Whinlatter Forest on your doorstep.

Discovery Travel (☎ 01904-632226; www.discovery travel.co.uk) Specialises in long distance cycling tours of the Sea to Sea Cycle Route (C2C) and Hadrian's Cycleway.

Mickledore Travel (☎ 017687-72335; www.mickle dore.co.uk) Three long-distance routes including the C2C, Hadrian's Cycleway and a 'Reiver's Route' taking in Carlisle, Cockermouth and Whitehaven.

Fishing

The Lake District has some excellent fishing, whether it's for rainbow and brown trout at Esthwaite Water or for pike, perch and Arctic char at Windermere. You'll need a valid rod licence, available from the **Environment Agency** (☎ 08708 506 506; www.environment-agency.gov .uk), local tourist offices and some post offices; not all lakes are open to fishing and some operate catch-and-release policies, so make sure you know what the score is before you cast a line. Live bait is prohibited in many lakes as it increases the risk of disease and pest species.

The website www.lakedistrictfishing.net is a good place for general angling-related info, with advice on fishing spots, recommended tackle, and links to local anglers who can provide tuition.

Bob Carlson (☎ 01539-733297, 07886-817770; www .flyfishingtuition.co.uk)

Cumbria Fly Fishing (☎ 016973-51752, 07808-563788; www.cumbriaflyfishing.co.uk)

English Lakes Fly Fishing (☎ 01229-889792; www .englishlakesflyfishing.co.uk)

Hemmingways (☎ 017687-78575, 07771-763067; www.hemmingwaysfish.co.uk)

Walking

If you want to extend your hill-walking skills and really become an accomplished walker, local hiking companies provide courses in map reading, navigation, compass skills and even mountain survival, while others can put together walk-and-sleep packages or provide guided walks to specific fells. For details on baggage transport services, see p232.

Contours (☎ 017684-80451; www.contours.co.uk) Big and very comprehensive provider, with organised tours to the Coast-to-Coast Walk, Cumbria Way and Dales Way, as well as 'rounds' of Ullswater and Coniston.

Discovery Travel (☎ 01904-766564; www.discovery travel.co.uk) National operator focusing on long-distance routes, including the Coast-to-Coast and the Cumbria Way.
Glenridding Walking Guides (☎ 01768-482797, 07762-637930; www.glenriddingguides.com; Glenridding) One of the best small-scale guiders; choose your fell and they'll provide someone to show you the way. Prices are £70 per half day (plus £10 for each extra person) or £120 per full day (plus £20 per extra person).
Knobbly Stick (☎ 01539-737576; www.knobblystick .com) Guided and unguided walking trips around several areas of the Lakes.
Striding Ahead (☎ 0845 638 1885; www.striding ahead.co.uk) Experienced operator providing guided walks to Coniston Old Man, the Langdale Pikes, Bowfell, Crinkle Crags, Blencathra, Helvellyn and Scafell Pike; if you want to work in some abseiling or climbing, no probs.
Touchstone Tours (☎ 017687-79599; www.touchstone tours.co.uk; Threlkeld) Navigation courses and specific fell walks (including Scafell Pike, Skiddaw and Helvellyn) – and dogs are welcome.

For general advice on walking in the Lakes, contact the **Ramblers Association** (☎ 0207-339-8500; www.ramblers.org.uk) or the **Lake District National Park Association** (☎ 01539-724555; www.lake-district .gov.uk), which organises lots of guided walks and rangers' talks throughout the year. It's also worth checking out some of the Lake District walking festivals, which are held in Ullswater, Ulverston, Coniston, Keswick and several other locations, and offer a varied program of guided walks to the summits of classic fells.

BUSINESS HOURS
Banks, Shops & Offices
Broadly speaking, most shops and businesses keep similar opening hours as the rest of England – 9am to 5.30pm Monday to Saturday, with many places also opening from around 10am to 4pm on Sunday. Supermarkets and convenience stores usually open earlier and close a bit later, from around 8am to 9pm on weekdays and Saturday, while post offices tend to stick to standard hours of 9am to 5.30pm Monday to Friday and 9am to 12.30pm on Saturday. Only a few banks open on Saturday, but you'll usually find a 24-hour ATM at most of the larger branches. We've used these hours as standard for all our listings throughout this book, and have only added specific opening hours if they differ greatly from the norm. In low season (especially in winter), and outside the larger towns,

opening hours tend to be a lot shorter – it's not uncommon for some village shops to shut up early for the day if things are quiet.

Museums & Sights
Museums and sights generally operate according to the same hours as other businesses, but hours tend to be longer in the summer months to cater for the extra visitors, and some places shut up shop completely for the winter season.

Pubs, Bars & Clubs
Despite the controversial introduction of round-the-clock licences, the vast majority of pubs still tend to stick to tried-and-tested hours. Most open for lunchtime punters from around noon, although some also open for morning coffee from around 10am; it's not unusual for pubs (especially those outside the main towns) to close after lunch, usually at 3pm, before reopening for the evening trade at 7pm. Kicking-out time is traditionally 11pm, but some pubs run a later licence until midnight, and some of the big-city boozers stay open till the wee small hours.

Restaurants & Cafes
Most cafes open from around 9am to 5.30pm Monday to Saturday, and sometimes on Sunday too; you might find some establishments also open a couple of nights at the weekend for dinner. Restaurants vary widely – standard hours for lunch are from noon till 2pm, and for dinner from 6pm to 10pm; most close at least one day a week, although not always on Sunday. It's worth booking ahead at the more popular places.

CHILDREN
Kids will be spoilt for choice for things to do in the Lake District – they could easily fill their days canoeing, cycling, kayaking, sailing, bike riding, horse riding, ghyll scrambling or practically any other outdoor activity you care to think of. For general information, advice and anecdotes, consult Lonely Planet's *Travel with Children*.

The two Go Ape parks at Grizedale (p122) and Whinlatter (p156) and the Keswick Climbing Wall (p149) are especially popular with little monkeys, while braver young 'uns might well love tackling the new high-altitude Via Ferrata walk at Honister Slate Mine (p163). Steam trains are another good

SAFE HIKING

While the Lakeland fells lack the stature of many of the world's larger mountains, they are certainly not without their dangers. The main cause of trouble comes from people not being properly prepared. Once you get off the beaten track in the Lake District, trails are often rough, exposed and indistinct, signposts are few and far between, and the weather can change dramatically without warning, so it pays to spend a little time preparing before you set out to avoid potential problems later on.

Firstly, pack the appropriate equipment and supplies including map, compass and rainwear, as well as insulating base layers that you can put on and remove easily according to the weather. Gore-Tex or an equivalent breathable material is recommended for outer layers as it allows moisture to evaporate from your skin and keep you cool. Pack plenty of food and water – at least 2L of water per person for a full-day hike – and carry a few energy bars for emergencies.

Next, prepare your route. Consult good-quality maps and guidebooks before you set out, and choose a route that's appropriate for your fitness and ability levels. Allow ample time for the walk, and ask around for local advice about any new hazards that may have cropped up along the route.

It's pointless carrying a compass unless you know how to use it, so if you're a novice walker, a day spent brushing up on your navigational skills with a local walking company (p218) might be a worthwhile investment.

On the day of your walk, check the weather forecast before you leave, hike in pairs or groups, let someone know your intended route and estimated time of return, and carry a mobile phone in case you need to call the emergency services. Most importantly, be prepared for rapid changes in the weather – the high fells can be difficult to navigate in mist and cloud, and every year there are cases of people becoming lost and wandering over the edge of an unseen crag.

bet for kids, especially the scenic Lakeside and Haverthwaite Railway (p71) and the teeny trains of the Ravenglass and Eskdale Railway (p130). There are good aquariums at Lakeside (p72) and Maryport (p192) as well as the Osprey Information Centre at Whinlatter (p156) if the weather takes a turn for the worse. And don't rule out the fells – if you pick your walk carefully, children can get a real kick out of the Lakeland scenery.

Local tourist offices sometimes offer specific events aimed at kids, such as guided walks with National Park Authority (NPA) staff and outdoor activity days, so ask around to find out what's available during your stay. Practically every visitor attraction offers discounted admission prices for children; consult relevant listings throughout the book.

Remember not all hotels and B&Bs accommodate children, so ask about their policy before you book to avoid any embarrassing moments later on. The same goes for pubs and restaurants; children are often not allowed in pubs after certain hours, so ask behind the bar before you sit down. Baby-changing facilities can also be tough to come by, although most of the larger attractions will have a child-friendly loo.

CLIMATE

If there's one word that sums up the Cumbrian weather, it's *changeable*. You'll often find all four seasons packed into a single day – bright sunshine can turn to thick mist and torrential showers in the space of an hour, so it's well worth keeping up to date with the forecast, especially if you're planning on spending any time outdoors. And while the Lake District is renowned as one of the most verdant corners of England, there's an obvious price to be paid for all that greenness – the region receives the highest annual rainfall of any of England's counties.

For more advice on the weather and how to prepare for it, see p18.

DANGERS & ANNOYANCES

Compared with many places, the Lake District is a safe place to travel, and as long as you apply the usual common sense rules, you shouldn't run into too much trouble. As always, don't carry around too much cash, keep your wits about you at cashpoints and ATM machines, and if you're travelling from overseas, carry separate copies of your passport, driving licence, travel insurance and other travel documents.

Theft from cars is one of the most common problems, especially since many hikers tend to leave their cars in remote places, often for several hours at a time. Make sure there are no valuables in view, take out your car stereo (and remember to turn off your headlights).

It's also worth remembering that most of the lakes are cold and deep, and currents can be surprisingly strong, so they're not really ideal for a paddle – many are also off limits to swimmers, so check up before you dive in.

DISCOUNT CARDS

The Lake District's perennial popularity means that prices tend towards the expensive end, but with a bit of forward planning you can pick up some handy discounts.

There are several regional travel passes covering trains, buses or both, which are outlined in detail in the Transport chapter (p226), and if you're planning on staying in several hostels a YHA membership card is also well worth having.

If you're doing a lot of sightseeing (especially if you're a fan of historic houses and gardens), membership of the **National Trust** (NT; ☎ 0870 458 4000; www.nationaltrust.org.uk) is a really worthwhile investment. Standard prices are £46/77/82 per adult/couple/family per year; children and young people from ages five to 25 cost £15.75, while under-fives are free. Pensioners who have been members of the NT for five years can rejoin for £32. You can usually get a discount by joining online and paying by direct debit, or join at any participating properties. The Trust owns a number of the area's most historic buildings, including Dove Cottage in Grasmere (p87), Wordsworth House in Cockermouth (p157) and Hill Top (p123), as well as a whole string of glorious gardens and beauty spots including Fell Foot Park (p71). National Trust membership also grants free parking in the Trust's many car parks. US visitors who belong to the **Royal Oak Foundation** (www.royal-oak.org) also qualify for free entry to National Trust properties.

English Heritage (EH; ☎ 0870 333 1181; www.english-heritage.org.uk) also owns several properties in Cumbria including Carlisle Castle (p197), Shap Abbey (p176), Lanercost Priory (p202) and Birdoswald Roman Fort (p203). An annual membership costs £42/73 per adult/couple, while under 19s and students can join for £32, and over 60s for £30/49 per person/couple.

FOOD

Stopping for sustenance is a real highlight of any visit to the Lakes, with plenty of hearty nosh to tuck into from farm-fresh cheese to tender fellbred lamb and tatie hotpot. Food is generally of a high standard, and there are usually veggie-friendly options on most menus – see p45 for details of some of the local specialities to look out for. Where appropriate, we've split our price ranges into budget categories based on a main course: budget up to £8, midrange £8 to £16 and top end over £16.

GAY & LESBIAN TRAVELLERS

The Lake District isn't really renowned for its gay scene, but equally you're unlikely to run into too much hostility either; life in the Lakes is pretty laid-back, and you'll find most places are fairly tolerant. There's a small gay scene in Carlisle, and you'll find the county's only gay pub at the **Steam Packet Inn** (☎ 01900-62186; Stanley St) in Workington. For more advice take a look at the handy websites www.gaycumbria.com and www.iknow-lakedistrict.co.uk/information/gay_friendly.htm.

HOLIDAYS

Nearly all banks and businesses close for official public holidays:
New Year's Day 1 January
Easter Good Friday and Easter Sunday, Mar/Apr
May Day First Monday in May
Spring Bank Holiday Last Monday in May
Summer Bank Holiday Last Monday in August
Christmas Day 25 December
Boxing Day 26 December

Many (but certainly not all) tourist attractions stay open on Bank Holidays to take advantage of the holiday trade. Practically everywhere shuts up shop on Christmas Day. Other busy times to look out for are the main school holidays, as well as the weeklong half-term breaks, when traffic jams and crowds are likely to be substantially worse – it's worth finding out the dates in advance if you prefer the quiet life. The dates vary every year, but are generally:
Christmas Mid-December to early January
Easter Week before and week after Easter
Summer Mid-July to early September

DIRECTORY

INSURANCE

A decent travel insurance policy is always a worthwhile investment. Check the policy carefully to make sure it covers you for common problems such as travel hold-ups, luggage loss, theft, and flight delays, and also on the extent of cover for less frequent events such as flooding and weather damage (rare, but not unprecedented in Cumbria). Unlike many European countries, you won't need a specific clause in your policy to cover you for rescue on the fells (mountain rescue in England is a voluntary service funded by charitable donations), but you will definitely need appropriate medical cover in case you need hospital treatment or emergency repatriation.

Worldwide travel insurance is available at www.lonelyplanet.com/travel_services. You can buy, extend and claim online anytime – even if you're already on the road.

INTERNATIONAL VISITORS
Entering the Region

If arriving from outside the UK at one of the nearby airports such as Manchester, Liverpool or Glasgow, a valid passport is necessary and a travel visa may be required. European Economic Area (EEA) citizens don't need a visa for either travel or work. Citizens of Australia, New Zealand, Canada and the US do not need a visa either, but are prohibited from working during their stay. Other passport holders should visit www.ukvisas.gov.uk or contact the local British embassy.

The gateway towns to the Lakes are Carlisle and Windermere, which connect with major train lines across the rest of the country, and Kendal and Penrith, both within easy access of the M6 motorway.

Money

Notes and coins from England and Scotland are legal tender in Cumbria. Notes are divided into £50, £20, £10 and £5 denominations. Coins are available in £2, £1, 50p, 20p, 10p, 5p, 2p and 1p denominations.

Credit and debit cards are both widely accepted, although many shops and businesses aren't set up to take American Express. 'Chip & PIN', where you enter a secret PIN at the till rather than signing a receipt, is now almost universal, and many supermarkets offer a 'cash back' service, where you can withdraw money at the till rather than having to find an ATM.

If you need to change money, most larger post offices offer currency exchange (usually commission free), as do nearly all branches of the major banks (although the exchange rates tend to be less favourable, and you may incur a commission charge). Travellers cheques, while useful, are a rarity in England – most banks will cash them for a fee.

Tipping at cafes and restaurants is not compulsory, but it's generally accepted practice to add 10% to 15% to the bill. Taxi drivers will expect around 10%.

Bargaining is generally only accepted practice at flea markets and jumble sales, or when buying high-value items (from an electrical store or antique shop, for example).

Post

Domestic and international postal services are handled by the Royal Mail, which provides services through local post offices. British post-boxes are painted an unmistakeable shade of scarlet. There are two main services: a First Class stamp (39p) is the most expensive, and generally guarantees domestic delivery for the next working day, while Second Class (30p) is cheaper and can take two or more days to arrive. International mail (including postcards) is best sent via First Class Airmail; a standard letter costs from 50p within the EU and from 56p worldwide. For the latest prices, visit www.royal mail.com.

Practicalities

True to their roots, the British have a bewilderingly inconsistent attitude to relatively simple things such as weighing themselves and measuring distances.

- Road distances are generally measured in miles but shorter distances are often measured in metres, while heights are usually given in feet and inches.
- Weights in shops and markets are usually given in pounds and ounces (although the equivalent in kilograms and grams is nearly always quoted).
- Petrol stations quote prices for both gallons and litres. Most other liquids are sold in litres or half-litres, except milk and beer – available in pints.
- The TV system in Britain is PAL. Analogue services are currently the norm, although the entire country will have switched over to a digital-only signal by 2012.

> **MOBILE BLUES**
>
> Mobile phone (or cell phone) coverage in the Lake District can be extremely patchy. The larger networks tend to have much better reception than some of the smaller operators, but it's sensible not to assume you'll automatically be able to get a crystal clear signal wherever you happen to be in the district.
>
> This is especially important when you're exploring the fells, where coverage is notoriously erratic – while it is always sensible to carry a mobile in case of emergencies, it's absolutely essential that you're not relying on it as your only back-up in case of emergency. A compass and map will never leave you stranded.

▪ British plugs have three flat parallel pins, and the electricity supply is 240V (50Hz AC). Adaptors for EU, US and Australian systems are widely available.

Telephone

Public telephones are widely available, although sadly the traditional red phone boxes are becoming an increasingly rare sight. Most public phones accept small change, and some also accept major credit or debit cards. Prepay phone cards can be bought from post offices and newsagents in £5, £10 and £20 denominations. Many pubs have a public telephone available for punters' use. The minimum call charge from public phones is 40p. For the operator dial ☎ 100, and for directory enquiries dial ☎ 118-118.

UK mobile phones use GSM 900/1800, which is compatible with both Europe and Australia, but often not with Japan or the US. You'll probably pay a small fortune in roaming charges if you use your phone abroad anyway, so you may be better off buying a temporary pay-as-you-go card (around £20 to £30) from newsagents or mobile phone shops.

Time

At least time in England is relatively uncomplicated – well, almost. Whichever part of the country you're in, you'll be slap-bang on GMT (Greenwich Mean Time) – one hour behind Paris, nine hours behind Tokyo, 11 hours behind Melbourne, or five hours ahead of New York. If you're here during British Summer Time from late March to early October, however, clocks are one hour ahead of GMT.

INTERNET ACCESS

The internet revolution has provided a much-needed communications lifeline for Cumbria (like many other rural areas in England), but since around 70% of the local population are hooked up to the net at home, the need for public cybercafes has declined greatly in recent years. Many hotels, B&Bs, restaurants and cafes will offer wi-fi access (usually, but not always, free of charge), but it's much rarer these days to see a modem port where you can plug in your laptop.

Many of the larger hostels also provide a computer for guests' use, but local libraries are one of the most convenient places to get online during your stay – practically all branches provide computer terminals with internet access for a small fee (at the time of writing £1 for the first half hour). You don't need to be a British citizen or a member of the library – just book yourself in at the reception desk and get surfing.

This book uses an internet icon (▣) to indicate a computer available for public internet use and a wi-fi icon (▢) to indicate wireless internet access. For online Lake District info, check out the Internet Resources section in the Getting Started chapter (p20).

MAPS

If you're planning on anything other than a low-level ramble, a good-quality map is not simply a useful accessory – it's absolutely essential. Relatively few Lakeland trails are waymarked along the route, and often signs at junctions simply indicate public bridleways or paths rather than specific trails, so maps provide a crucial reference tool. It's also vitally important that you're familiar with at least the basic skills of using a map and compass to navigate, just in case you get lost along your route – one of the major causes of call outs for the mountain rescue teams is people getting lost on the fells, so packing a compass (and knowing how to use it) is an absolute must.

Two companies produce detailed maps suitable for hiking, cycling and general exploring. The traditionalist's choice is **Ordnance Survey** (OS; www.ordnancesurvey.co.uk), which covers Cumbria and the wider Lake District with its orange-jacketed 1:25,000

DIRECTORY

WHAT'S UP WITH THE WEATHER?

There are several places you can go to check up on what the weather's likely to do – an absolutely essential pre-hike precaution – but you should always take the predictions with a hefty pinch of salt. The Lakeland weather is predictably unpredictable – so be prepared for all eventualities, just in case.

The **Lake District Weatherline** (☎ 0870 055 0575; www.lake-district.gov.uk/weatherline) provides a five-day forecast courtesy of the National Park Authority (NPA), while the **Mountain Weather Information Service** (www.mwis.org.uk) provides a downloadable forecast for the Lake District and Britain's other mountain parks. Meanwhile the **Met Office** (www.met-office.gov.uk) provides tailored forecasts for specific areas; you can search by region or input a town or postcode, and get predictions for weather, wind, rainfall, cloud, pressure, temperature and UV risk.

Explorer series. The level of detail is astonishing – public bridleways, trails, gradients and hill contours are all marked alongside even the smallest tarns, farmhouses and copses, not to mention hostels, inns, churches, bike-hire locations and major points of interest. Four maps (OL4 to OL7) cover the most popular Lake District areas; the standard copies are printed on high-quality fold-out paper, or there are more expensive waterproof versions.

Many walkers prefer the 1:25,000 *Superwalker* series, published by **Harvey** (www.harveymaps.co.uk), specifically developed to provide clear, accurate mapping for hikers. There are six maps *(North, East, Central, Southeast, Southwest* and *West)*. All the main trails and routes are marked with bright, stand-out colours, with Wainwright's 214 official fells marked in bold red text. Although they sacrifice some of the finer landscape detail for clarity, they're arguably easier to use when you're out on the trail. They're also (theoretically) waterproof and tear proof.

If you're tackling a well-known walk, it's worth looking out for specific route guides in local tourist offices and bookshops. Altos produces a range of leaflets containing full route descriptions and 1:25,000 maps of some of the classic fells, including Helvellyn and Fairfield, Coniston and Langdale, and Scafell Pike and Great Gable, all cross-referenced with the relevant Wainwright guide.

For general use the Ordnance Survey 1:110,000 *Cumbria and the Lake District Travel Map* or the slightly more detailed 1:50,000 *Landranger* series (denoted by pink jackets) are worthwhile investments, while the *A-Z Lake District Visitors' Atlas & Guide* makes a handy tome to have stashed on the dashboard.

SOLO TRAVELLERS

There are no really specific dangers to look out for if you're travelling solo, apart from the damage it's going to do to your wallet. While some B&Bs have single-specific rooms, the vast majority of places (and nearly all hotels) just rent out a double room at a slightly reduced rate (usually between half and three-quarters of the standard price). Hostels are an obvious exception since dorms are shared and usually arranged along gender lines. Female travellers should take the usual precautions when walking alone at night, especially in Carlisle and the other larger towns.

TOURIST INFORMATION

The main regional tourist board for the Lake District is **Go Lakes** (www.golakes.co.uk), while there's comprehensive county-wide information available from **Visit Cumbria** (www.visitcumbria.com). There are tourist offices dotted all over the national park, although cutbacks in recent years have led to a number of controversial closures; we've listed all the relevant offices in the appropriate chapters. Useful websites:

Historic Carlisle (☎ 01228-625600; www.historic-carlisle.org.uk) Carlisle and Hadrian's Wall country.

I Know Lake District (www.iknow-lakedistrict.co.uk) Mainly accommodation listings split up by area.

Keswick (www.keswick.org) Keswick-specific site run by local tourism association.

Lake District National Park Authority (☎ 01539-724555; www.lake-district.gov.uk) Online portal for the NPA.

Lake District Peninsulas (☎ 01229-580742; www.lake-district-peninsulas.co.uk) Info on the southern coastal area around Coniston, Cartmel, Grange, Ulverston and Barrow.

South Lakeland (www.southlakeland.gov.uk) Council-run website covering the southeastern area between Kendal and Windermere.

Visit Eden (www.eden.gov.uk/tourism) Eden Valley and Penrith area information on the Eden District council site.

Western Lake District (☎ 01900-818741; www .western-lakedistrict.co.uk) Specific advice for the western national park.

TRAVELLERS WITH DISABILITIES

As in much of England, access for people with disabilities isn't always as good as it should be. Most of the better-known attractions have made a concerted effort to facilitate entry for wheelchair users, and to provide facilities for people with sight and hearing difficulties, but in many places the nature of the building inherently limits what can be achieved. Other attractions, such as the cruise boats, struggle to accommodate wheelchair users – the best advice is to phone ahead and ask what the specific operator thinks they'll be able to do (at least that way you'll save a wasted journey).

The same goes for B&Bs, hotels and restaurants – modern developments are legally required to offer wheelchair access, but the same rules don't apply to older buildings. Again, heritage and geography doesn't always make things easy – many pubs, restaurants and older guest houses simply can't convert the existing architecture to make it appropriate for disabled visitors. Local tourist offices often have lists of disabled-friendly accommodation, so they should probably be your first port of call for advice. There's also a searchable directory of wheelchair-friendly accommodation at www.iknow-lakedistrict .co.uk/information/disabled_access.htm.

The **Lake District NPA** (☎ 01539-724555; www .lake-district.gov.uk) has tried hard to improve its service for disabled customers. There are 21 specific 'Miles Without Stiles' routes that have been 'road tested' for buggy pushers and wheelchair users, including Tarn Hows and the Grasmere Riverside Path – details can be found at www.lake-district.gov.uk/index/ enjoying. The visitor centre at Brockhole is another place with excellent disabled access – push-wheelchairs are available for use inside the house, with electric-powered ones for use in the gardens, and there's a 'Brockmobile' electric bus to transport visitors from the car park to the visitor centre. A limited number of electric scooters are available for hire from the Bowness and Ullswater visitor centres.

Most buses and coaches, unfortunately, aren't set up to accommodate wheelchairs, although National Express will do its best to assist disabled travellers. Most modern trains have at least one carriage that is wheelchair-accessible, and often signs are in Braille – although the same can't be said for many station platforms.

National sources of information:

All Go Here (www.allgohere.com) Hotels and businesses that are certified disabled-friendly.

Disability UK (www.disabilityuk.com) Huge online directory including details of Shopmobility schemes.

VOLUNTEERING

Looking to do a little bit more than just sit back and savour the scenery? Volunteering has a long and distinguished heritage in the Lake District, and there are plenty of schemes that allow you to get involved in looking after the unique Lakeland landscape in a hands-on way. You could find yourself patching up a drystone wall, pulling out invasive plants or participating in a red squirrel spot – as long as you're prepared for some good old-fashioned graft (not to mention the whims of the Lakeland weather), you'll certainly feel fulfilled once the day is through.

Cumbria Wildlife Trust (☎ 01539-816300; www .cumbriawildlifetrust.org.uk) Conservation charity that runs programs in wildlife monitoring, tree planting, scrub clearance and boardwalk building.

Fix the Fells (☎ 015394-34633; www.fixthefells.co.uk) An ambitious project to repair hundreds of miles of damaged footpaths in the Lake District, run in conjunction with the National Trust. Group volunteer programs are offered at High Wray Basecamp, with shorter individual programs sometimes available.

Friends of the Lake District (☎ 01539-720788; www.fld.org.uk) Community-based charity that runs volunteer conservation days practically every week of the year. Brush up your skills in bracken control, hedge laying and woodland management.

National Park Authority Volunteer Scheme (☎ 01539-724555; www.lake-district.gov.uk) Official conservation programs run by the National Park, including wildlife surveys, litter clearing, tree replanting and footpath repair.

National Trust Working Holidays (☎ 0844 800 3099; www.nationaltrust.org.uk/workingholidays) The NT organises regular working holidays in the Lake District offering opportunities for everything from scrub clearing to drystone walling. Places are limited so you'll need to apply well ahead.

Transport

TRANSPORT

CONTENTS

Once upon a time Cumbria and the Lake District was one of the least accessible areas of England – the only route into the county from the south was via the treacherous trek across the sands of Morecambe Bay (a tradition still maintained by the Queen's Guide, see p182), and the northern roads were regularly harried by bands of bloodthirsty bandits from across the Scottish border. But ever since the arrival of the railway in 1847, this corner of England has become one of the nation's favourite rural getaways, and you'll find travel to the main Lakeland gateways of Kendal, Carlisle and Windermere is a doddle, with regular bus and train connections from both north and south.

For travel inside the national park, you'll be relying on either the local bus network or self-powered travel (whether that means car, bicycle or shanks' pony), since the railway comes to a dead halt at Windermere.

GETTING THERE & AWAY

AIR

Cumbria doesn't have its own airport, but there are several within a couple of hours' travel. The most useful is Manchester Airport, which has its own railway station offering direct train, coach and bus connections north to Windermere and Barrow-in-Furness. Other regional airports close by include Blackpool, Glasgow, Liverpool and Newcastle.

LAND

Bicycle

Several long-distance bike routes run through Cumbria, including the classic cross-Britain **Sea to Sea** (C2C; www.c2c-guide.co.uk) between Workington or Whitehaven and Sunderland or Tynemouth, the **Pennine Cycleway** (www.cycle-routes.org/penninecycleway), which travels through Kendal, Appleby and Penrith, **Hadrian's Cycleway** (www.cycle-routes.org/hadrians cycleway) from Ravenglass via the Cumbrian Coast and Carlisle to Tynemouth, and the **Walney to Wear** (www.cyclingw2w.info) between Walney Island, near Barrow-in-Furness, and Whitby in Northumberland. The popular **Reivers Route** (www.reivers-guide.co.uk) travels from Whitehaven via Caldbeck and Carlisle, before venturing east all the way to Tynemouth.

Sustrans (☎ 0845 113 0065; www.sustrans.org.uk) publishes comprehensive guidebooks and detailed maps to many of these routes.

For information on taking your bike on public transport, see the Bicycle section under Getting Around (p229).

Bus & Coach

National Express (www.nationalexpress.com) runs a coach up and down the M6, connecting London's Victoria Coach Station with Windermere (single/return £33/49, eight hours, one daily) via Birmingham, Preston, Lancaster, Carnforth and Kendal. From Windermere, the bus continues on to Ambleside, Grasmere and Keswick.

There are at least five buses a day from Manchester to Carlisle (single/return £24.50/37, three hours). Several buses travel via Preston, where you can catch the onward bus to Windermere and the Lakes (single/return £20.40/31.50). Services from other destinations, including Leeds, Liverpool, York and Manchester Airport, usually change at Manchester city centre and connect through Preston on to the Lake District. If you're travelling from the south of England, you'll need to change coaches at London or Birmingham for the daily bus north to the Lakes.

From Scotland, there are several services from Glasgow and Edinburgh to Carlisle (£17.70, two hours, nine daily). If you're heading on to the Lakes, you're better off catching a local bus or train from Carlisle, since the National Express coach travels south to Preston before linking up with the daily bus into the Lake District en route from London and Birmingham (adding at least three hours onto your journey).

Car & Motorcycle

The M6 cuts through the east side of Cumbria, passing close to the Lake District's three gateway towns: Kendal (southbound take junction 39 onto the A6, northbound take junction 36 onto the A590), Penrith (junction 40) and Carlisle (follow junction 43 for the city centre). Count on a journey of around five hours from London, an hour and a half from Manchester or Liverpool, and a couple of hours from Glasgow or Edinburgh, and allow extra time for traffic once you get to the Lakes (especially during the peak season from July to August and Bank Holiday weekends). BBC Radio Cumbria and other local radio stations carry regular traffic reports that can give you the heads-up on traffic black spots.

Train

Despite the omnipresent delays, diversions and dreaded 'engineering works', there's no doubt that travelling by train is one of the most convenient and hassle-free ways to arrive in Cumbria. In general the main intercity trains are reliable, comfortable and efficient.

Virgin Trains (☎ 08457 222 333; www.virgintrains .co.uk) is the major intercity operator, owned and run by Richard Branson's Virgin empire. Virgin runs the main West Coast line between London Euston and Scotland, which zips up England's western edge stopping at Manchester, Preston, Lancaster, Oxenholme, Penrith and Carlisle, before continuing to either Glasgow or Edinburgh. For travel to the Lake District, there's a branch line from Oxenholme via Kendal, Burneside, Staveley and Windermere; some trains travel direct, for others you'll need to change at Oxenholme or Lancaster.

Intercity trains run hourly Monday to Friday, with around five to seven direct trains on weekends. It's a journey of around 3½ hours from London to Windermere, and between two and three hours from either Edinburgh or Glasgow. Most services are provided by Virgin's 'Pendolino' or 'Super Voyager' trains, with power points for charging laptops and mobile phones and a multi-channel entertainment system. Sample fares into the Lake District: London to Oxenholme to Windermere costs £82.30 off-peak and £133 anytime; Manchester to Oxenholme

CLIMATE CHANGE & TRAVEL

Climate change is a serious threat to the ecosystems that humans rely upon, and air travel is the fastest-growing contributor to the problem. Lonely Planet regards travel, overall, as a global benefit, but believes we all have a responsibility to limit our personal impact on global warming.

Flying & Climate Change

Pretty much every form of motor travel generates CO_2 (the main cause of human-induced climate change) but planes are far and away the worst offenders, not just because of the sheer distances they allow us to travel, but because they release greenhouse gases high into the atmosphere. The statistics are frightening: two people taking a return flight between Europe and the US will contribute as much to climate change as an average household's gas and electricity consumption over a whole year.

Carbon Offset Schemes

Climatecare.org and other websites use 'carbon calculators' that allow jetsetters to offset the greenhouse gases they are responsible for with contributions to energy-saving projects and other climate-friendly initiatives in the developing world – including projects in India, Honduras, Kazakhstan and Uganda.

Lonely Planet, together with Rough Guides and other concerned partners in the travel industry, supports the carbon offset scheme run by climatecare.org. Lonely Planet offsets all of its staff and author travel.

For more information check out our website: lonelyplanet.com.

TRANSPORT

to Windermere costs £18.80 off-peak and £28.40 anytime; Glasgow to Oxenholme to Windermere costs £33.20 off-peak and £42 anytime – for other destinations consult the relevant chapters.

First Transpennine Express (www.tpexpress.co.uk) is the region's second major operator. The main line into Cumbria starts at Manchester Airport; there are direct trains via Manchester city centre (Piccadilly and Oxford Rd), Preston, Lancaster, Oxenholme, Penrith and Carlisle en route to Edinburgh or Glasgow. A second, wonderfully scenic route (known as the Furness Railway) veers off at Lancaster and heads across Morecambe Bay via Carnforth, Arnside, Grange-over-Sands and Ulverston before terminating at Barrow-in-Furness.

Northern Rail (☎ 0845 000 0125; www.northernrail .org) handles services across much of northern England. Useful services for Cumbria and the Lake District include the Tyne Valley line (sometimes referred to as the Hadrian's Wall line) between Newcastle-upon-Tyne and Carlisle, the historic Settle-Carlisle Railway (see boxed text, p201), and the equally lovely Cumbrian Coast line. Single fares from Newcastle to Carlisle start at around £12.10 for anytime travel; Day Ranger tickets on the Cumbrian Coast line cost £15/7.50 per adult/child, while tickets on the Settle-Carlisle Railway cost £23.10/27.80 for a single/return from Leeds to Carlisle, or £16.80/20 from Settle.

CLASSES
Most intercity trains have 1st and 2nd class carriages; paying the premium entitles you to more legroom, comfier seats and usually a dining car or buffet. On certain weekend trains you might be able to upgrade to 'weekend 1st' for between £10 and £20, either at the station or from the conductor. Note that advance tickets don't qualify for the weekend 1st upgrade; it's only available to off-peak or anytime ticket holders.

TICKETS & RAILCARDS
If you're travelling by train, it's worth booking as far in advance as possible. Due to recent price restructuring it's now eye-wateringly expensive to delay buying your tickets until the day of travel (often two or three times the standard off-peak fare). You'll need to book a week or more in advance to secure the cheapest deals.

THE LAKES ARE YOUR OYSTER

The best-value ticket for general all-round travel on public transport within the Lake District has to be the **Lakes Day Ranger** (adult/child/railcard/family £17/8.50/11.20/33), which is valid on all trains (including the Lancaster–Oxenholme–Windermere–Penrith line and the Cumbrian Coast line from Lancaster to Workington) and all Stagecoach buses within Cumbria, and also includes a boat trip with Windermere Lake Cruises. It even allows you a 20% discount on cruises on Coniston Water, Ullswater and Derwent Water. Shame it's only valid for a day really…

There are three categories – advance and off-peak tickets are the cheapest, but are valid only on the date and time specified on the ticket, while anytime tickets are more expensive but allow travel on any train. Bizarrely, buying two single tickets often works out cheaper than a standard return.

If you're undertaking a lot of train travel, a National Railcard may be a useful investment, entitling you to one-third off standard fares. Railcards are available for under-25s, family groups, over 60s, disabled travellers and HM Forces members. Railcards can be bought at most mainline stations – you'll need proof of identity and some passport photos.

For timetables, fares and full travel details for any of Britain's train networks, contact **National Rail Enquiries** (☎ 08457 484950; www .nationalrail.co.uk) or the **Trainline** (☎ 0870 010 1296; www.thetrainline.com).

RAIL PASSES
Rail Rover tickets are worth considering if you're visiting the Lakes as part of a grand British tour. These tickets are valid from 8.45am on weekdays and anytime on weekends on any of northern England's train services, and can be purchased in advance from any staffed train station.

Freedom of the Northwest Also known as the Northwest Rover; allows four days' travel in eight throughout Northwest England for £57/28.50/37.60 per adult/child/ railcard holder; the seven-day version costs £70/35/46.20.

North Country Rover Coast-to-coast ticket valid for travel anywhere north of Leeds/Preston and south of Carlisle/Newcastle; four days' travel in eight consecutive days costs £72/36/47.50 per adult/child/railcard holder.

Settle-Carlisle Rover Valid for travel between Leeds, Shipley, Skipton, Settle, Ribblehead, Kirkby Stephen, Appleby and Carlisle. Four days' travel in eight costs £44/22/29.05. For more detail on the Settle-Carlisle Railway line, see p201.

For Day Ranger tickets and passes for travel within Cumbria, consult the Train section under Getting Around (p233).

Flights, tours and rail tickets can be booked online at www.lonelyplanet.com/travel_services.

GETTING AROUND

Cumbria is a compact county, with practically all the main attractions located within an hour's drive of each other. For most journeys, buses are by far the cheapest and most convenient way of getting around; all but the most remote corners of the county are accessible by some kind of regular bus service.

Train services for the Lake District terminate at Windermere; Penrith and Carlisle are both on the main West Coast railway line, and there's a handy coastal rail route that travels through all of the main coastal towns including Grange-over-Sands, Ulverston and Whitehaven (not to mention a cluster of fantastic scenic railways – see p232).

But despite the decent public transport links, the vast majority of people still end up travelling to the region by car. The National Park Authority and Cumbria Council have made a concerted effort to wean people off their addiction to the internal combustion engine, and there are some great-value daily and weekly travel passes available, as well as a handy cross-park travel network called the Cross-Lakes Shuttle connecting Windermere and Coniston with a combination of minibuses, local bus services and cruise boats.

For general transport information, fares and timetables, contact the national **Traveline** (☎ 0871 200 22 33); there's a specific site for the North East and Cumbria at www.travelinenortheast.info.

BICYCLE

There's no greener way to explore the Lake District than by bicycle, and it's becoming an increasingly popular method of getting around as carbon footprints and environmental issues gain greater importance in people's travel plans. Long-haul cyclists and mountain bikers are spoilt for choice, but for something more sedate, bookshops and local tourist offices stock plenty of guidebooks and booklets detailing routes to suit all abilities. Bike-hire shops and equipment suppliers are readily available throughout the region, and the excellent website at www.cyclingcumbria.co.uk is packed with route suggestions and general biking advice. We've detailed a few choice bike rides throughout the book, with more cycling suggestions in the Outdoors chapter (p104).

Cycling in the Lakes certainly isn't without its drawbacks – heavy summer traffic, leg-shredding hills and the unreliable English weather all present potential problems, but by planning your route carefully and sticking to the quieter roads, there are few better ways to experience the Lake District scenery.

Bikes can be transported on most trains, but space is limited (tandems, tricycles and trailers are likely to be met with steely smiles). Northern Rail operates on a first-come, first-served basis, and usually has space for two bikes. Virgin can carry four, and First Transpennine up to two on selected services; for both companies you'll need to make a free advance reservation by phone or when buying your ticket.

Relatively few buses have space to carry bikes. One notable exception is the 505 Windermere to Coniston bus, which has guaranteed space for two bicycles; phone ☎ 015394-722143 to make a (free) reservation with details of the bus you're catching and where you're joining the service to make sure there's space. Bikes can be loaded at Windermere Station, Ambleside (Kelsick Rd), Hawkshead and Coniston. The AD 122

TRANSPORT

THINGS CHANGE...

The information in this chapter is particularly vulnerable to change. Check directly with the travel operator or agent to make sure you understand how a fare (and ticket you may buy) works and be aware of the security requirements for international travel. Shop carefully. The details given in this chapter should be regarded as pointers and are not a substitute for your own careful, up-to-date research.

TRANSPORT

Hadrian's Wall bus also has room for two bikes (call ☎ 01434-32022 to book a spot), while the Cross-Lakes Shuttle (see boxed text, p70) can carry up to five.

Ullswater 'Steamers', Windermere Cruise Boats and the Coniston Launch will all happily carry bikes for free when space is available.

BOAT

Windermere, Derwent Water, Ullswater and Coniston all boast their own ferry services, most of which allow you to break up your trip so that you can indulge in a bit of hiking or biking. If you prefer to travel under your own steam, row boats and motor boats are available on most of the larger lakes, and some also have boating marinas offering yachting or windsurfing – see the relevant chapter for full details.

Coniston Launch (☎ 017687-75753; www.coniston launch.co.uk) Two solar-powered cruise boats offering a selection of trips around Coniston Water.

Keswick Launch (☎ 017687-72263; www.keswick -launch.co.uk) Regular ferry boats stopping at seven boat landings around the lake.

Steam Yacht Gondola (☎ 015394-63831; www .nationaltrust.org.uk/gondola) Historic steam yacht restored by the National Trust, with trips on Coniston Water.

Ullswater 'Steamers' (☎ 017684-82229; www .ullswater-steamers.co.uk) Three restored cruise boats plying Ullswater between Glenridding, Howtown and Pooley Bridge.

Windermere Cruise Boats (☎ 015394-43360; www .windermere-lakecruises.co.uk) The original Lakeland boat company offers a choice of four main colour-coded cruise routes around Windermere.

In addition to the cruises, Windermere also has a cross-lake ferry that carries cars, bikes, foot passengers and even horses from a jetty south of Bowness-on-Windermere to Ferry House at Far Sawrey on the lake's western shore. It runs year round (except on Christmas Day and Boxing Day), and can carry up to 18 cars and 100 passengers; current single fares are £3.50 for motor vehicles, £1.50 for motorbikes and horses, £1 for bicycles and 50p for foot passengers.

BUS

Cumbria's bus network has come on in leaps and bounds, and it's now perfectly possible to travel around locally within Cumbria and the Lake District solely by charabanc. Buses

remain perennially popular among Lakeland hikers – most of the classic trailheads lie within easy range of at least one bus service, so don't be surprised if you find yourself jostling for space with assorted rucksacks, thermos flasks, walking poles, map cases and muddy boots. In fact overcrowding has become a bit of a headache for local authorities – if the sun's shining and the weather's warm, you might struggle to find a seat on some of the more popular routes.

Stagecoach (www.stagecoachbus.com) is the main operator. Perhaps the most useful service is the 555 (Lakeslink) – quite possibly the only bus service in England to have had a book written about it (*55 555 Walks* by Robert Swain). The service runs between Lancaster and Keswick via nearly all the main Lakeland towns, including Staveley, Windermere, Troutbeck, Ambleside and Grasmere; a couple of daily buses run on to Carlisle via Wigton (when the bus changes number to the 554).

Other useful buses include the 505 (Coniston Rambler), linking Kendal, Windermere, Ambleside and Coniston; the open-top 599 (Lakesrider) between Bowness and Grasmere; the X4/X5 (Trans-Cumbrian) from Penrith to Workington via Troutbeck, Keswick and Cockermouth; the 77 (Honister Rambler) from Keswick to Buttermere; and the 79 (Borrowdale Rambler) from Keswick to Borrowdale. We've detailed other local services in the relevant chapters.

Stagecoach publishes a handy free booklet, *The Cumbria & Lakesrider*, which contains full timetables for all its routes. Also look out for the *A to B to SEE* 'scenic guide' leaflets, detailing points of interest to look out for during your bus journey, and the *Give the Driver a Break* series, which combine a bus timetable with suggestions for local sights and walks.

You can pick up these free booklets at bus stations and tourist offices, or download timetables at www.stagecoachbus.com/north west/timetables.php or www.cumbria.gov .uk/roads-transport. We've given bus times throughout the guide based on summer timetables; most routes run a drastically reduced winter service, and some only run between Easter and October.

For details of the Cross-Lakes Shuttle between Windermere, Hawkshead and Coniston, see p70.

Bus Passes

Several bus passes are available for individual areas of Cumbria, useful if you're planning on mainly travelling within a limited area; otherwise, you might as well splash out on the **North West Explorer** ticket (adult one/four/seven days £9.50/21/30, child £6.25/14.50/20.50, disabled and senior citizens day pass £5.75, family day pass £19), which gives unlimited travel on services in Cumbria and Lancashire, or the **All Cumbria** pass (all age groups seven/28 days £23/80), valid on any Cumbria bus. All tickets are available on the bus from the driver or from larger bus stations.

Other local bus passes:

Borrowdale Dayrider (adult/child £5.25/4) Valid on bus 79 between Keswick and Seatoller.

Carlisle Dayrider (adult £3) Unlimited travel in Carlisle.

Central Lakes Dayrider (adult/child/family £6.30/4.70/12.50) Covers Bowness, Ambleside, Grasmere, Langdale and Coniston; includes the 599, 505 and 516.

Hadrian's Wall Day Rover (adult/child/family £7.50/4.80/15) Unlimited travel on the Hadrian Wall routes between Carlisle and Newcastle, including the AD122/185 and 685. Three-day passes cost £15/9.60/30; seven-day passes cost £30/19.20/60.

Honister Dayrider (adult/child £6.25/4.50) Valid on bus 77/77A between Keswick, Buttermere and Borrowdale.

Ruskin Explorer (adult/child £14.50/6.85) Includes travel on the 505, a cruise on the Coniston Launch and entry to Brantwood.

West Cumbria Dayrider/Megarider (1/7 day £3.95/14) Valid for buses in West Cumbria.

CAR & MOTORCYCLE

Over 90% of visitors end up travelling to the Lake District by car, and while it's undoubtedly convenient to have your own wheels, you might end up rueing the decision once you've spent a few days negotiating the summertime snarl-ups. If you do bring your own motor, it's worth thinking about leaving it parked up wherever you're staying and travelling around by bus.

Hire

Expect to pay between £30 and £50 per day for a small- to medium-sized car, or between £220 and £250 a week. You'll find rental offices for most of the big firms in Carlisle or contact the national call centres:

Avis (☎ 0844 581 1047; www.avis.co.uk)

Europcar (☎ 0845 758 5375; www.europcar.co.uk)

Hertz (☎ 0870 850 2677; www.hertz.co.uk)

National (☎ 0800 227 7368; www.nationalcar.com)

For something a little more memorable, **Lakes & Dales** (☎ 01768-879091; www.lakesanddales.co.uk) hires a fleet of classic soft-top cars, including Austin Healeys, Morgans and Triumphs, while **Rainbow Camper Hire** (☎ 017687-80413; www.vwcamperhire.net; Keswick) lets you live out the hippie dream with its lovingly restored VW camper vans.

Parking

There's no getting around it – parking in the Lakes can be a pain. On busy summer mornings practically all the major car parks (especially the ones near well-known trailheads) are bumper-to-bumper by around 9am. Parking is not only tricky, it's also pricey – expect to shell out around £2 to £3 for an hour's stay, and anything upwards of £5 to £8 for all-day stays. Theft from parked cars is a growing problem – make sure there are no valuables on display in your car, and remove your car stereo.

On-street parking in many Cumbrian towns is limited to one or two hours, and is regulated by a 'timed disc' system. You can pick up the discs free from many shops, post offices and tourist offices; turn the disc dial to your arrival time, pop it on your dashboard, and make sure you don't overstay the duration indicated on nearby lamp posts.

Road Rules

All EU (and most other international) driving licences are valid in England for up to 12 months, but if you're bringing your car from overseas you will require (at least) third-party insurance. Other important rules to remember:

- drive on the left
- give way to your right at junctions and roundabouts
- use the left-hand lane unless overtaking
- wear fitted seatbelts in cars
- children up to three years old must always travel in an appropriate child seat
- children aged three to 12, or up to 135cm in height, must use an appropriate child restraint in the front seat, and if possible when travelling in the rear seat
- don't use mobile phones or other devices while at the wheel

Standard speed limits (unless otherwise indicated) are 30mph in built-up areas, 60mph on main roads and single carriageways, and 70mph on dual carriageways and motorways.

TRANSPORT

TRANSPORT

Avoid drinking and driving; the legal blood-alcohol limit is 80mg per 100ml (.08%), and if you're caught over the limit you could face a fine of up to £5000 and/or six months in the clink. Not the way to start a holiday.

HITCHING

Hitching around Cumbria and the Lake District is possible, although you might find yourself facing some lengthy waits – British drivers are much less likely to stop to pick up hitchers than they once were. Travellers (especially solo females) should understand that they're taking a small but potentially serious risk, and we don't recommend it. If you decide to go by thumb, remember that hitching on British motorways is illegal – you're better off trying your luck at service stations or dual carriageway lay-bys.

LOCAL TRANSPORT
Shuttle Buses & Baggage Couriers

From Easter to October, the YHA Shuttle Bus connects eight Lake District hostels, and provides a baggage transport service for guests. Hostels on the route include Windermere, Hawkshead, Coniston Holly How, Elterwater, Langdale, Butharlyp Howe and Grasmere. Hostel-to-hostel transport costs £3, or £2.50 for bags; transport from Windermere Station costs £2 to Windermere YHA and £2.50 to Ambleside YHA.

Several other companies offer short-haul minibus transfers and/or a baggage courier service between hotels, B&Bs and campsites, handy for hikers and bikers who don't fancy carting their luggage along the trail. Most companies operate along all the major long-distance routes, including the Coast-to-Coast, Cumbria Way, Hadrian's Wall path, Dales Way and the Sea to Sea Cycle Route. Prices start at around £6 to £8 per 20kg bag.

Brigantes (☎ 01729-830463; www.brigantesenglish walks.com)

Coast-to-Coast Packhorse (☎ 017683-71777; www .cumbria.com/packhorse)

Sherpa Van (☎ 0871 520 0124; www.sherpavan.com)

Taxi

Taxis can be a useful way of covering short distances, especially if you're in a small group, but if you're travelling any further than 10 miles or so, it quickly starts to become an expensive option. Unlike in the cities, you won't usually be able to flag down a cab in Cumbria;

you'll either have to find a taxi rank (such as the ones at most train stations), or contact a local cab company. Consult the relevant chapter for listings.

TOURS

If you've got a limited time to spend in the park, or you just prefer letting someone else do the planning, taking an organised tour can be a great way of cramming in the sights. Most are conducted in small minibuses or coaches, usually with a guided commentary, but they pack a lot in, so there won't be much time for dawdling. There's usually a minimum-person limit, so it's worth hooking up with friends if you can; admission charges to sights aren't always included, so ask before you book.

We've suggested operators for specific guides or activities (eg hiking, biking and rock climbing) in the Directory chapter (p217).

Lake District Tours (☎ 015395-52106; www.lake districttours.co.uk; Witherslack) Small family-run operator, with several well-guided tours: Wordsworth and Beatrix Potter (adult/child £29.50/10); a nature tour including Colwith and Skelwith Forces, Blea Tarn and Orrest Head (adult/child £36.50/35); and a scenic gardens tour including Gummers How, Cartmel and Holker Hall (adult/child £44/28).

Lakes Supertours (☎ 015394-42751; www.lakes -supertours.co.uk; 1 High St, Windermere) Eleven- and 16-seat minibuses with full-day trips to Borrowdale, Buttermere and Ullswater, including an Ullswater lake cruise (adult/child £30/20); a Wordsworth and Beatrix Potter tour including a Keswick cruise (adult/child £30/20); a trip to the western lakes and Duddon Valley (adult/child £30/20); and several other options.

Mountain Goat (☎ 015394-45161; www.mountain -goat.co.uk; Windermere) One of the oldest and most experienced operators, offering private charters and daily tours including a 10-lakes tour (adult/child £33.50/23.50); a Beatrix Potter tour (adult/child £33.50/23.50); a trip around the Lake District's highest passes (adult/child £33.50/23.50); and an afternoon tour taking in nine lakes and a visit to Hill Top (adult/child £33.50/18.50).

Touchstone Tours (☎ 017687-79599; www.touchstone tours.co.uk; Threlkeld) Another reliable minibus operator, operating almost identical trips to Mountain Goat for the same prices, as well as private charters and guided walks.

TRAIN

During the 19th century, like many northern counties, Cumbria was at the heart of the Industrial Revolution. Pioneering industrialists constructed several railways to speed up the transfer of manufactured goods, a handful of which still clatter around the county. The Oxenholme–Windermere branch line via Kendal, Burneside and Staveley remains one of the main routes into the Lakes for many visitors; trains run at least hourly every day of the week, and link up with the main West Coast line north via Penrith to Scotland and south to Birmingham and London. Sample fares from Oxenholme to Windermere are £4.40/5.60 for an anytime single/return.

Another of Cumbria's most famous (and spectacular) vintage railways is the Settle-Carlisle Railway (p201), whose 72 miles of track, 20 viaducts and 14 tunnels traverse the breathtaking countryside of the Yorkshire Dales and eastern Cumbria. Equally stunning is the Cumbrian Coast line, which makes an unforgettable circuit around Cumbria's coastline before reaching journey's end in Carlisle.

Steam addicts have three lines to choose from: the **South Tynedale Railway** (www.strps.org .uk) cuts through the bleakly beautiful landscapes of the North Pennines; the **Lakeside and Haverthwaite Railway** (p71; www.lakesiderailway .co.uk), chugs its way from Haverthwaite to the shores of Windermere; and last, but certainly not least, are the mini-trains of the **Ravenglass and Eskdale Railway** (La'al Ratty; p130; www.ravenglass -railway.co.uk), originally built to ferry iron ore and now arguably the ultimate toy train set.

Rail Passes

Several rail passes are available for specific train lines in and around Cumbria; for general travel, the Lakes Day Ranger pass (see boxed text, p228) represents the best value.

Cumbria Round Robin (adult/child £25/12.50) Valid for a circular trip in either direction between Carlisle, Oxenholme, Lancaster, Grange-over-Sands, Barrow-in-Furness, Whitehaven and Carlisle.

Cumbrian Coast Day Ranger (adult/child £16/8) Buys a day's travel between all stations along the Cumbrian Coast line.

Dales Railcard (£10) Offers a one-third discount on standard fares on the Settle-Carlisle Railway line. Available from Carlisle and Appleby stations or www.settle-carlisle .co.uk/railcard_info.cfm.

Hadrian's Wall Day Ranger (adult/child £15/7.50) Valid for travel on the Hadrian's Wall line between Whitehaven, Workington, Carlisle, Hexham, Newcastle and Sunderland.

Northern Duo Buys one return ticket plus a second for half price when two adults travel together on certain Northern Rail routes.

Health

CONTENTS

While it often receives bad press, England's National Health Service (NHS) is still one of the top health-care systems in the world, providing first-rate care free at the point of delivery (at least for British residents). Cumbria and the Lake District is a healthy place to travel and hygiene standards are high; the region's main hospitals are in Carlisle (the Cumberland Infirmary), Barrow-in-Furness (the Furness General Hospital) and Kendal (the Westmorland General).

AVAILABILITY & COST OF HEALTH CARE

Health care is readily available and for minor ailments pharmacists dispense advice and over-the-counter medication. For general advice contact the 24-hour helpline **NHS Direct** (☎ 0845 46 47; www.nhsdirect.nhs.uk).

ENVIRONMENTAL HAZARDS
Heat Exhaustion

Heat exhaustion occurs following excessive fluid loss with inadequate replacement of fluids and salt. Symptoms include headache, dizziness and tiredness. Dehydration is already happening by the time you feel thirsty – aim to drink sufficient water to produce pale, diluted urine. To treat heat exhaustion, replace lost fluids by drinking water and/or fruit juice, and cool the body with cold water and fans. Treat salt loss with salty fluids such as soup or Bovril, or add a little more table salt to foods than usual.

Hypothermia

The high fells are exposed and can be prone to sudden extremes of weather. It's important to be well prepared and to get an up-to-date weather forecast before you set out. Even on a hot day the weather can change rapidly; carry waterproof garments, warm layers and a reflective survival blanket and remember to inform others of your intended route and what time you plan to return.

Hypothermia is a possibility if you are exposed to extremes of wind or cold. Acute hypothermia follows a sudden drop of temperature over a short time. Chronic hypothermia is caused by a gradual loss of temperature over hours. Hypothermia starts with shivering, loss of judgment and clumsiness, followed by apathy, confusion and coma. Prevent further heat loss by seeking shelter, warm clothing, hot sweet drinks and shared bodily warmth.

Insect Bites & Stings

Bee and wasp stings are uncomfortable, but only dangerous to those with a severe allergy (anaphylaxis); carry an 'epipen' or similar adrenaline injection if you're allergic.

Ticks are carried by many sheep and cattle and can be found in many grassy or wooded areas. Some ticks carry Lyme Disease, which can be a serious illness if left untreated, and may appear as an expanding, reddish rash up to 30 days after the initial bite. Symptoms include influenza, mild headaches and aching muscles and joints. If you have been bitten by a tick and experience any of these symptoms, see a doctor.

To avoid being bitten, wear long trousers tucked into socks and long-sleeved shirts. At the end of the day check yourself carefully, especially around the groin and armpits. If you find a tick remove it by grasping it firmly with tweezers, as close to the skin as possible, and pulling directly up. Don't burn it off or crush it, as this encourages the tick to regurgitate into your bloodstream. If this happens, or the tick's head remains in your skin, seek medical attention.

Sunburn

Sunburn is possible even on a relatively cloudy day. Cover up, use suncream of an appropriate SPF rating for your skin, and wear a hat. If you get burnt, treat the affected area with an aloe vera or calamine lotion and stay out of the sun.

Water

Tap water quality in Britain is high and you should have no problem drinking it, but don't drink from any streams, lakes, tarns or ponds in the countryside – you can't be sure what's in the water, or what it's flowed through. If you're camping, make sure any water taps are labelled safe to drink, as some are intended only for animal use.

FURTHER READING

Health Advice for Travellers (currently called the T6 leaflet) is available from post offices. It contains general health information, recommended vaccines, reciprocal health agreements and a European Health Insurance Card (EHIC) application form.

INSURANCE

If you're an EU citizen, a European Health Insurance Card, available from doctor's surgeries and post offices, covers you for most medical care, but not for non-emergencies or emergency repatriation.

Non-EU citizens should ask about reciprocal healthcare arrangements before travelling, or take out appropriate travel insurance covering healthcare costs and emergency repatriation. Find out in advance if your insurance will make payments directly to providers or reimburse you later.

TRAVEL HEALTH WEBSITES

If visiting England from overseas it's usually a good idea to consult your government's travel-health website before departure.

- Australia (www.smartraveller.gov.au)
- Canada (www.hc-sc.gc.ca)
- USA (www.cdc.gov/travel)

RECOMMENDED VACCINATIONS

The World Health Organization (WHO) recommends that all travellers should be covered for diphtheria, tetanus, measles, mumps, rubella and polio.

TRAVELLING WITH CHILDREN

All travellers with children should know how to treat minor ailments and when to seek medical treatment. Make sure the children are up to date with routine vaccinations. Be wary of any dogs or other animals you don't know – not all are accustomed to children and might react suddenly and unpredictably (the same rules apply to theoretically harmless animals such as sheep, pigs, donkeys, goats and cows, of which there are many in the Lake District). Any bite or scratch should be immediately cleaned and disinfected; if in doubt, seek qualified medical help.

HEALTH

Glossary

beck – river or stream, from Old Norse *bekkr*
black pudding – type of blood sausage
butty – slang for sandwich

char – type of fish found in some Cumbrian lakes, related to the salmon
cob – rustic building material, usually made from compacted earth, clay and straw
coppice – small area of woodland
crag – outcrop of rock, derived from the Celtic word *creic*, meaning rock
Cumberland sausage – traditional Cumbrian coiled sausage made of pork

dale – valley, from Old Norse *dalr*
damson – a soft fruit related to the plum, used to make jams, chutneys and gin
drystone wall – a traditional form of wall built without the use of mortar

fell – mountain, from Old Norse *fjall*
force – waterfall, from Old Norse *fors*
full English – fried breakfast, usually with bacon, sausage, tomatoes, mushrooms, baked beans and black pudding

ghyll – ravine, from Old Norse *gil*
grange – old dialect word for farm
gurn – to pull a face

heaf – sheep's territory, customarily passed down from ewe to lamb

Herdwick – native Lakeland sheep, distinguished by its black fleece and white face
holm – island, from Old Norse *holmr*

la'al – Cumbrian word for little, as in La'al Ratty

menhir – upright stone fashioned by prehistoric builders
mere – a pond or lake
mintcake – hard Cumbrian sweet made of boiled sugar, traditionally made in Kendal
motte-and-bailey – early form of castle, usually consisting of a keep or fort on a raised hill

Roundhead – alternative word for Parliamentarian during the English Civil War

sarnie – slang for sandwich
scree – broken rock and gravel found on steep mountain sides

tallow – animal fat, used to make candles
tarn – mountain lake
tatie – potato
thwaite – Old Norse word for clearing

vendace – endangered species of whitefish native to the Lake District and parts of Scotland

Westmorland slate – distinctive grey-green slate mined around the Lake District

Behind the Scenes

THIS BOOK

This is the exciting 1st edition of Lonely Planet's *Lake District* guidebook. It was commissioned in Lonely Planet's London office, and produced by the following:

Commissioning Editor Clifton Wilkinson
Coordinating Editor Saralinda Turner
Coordinating Cartographer Anthony Phelan
Coordinating Layout Designer Paul Iacono
Managing Editor Bruce Evans
Managing Cartographers Alison Lyall, Mark Griffiths
Managing Layout Designer Laura Jane
Assisting Editors Fionnuala Twomey, Kate Evans
Assisting Cartographers Fatima Basic, Hunor Csutoros, Piotr Czajkowski, Marc Milinkovic
Cover Designer Pepi Bluck
Project Manager Rachel Imeson

Thanks to Yvonne Bischofberger, Katrina Browning, Helen Christinis, Melanie Dankel, Craig Kilburn, Katie Lynch, Clara Monitto, Susan Paterson, Carlos Solarte, Laura Stansfeld, Glenn van der Knijff

THANKS
OLIVER BERRY

As always, too many people to thank in such a short space. Top of the list is Susie Berry for moral support and late night grub. Thanks to Mark, Si and Brett for holding the o-region boat afloat in my absence, to the Hobo for always being on my shoulder, and to TSP for long-distance Skyping. Extra special thanks to Ashley Cooper from the Langdale and Ambleside Mountain Rescue Team, to Gillian Hodgson from the Coniston Launch, and to Nathan Fox from the Bassenthwaite Osprey Project for taking the time to answer my questions and proof my text. Thanks to everyone at Lonely Planet, especially Cliff Wilkinson for steering the ship, reading my stuff and giving me the gig in the first place, to Saralinda Turner for saintly patience and eagle-eyed editing, to all the cartos for making it through the mapping nightmare, and to everyone in London and Melbourne who poured so much time and effort into making this book what it is. And no thanks list would be complete without the two Ws, Wainwright and Wordsworth; it's been an honour to follow in your footsteps, lads.

ACKNOWLEDGMENTS
Many thanks to the following for the use of their content:

Globe on title page ©Mountain High Maps 1993 Digital Wisdom, Inc.

Internal photographs by Stephen Bradley/Alamy p6 (#3); Robert Harding Picture Library Ltd/Alamy

---

THE LONELY PLANET STORY

Fresh from an epic journey across Europe, Asia and Australia in 1972, Tony and Maureen Wheeler sat at their kitchen table stapling together notes. The first Lonely Planet guidebook, *Across Asia on the Cheap,* was born.

Travellers snapped up the guides. Inspired by their success, the Wheelers began publishing books to Southeast Asia, India and beyond. Demand was prodigious, and the Wheelers expanded the business rapidly to keep up. Over the years, Lonely Planet extended its coverage to every country and into the virtual world via lonelyplanet.com and the Thorn Tree message board.

As Lonely Planet became a globally loved brand, Tony and Maureen received several offers for the company. But it wasn't until 2007 that they found a partner whom they trusted to remain true to the company's principles of travelling widely, treading lightly and giving sustainably. In October of that year, BBC Worldwide acquired a 75% share in the company, pledging to uphold Lonely Planet's commitment to independent travel, trustworthy advice and editorial independence.

Today, Lonely Planet has offices in Melbourne, London and Oakland, with over 500 staff members and 300 authors. Tony and Maureen are still actively involved with Lonely Planet. They're travelling more often than ever, and they're devoting their spare time to charitable projects. And the company is still driven by the philosophy of *Across Asia on the Cheap*: 'All you've got to do is decide to go and the hardest part is over. So go!'

SEND US YOUR FEEDBACK

We love to hear from travellers – your comments keep us on our toes and help make our books better. Our well-travelled team reads every word on what you loved or loathed about this book. Although we cannot reply individually to postal submissions, we always guarantee that your feedback goes straight to the appropriate authors, in time for the next edition. Each person who sends us information is thanked in the next edition – and the most useful submissions are rewarded with a free book.

To send us your updates – and find out about Lonely Planet events, newsletters and travel news – visit our award-winning website: **lonelyplanet.com/contact**.

Note: we may edit, reproduce and incorporate your comments in Lonely Planet products such as guidebooks, websites and digital products, so let us know if you don't want your comments reproduced or your name acknowledged. For a copy of our privacy policy visit lonelyplanet.com/privacy.

p8 (#1); Stephen Saks Photography/Alamy p9 (#2); Patrick Ward/Alamy p9 (#3); Ashley Cooper/Alamy p10 (#1); Stan Pritchard/Alamy p11 (#2); Jeff Greenberg/Alamy p12 (#1); Numb/Alamy p12 (#2). All other photographs by Lonely Planet Images, and by Hugh Watts p5; David Tomlinson p6 (#1), p7 (#2); Eoin Clarke p10 (#3).

All images are the copyright of the photographers unless otherwise indicated. Many of the images in this guide are available for licensing from Lonely Planet Images: www.lonelyplanet images.com.

Index

GREENDEX

The Lake District has a long and distinguished tradition of environmental protection, but in a world facing up to climate change, spiralling pollution and dwindling resources, it's vitally important that everyone keeps up the good work. Throughout the book we've highlighted places that are doing their bit to make the planet a better place – whether by employing ecofriendly technologies, championing the virtues of small-scale producers, cutting down on energy use or sourcing produce from local, organic or ethical suppliers.

We're keen to continue developing our ideas for sustainable travel, so if you think we've missed a green gem, email us at www.lonelyplanet.com/feedback. For more information about responsible travel, check out our website at www.lonelyplanet.com/responsibletravel.

MAP LEGEND

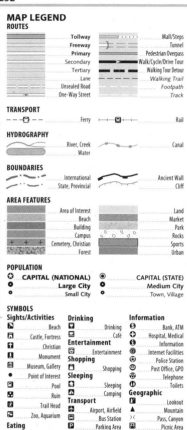

ROUTES

Tollway
Freeway
Primary
Secondary
Tertiary
Lane
Unsealed Road
One-Way Street

Mall/Steps
Tunnel
Pedestrian Overpass
Walk/Cycle/Drive Tour
Walking Tour Detour
Walking Trail
Footpath
Track

TRANSPORT

Ferry
Rail

HYDROGRAPHY

River, Creek
Water
Canal

BOUNDARIES

International
State, Provincial
Ancient Wall
Cliff

AREA FEATURES

Area of Interest
Beach
Building
Campus
Cemetery, Christian
Forest

Land
Market
Park
Rocks
Sports
Urban

POPULATION

CAPITAL (NATIONAL)
Large City
Small City

CAPITAL (STATE)
Medium City
Town, Village

SYMBOLS

Sights/Activities
Beach
Castle, Fortress
Christian
Monument
Museum, Gallery
Point of Interest
Pool
Ruin
Trail Head
Zoo, Aquarium

Eating
Eating

Drinking
Drinking
Café

Entertainment
Entertainment

Shopping
Shopping

Sleeping
Sleeping
Camping

Transport
Airport, Airfield
Bus Station
Parking Area
Petrol Station

Information
Bank, ATM
Hospital, Medical
Information
Internet Facilities
Police Station
Post Office, GPO
Telephone
Toilets

Geographic
Lookout
Mountain
Pass, Canyon
Picnic Area
Waterfall

LONELY PLANET OFFICES

Australia
Head Office
Locked Bag 1, Footscray, Victoria 3011
☎ 03 8379 8000, fax 03 8379 8111
talk2us@lonelyplanet.com.au

USA
150 Linden St, Oakland, CA 94607
☎ 510 250 6400, toll free 800 275 8555
fax 510 893 8572
info@lonelyplanet.com

UK
2nd fl, 186 City Rd,
London EC1V 2NT
☎ 020 7106 2100, fax 020 7106 2101
go@lonelyplanet.co.uk

Published by Lonely Planet Publications Pty Ltd
ABN 36 005 607 983

© Lonely Planet Publications Pty Ltd 2009

© photographers as indicated 2009

Cover photograph: Bleached by the elements: a weather-stained pier on Derwent Water, Cumbria, England, Chris Simpson/Getty Images. Many of the images in this guide are available for licensing from Lonely Planet Images: www.lonelyplanetimages.com.

Printed through Colorcraft Ltd, Hong Kong.
Printed in China.

Mixed Sources
Product group from well-managed forests and other controlled sources
www.fsc.org Cert no. SGS-COC-005002
© 1996 Forest Stewardship Council
FSC